Martin F. Tupper

TUPPER'S

COMPLETE

POETICAL WORKS:

CONTAINING

"PROVERBIAL PHILOSOPHY," "A THOUSAND LINES," "HACTENUS," "GERALDINE," AND "MISCELLANEOUS POEMS:"

WITH A PORTRAIT OF THE AUTHOR.

A NEW EDITION.

BOSTON:
PHILLIPS, SAMPSON AND COMPANY,
110 WASHINGTON STREET.
1851.

CONTENTS.

PROVERBIAL PHILOSOPHY.

FIRST SERIES.

SECOND SERIES.

A THOUSAND LINES.

HACTENUS:

SUNDRY OF MY LYRICS HITHERTO.

GERALDINE,

AND OTHER POEMS.

MISCELLANEOUS POEMS.

PROVERBIAL PHILOSOPHY.

FIRST SERIES.

PROVERBIAL PHILOSOPHY.

PREFATORY.

THOUGHTS, that have tarried in my mind, and peopled its inner chambers,
The sober children of reason, or desultory train of fancy;
Clear running wine of conviction, with the scum and the lees of speculation;
Corn from the sheaves of Science, with stubble from mine own garner,
Searchings after Truth, that have tracked her secret lodes,
And come up again to the surface-world with a knowledge grounded deeper;
Arguments of high scope, that have soared to the keystone of heaven,
And thence have swooped to their certain mark, as the falcon to its quarry;
The fruits I have gathered of prudence, the ripened harvest of my musings,
These commend I unto thee, O docile scholar of Wisdom,
These I give to thy gentle heart, thou lover of the right.

What though a guilty man renew that hallowed theme,
And strike with feebler hand the harp of Sirach's son?
What, though a youthful tongue take up that ancient parable,
And utter faintly forth dark sayings as of old?
Sweet is the virgin honey, though the wild bee have stored it in a reed;
And bright the jewelled band, that circleth an Ethiop's arm;
Pure are the grains of gold in the turbid stream of Ganges,
And fair the living flowers, that spring from the dull cold sod.
Wherefore, thou gentle student, bend thine ear to my speech,
For I also am as thou art; our hearts can commune together;
To meanest matters will I stoop, for mean is the lot of mortal;
I will rise to noblest themes, for the soul hath an heritage of glory:

The passions of puny man; the majestic characters of God;
The feverish shadows of time, and the mighty substance of eternity.

Commend thy mind unto candour, and grudge not as though thou hadst a teacher,
Nor scorn angelic Truth for the sake of her evil herald;
Heed not him, but hear his words, and care not whence they come;
The viewless winds might whisper them, the billows roar them forth,
The mean unconscious sedge sigh them in the ear of evening,
Or the mind of pride conceive, and the mouth of folly speak them.
Lo now, I stand not forth laying hold on spear and buckler,
I come a man of peace, to comfort, not to combat;
With soft persuasive speech to charm thy patient ear,
Giving the hand of fellowship, acknowledging the heart of sympathy:
Let us walk together as friends in the shaded paths of meditation,
Nor judgment set his seal until he hath poised his balance;
That the chastenings of mild reproof may meet unwitting error,
And charity not be a stranger at the board that is spread for brothers.

THE WORDS OF WISDOM.

Few and precious are the words which the lips of Wisdom utter:
To what shall their rarity be likened? What price shall count their worth?
Perfect and much to be desired, and giving joy with riches,
No lovely thing on earth can picture all their beauty.
They be chance pearls, flung among the rocks by the sullen waters of Oblivion.
Which Diligence loveth to gather, and hang round the neck of Memory;
They be white-winged seeds of happiness, wafted from the islands of the blessed,
Which Thought carefully tendeth, in the kindly garden of the heart;
They be sproutings of an harvest for eternity, bursting through the tilth of time,
Green promise of the golden wheat, that yieldeth angels' food;
They be drops of the crystal dew, which the wings of seraphs scatter,
When on some brighter Sabbath, their plumes quiver most with delight;
Such, and so precious, are the words which the lips of Wisdom utter.

Yet more, for the half is not said, of their might, and dignity, and value,
For live-giving be they and glorious, redolent of sanctity and heaven:
As the fumes of hallowed incense, that veil the throne of the Most High;
As the beaded bubbles that sparkle on the rim of the cup of Immortality;
As wreaths of the rainbow spray, from the pure cataracts of Truth.
Such, and so precious, are the words which the lips of Wisdom utter.

Yet once again, loving student, suffer the praises of thy teacher.
For verily the sun of the mind, and the life of the heart, is Wisdom:
She is pure and full of light, crowning gray hairs with lustre,
And kindling the eye of youth with a fire not its own;
And her words, whereunto canst thou liken them? for earth cannot show their peers:

They be grains of the diamond sand, the radiant floor of heaven,
Rising in sunny dust behind the chariot of God;
They be flashes of the day-spring from on high, shed from the windows of the skies;
They be streams of living waters, fresh from the fountain of Intelligence;
Such and so precious, are the words which the lips of Wisdom utter.

For these shall guide thee well, and guard thee on thy way;
And wanting all beside, with these shalt thou be rich:
Though all around be woe, these shall make thee happy;
Though all within be pain, these shall bring thee health;
Thy good shall grow into ripeness, thine evil wither and decay,
And Wisdom's words shall sweetly charm thy doubtful into virtues:
Meanness shall then be frugal care; where shame was, thou art modest;
Cowardice riseth into caution, rashness is sobered into courage;
The wrathful spirit, rendering a reason, standeth justified in anger
The idle hand hath fair excuse, propping the thoughtful forehead.
Life shall have no labyrinth but thy steps can track it,
For thou hast a silken clue, to lead thee through the darkness:
The rampant Minotaur of ignorance shall perish at thy coming,
And thine enfranchised fellows hail thy white victorious sails. ([1])
Wherefore, friend and scholar, hear the words of Wisdom;
Whether she speaketh to thy soul in the full chords of revelation;
In the teaching earth, or air, or sea; in the still melodies of thought,
Or, haply, in the humbler strains that would detain thee here.

OF TRUTH IN THINGS FALSE.

ERROR is a hardy plant; it flourisheth in every soil;
In the heart of the wise and good, alike with the wicked and foolish;
For there is no error so crooked, but it hath in it some lines of truth;
Nor is any poison so deadly, that it serveth not some wholesome use:
And the just man, enamoured of the right, is blinded by the speciousness of wrong.
And the prudent, perceiving an advantage, is content to overlook the harm.
On all things created remaineth the half-effaced signature of God,

Somewhat of fair and good, though blotted by the finger of corruption:
And if error cometh in like a flood, it mixeth with streams of truth,
And the Adversary loveth to have it so, for thereby many are decoyed.
Providence is dark in its permissions; yet one day, when all is known,
The universe of reason shall acknowledge how just and good were they;
For the wise man leaneth on his wisdom, and the righteous trusteth to his righteousness,
And those who thirst for independence, are suffered to drink of disappointment.
Wherefore?—to prove and humble them; and to teach the idolaters of truth,
That it is but the ladder unto Him, on whom only they should trust.

There is truth in the wildest scheme that imaginative heat hath engendered,
And a man may gather somewhat from the crudest theories of fancy:
The alchemist laboureth in folly, but catcheth chance gleams of wisdom.
And findeth out many inventions, though his crucible breed not gold;
The sinner, toying with witchcraft, thinketh to delude his fellows,
But there be very spirits of evil, and what if they come at his bidding;
He is a bold bad man who dareth to tamper with the dead;
For their whereabout lieth in a mystery—that vestibule leading to Eternity,
The waiting-room for unclad ghosts, before the presence-chamber of their King:
Mind may act upon mind, though bodies be far divided;
For the life is in the blood, but souls communicate unseen:
And the heat of an excited intellect, radiating to its fellows,
Doth kindle dry leaves afar off, while the green wood around it is unwarmed.
The dog may have a spirit as well as his brutal master;
A spirit to live in happiness; for why should he be robbed of his existence?
Hath he not a conscience of evil, a glimmer of moral sense,
Love and hatred, courage and fear, and visible shame and pride?
There may be a future rest for the patient victims of the cruel;
And a season allotted for their bliss, to compensate for unjust suffering.
Spurn not at seeming error, but dig below its surface for the truth;
And beware of seeming truths, that grow on the roots of error:
For comely are the apples that spring from the Dead Sea's cursed shore:
But within are they dust and ashes, and the hand that plucked them shall rue it.

A frequent similar effect argueth a constant cause:
Yet who hath counted the links that bind an omen to its issue?
Who hath expounded the law that rendereth calamities gregarious,
Pressing down with yet more woes the heavy-laden mourner?
Who knoweth wherefore a monsoon should swell the sails of the prosperous,
Blithely speeding on their course the children of good luck?
Who hath companioned a vision from the horn or ivory gate, (2)
Or met an other's mind in his, and explained its presence?
There is a secret somewhat in antipathies; and love is more than fancy;
Yea, and a palpable notice warneth of an instant danger;
For the soul hath its feelers, cobwebs floating on the wind,
That catch events in their approach with sure and apt presentiment,
So that some halo of attraction heraldeth a coming friend.
Investing, in his likeness, the stranger that passed on before;
And while the word is in thy mouth, behold thy word fulfilled,
And he of whom we spake can answer for himself.
O man, little hast thou learnt of truth in things most true,
How therefore shall thy blindness wot of truth in things most false?
Thou hast not yet perceived the causes of life or motion;
How then canst thou define the subtle sympathies of mind?
For the spirit, sharpest and strongest when disease hath rent the body,
Hath welcomed kindred spirits in nightly visitations,
Or learnt from restless ghosts dark secrets of the living,
And helped slow justice to her prey by the dreadful teaching of a dream.

Verily, there is nothing so true, that the damps of error have not warped it;
Verily, there is nothing so false, that a sparkle of truth is not in it.
For the enemy, the father of lies, the giant Upas of creation,
Whose deadly shade hath blasted this once green garden of the Lord,
Can but pervert the good, but may not create the evil;
He destroyeth, but cannot build; for he is not antagonist deity:
Mighty in his stolen power, yet is he a creature and a subject;
Not a maker of abstract wrong, but a spoiler of concrete right:
The fiend hath not a royal crown; he is but a prowling robber,
Suffered, for some mysterious end, to haunt the King's highway;
And the keen sword he beareth, once was a simple ploughshare;
Yea, and his panoply of error is but a distortion of the truth:

The sickle that once reaped righteousness, beaten from its useful curve,
With axe, and spike, and bar, headeth the marauder's halbert.
Seek not further, O man, to solve the dark riddle of sin;
Suffice it, that thine own bad heart is to thee thine origin of evil.

OF ANTICIPATION.

Thou hast seen many sorrows, travel-stained pilgrim of the world,
But that which hath vexed thee most, hath been the looking for evil;
And though calamities have crossed thee, and misery been heaped on thy head,
Yet ills that never happened, have chiefly made thee wretched.
The sting of pain and the edge of pleasure are blunted by long expectation.
For the gall and the balm alike are diluted in the waters of patience:
And often thou sippest sweetness, ere the cup is dashed from thy lip;
Or drainest the gall of fear, while evil is passing by thy dwelling.
A man too careful of danger liveth in continual torment;
But a cheerful expecter of the best hath a fountain of joy within him:
Yea, though the breath of disappointment should chill the sanguine heart,
Speedily gloweth it again, warmed by the live embers of hope;
Though the black and heavy surge close above the head for a moment,
Yet the happy buoyancy of Confidence riseth superior to Despair.
Verily, evils may be courted, may be wooed and won by distrust;
For the wise Physician of our weal loveth not an unbelieving spirit;
And to those giveth he good, who rely on his hand for good;
And those leaveth he to evil, who fear, but trust him not.
Ask for good, and hope it; for the ocean of good is fathomless;
Ask for good, and have it; for thy Friend would see thee happy:
But to the timid heart, to the child of unbelief and dread,
That leaneth on his own weak staff, and trusteth the sight of his eyes,
The evil he feared shall come, for the soil is ready for the seed;
And suspicion hath coldly put aside the hand that was ready to help him;
Therefore look up, sad spirit, be strong, thou coward heart,
Or fear will make thee wretched, though evil follow not behind:
Cease to anticipate misfortune,—there are still many chances of escape;
But if it come, be courageous; face it, and conquer thy calamity.

There is not an enemy so stout as to storm and take the fortress of the mind,
Unless its infirmity turn traitor, and Fear unbar the gates.
The valiant standeth as a rock, and the billows break upon him;
The timorous is a skiff unmoored, tost and mocked at by a ripple;
The valiant holdeth fast to good, till evil wrench it from him;
The timorous casteth it aside, to meet the worst half way:
Yet oftentimes is evil but a braggart, that provoketh and will not fight;
Or the feint of a subtle fencer, who measureth his thrust elsewhere:
Or perchance a blessing in a masque, sent to try thy trust,
The precious smiting of a friend, whose frowns are all in love:
Often the storm threateneth, but is driven to other climes,
And the weak hath quailed in fear, while the firm hath been glad in his confidence.

OF HIDDEN USES.

The sea-wort ([3]) floating on the waves, or rolled up high along the shore,
Ye counted useless and vile, heaping on it names of contempt:
Yet hath it gloriously triumphed, and man been humbled in his ignorance,
For health is in the freshness of its savour, and it cumbereth the beach with wealth;
Comforting the tossings of pain with its violet-tinctured essence,
And by its humbler ashes enriching many proud.
Be this then a lesson to thy soul, that thou reckon nothing worthless,
Because thou heedest not its use, nor knowest the virtues thereof.
And herein, as thou walkest by the sea, shall weeds be a type and an earnest
Of the stored and uncounted riches lying hid in all creatures of God:
There be flowers making glad the desert, and roots fattening the soil,
And jewels in the secret deep, scattered among groves of coral,
And comforts to crown all wishes, and aids unto every need,
Influences yet unthought, and virtues, and many inventions,
And uses above and around, which man hath not yet regarded.
Not long to charm away disease, hath the crocus ([4]) yielded up its bulb,
Nor the willow lent its bark, nor the nightshade its vanquished poison;

Not long hath the twisted leaf, the fragrant gift of China,
Nor that nutritious root, the boon of far Peru,
Nor the many-coloured dahlia, nor the gorgeous flaunting cactus,
Nor the multitude of fruits and flowers, ministered to life and luxury;
Even so, there be virtues yet unknown in the wasted foliage of the elm,
In the sun-dried harebell of the downs, and the hyacinth drinking in the meadow,
In the sycamore's winged fruit, and the facet-cut cones of the cedar;
And the pansy and bright geranium live not alone for beauty,
Nor the waxen flower of the arbute, though it dieth in a day,
Nor the sculptured crest of the fir, unseen but by the stars;
And the meanest weed of the garden serveth unto many uses,
The salt tamarisk, and juicy flag, the freckled orchis, and the daisy.
The world may laugh at famine when forest-trees yield bread,
When acorns give out fragrant drink, (5) and the sap of the linden is as fatness:
For every green herb, from the lotus to the darnel,
Is rich with delicate aids to help incurious man.

Still, Mind is up and stirring, and pryeth in the corners of contrivance,
Often from the dark recesses picking out bright seeds of truth:
Knowledge hath clipped the lightning's wings, and mewed it up for a purpose,
Training to some domestic task the fiery bird of heaven;
Tamed is the spirit of the storm, to slave in all peaceful arts,
To walk with husbandry and science; to stand in the vanguard against death:
And the chemist balanceth his elements with more than magic skill,
Commanding stones that they be bread, and draining sweetness out of wormwood.
Yet man, heedless of a God, counteth up vain reckonings,
Fearing to be jostled and starved out, by the too prolific increase of his kind;
And asketh, in unbelieving dread, for how few years to come
Will the black cellars of the world yield unto him fuel for his winter.
Might not the wide-waste sea be pent within narrower bounds?
Might not the arm of diligence make the tangled wilderness a garden?
And for aught thou canst tell, there may be a thousand methods
Of comforting thy limbs in warmth, though thou kindle not a spark.

Fear not, son of man, for thyself nor thy seed:—with a multitude is plenty;
God's blessing giveth increase, and with it larger than enough.

Search out the wisdom of nature, there is depth in all her doings;
She seemeth prodigal of power, yet her rules are the maxims of frugality:
The plant refresheth the air, and the earth filtereth the water,
And dews are sucked into the cloud, dropping fatness on the world:
She hath, on a mighty scale, the general use of all things;
Yet hath she specially for each its microscopic purpose:
There is use in the prisoned air, that swelleth the pods of the laburnum;
Design in the venomed thorns, that sentinel the leaves of the nettle;
A final cause for the aromatic gum, that congealeth the moss around a rose:
A reason for each blade of grass, that reareth its small spire.
How knoweth discontented man what a train of ills might follow,
If the lowest menial of nature knew not her secret office?
If the thistle never sprang up, to mock the loose husbandry of indolence,
Or the pestilence never swept away an unknown curse from among men?
Would ye crush the buzzing myriads that float on the breath of the evening?
Would ye trample the creatures of God that people the rotting fruit?
Would ye suffer no mildew forest to stain the unhealthy wall,
Nor a noisome savour to exhale from the pool that breedeth disease?
Pain is useful unto man, for it teacheth him to guard his life,
And the fetid vapours of the fen warn him to fly from danger:
And the meditative mind, looking on, winneth good food for its hunger,
Seeing the wholesome root bring forth a poisonous berry;
For otherwhile falleth it out that truth, driven to extremities,
Yieldeth bitter folly as the spoilt fruit of wisdom.
O, blinded is thine eye, if it see not just aptitude in all things;
O, frozen is thy heart, if it glow not with gratitude for all things:
In the perfect circle of creation not an atom could be spared,
From earth's magnetic zone to the bindweed round a hawthorn.

The sage, and the beetle at his feet, hath each a ministration to perform;
The brier and the palm have the wages of life, rendering secret service.
Neither is it thus alone with the definite existences of matter;
But motion and sound, circumstance and quality, yea, all things have their office.
The zephyr playing with an aspen leaf,—the earthquake that rendeth a continent;

The moonbeam silvering a ruined arch,—the desert wave dashing up a pyramid;
The thunder of jarring icebergs,—the stops of a shepherd's pipe;
The howl of the tiger in the glen,—and the wood-dove calling to her mate;
The vulture's cruel rage,—the grace of the stately swan;
The fierceness looking from the lynx's eye, and the dull stupor of the sloth.
To these, and to all, is there added each its USE, though man considereth it lightly;
For Power hath ordained nothing which Economy saw not needful.

All things being are essential to the vast ubiquity of God;
Neither is there one thing overmuch, nor freed from honourable servitude.
Were there not a need-be of wisdom, nothing would be as it is;
For essence without necessity argueth a moral weakness.
We look through a glass darkly, we catch but glimpses of truth;
But, doubtless, the sailing of a cloud hath Providence to its pilot,
Doubtless, the root of an oak is gnarled for a special purpose,
The foreknown station of a rush is as fixed as the station of a king,
And chaff from the hand of a winnower, steered as the stars in their courses
Man liveth only in himself, but the Lord liveth in all things;
And his pervading unity quickeneth the whole creation.
Man doeth one thing at once, nor can he think two thoughts together;
But God compasseth all things, mantling the globe like air:
And we render homage to His wisdom, seeing use in all His creatures,
For, perhance, the universe would die, were not all things as they are.

OF COMPENSATION.

EQUAL is the government of heaven in allotting pleasures among men,
And just the everlasting law, that hath wedded happiness to virtue:
For verily on all things else broodeth disappointment with care,
That childish man may be taught the shallowness of earthly enjoyment.
Wherefore, ye that have enough, envy ye the rich man his abundance?
Wherefore, daughters of affluence, covet ye the cottager's content?
Take the good with the evil, for ye all are pensioners of God,
And none may choose or refuse the cup his wisdom mixeth.

The poor man rejoiceth at his toil, and his daily bread is sweet to him:
Content with present good, he looketh not for evil to the future:
The rich man languisheth with sloth, and findeth pleasure in nothing,
He locketh up care with his gold, and feareth the fickleness of fortune
Can a cup contain within itself the measure of a bucket?
Or the straitened appetites of man drink more than their fill of luxury?
There is a limit to enjoyment, though the sources of wealth be boundless;
And the choicest pleasures of life lie within the ring of moderation.

Also though penury and pain be real and bitter evils,
I would reason with the poor afflicted, for he is not so wretched as he seemeth.
What right hath an offender to complain, though others escape punishment,
If the stripes of earned misfortune overtake him in his sin?
Wherefore not endure with resignation the evils thou canst not avert?
For the coward pain will flee, if thou meet him as a man:
Consider, whatever be thy fate, that it might and ought to have been worse,
And that it lieth in thy hand to gather even blessings from afflictions:
Bethink thee, wherefore were they sent? and hath not use blunted their keeness?
Need hope, and patience, and courage, be strangers to the meanest hovel?
Thou art in an evil case,—it were cruel to deny to thee compassion,
But there is not unmitigated ill in the sharpest of this world's sorrows:
I touch not the sore of thy guilt; but of human griefs I counsel thee,
Cast off the weakness of regret, and gird thee to redeem thy loss.
Thou hast gained, in the furnace of affliction, self-knowledge, patience, and humility,
And these be as precious ore, that waiteth the skill of the coiner:
Despise not the blessings of adversity, nor the gain thou hast earned so hardly,
And now thou hast drained the bitter, take heed that thou lose not the sweet.

Power is seldom innocent, and envy is the yoke-fellow of eminence;
And the rust of the miser's riches wasteth his soul as a canker.
The poor man counteth not the cost at which such wealth hath been purchased;
He would be on the mountain's top without the toil and travail of the climbing.

But equity demandeth recompense; for high-place, calumny and care;
For state, comfortless splendour eating out the heart of home ;
For warrior fame, dangers and death; for a name among the learned, a spirit overstrained;
For honour of all kinds, the goad of ambition; on every acquirement, the tax of anxiety.
He that would change with another, must take the cup as it is mixed:
Poverty, with largeness of heart; or a full purse, with a sordid spirit:
Wisdom, in an ailing body; or a common mind with health:
Godliness, with man's scorn; or the welcome of the mighty, with guilt:
Beauty, with a fickle heart; or plainness of face, with affection.
For so hath Providence determined, that a man shall not easily discover
Unmingled good or evil, to quicken his envy or abhorrence.
A bold man or a fool must he be, who would change his lot with another;
It were a fearful bargain, and mercy hath lovingly refused it;
For we know the worst of ourselves, but the secrets of another we see not,
And better is certain bad, than the doubt and dread of worse.

Just, and strong, and opportune is the moral rule of God;
Ripe in its times, firm in its judgments, equal in the measure of its gifts,
Yet men, scanning the surface, count the wicked happy:
Nor heed the compensating peace which gladdeneth the good in his afflictions.
They see not the frightful dreams that crowd a bad man's pillow,
Like wreathed adders crawling round his midnight conscience;
They hear not the terrible suggestions, that knock at the portal of his will,
Provoking to wipe away from life the one weak witness of the deed;
They know not the torturing suspicions that sting his panting breast,
When the clear eye of penetration quietly readeth off the truth.
Likewise of the good what know they? the memories bringing pleasure,
Shrined in the heart of the benevolent, and glistening from his eye;
The calm self-justifying reason that establisheth the upright in his purpose;
The warm and gushing bliss that floodeth all the thoughts of the religious.
Many a beggar at the cross-way, or gray-haired shepherd on the plain,
Hath more of the end of all wealth, than hundreds who multiply the means.

Moreover, a moral compensation reacheth to the secrecy of thought;
For if thou wilt think evil of thy neighbour, soon shalt thou have him for thy foe.

And yet he may know nothing of the cause that maketh thee distasteful to his soul,—
The cause of unkind suspicion, for which thou hast thy punishment:
And if thou think of him in charity, wishing or praying for his weal,
He shall not guess the secret charm that lureth his soul to love thee.
For just is retributive ubiquity: Samson did sin with Dalilah,
And his eyes and captive strength were forfeit to the Philistine:
Jacob robbed his brother, and sorrow was his portion to the grave:
David must fly before his foes, yea, though his guilt is covered:
And He, who seeming old in youth, (6) was marred for others' sin,
For every special crime must bear its special penalty:
By luxury, or rashness, or vice, the member that hath erred suffereth,
And therefore the Sacrifice for all was pained at every pore.

Alike to the slave and his oppressor cometh night with sweet refreshment,
And half of the life of the most wretched is gladdened by the soothings of sleep.
Pain addeth zest unto pleasure, and teacheth the luxury of health:
There is a joy in sorrow, which none but a mourner can know;
Madness hath imaginary bliss, and most men have no more;
Age hath its quiet calm, and youth enjoyeth not for haste;
Daily, in the midst of its beatitude, the righteous soul is vexed;
And even the misery of guilt doth attain to the bliss of pardon.
Who, in the face of the born-blind, ever looked on other than content?
And the deaf ear listeneth within to the silent music of the heart.
There is evil poured upon the earth from the overflowings of corruption,—
Sickness, and poverty, and pain, and guilt, and madness, and sorrow;
But, as the water from a fountain riseth and sinketh to its level,
Ceaselessly toileth justice to equalize the lots of men:
For, habit, and hope, and ignorance, and the being but one of a multitude
And strength of reason in the sage, and dulness of feeling in the fool,
And the light elasticity of courage, and the calm resignation of meekness
And the stout endurance of decision, and the weak carelessness of apathy
And helps invisible but real, and ministerings not unfelt,
Angelic aid with worldly discomfiture, bodily loss with the soul's gain,
Secret griefs, and silent joys, thorns in the flesh, and cordials for the spirit,
(—Short of the insuperable barrier dividing innocence from guilt,—)
Go far to level all things, by the gracious rule of Compensation.

OF INDIRECT INFLUENCES.

Face thy foe in the field, and perchance thou wilt meet thy master,
For the sword is chained to his wrist, and his armour buckled for the battle;
But find him when he looketh not for thee, aim between the joints of his harness,
And the crest of his pride will be humbled, his cruelty will bite the dust.
Beard not a lion in his den, but fashion the secret pitfall,
So shalt thou conquer the strong, thyself triumphing in weakness.
The hurricane rageth fiercely, and the promontory standeth in its might,
Breasting the artillery of heaven, as darts glance from the crocodile;
But the small continual creeping of the silent footsteps of the sea
Mineth the wall of adamant, and stealthily compasseth its ruin.
The weakness of accident is strong, where the strength of design is weak:
And a casual analogy convinceth, when a mind beareth not argument.
Will not a man listen? be silent; and prove thy maxim by example:
Never fear, thou losest not thy hold, though thy mouth doth not render a reason.
Contend not in wisdom with a fool, for thy sense maketh much of his conceit;
And some errors never would have thriven, had it not been for learned refutation;
Yea, much evil hath been caused by an honest wrestler for truth,
And much of unconscious good, by the man that hated wisdom:
For the intellect judgeth closely, and if thou overstep thy argument,
Or seem not consistent with thyself, or fail in thy direct purpose,
The mind that went along with thee, shall stop and return without thee,
And thou shalt have raised a foe, where thou mightest have won a friend.

Hints, shrewdly strown, mightily disturb the spirit,
Where a barefaced accusation would be too ridiculous for calumny:
The sly suggestion toucheth nerves, and nerves contract the fronds,
And the sensitive mimosa of affection trembleth to its root;
And friendships, the growth of half a century, those oaks that laugh a storms,
Have been cankered in a night by a worm, even as the prophet's gourd.
Hast thou loved, and not known jealousy? for a sidelong look
Can please or pain thy heart more than the multitude of proofs:

Hast thou hated, and not learned that thy silent scorn
Doth deeper aggravate thy foe than loud-cursing malice?—
A wise wise man prevaileth in power, for he screeneth his battering engine,
But a fool tilteth headlong, and his adversary is aware.

Behold those broken arches, that oriel all unglazed,
That crippled line of columns bleaching in the sun,
The delicate shaft stricken midway, and the flying buttress
Idly stretching forth to hold up tufted ivy:
Thinkest thou the thousand eyes that shine with rapture on a ruin,
Would have looked with half their wonder on the perfect pile?
And wherefore not—but that light hints, suggesting unseen beauties,
Fill the complacent gazer with self-grown conceits?
And so, the rapid sketch winneth more praise to the painter,
Than the consummate work elaborated on his easel:
And so, the Helvetic lion caverned in the living rock
Hath more of majesty and force, than if upon a marble pedestal.

Tell me, daughter of taste, what hath charmed thine ear in music?
Is it the laboured theme, the curious fugue or cento,—
Nor rather the sparkles of intelligence flashing from some strange note
Or the soft melody of sounds far sweeter for simplicity?
Tell me, thou son of science, what hath filled thy mind in reading?
Is it the volume of detail where all is orderly set down,
And they that read may run, nor need to stop and think;
The book carefully accurate, that counteth thee no better than a fool,
Gorging the passive mind with annotated notes;—
Nor rather the half-suggested thoughts, the riddles thou mayest solve,
The fair ideas, coyly peeping like young loves out of roses,
The quaint arabesque conceptions, half cherub and half flower,
The light analogy, or deep allusion, trusted to thy learning,
The confidence implied in thy skill to unravel meaning mysteries?
For ideas are ofttimes shy of the close furniture of words,
And thought, wherein only is power, may be best conveyed by a suggestion;
The flash that lighteth up a valley, amid the dark midnight of a storm,
Coineth the mind with that scene sharper than fifty summers.

A worldly man boasteth in his pride that there is no power but of money:
And he judgeth the characters of men by the differing measures of their means:

He stealeth all goodly names, as worth, and value, and substance,
Which be the ancient heritage of Virtue, but such an one ascribeth unto Wealth:
He spurneth the needy sage, whose wisdom hath enriched nations,
And the sons of poverty and learning, without whom earth were a desert:
Music, the soother of cares, the tuner of the dank discordant heart-strings,
It is nought unto such an one but sounds, whereby some earn their living:
The poem, and the picture, and the statue, to him seem idle baubles,
Which wealth condescendeth to favour, to gain him the name of patron.
But little wotteth he the might of the means his folly despiseth;
He considereth not that these be the wires which move the puppets of the world.
A sentence hath formed a character, (7) and a character subdued a kingdom;
A picture hath ruined souls, or raised them to commerce with the skies:
The pen hath shaken nations, and stablished the world in peace;
And the whole full horn of plenty been filled from the vial of science.
He regardeth man as sensual, the monarch of created matter,
And careth not aught for mind, that linketh him with spirits unseen:
He feedeth his carcass and is glad, though his soul be faint and famished,
And the dull brute power of the body bindeth him a captive to himself.

Man liveth from hour to hour, and knoweth not what may happen;
Influences circle him on all sides, and yet must he answer for his actions,
For the being that is master of himself, bendeth events to his will,
But a slave to selfish passion is the wavering creature of circumstance.
To this man temptation is a poison, to that man it addeth vigour;
And each may render to himself influences good or evil.
As thou directest the power, harm or advantage will follow;
And the torrent that swept the valley, may be led to turn a mill;
The wild electric flash, that could have kindled comets,
May by the ductile wire give ease to an ailing child.
For outward matter or event, fashion not the character within,
But each man, yielding or resisting, fashioneth his mind for himself.

Some have said, What is in a name?—most potent plastic influence;
A name is a word of character, and repetition stablisheth the fact;
A word of rebuke, or of honour, tending to obscurity or fame;
And greatest is the power of a name, when its power is least suspected.

A low name is a thorn in the side, that hindereth the footman in his running;
But a name of ancestral renown shall often put the racer to his speed.
Few men have grown unto greatness whose names are allied to ridicule,
And many would never have been profligate, but for the splendour of a name.
A wise man scorneth nothing, be it never so small or homely,
For he knoweth not the secret laws that may bind it to great effects.
The world in its boyhood was credulous, and dreaded the vengeance of the stars,
The world in its dotage is not wiser, fearing not the influence of small things:
Planets govern not the soul, nor guide the destinies of man,
But trifles, lighter than straws, are levers in the building up of character.
A man hath the tiller in his hand, and may steer against the current,
Or may glide down idly with the stream, till his vessel founder in the whirlpool.

OF MEMORY.

Where art thou, storehouse of the mind, garner of facts and fancies,—
In what strange firmament are laid the beams of thine airy chambers?
Or art thou that small cavern, (8) the centre of the rolling brain,
Where still one sandy morsel testifieth man's original?
Or hast thou some grand globe, some common hall of intellect,
Some spacious market-place for thought, where all do bring their wares,
And gladly rescued from the littleness, the narrow closet of a self,
The privileged soul hath large access,-coming in the livery of learning?
Live we as isolated worlds, perfect in substance and spirit,
Each a sphere, with a special mind, prisoned in its shell of matter?
Or rather, as converging radiations, parts of one majestic whole,
Beams of the Sun, streams from the River, branches of the mighty Tree,
Some bearing fruit, some bearing leaves, and some diseased and barren,—
Some for the feast, some for the floor, and some—how many—for the fire?
Memory may be but a power of coming to the treasury of Fact,

A momentary self-desertion, an absence in spirit from the now,
An actual coursing hither and thither, by the mind, slipped from its leash,
A life, as in the mystery of dreams, spent within the limits of a moment.

A brutish man knoweth not this, neither can a fool comprehend it,
But there be secrets of the memory, deep, wondrous, and fearful.
Were I at Petra, could I not declare, My soul hath been here before me?
Am I strange to the columned halls, the calm dead grandeur of Palmyra?
Know I not thy mount, O Carmel! Have I not voyaged on the Danube?
Nor seen the glare of Arctic snows,—nor the black tents of the Tartar?
Is it then a dream, that I remember the faces of them of old,
While wandering in the grove with Plato, and listening to Zeno in the porch?
Paul have I seen, and Pythagoras, and the Stagyrite hath spoken me friendly,
And His meek eye looked also upon me, standing with Peter in the palace.
Athens and Rome, Persepolis and Sparta, am I not a freeman of you all?
And chiefly can my yearning heart forget thee, O Jerusalem?
For the strong magic of conception, mingled with the fumes of memory,
Giveth me a life in all past time, yea, and addeth substance to the future.
Be ye my judges, imaginative minds, full-fledged to soar into the sun,
Whose grosser natural thoughts the chemistry of wisdom hath sublimed,
Have ye not confessed to a feeling, a consciousness, strange and vague,
That ye have gone this way before, and walk again your daily life,
Tracking an old routine, and on some foreign strand,
Where bodily ye have never stood, finding your own footsteps?
Hath not at times some recent friend looked out an old familiar,
Some newest circumstance or place teemed as with ancient memories?
A startling sudden flash lighteth up all for an instant,
And then it is quenched, as in darkness, and leaveth the cold spirit trembling.

Memory is not wisdom; idiots can rote volumes:
Yet, what is wisdom without memory? a babe that is strangled in its birth;
The path of the swallow in the air; the path of the dolphin in the waters;
A cask running out; a bottomless chasm: such is wisdom without memory.
There be many wise, who cannot store their knowledge;
Yet from themselves are they satisfied, for the fountain is within.

There be many who store, but have no wisdom of their own,
Lumbering their armory with weapons their muscles cannot lift:
There be many thieves and robbers, who glean and store unlawfully,
Calling in to memory's help some cunningly devised Cabala:
But to feed the mind with fatness, to fill thy granary with corn,
Nor clog with chaff and straw the threshing-floor of reason,
Reap the ideas, and house them well; but leave the words high stubble,
Strive to store up what was thought, despising what was said.
For the mind is a spirit, and drinketh in ideas, as flame melteth into flame,
But for words, it must pack them as on floors, cumbrous and perishable merchandise.

To be pained for a minute, to fear for an hour, to hope for a week—how long and weary!
But to remember fourscore years, is to look back upon a day.
An avenue seemeth to lengthen in the eyes of the wayfaring man,
But let him turn, those stationed elms crowd up within a yard;
Pace the lamp-lit streets of some sleeping city,
The multitude of cressets shall seem one, in the false picture of perspective;
Even so, in sweet treachery, dealeth the aged with himself,
He gazeth on the green hill-tops, while the marshes beneath are hidden;
And the partial telescope of memory pierceth the blank between,
To look with lingering love at the fair star of childhood.
Life is as the current spark on the miner's wheel of flints:
Whiles it spinneth there is light; stop it, all is darkness:
Life is as a morsel of frankincense burning in the hall of Eternity;
It is gone, but its odorous cloud curleth to the lofty roof!
Life is as a lump of salt, melting in the temple-laver;
It is gone,—yet its savour reacheth to the farthest atom;
Even so, for evil or for good, is life the criterion of a man,
For its memories of sanctity or sin pervade all the firmament of being,
There is but the flitting moment wherein to hope or to enjoy,
But in the calendar of memory, that moment is all time.

THE DREAM OF AMBITION.

I LEFT the happy fields that smile around the village of Content,
And sought with wayward feet the torrid desert of Ambition.
Long time, parched and weary, I travelled that burning sand,
And the hooded basilisk and adder were strewed in my way for palms;
Black scorpions thronged me round, with sharp uplifted stings,
Seeming to mock me as I ran; (then I guessed it was a dream,—
But life is oft so like a dream, we know not where we are.)
So I toiled on, doubting in myself, up a steep gravel cliff,
Whose yellow summit shot up far into the brazen sky;
And quickly, I was wafted to the top, as upon unseen wings
Carrying me upward like a leaf: (then I thought it was a dream,—
Yet life is oft so like a dream, we know not where we are.)
So I stood on the mountain, and behold! before me a giant pyramid,
And I clomb with eager haste its high and difficult steps;
For, I longed, like another Belus, to mount up, yea to heaven,
Nor sought I rest until my feet had spurned the crest of earth.

Then I sat on my granite throne under the burning sun,
And the world lay smiling beneath me, but I was wrapt in flames;
(And I hoped in glimmering consciousness, that all this torture was a dream,—
Yet life is oft so like a dream, we know not where we are.)
And anon, as I sat scorching, the pyramid shuddered to its root,
And I felt the quarried mass leap from its sand foundations:
Awhile it tottered and tilted, as raised by invisible levers,—
(And now my reason spake with me; I knew it was a dream;
Yet I hushed that whisper into silence, for I hoped to learn of wisdom,
By tracking up my truant thoughts, whereunto they might lead.)
And suddenly, as rolling upon wheels, adown the cliff it rushed,
And I thought, in my hot brain, of the Muscovites' icy slope;
A thousand yards in a moment we ploughed the sandy seas,
And crushed those happy fields, and that smiling village,
And onward, as a living thing, still rushed my mighty throne,
Thundering along, and pounding, as it went, the millions in my way:
Before me all was life, and joy, and full-blown summer,

Behind me death and woe, the desert and simoom.
Then I wept and shrieked aloud, for pity and for fear;
But might not stop, for, comet-like, flew on the maddened mass
Over the crashing cities, and falling obelisks and towers,
And columns, razed as by a scythe, and high doomes, shivered as an egg-shell,
And deep embattled ranks, and women, crowded in the streets,
And children, kneeling as for mercy, and all I had ever loved,
Yea, over all, mine awful throne rushed on with seeming instinct,
And over the crackling forests, and over the rugged beach,
And on with a terrible hiss through the foaming wild Atlantic
That roared around me as I sat, but could not quench my spirit,—
Still on, through startled solitudes we shattered the pavement of the sea,
Down, down, to that central vault, the bolted doors of hell;
And these, with horrid shock, my huge throne battered in,
And on to the deepest deep, where the fierce flames were hottest,
Blazing tenfold as conquering furiously the seas that rushed in with me,—
And there I stopped; and a fearful voice shouted in mine ear,
"Behold the home of Discontent; behold the rest of Ambition!"

OF SUBJECTION.

Law hath dominion over all things, over universal mind and matter;
For there are reciprocities of right, which no creature can gainsay.
Unto each there was added by its Maker, in the perfect chain of being,
Dependencies and sustentations, accidents, and qualities, and powers;
And each must fly forward in the curve, unto which it was forced from the beginning;
Each must attract and repel, or the monarchy of Order is no more.
Laws are essential emanations from the self-poised character of God
And they radiate from that sun, to the circling edges of creation.
Verily, the mighty Lawgiver hath subjected Himself unto laws,
And God is the primal grand example of free unstrained obedience:
His perfection is limited by right, and cannot trespass into wrong,
Because He hath established Himself as the fountain of only good,
And in thus much is bounded, that the evil hath he left unto another,

And that dark other hath usurped the evil which Omnipotence laid down.
Unto God there exist impossibilities; for the True One cannot lie,
Nor the Wise One wander from the track which he hath determined for himself:
For his will was purposed from eternity, strong in the love of order;
And that will altereth not, as the law of the Medes and Persians.
God is the origin of order, and the first exemplar of his precept;
For there is subordination of his Essence, self-guided unto holiness;
And there is subordination of his Persons, in due procession of dignity;
For the Son, as a son, is subject; and to him doth the Spirit minister;
But these things be mysteries to man, he cannot reach nor fathom them,
And ever must he speak in paradox, when labouring to expound his God;
For, behold, God is Alone, mighty in unshackled freedom;
And with those wondrous Persons abideth eternal equality.

So then, start ye from the fountain and follow the river of existence,
For its current is bounded throughout by the banks of just subordination:
Thrones, and dominions, and powers, Archangels, Cherubim and Seraphim,
Angels, and flaming ministers, and breathing chariots and harps.
For there are degrees in heaven, and varied capabilities of bliss,
And steps in the ladder of intelligence, and ranks in approaches to Perfection:
Doubtless, reverence is given, as their due, to the masters in wisdom;
Doubtless, there are who serve; or a throne would have small glory.
Regard now the universe of matter, the substance of visible creation,
Which of old, with well-observing truth, the Greek hath surnamed ORDER; (*)
Where is there an atom out of place? or a particle that yieldeth not obedience?
Where is there a fragment that is free? or one thing the equal of another?
The chain is unbroken down to man, and beyond him the links are perfect:
But he standeth solitary sin, a marvel of permitted chaos.

And shall this seeming error in the scale of due subordination
Be a spot of desert unreclaimed, in the midst of the vineyard of the Lord?
Shall his presumptuous pride snap the safe tether of connexion,
And his blind selfish folly refuse the burden of maintenance?
O man, thou art a creature; boast not thyself above the law:
Think not of thyself as free: thou art bound in the trammels of dependence.

What is the sum of thy duty, but obedience to righteous rule,
To the great commanding oracle, uttered by delegated organs?
Thou canst not render homage to abstract Omnipresent power,
Save through the concrete symbol of visible ordained authority.
Those who obey not man are oftenest found rebels againest God;
And seldom is the delegate so bold, as to order what he knoweth to be wrong.
Yet mark me, proud gainsayer! I say not, obey unto sin;
But, where the Principal is silent, take heed that thou despise not the Deputy:
And he that loveth order will bless thee for thy faith,
If thou recognize his sanction in the powers that fashion human laws.
Thou, the vicegerent of the Lord, his high anointed image,
Toward whom a good man's loyalty floweth from the hearts of his religion,
Thou, whose deep responsibilities are fathomed by a nation's prayers,
Whom wise men fear for while they live, and envy thee nothing but thy virtues,
From thy dizzy pinnacle of greatness, remember thou also art a subject,
And the throne of thine earthly glory is itself but the footstool of thy God.
The homage thy kingdoms yield thee, regard thou as yielded unto Him;
And while girt with all the majesty of state, consider thee the Lord's chief servant;
So shalt thou prosper, and be strong, grafted on the strength of another;
So shall thy virgin heart be happy, in being humble.
And thou shalt flourish as an oak, the monarch of thine island forests,
Whose deep-dug roots are twisted around the stout ribs of the globe,
That mocketh at the fury of the storm, and rejoiceth in summer sunshine,
Glad in the smiles of heaven, and great in the stability of earth.

A ruler hath not power for himself, neither is his pomp for his pride;
But benėath the ermine of his office should he wear the rough hair-cloth of humility.
Nevertheless, every way obey him, so thou break not a higher commandment;
For Nero was an evil king, yet Paul prescribeth subjection.
If the rulers of a nation be holy, the Lord hath blessed that nation;
If they be lewd and impious, chastisement hath come upon that people:
For the bitterest scourge of a land is ungodliness in them that govern it,
And the guilt of the sons of Josiah drove Israel weeping into Babylon.

Yet be thou resolute against them, if they change the mandates of thy God,
If they touch the ark of his covenant, wherein all his mercies are enshrined:
Be resolute, but not rebellious; lest thou be of the company of Korah:
Set thy face against them as a flint: but be not numbered with Abiram.
Daniel nobly disobeyed; but not from a spirit of sedition;
And Azarias shouted from the furnace,—I will not bow down, O KING.
If truth must be sacrificed to unity, then faithfulness were folly;
If man must be obeyed before God, the martyrs have bled in vain:
Yet none of that blessed army reviled the rulers of the land;
They were loud and bold against the sin, but bent before the ensign of authority.
Honesty, scorning compromise, walketh most suitably with Reverence;
Otherwise righteous daring may show but as obstinate rebellion;
Therefore, suffer not thy censure to lack the savour of courtesy,
And remember the mortal sinneth, but the staff of his power is from God.

Man, thou hast a social spirit, and art deeply indebted to thy kind:
Therefore claim not all thy rights; but yield, for thine own advantage.
Society is a chain of obligations, and its links must support each other:
The branch cannot but wither, that is cut from the parent vine.
Wouldst thou be a dweller in the woods, and cast away the cords that bind thee,
Seeking, in thy bitterness or pride, to be exiled from thy fellows?
Behold, the beasts shall hunt thee, weak, naked, houseless outcast;
Disease and Death shall track thee out, as bloodhounds, in the wilderness:
Better to be vilest of the vile, in the hated company of men,
Than to live a solitary wretch, dreading and wanting all things;
Better to be chained to thy labour, in the dusky thoroughfares of life,
Than to reign monarch of Sloth, in lonesome savage freedom.

Whence then cometh the doctrine that all should be equal and free?—
It is the lie that crowded hell, when Seraphs flung away subjection.
No man is his neighbour's equal, for no two minds are similar,
And accidents, alike with qualities, have every shade but sameness:
The lightest atom of difference shall destroy the nice balance of equality,
And all things, from without and from within, make one man to differ from another.

We are equal and free! was the watchword that spirited the legions of Satan,
We are equal and free! is the double lie that entrappeth to him conscripts from earth:
The messengers of that dark despot will pander to thy license and thy pride,
And draw thee from the crowd where thou art safe, to seize thee in the solitary desert.
Woe unto him whose heart the syren song of Liberty hath charmed;
Woe unto him whose mind is bewitched by her treacherous beauty;
In mad zeal flingeth he away the fetters of duty and restraint,
And yieldeth up the holocaust of self to that fair idol of the damned.
No man hath freedom in aught save in that from which the wicked would be hindered,
He is free toward God and good; but to all else a bondman.

Thou art in a middle sphere, to render and receive honour,
If thy king commandeth, obey; and stand not in the way with rebels;
But if need be, lay thy hand upon thy sword, and fear not to smite a traitor,
For the universe acquitteth thee with honour, fighting in defence of thy king.
If a thief break thy dwelling, and thou take him, it were sin in thee to let him go;
Yea, though he pleadeth to thy mercy, thou canst not spare him and be blameless;
For his guilt is not only against thee, it is not thy moneys or thy merchandise,
But he hath done damage to the law, which duty constraineth thee to sanction.
Feast not thine appetite of vengeance, remembering thou also art a man,
But weep for the sad compulsion, in which the chain of Providence hath bound thee:
Mercy is not thine to give; wilt thou steal another's privilege?
Or send abroad among thy neighbours, a felon whom impunity hath hardened?
Remember the Roman father, strong in his stern integrity,
And let not thy slothful self-indulgence make thee a conniver at the crime.
Also, if the knife of the murderer be raised against thee or thine,

And through good Providence and courage, thou slay him that would have slain thee,
Thou losest not a tittle of thy rectitude, having executed sudden justice;
Still mayst thou walk among the blessed, though thy hands be red with blood.
For thyself, thou art neither worse nor better; but thy fellows should count thee their creditor:
Thou hast manfully protected the right, and the right is stronger for thy deed.
Also, in the rescuing of innocence, fear not to smite the ravisher;
What though he die at thy hand? for a good name is better than the life;
And if Phineas had everlasting praise in the matter of Salu's son,
With how much greater honour standeth such a rescuer acquitted?
Uphold the laws of thy country, and fear not to fight in their defence;
But first be convinced in thy mind: for herein the doubter sinneth.
Above all things look thou well around, if indeed stern duty forceth thee
To draw the sword of justice, and stain it with the slaughter of thy fellows.

She that lieth in thy bosom, the tender wife of thy affections,
Must obey thee, and be subject, that evil drop not on thy dwelling.
The child that is used to constraint, feareth not more than he loveth;
But give thy son his way, he will hate thee and scorn thee together.
The master of a well-ordered home, knoweth to be kind to his servants;
Yet he exacteth reverence, and each one feareth at his post.
There is nothing on earth so lowly, but duty giveth it importance;
No station so degrading, but it is ennobled by obedience:
Yea, break stones upon the highway, acknowledging the Lord in thy lot,
Happy shalt thou be, and honourable, more than many children of the mighty.
Thou that despisest the outward forms, beware thou lose not the inward spirit;
For they are as words unto ideas, as symbols to things unseen.
Keep then the form that is good: retain, and do reverence to example;
And in all things observe subordination, for that is the whole duty of man.

A horse knoweth his rider, be he confident or timid,
And the fierce spirit of Bucephalus stoopeth unto none but Alexander;
The tigress roused in the jungle by the prying spaniels of the fowler,
Will quail at the eye of man, so he assert his dignity;

Nay, the very ships, those giant swans breasting the mighty waters,
Roll in the trough, or break the wave, to the pilot's fear or courage:
How much more shall man, discerning the Fountain of authority,
Bow to superior commands, and make his own obeyed.
And yet, in travelling the world, hast thou not often known
A gallant host led on to ruin by a feeble Xerxes?
Hast thou not often seen the wanton luxury of indolence
Sullying with its sleepy mist the tarnished crown of headship?
Alas! for a thousand fathers, whose indulgent sloth
Hath emptied the vial of confusion over a thousand homes:
Alas! for the palaces and hovels, that might have been nurseries for heaven,
By hot intestine broils blighted into schools for hell:
None knoweth his place, yet all refuse to serve,
None weareth the crown, yet all usurp the sceptre:
And perhance some fiercer spirit, of natural nobility of mind,
That needed but the kindness of constraint to have grown up great and good,
Now,—the rich harvest of his heart choked by unweeded tares,—
All bold to dare and do, unchecked by wholesome fear,
A scoffer about bigotry and priestcraft, a rebel against government and God,
And standard-bearer of the turbulent, leading on the sons of Belial:
Such an one is king of that small state, head tyrant of the thirty,
Brandishing the torch of discord in his village-home:
And the timid Eli of the house, yon humble parish-priest,
Liveth in shame and sorrow, fearing his own handy-work;
The mother, heart-stricken years agone, hath dropped into an early grave,
The silent sisters long to leave a home they cannot love;
The brothers, casting off restraint, follow their wayward wills;
And the chance guest, early departing, blesseth his kind stars,
That on his humbler home hath brooded no domestic curse.
Yet is that curse the fruit; wouldest thou the root of the evil?
A kindness—most unkind, that hath always spared the rod;
A weak and numbing indecision in the mind that should be master;
A foolish love, pregnant of hate, that never frowned on sin;
A moral cowardice of heart, that never dared command.

A kingdom is a nest of families, and a family a small kingdom;
And the government of whole or part differeth in nothing but extent.
The house, where the master ruleth, is strong in united subjection.
And the only commandment with promise, being honoured, is a blessing to that house;

But and if he yieldeth up the reins, it is weak in discordant anarchy,
And the bonds of love aud union melt away, as ropes of sand.
The realm, that is ruled with vigour, lacketh neither peace nor glory,
It dreadeth not foes from without, nor the sons of riot from within:
But the meanness of temporizing fear robbeth a kingdom of its honour,
And the weakness of indulgent sloth ravageth its bowels with discord.
The best of human governments is the patriarchal rule;
The authorized supremacy of one, the prescriptive subjection of many:
Therefore, the children of the East have thriven from age to age,
Obeying, even as a god, the royal father of Cathay:
Therefore, to this our day, the Rechabite wanteth not a man, (10)
But they stand before the Lord, forsaking not the mandate of their sire.
Therefore shall Magog among the nations arise from his northern lair,
And rend, in the fury of his power, the insurgent world beneath him:
For the thunderbolt of concentrated strength can be hurled by the will of one,
While the dissipated forces of many are harmless as summer lightning.

OF REST. (11)

In the silent watches of the night, calm night that breedeth thoughts, (*)
When the task-weary mind disporteth in the careless play-hours of sleep,
I dreamed; and behold, a valley, green and sunny and well watered,
And thousands moving across it, thousands and tens of thousands:
And though many seemed faint and toil-worn, and stumbled often, and fell,
Yet moved they on unresting, as the ever-flowing cataract.
Then I noted adders in the grass, and pitfalls under the flowers,
And chasms yawned among the hills, and the ground was cracked and slippery:
But Hope and her brother Fear suffered not a foot to linger;
Bright phantoms of false joys beckoned alluringly forward,
While yelling grisly shapes of dread came hunting on behind:
And ceaselessly, like Lapland swarms, that miserable crowd sped along
To the mist-involved banks of a dark and sullen river.
There saw I, midway in the water, standing a giant fisher,
And he held many lines in his hand, and they called him Iron Destiny.
So I tracked those subtle chains, and each held one among the multitude:

Then I understood what hindered, that they rested not in their path:
For the fisher had sport in his fishing, and drew in his lines continually,
And the new-born babe, and the aged man, were dragged into that dark river:
And he pulled all those myriads along, and none might rest by the way,
Till many, for sheer wearinsss, were eager to plunge into the drowning stream.

So I knew that valley was Life, and it sloped to the waters of Death.
But far on the thither side spread out a calm and silent shore,
Where all was tranquil as a sleep, and the crowded strand was quiet:
And I saw there many I had known, but their eyes glared chillingly upon me,
As set in deepest slumber; and they pressed their fingers to their lips.
Then I knew that shore was the dwelling of Rest, where spirits held their Sabbath,
And it seemed they would have told me much, but they might not break that silence;
For the law of their being was mystery: they glided on, hushing as they went.
Yet further, under the sun, at the roots of purple mountains,
I noted a blaze of glory, as the night-fires on northern skies;
And I heard the hum of joy, as it were a sea of melody;
And far as the eye could reach, were millions of happy creatures
Basking in the golden light; and I knew that land was Heaven.
Then the hill whereon I stood split asunder, and a crater yawned at my feet,
Black, and deep, and dreadful, fenced round with ragged rocks:
Dimly was the darkness lit up by spires of distant flame:
And I saw below a moving mass of life, like reptiles bred in corruption,
Where all was terrible unrest, shrieks and groans and thunder.

So I woke, and I thought upon my dream: for it seemed of wisdom's ministration.
What man is he that findeth rest, though he hunt for it year after year?
As a child he had not yet been wearied, and cared uot then to court it;
As a youth he loved not to be quiet, for excitement spurred him into strife;
As a man he tracketh rest in vain, toiling painfully to catch it,
But still is he pulled from the pursuit, by the strong compulsion of his fate.
So he hopeth to have peace in old age, as he cannot rest in manhood,
But troubles thicken with his years, till Death hath dogged him to the grave.

There remaineth a rest for the spirit on the shadowy side of life;
But unto this world's pilgrim no rest for the sole of his foot.
Ever, from stage to stage, he travelleth wearily forward,
And though he pluck flowers by the way, he may not sleep among the flowers.
Mind is the perpetual motion; for it is a running stream
From an unfathomable source, the depth of the divine Intelligence:
And though it be stopped in its flowing, yet hath it a current within,
The surface may sleep unruffled, but underneath are whirlpools of contention.
Seekest thou rest, O mortal?—seek it no more on earth,
For destiny will not cease from dragging thee through the rough wilderness of life;
Seekest thou rest, O immortal?—hope not to find it in Heaven,
For sloth yieldeth not happiness; the bliss of a spirit is action.
Rest dwelleth only on an island in the midst of the ocean of existence,
Where the world-weary soul for a while may fold its tired wings,
Until, after short sufficient slumber, it is quickened unto deathless energy,
And speedeth in eagle-flight to the Sun of unapproachable perfection.

OF HUMILITY.

Vice is grown aweary of her gawds, and donneth russet garments,
Loving for change to walk as a nun, beneath a modest veil:
For Pride hath noted how all admire the fairness of Humility,
And to clutch the praise he coveteth, is content to be drest in hair-cloth;
And wily Lust tempteth the young heart, that is proof against the bravery of harlots,
With timid tears and retiring looks of an artless seeming maid;
And indolent Apathy, sleepily ashamed of his dull lack-lustre face,
Is glad of the livery of meakness, that charitable cloak and cowl;
And Hatred hideth his demon frown beneath a gentle mask;
And Slander, snake-like, creepeth in the dust, thinking to escape recrimination.
But the world hath gained somewhat from its years, and is quick to penetrate disguises:

Neither in all these is it easily deceived, but rightly divideth the true from the false.

Yet there is a meanness of spirit that is fair in the eyes of most men,
Yea, and seemeth fair unto itself, loving to be thought Humility.
Its choler is not roused by insolence, neither do injuries disturb it:
Honest indignation is strange unto its breast, and just reproof unto its lip.
It shrinketh, looking fearfully on men, fawning at the feet of the great;
The breath of calumny is sweet unto its ear, and it courteth the rod o persecution.
But what! art thou not a man, deputed chief of the creation?
Art thou not a soldier of the right, militant for God and good?
Shall virtue and truth be degraded, because thou art too base to uphold them?
Or Goliath be bolder in blaspheming for want of a David in the camp?
I say not, avenge injuries; for the ministry of vengeance is not thine;
But wherefore rebuke not a liar? wherefore do dishonour to thyself?
Wherefore let the evil triumph, when the just and the right are on thy side?
Such Humility is abject, it lacketh the life of sensibility,
And that resignation is but mock, where the burden is not felt:
Suspect thyself and thy meekness: thou art mean and indifferent to sin;
And the heart that should grieve and forgive, is case-hardened and forgetteth.

Humility mainly becometh the converse of man with his Maker,
But oftentimes it seemeth out of place in the intercourse of man with man:
Yet, it is the cringer to his equal, that is chiefly seen bold to his God,
While a martyr, whom a world cannot browbeat, is humble as a child before Him.
Render unto all men their due, but remember thou also art a man,
And cheat not thyself of the reverence which is owing to thy reasonable being.
Be courteous, and listen, and learn: but teach and answer if thou canst:
Serve thee of thy neighbour's wisdom, but be not enslaved as to a master.
Where thou perceivest knowledge, bend the ear of attention and respect;
But yield not further to the teaching, than as thy mind is warranted by reasons.
Better is an obstinate disputant, that yieldeth inch by inch,
Than the shallow traitor to himself, who surrendereth to half an argument.

Modesty winneth good report, but scorn cometh close upon servility;

Therefore use meekness with discretion, casting not pearls before swine.
For a fool will tread upon thy neck, if he seeth thee lying in the dust;
And there be companies and seasons where resolute bearing is but duty.
If a good man discloseth his secret failings unto the view of the profane,
What doeth he but harm unto his brother, confirming him in his sin:
There is a concealment that is right, and an open-mouthed humility that erreth;
There is a candour near akin to folly, and a meekness looking like shame.
Masculine sentiments, vigorously holden, well become a man;
But a weak mind hath a timorous grasp, and mistaketh it for tenderness of conscience.
Many are despised for their folly, who put it to the account of their religion,
And because men treat them with contempt, they look to their God for glory:
But contempt shall still be their reward, who betrayed their Master unto ridicule,
Reflecting on Him in themselves, meanness and ignorance and cowardice.
A Christian hath a royal spirit, and need not be ashamed but unto One:
Among just men walketh he softly, but the world should see him as a champion.
His humbleness is far unlike the shame that covereth the profligate and weak,
When the sober reproof of virtue hath touched their tingling ears;
It is born of love and wisdom, and is worthy of all honour,
And the sweet persuasion of its smile changeth contempt into reverence.

A man of a haughty spirit is daily adding to his enemies:
He standeth as the Arab in the desert, and the hands of all men are against him:
A man of a base mind daily subtracteth from his friends,
For he holdeth himself so cheaply, that others learn to despise him.
But where the meekness of self-knowledge veileth the front of self-respect,
There look thou for the man, whom none can know but they will honour.
Humility is the softening shadow before the stature of Excellence,
And lieth lowly on the ground, beloved and lovely as the violet:
Humility is the fair-haired maid, that calleth Worth her brother,
The gentle silent nurse, that fostereth infant virtues:
Humility bringeth no excuse; she is welcome to God and man:
Her countenance is needful unto all, who would prosper in either world;
And the mild light of her sweet face is mirrored in the eyes of her companions,

And straightway stand they accepted, children of penitence and love.
As when the blind man is nigh unto a rose, its sweetnes is the herald of its beauty,
So when thou savourest humility, be sure thou art nigh unto merit.
A gift rejoiceth the covetous, and praise fatteneth the vain,
And the pride of man delighteth in the humble bearing of his fellow,
But to the tender benevolence of the unthanked Almoner of good,
Humility is queen among the graces, for she giveth Him occasion to bestow.

OF PRIDE.

Deep is the sea, and deep is hell, but Pride mineth deeper;
It is coiled as a poisonous worm about the foundations of the soul.
If thou expose it in thy motives, and track it in thy springs of thought,
Complacent in its own detection, it will seem indignant virtue;
Smoothly will it gratulate thy skill, O subtle anatomist of self,
And spurn at its very being, while it nestleth the deeper in thy bosom
Pride is a double traitor, and betrayeth itself to entrap thee,
Making thee vain of thy self-knowledge; proud of thy discoveries of pride.
Fruitlessly thou strainest for humility, by darkly diving into self;
Rather look away from innate evil, and gaze upon extraneous good:
For in sounding the deep things of the heart, thou shalt learn to be vain of its capacities,
But in viewing the heights above thee, thou shalt be taught thy littleness;
Could an emmet pry into itself, it might marvel at its own anatomy,
But let it look on eagles, to discern how mean a thing it is.
And all things hang upon comparison; to the greater, great is small:
Neither is there any thing so vile, but somewhat yet is viler:
On all sides is there an infinity: the culprit at the gallows hath his worse,
And the virgin martyr at the stake need not look far for a better.
Therefore see thou that thine aim reacheth unto higher than thyself:
Beware that the standard of thy soul wave from the loftiest battlement:
For pride is a pestilent meteor, flitting on the marshes of corruption,
That will lure thee forward to thy death, if thou seek to track it to its source:

Pride is a gloomy bow, arching the infernal firmament,
That will lead thee on, if thou wilt hunt it, even to the dwelling of despair.
Deep calleth unto deep, and mountain overtoppeth mountain,
And still shalt thou fathom to no end the depth and the height of pride;
For it is the vast ambition of the soul, warped to an idle object,
And nothing but a Deity in Self can quench its insatiable thirst.

Be aware of the smiling enemy, that openly sheatheth his weapon,
But mingleth poison in secret with the sacred salt of hospitality:
For pride will lie dormant in thy heart, to snatch its secret opportunity,
Watching, as a lion-ant, in the bottom of its toils.
Stay not to parley with thy foe, for his tongue is more potent than his arm,
But be wiser, fighting against pride in the simple panoply of prayer.
As one also of the poets hath said, let not the Proteus escape thee; (13)
For he will blaze forth as fire, and quench himself in likeness of water;
He will fright thee as a roaring beast, or charm thee as a subtle reptile.
Mark, amid all his transformations, the complicate deceitfulness of pride,
And the more he striveth to elude thee, bind him the closer in thy toils.
Prayer is the net that snareth him; prayer is the fetter that holdeth him:
Thou canst not nourish pride, while waiting as an almsman on thy God,—
Waiting in sincerity and trust, or pride shall meet thee even there:
Yea, from the palaces of Heaven, hath pride cast down his millions.
Root up the mandrake from thy heart, though it cost thee blood and groans,
Or the cherished garden of thy graces will fade and perish utterly.

OF EXPERIENCE.

I KNEW that age was enriched with the hard-earned wages of knowledge,
And I saw that hoary wisdom was bred in the school of disappointment:
I noted that the wisest of youth, though provident and cautious of evil,
Yet sailed along unsteadily, as lacking some ballast of the mind:
And the cause seemed to lie in this, that while they considered around them;
And warded off all dangers from without, they forgat their own weakness within.
So steer they in self-confidence, until, from the multitude of perils,

They begin to be wary of themselves, and learn the first lesson of Experience.
I knew that in the morning of life, before its wearisome journey,
The youthful soul doth expand, in the simple luxury of being;
It hath not contracted its wishes, nor set a limit to its hopes;
The wing of fancy is unclipt, and sin hath not seared its feelings:
Each feature is stamped with immortality, for all its desires are infinite,
And it seeketh an ocean of happiness, to fill the deep hollow within.
But the old and the grave look on, pitying that generous youth,
For they also have tasted long ago the bitterness of hope destroyed:
They pity him, and are sad, remembering the days that are past,
But they know he must taste for himself, or he will not give ear to their wisdom.
For Experience hath another lesson, which a man will do well if he learn.
By checking the flight of expectation, to cheat disappointment of its pain.

Experience teacheth many things, and all men are his scholars:
Yet is he a strange tutor, unteaching that which he hath taught.
Youth is confident, manhood wary, and old age confident again:
Youth is kind, manhood cold, and age returneth unto kindness.
For youth suspecteth nought, till manhood, bitterly learned,
Mistrusteth all, overleaping the mark; and age correcteth his excess.
Suspicion is the scaffold unto faith, a temporary needful eyesore,
By which the strong man's dwelling is slowly builded up behind;
But soon as the top-stone hath been set to the well-proved goodly pyramid,
The scaffold is torn down, and well-timed trust taketh its long leave of suspicion.
A thousand volumes in a thousand tongues, enshrine the lessons of Experience,
Yet a man shall read them all, and go forth none the wiser:
For self-love lendeth him a glass, to colour all he conneth,
Lest in the features of another he find his own complexion.
And we secretly judge of ourselves, as differing greatly from all men,
And love to challenge causes, to show how we can master their effects:
Pride is pampered in expecting that we need not fear a common fate,
Or wrong-headed prejudice exulteth, in combating old experience;
Or perchance caprice and discontent are the spurs that goad us into danger
Careless, and half in hope to find there an enemy to joust with.
Private experience is an unsafe teacher, for we rarely learn both sides,

And from the gilt surface reckon not on steel beneath:
The torrid sons of Guinea think scorn of icy seas,
And the frostbitten Greenlander disbelieveth suns too hot.
But thou, student of Wisdom, feed on the marrow of the matter;
If thou wilt suspect, let it be thyself; if thou wilt expect, let it not be gladness.

OF ESTIMATING CHARACTER.

Rashly, nor ofttimes truly, doth man pass judgment on his brother;
For he seeth not the springs of the heart, nor heareth the reasons of the mind.
And the world is not wiser than of old, when justice was meted by the sword,
When the spear avenged the wrong, and the lot decided the right;
When the footsteps of blindfold innocence were tracked by burning ploughshares,
And the still condemning water delivered up the wizard to the stake:
For we wait, like the sage of Salamis, to see what the end will be, ([14])
Fixing the right or the wrong, by the issues of failure or success.
Judge not of things by their events; neither of character by providence;
And count not a man more evil because he is more unfortunate;
For the blessings of a better covenant lie not in the sunshine of prosperity;
But pain and chastisement the rather show the wise Father's love.

Behold that daughter of the world; she is full of gaiety and gladness;
The diadem of rank is on her brow, uncounted wealth is in her coffers:
She tricketh out her beauty like Jezebel, and is welcome in the courts of kings;
She is queen of the fools of fashion, and ruleth the revels of luxury:
And though she sitteth not as Tamar, nor standeth in the ways as Rahab,
Yet in the secret of her chamber, she shrinketh not from dalliance and guilt.
She careth not if there be a God, or a soul, or a time of retribution;
Pleasure is the idol of her heart: she thirsteth for no purer heaven.
And she laugheth with light good humour, and all men praise her gentleness;

They are glad in her lovely smile, and the river of her bounty filleth them.
So she prospered in the world: the worship and desire of thousands;
And she died even as she had lived, careless and courteous and liberal.
The grave swallowed up her pomp, the marble proclaimed her virtues,
For men esteemed her excellent, and charities sounded forth her praise;
But elsewhere far other judgment setteth her—with infidels and harlots!
She abused the trust of her splendour: and the wages of her sin shall be hereafter.

Look again on this fair girl, the orphan of a village pastor
Who is dead, and hath left her his all,—his blessing, and a name unstained;
And friends, with busy zeal, that their purses be not taxed,
Place the sad mourner in a home, poor substitute for that she hath lost.
A stranger among strange faces, she drinketh the wormwood of dependence;
She is marked as a child of want; and the world hateth poverty.
Prayer is not heard in that house; the day she hath loved to hallow
Is noted but by deeper dissipation, the riot of luxury and gaming:
And wantonness is in her master's eye, and she hath nowhere to flee to;
She is cared for by none upon earth, and her God seemeth to forsake her.
Then cometh, in fair show, the promise, and the feint of affection,
And her heart, long unused to kindness, remembereth her father, and loveth.
And the villain hath wronged her trust, and mocked, and flung her from him,
And men point at her and laugh: and women hate her as an outcast:
But elsewhere, far other judgment seateth her—among the martyrs!
And the Lord, who seemed to forsake, giveth double glory to the fallen.

Once more, in the matter of wealth: if thou throw thine all on a chance,
Men will come around thee, and wait, and watch the turning of the wheel;
And if, in the lottery of life, thou hast drawn a splendid prize,
What foresight hadst thou, and skill! yea, what enterprise and wisdom!
But if it fall out against thee, and thou fail in thy perilous endeavour,
Behold, the simple did sow, and hath reaped the right harvest of his folly:
And the world will be glaldly accused, nor will reach out a finger to help;
For why should this speculative dullard be a whirlpool to all around him?
Go to, let him sink by himself: we knew what the end of it would be:—
For the man hath missed his mark, and his fellows look no further.

Also, touching guilt and innocence: a man shall walk in his uprightness,
Year after year without reproach, in charity and honesty with all:
But in one evil hour the enemy shall come in like a flood;
Shall track him and tempt him, and hem him,—till he knoweth not whither to fly.
Perchance his famishing little ones shall scream in his ears for bread,
And, maddened by that fierce cry, he rusheth as a thief upon the world:
The world that hath left him to starve, itself wallowing in plenty,—
The world, that denieth him his rights,—he daringly robbeth it of them.
I say not, such an one is innocent: but, small is the measure of his guilt
To that of his wealthly neighbour, who would not help him at his need;
To that of the selfish epicure, who turned away with coldness from his tale;
To that of unsuffering thousands, who look with complacence on his fall.

Or perchance the continual dropping of the venomed words of spite,
Insult and injury and scorn, have galled and pierced his heart;
Yet, with all long-suffering and meekness, he forgiveth unto seventy times seven:
Till, in some weaker moment, tempted beyond endurance,
He striketh, more in anger than in hate; and, alas! for his heavy chance,
He hath smitten unto instant death his spiteful, life-long enemy!
And none was by to see it; and all men knew of their contentions:
Fierce voices shout for his blood, and rude hands hurry him to judgment.
Then man's verdict cometh,—Murderer, with forethought malice;
And his name is a note of execration; his guilt is too black for devils.
But to the righteous Judge, seemeth he the suffering victim:
For his anger was not unlawful, but became him as a Christian and a man;
And though his guilt was grievous when he struck that heavy bitter blow,
Yet light is the sin of the smiter, and verily kicketh the beam,
To the weight of that man's wickedness, whose slow relentless hatred
Met him at every turn, with patient continuance in evil.
Doubtless, eternal wrath shall be heaped upon that spiteful enemy.

It is in vain, it is in vain, saith the preacher; there be none but the righteous and the wicked,
Base rebels, and stanch allies, the true knight, and the traitor;
And he beareth strong witness among men, There is no neutral ground,

The broad highway and narrow path map out the whole domain;
Sit here among the saints, these holy chosen few,
Or grovel there a wretch condemned, to die among the million.
And verily for ultimate results, there be but good and bad;
Heaven hath no dusky twilight; hell is not gladdened with a dawn.
Yet looking round among his fellows, who can pass righteous judgment,
Such an one is holy and accepted, and such an one reprobate and doomed?
There is so much of good among the worst, so much of evil in the best,
Such seeming partialities in providence, so many things to lessen and expand,
Yea, and with all man's boast, so little real freedom of his will,—
That, to look a little lower than the surface, garb or dialect or fashion,
Thou shalt feebly pronounce for a saint, and faintly condemn for a sinner.
Over many a heart good and true, fluttereth the Great King's pennant:
By many an iron hand, the pirate's black banner is unfurled:
But there be many more besides, in the yacht and the trader and the fishing boat,
In the feather'd war-canoe, and the quick mysterious gondola:
And the army of that Great King hath no stated uniform;
Of mingled characters and kinds goeth forth the countless host;
There is the turbaned Damascene, with his tattooed Zealand brother,
There the slim bather in the Ganges, with the sturdy Russian boor,
The sluggish inmate of a polar cave, with the fire-souled daughter of Brazil,
The embruted slave from Cuba, and the Briton of gentle birth.
For all are His inheritance, of all He taketh tithe:
And the Church, his mercy's ark, hath some of every sort.
Who art thou, O man, that art fixing the limits of the fold?
Wherefore settest thou stakes to spread the tent of heaven?
Lay not the plummet to the line: religion hath no landmarks:
No human keenness can discern the subtle shades of faith:
In some it is as earliest dawn, the scarce diluted darkness;
In some as dubious twilight, cold and gray and gloomy;
In some the ebon east is streaked with flaming gold:
In some the dayspring from on high breaketh in all its praise.
And who hath determined the when, separating light from darkness?
Who shall pluck from earliest dawn the promise of the day?
Leave that care to the Husbandman, lest thou garner tares;
Help thou the Shepherd in his seeking, but to separate be his:
For I have often seen the noble erring spirit
Wrecked on the shoals of passion, and numbered of the lost;

Often the generous heart, lit by unhallowed fire,
Counted a brand among the burning, and left uncared-for, in his sin:
Yet I waited a little year, and the mercy thou hadst forgotten
Hath purged that noble spirit, washing it in waters of repentance;
That glowing generous heart, having burnt out all its dross,
Is as a golden censer, ready for the aloes and cassia:
While thou, hard-visaged man, unlovely in thy strictness,
Who turned from him thy sympathies with self-complacent pride,
How art thou shamed by him! his heart is a spring of love,
While the dry well of thine affections is choked with secret mammon.

Sometimes at a glance thou judgest well: years could add little to thy knowledge:
When charity gloweth on the cheek, or malice is lowering in the eye,
When honesty's open brow, or the weasel-face of cunning is before thee,
Or the loose lip of wantonness, or clear bright forehead of reflection.
But often, by shrewd scrutiny, thou judgest to the good man's harm:
For it may be his hour of trial, or he slumbereth at his post,
Or he hath slain his foe, but not yet levelled the stronghold,
Or barely recovered of the wounds, that fleshed him in his fray with passion.
Also, of the worst, through prejudice, thou loosely shalt think well:
For none is altogether evil, and thou mayst catch him at his prayers.
There may be one small prize, though all beside be blanks;
A silver thread of goodness in the black sergecloth of crime.

There is to whom all things are easy: his mind, as a master-key,
Can open, with intuitive address, the treasuries of art and science:
There is to whom all things are hard; but industry giveth him a crow-bar,
To force, with groaning labour, the stubborn lock of learning:
And often when thou lookest on an eye, dim in native dulness,
Little shalt thou wot of the wealth diligence hath gathered to its gaze;
Often the brow that should be bright with the dormant fire of genius,
Within its ample halls, hath ignorance the tenant.
Yet are not the sons of men cast as in moulds by the lot?
The like in frame and feature hath much alike in spirit;
Such a shape hath such a soul, so that a deep discerner
From his make will read the man, and err not far in judgment:
Yea, and it holdeth in the converse, that growing similarity of mind
Findeth or maketh for itself an apposite dwelling in the body:

Accident may modify, circumstance may bevil, externals seem to change it,
But still the primitive crystal is latent in its many variations:
For the map of the face, and the picture of the eye, are traced by the pen of passion;
And the mind fashioneth a tabernacle suitable for itself.
A mean spirit boweth down the back, and the bowing fostereth meanness;
A resolute purpose knitteth the knees, and the firm tread nourisheth decision;
Love looketh softly from the eye, and kindleth love by looking;
Hate furroweth the brow, and a man may frown till he hateth:
For mind and body, spirit and matter, have reciprocities of power,
And each keepeth up the strife; a man's works make or mar him.

There be deeper things than these, lying in the twilight of truth;
But few can discern them aright, from surrounding dimness of error.
For perchance, if thou knewest the whole, and largely with comprehensive mind
Couldst read the history of character, the chequered story of a life,
And into the great account, which summeth a mortal's destiny,
Wert to add the forces from without, dragging him this way and that,
And the secret qualities within, grafted on the soul from the womb,
And the might of other men's example, among whom his lot is cast,
And the influence of want, or wealth, of kindness, or harsh ill-usage,
Of ignorance he cannot help, and knowledge found for him by others,
And first impressions, hard to be effaced, and leadings to right or to wrong,
And inheritance of likeness from a father, and natural human frailty,
And the habit of health or disease, and prejudices poured into his mind,
And the myriad little matters none but Omniscience can know,
And accidents that steer the thoughts, where none but Ubiquity can trace them;—
If thou couldst compass all these, and the consequents flowing from them,
And the scope to which they tend, and the necessary fitness of all things,
Then shouldst thou see as He seeth, who judgeth all men equal,—
Equal, touching innocence and guilt; and different alone in this,
That one acknowledgeth his evil, and looketh to his God for mercy;
Another boasteth of his good, and calleth on his God for justice;
So He, that sendeth none away, is largely munificent to prayer,
But, in the heart of presumption, sheatheth the sword of vengeance.

OF HATRED AND ANGER.

Blunted unto goodness is the heart which anger never stirreth,
But that which hatred swelleth, is keen to carve out evil.
Anger is a noble infirmity, the generous failing of the just,
The one degree that riseth above zeal, asserting the prerogatives of virtue:
But hatred is a slow continuing crime, a fire in the bad man's breast,
A dull and hungry flame, for ever craving insatiate.
Hatred would harm another; anger would indulge itself:
Hatred is a simmering poison; anger, the opening of a valve:
Hatred destroyeth as the upas-tree; anger smiteth as a staff:
Hatred is the atmosphere of hell; but anger is known in heaven.
Is there not a righteous wrath, an anger just and holy,
When goodness is sitting in the dust, and wickedness enthroned on Babel?
Doth pity condemn guilt?—is justice not a feeling but a law
Appealing to the line and to the plummet, incognizant of moral sense?
Thou that condemnest anger, small is thy sympathy with angels;
Thou that hast accounted it for sin, cold is thy communion with heaven.

Beware of the angry in his passion; but fear not to approach him afterward;
For if thou acknowledge thine error, he himself will be sorry for his wrath
Beware of the hater in his coolness; for he meditateth evil against thee;
Commending the resources of his mind calmly to work thy ruin.
Deceit and treachery skulk with hatred, but an honest spirit flieth with anger:
The one lieth secret, as a serpent; the other chaseth, as a leopard.
Speedily be reconciled in love, and receive the returning offender,
For wittingly prolonging anger, thou tamperest unconsciously with hatred.
Patience is power in a man, nerving him to rein his spirit:
Passion is as palsy to his arm, while it yelleth on the coursers to their speed:
Patience keepeth counsel, and standeth in solid self-possession,
But the weakness of sudden passion layeth bare the secrets of the soul.
The sentiment of anger is not ill, when thou lookest on the impudence of vice,

Or savourest the breath of calumny, or hast earned the hard wages of injustice,
But see thou that thou curb it in expression, rendering the mildness of rebuke,
So shalt thou stand without reproach, mailed in all the dignity of virtue.

OF GOOD IN THINGS EVIL.

I HEARD the man of sin reproaching the goodness of Jehovah,
Wherefore, if he be Almighty Love, permitteth he misery and pain?
I saw the child of hope vexed in the labyrinth of doubt,
Wherefore, O holy One and just, is the horn of thy foul foe so high exalted?—
And, alas! for this our groaning world, for that grief and guilt are here;
Alas! for that Earth is the battle-field, where good must combat with evil:
Angels look on and hold their breath, burning to mingle in the conflict,
But the troops of the Captain of Salvation may be none but the soldiers of the cross:
And that slender band must fight alone, and yet shall triumph gloriously,
Enough shall they be for conquest, and the motto of their standard is ENOUGH.
Thou art sad, O denizen of earth, for pains and diseases and death,
But remember, thy hand hath earned them; grudge not at the wages of thy doings:
Thy guilt, and thy fathers' guilt, must bring many sorrows in their company,
And if thou wilt drink sweet poison, doubtless it shall rot thee to the core.
Who art thou but the heritor of evil, with a right to nothing good?
The respite of an interval of ease were a boon which Justice might deny thee:
Therefore lay thy hand upon thy mouth, O man much to be forgiven,
And wait, thou child of hope, for time shall teach thee all things.
Yet hear, for my speech shall comfort thee; reverently, but with boldness,
I would raise the sable curtain, that hideth the symmetry of Providence.
Pain and sin are convicts, and toil in their fetters for good;
The weapons of evil are turned against itself, fighting under better banners:

The leech delighteth in stinging, and the wicked loveth to do harm,
But the wise Physician of the universe useth that ill tendency for health.
Verily from others' griefs are gendered sympathy and kindness;
Patience, humility, and faith, spring not seldom from thine own:
An enemy, humbled by his sorrows, cannot be far from thy forgiveness,
A friend who hath tasted of calamity, shall fan the dying incense of thy love:
And for thyself, is it a small thing, so to learn thy frailty,
That from an aching bone thou savest the whole body?
The furnace of affliction may be fierce, but if it refineth thy soul,
The good of one meek thought shall outweigh years of torment.
Nevertheless, wretched man, if thy bad heart be hardened in the flame,
Being earth-born, as of clay, and not of moulded wax,
Judge not the hand that smiteth, as if thou wert visited in wrath;
Reproach thyself, for He is Justice: repent thee, for He is Mercy.

Cease, fond caviller at wisdom, to be satisfied that every thing is wrong:
Be sure there is good necessity, even for the flourishing of evil.
Would the eye delight in perpetual noon? or the ear in unqualified harmonies?
Hath winter's frost no welcome, contrasting sturdily with summer?
Couldst thou discern benevolence, if there were no sorrows to be soothed?
Or discover the resources of contrivance, if nothing stood opposed to the means?
What were power without an enemy? or mercy without an object?
Or truth, where the false were impossible? or love, where love were a debt?
The characters of God were but idle, if all things around him were perfection,
And virtues might slumber on like death, if they lacked the opportunities of evil.
There is one all-perfect, and but one; man dare not reason of His Essence.
But there must be deficiencies in heaven, to leave room for progression in bliss:
A realm of unqualified BEST were a stagnant pool of being,
And the circle of absolute perfection, the abstract cipher of indolence.
Sin is an awful shadow, but it addeth new glories to the light;
Sin is a black foil, but it setteth off the jewelry of heaven;
Sin is the traitor that hath dragged the majesty of mercy into action;

Sin is the whelming argument, to justify the attribute of vengeance.
It is a deep dark thought, and needeth to be diligently studied,
But perchance evil was essential, that God should be seen of his creatures:
For where perfection is not, there lacketh possible good,
And the absence of better that might be, taketh from the praise of it is well:
And creatures must be finite, and finite cannot be perfect;
Therefore, though in small degree, creation involveth evil,
He chargeth his angels with folly, and the heavens are not clean in His sight:
For every existence in the universe hath either imperfection or Godhead:
And the light that blazeth but in One, must be softened with shadow for the many.
There is then good in evil; or none could have known his Maker;
No spiritual intellect or essence could have gazed on his high perfections,
No angel harps could have tuned the wonders of his wisdom,
No ransomed souls have praised the glories of his mercy,
No howling fiends have shown the terrors of his justice,
But God would have dwelt alone in the fearful solitude of holiness.

Nevertheless, O sinner, harden not thine heart in evil;
Nor plume thee in imaginary triumph, because thou art not valueless as vile;
Because thy dark abominations add lustre to the charity of Light;
Because a wonder-working alchemy draineth elixir out of poisons;
Because the same fiery volcano that scorcheth and ravageth a continent,
Hath in the broad blue bay cast up some petty island;
Because to the full demonstration of the qualities and accidents of good,
The swarthy legions of the devil have toiled as unwitting pioneers:
For sin is still sin; so hateful Love doth hate it;
A blot on the glory of creation, which justice must wipe out.
Sin is a loathsome leprosy, fretting the white robe of innocence;
A rottenness, eating out the heart of the royal cedars of Lebanon;
A pestilential blast, the terror of that holy pilgrimage;
A rent in the sacred veil, whereby God left his temple.
Therefore, consider thyself, thou that dost not sorrow for thy guilt:
Fear evil, or face its enemy: dread sin, or dare justice.

Yea, saith the Spirit: and their works do follow them;

Habits, and thoughts, and deeds, are shadows and satellites of self.
What! shall the claimant to a throne stand forward with a rabble rout,—
Meanness, impiety, and lust; riot and indolence and vanity?
Nay, man! the train wherewith thou comest attend whither thou shalt go;
A throne for a king's son, but an inner dungeon for the felon.
For a man's works do follow him: bodily, standing in the judgment,
Behold the false accuser, behold the slandered saint;
The slave, and his bloody driver; the poor, and his generous friend;
The simple dupe, and the crafty knave: the murderer, and—his victim!
Yet all are in many characters the best stand guilty at the bar;
And he that seemed the worst may have most of real excuse.
The talents unto which a man is born, be they few or many,
Are dropped into the balance of account, working unlooked-for changes,
And perchance the convict from the galleys may stand above the hermit from his cell,
For that the obstacles in one outweigh the propensions in the other.
There be, who have made themselves friends, yea, by unrighteous mammon,—
Friends, ready waiting as an escort to those everlasting habitations;
Embodied in living witnesses, thronging to meet them in a cloud,
Charity, meekness and truth, zeal, sincerity and patience.
There be, who have made themselves foes, yea, by honest gain,
Foes, whose plaint must have its answer, before the bright portal is unbarred:
Pride, and selfishness, and sloth, apathy, wrath, and falsehood,
Bind to their everlasting toil many that must weary in the fires.
Love hath a power and a longing to save the gathered world,
And rescue universal man from the hunting hell-hounds of his doings:
Yet few, here one and there one, scanty as the gleaning after harvest,
Are glad of the robes of praise which Mercy would fling around the naked;
But wrapping closer to their skin the poisoned tunic of their works,
They stand in self-dependence to perish in abandonment of God.

OF PRAYER.

A WICKED man scorneth prayer, in the shallow sophistry of reason,
He derideth the silly hope, that God can be moved by supplication:—
Can the unchangeable be changed, or waver in his purpose?
Can the weakness of pity affect him? Should he turn at the bidding of a man?
Methought he ruled all things, and ye called his decrees immutable,
But if thus he listeneth to words, wherein is the firmness of his will?—
So I heard the speech of the wicked, and, lo, it was smoother than oil;
But I knew that his reasonings were false, for the promise of the Scripture is true:
Yet was my soul in darkness, for his words were too hard for me;
Till I turned to my God in prayer, for I know he heareth always.
Then I looked abroad on the earth, and, behold, the Lord was in all things,
Yet saw I not his hand in aught, but perceived that he worketh by means;
Yea, and the power of the mean proveth the wisdom that ordained it;
Yea, and no act is useless, to the hurling of a stone through the air.
So I turned my thoughts to supplication, and beheld the mercies of Jehovah,
And I saw sound argument was still the faithful friend of godliness;
For as the rock of the affections is the solid approval of reason,
Even so the temple of Religion is founded on the basis of Philosophy.

Scorner, thy thoughts are weak, they reach not the summit of the matter.
Go to, for the mouth of a child might show thee the mystery of prayer:
Verily, there is no change in the counsels of the Mighty Ruler:
Verily, his purpose is strong, and rooted in the depths of necessity:
But who hath shown thee his purpose, who hath made known to thee his will?
When, O gainsayer, hast thou been schooled in the secrets of wisdom?
Fate is a creature of God, and all things move in their orbits,
And that which shall surely happen is known unto him from eternity;
But as, in the field of nature, he useth the sinews of the ox,
And commandeth diligence and toil, himself giving the increase,
So, in the kingdom of his grace, granteth he omnipotence to prayer,
For he knoweth what thou wilt ask, and what thou wilt ask aright.

No man can pray in faith, whose prayer is not grounded on a promise:
Yet a good man commendeth all things to the righteous wisdom of his God:
For those who pray in faith, trust the immutable Jehovah,
And they who ask blessings unpromised, lean on uncovenanted mercy.

Man, regard thy prayers as a purpose of love to thy soul;
Esteem the providence that led to them as an index of God's good-will:
So shalt thou pray aright, and thy words shall meet with acceptance.
Also, in pleading for others, be thankful for the fullness of thy prayer.
For if thou art ready to ask, the Lord is more ready to bestow.
The salt preserveth the sea, and the saints uphold the earth;
Their prayers are the thousand pillars that prop the canopy of nature.
Verily, an hour without prayer, from some terrestrial mind,
Were a curse in the calendar of time, a spot of the blackness of darkness.
Perchance the terrible day, when the world must rock into ruins,
Will be one unwhitened by prayer,—shall He find faith on the earth?
For there is an economy of mercy, as of wisdom, and power, and means;
Neither is one blessing granted, unbesought from the treasury of good;
And the charitable heart of the Being, to depend upon whom is happiness,
Never withholdeth a bounty, so long as his subject prayeth;
Yea, ask what thou wilt, to the second throne in heaven,
It is thine, for whom it was appointed; there is no limit unto prayer:
But and if thou cease to ask, tremble, thou self-suspended creature,
For thy strength is cut off as was Samson's: and the hour of thy doom is come.

Frail art thou, O man, as a bubble on the breaker,
Weak and governed by externals, like a poor bird caught in the storm;
Yet thy momentary breath can still the raging waters,
Thy hand can touch a lever that may move the world.
O Merciful, we strike eternal covenant with thee,
For man may take for his ally the King who ruleth kings;
How strong, yet how most weak, in utter poverty how rich,
What possible omnipotence to good is dormant in a man!
Behold that fragile form of delicate transparent beauty,
Whose light-blue eye and hectic cheek are lit by the balefires of decline,
All droopingly she lieth, as a dew-laden lily,
Her flaxen tresses, rashly luxuriant, dank with unhealthy moisture:
Hath not thy heart said of her, Alas! poor child of weakness?

Thou hast erred; Goliath of Gath stood not in half her strength:
Terribly she fighteth in the van as the virgin daughter of Orleans,
She beareth the banner of heaven, her onset is the rushing cataract,
Seraphim rally at her side, and the captain of that host is God,
And the serried ranks of evil are routed by the lightning of her eye;
She is the King's remembrancer, and steward of many blessings,
Holding the buckler of security over her unthankful land;
For that weak fluttering heart is strong in faith assured,
Dependence is her might, and behold—she prayeth.

Angels are round the good man, to catch the incense of his prayers,
And they fly to minister kindness to those for whom he pleadeth;
For the altar of his heart is lighted, and burneth before God continually,
And he breatheth, conscious of his joy, the native atmosphere of heaven;
Yea, though poor, and comtemned, and ignorant of this world's wisdom;
Ill can his fellows spare him, though they know not of his value;
Thousands bewail a hero, and a nation mourneth for its king,
But the whole universe lamenteth the loss of a man of prayer.
Verily, were it not for One, who sitteth on his rightful throne,
Crowned with a rainbow of emerald, ([15]) the green memorial of earth,—
For one, a mediating man, that hath clad his Godhead with mortality,
And offereth prayer without ceasing, the royal priest of Nature,
Matter and life and mind had sunk into dark annihilation,
And the lightning frown of Justice withered the world into nothing.

Thus, O worshipper of reason, thou hast heard the sum of the matter;
And woe to his hairy scalp that restraineth prayer before God.
Prayer is a creature's strength, his very breath and being;
Prayer is the golden key that can open the wicket of Mercy;
Prayer is the magic sound that saith to Fate, So be it;
Prayer is the slender nerve that moveth the muscles of Omnipotence.
Wherefore, pray, O creature, for many and great are thy wants;
Thy mind, thy conscience, and thy being, thy rights commend thee unto prayer,
The cure of all cares, the grand panacea for all pains,
Doubt's destroyer, ruin's remedy, the antidote to all anxieties.

So then, God is true, and yet He hath not changed:
It is he that sendeth the petition, to answer it according to his will.

THE LORD'S PRAYER.

INQUIREST thou, O man, wherewithal may I come unto the Lord?
And with what wonder-working sounds may I move the majesty of heaven?
There is a model to thy hand; upon that do thou frame thy supplication;
Wisdom hath measured its words, and redemption urgeth thee to use them.
Call thy God thy Father, and yet not thine alone,
For thou art but one of many, thy brotherhood is with all:
Remember his high estate, that he dwelleth King of Heaven;
So shall thy thoughts be humbled, nor love be unmixed with reverence:
Be thy first petition unselfish, the honour of Him who made thee,
And that in the depths of thy heart his memory be shrined in holiness:
Pray for that blessed time when good shall triumph over evil,
And one universal temple echo the perfections of Jehovah:
Bend thou to his good-will, and subserve his holy purposes,
Till in thee, and those around thee, grow a little heaven upon earth:
Humbly as a grateful almsman, beg thy bread of God,—
Bread for thy triple estate, for thou hast a trinity of nature:
Humility smootheth the way, and gratitude softeneth the heart,
Be then thy prayer for pardon mingled with the tear of penitence;
Yea, and while, all unworthy, thou leanest on the hand that should smite,
Thou canst not from thy fellows withhold thy less forgiveness.
To thy Father thy weaknesses are known, and thou hast not hid thy sin,
Therefore ask him, in all trust, to lead thee from the dangers of temptation;
While the last petition of the soul that breatheth on the confines of prayer
Is deliverance from sin and the evil one, the miseries of earth and hell.
And wherefore, child of hope, should the rock of thy confidence be sure?
Thou knowest that God heareth, and promiseth an answer of peace;
Thou knowest that he is King, and none can stay his hand;
Thou knowest his power to be boundless, for there is none other:
And to Him thou givest glory, as a creature of his workmanship and favour,
For the never-ending term of thy saved and bright existence.

OF DISCRETION.

For what then was I born?—to fill the circling year
With daily toil for daily bread, with sordid pains and pleasures?—
To walk this chequered world, alternate light and darkness,
The day dreams of deep thought followed by the night-dreams of fancy?—
To be one in a full procession?—to dig my kindred clay?—
To decorate the gallery of art?—to clear a few acres of forest?
For more than these, my soul, thy God hath lent thee life.
Is then that noble end to feed this mind with knowledge,
To mix for mine own thirst the sparkling wine of wisdom,
To light with many lamps the caverns of my heart,
To reap, in the furrows of my brain, good harvest of right reasons?—
For more than these, my soul, thy God hath lent thee life.
Is it to grow stronger in self-government, to check the chafing will,
To curb with tightening rein the mettled steeds of passion,
To welcome with calm heart, far in the voiceless desert,
The gracious visitings of heaven that bless my single self?
For more than these, my soul, thy God hath lent thee life.
To aim at thine own happiness, is an end idolatrous and evil:
In earth, yea in heaven, if thou seek it for itself, seeking thou shalt not find.
Happiness is a roadside flower, growing on the highways of Usefulness;
Plucked, it shall wither in thy hand; passed by, it is fragrance to thy spirit;
Love not thine own soul, regard not thine own weal,
Trample the thyme beneath thy feet; be useful, and be happy!

Thus unto fair conclusions argueth generous youth,
And quickly he starteth on his course, knight-errant to do good.
His sword is edged with arguments, his vizor terrible with censures;
He goeth full mailed in faith, and zeal is flaming at his heart.
Yet one thing he lacketh, the Mentor of the mind.
The quiet whisper of Discretion—Thy time is not yet come.
For he smiteth an oppressor; and vengeance for that smiting
Is dealt in double stripes on the faint body of the victim:
He is glad to give and to distribute; and clamorous pauperism feasteth,
While honest labour, pining, hideth his sharp ribs:
He challengeth to a fair field that subtle giant Infidelity,

And worsted in the unequal fight, strengtheneth the hands of error:
He hasteth to teach and preach, as the war-horse rusheth to the battle,
And to pave a way for truth, would break up the Apennines of prejudice:
He wearieth by stale proofs, where none looked for a reason,
And to the listening ear will urge the false argument of feeling.
So hath it often been, that, judging by results,
The hottest friends of truth have done her deadliest wrong.
Alas! for there are enemies without, glad enough to parley with a traitor,
And a zealot will let down the drawbridge, to prove his own prowess:
Yea, from within will he break away a breach in the citadel of truth
That he may fill the gap, for fame, with his own weak body.

Zeal without judgment is an evil, though it be zeal unto good:
Touch not the ark with unclean hand, yea, though it seem to totter.
There are evil who work good, and there are good who work evil,
And foolish backers of wisdom have brought on her many reproaches.
Truth hath more than enough to combat in the minds of all men,
For the mist of sense is a thick veil, and sin hath warped their wills;
Yet doth an officious helper awkwardly prevent her victory,—
These thy wounded hands were smitten in the house of friends:—
To point out a meaning in her words, he will blot those words with his finger;
And winnow chaff into the eyes, before he hath wheat to show:
He will heap sturdy logs on a faint expiring fire,
And with a room in flames, will cast the casement open;
By a shoulder to the wheel downhill harasseth the labouring beast,
And where obstruction were needed, will harm by an ill-judged thrusting-on.
A vessel foundereth at sea, if a storm have unshipped the rudder;
And a mind with much sail shall require heavy ballast.
Take a lever by the middle, thou shalt seem to prove it powerless,
Argue for truth indiscreetly, thou shalt toil for falsehood.
There is plenty of room for a peaceable man in the most thronged assembly;
But a quarrelsome spirit is straitened in the open field:
Many a teacher, lacking judgment, hindereth his own lessons;
And the savoury mess of pottage is spoiled by a bitter herb:
The garment woven of a piece is rashly torn by schism,
Because its unwise claimants will not cast lots for its possession.

Discretion guide thee on thy way, noble-minded youth,

Help thee to humour infirmities, to wink at innocent errors,
To take small count of forms, to bear with prejudice and fancy:
Discretion guard thine asking, discretion aid thine answer,
Teach thee that well-timed silence hath more eloquence than speech,
Whisper thee, thou art Weakness, though *thy* cause be strength,
And tell thee, the keystone of an arch can be loosened with least labour from within.
The snows of Hecla lie around its troubled smoking Geysers;
Let the cool streams of prudence temper the hot spring of zeal:
So shalt thou gain thine honourable end, nor lose the midway prize;
So shall thy life be useful, and thy young heart happy.

OF TRIFLES.

YET once more, saith the fool, yet once, and is it not a little one?
Spare me this folly yet an hour, for what is one among so many?
And he blindeth his conscience with lies, and stupefieth his heart with doubts;—
Whom shall I harm in this matter? and a little ill breedeth much good;
My thoughts, are they not mine own? and they leave no mark behind them;
And if God so pardoneth crime, how should these petty sins affect him?—
So he transgresseth yet again, and falleth by little and little,
Till the ground crumble beneath him, and he sinketh in the gulf despairing.
For there is nothing in the earth so small that it may not produce great things,
And no swerving from a right line, that may not lead eternally astray.
A landmark tree was once a seed, and the dust in the balance maketh a difference;
And the cairn is heaped high by each one flinging a pebble:
The dangerous bar in the harbour's mouth is only grains of sand;
And the shoal that hath wrecked a navy is the work of a colony of worms:
Yea, and a despicable gnat may madden the mighty elephant;
And the living rock is worn by the diligent flow of the brook.
Little art thou, O man, and in trifles thou contendest with thine equals,
For atoms must crowd upon atoms, ere crime groweth to be a giant.

What, is thy servant a dog?—not yet wilt thou grasp the dagger,
Not yet wilt thou laugh with the scoffers, not yet betray the innocent:
But, if thou nourish in thy heart the reveries of injury or passion,
And travel in mental heat the mazy labyrinths of guilt,
And then conceive it possible, and then reflect on it as done,
And use, by little and little, thyself to regard thyself a villain,
Not long will crime be absent from the voice that doth invoke him to thy heart,
And bitterly wilt thou grieve, that the buds have ripened into poison.

A spark is a molecule of matter, yet it may kindle the world;
Vast is the mighty ocean, but drops have made it vast.
Despise not thou a small thing, either for evil or for good;
For a look may work thy ruin, or a word create thy wealth:
The walking this way or that, the casual stopping or hastening,
Hath saved life, and destroyed it, hath cast down and built up fortunes.
Commit thy trifles unto God, for to him is nothing trivial;
And it is but the littleness of man that seeth no greatness in a trifle.
All things are infinite in parts, and the moral is as the material,
Neither is any thing vast, but it is compacted of atoms.
Thou art wise, and shalt find comfort, if thou study thy pleasure in trifles,
For slender joys, often repeated, fall as sunshine on the heart:
Thou art wise, if thou beat off petty troubles, nor suffer their stinging to fret thee:
Thrust not thine hand among the thorns, but with a leathern glove.
Regard nothing lightly which the wisdom of Providence hath ordered;
And therefore, consider all things that happen unto thee or unto others.
The warrior that stood against a host, may be pierced unto death by a needle;
And the saint that feareth not the fire, may perish the victim of a thought.
A mote in the gunner's eye is as bad as a spike in the gun;
And the cable of a furlong is lost through an ill-wrought inch.
The streams of small pleasures fill the lake of happiness:
And the deepest wretchedness of life is continuance of petty pains.
A fool observeth nothing, and seemeth wise unto himself;
A wise man heedeth all things, and in his own eyes is a fool:
He that wondereth at nothing hath no capabilities of bliss;
But he that scrutinizeth trifles hath a store of pleasure to his hand.
If pestilence stalk through the land, ye say, This is God's doing;

.s it not also His doing, when an aphis creepeth on a rose-bud ?—
If an avalanche roll from its Alp, ye tremble at the will of Providence;
Is not that will concerned when the sear leaves fall from the poplar ?—
A thing is great or little only to a mortal's thinking,
But abstracted from the body, all things are alike important:
The Ancient of Days noteth in his book the idle converse of a creature
And happy and wise is the man to whose thought existeth not a trifle.

OF RECREATION.

To join advantage to amusement, to gather profit with pleasure,
Is the wise man's necessary aim, when he lieth in the shade of recreation,
For he cannot fling aside his mind, nor bar up the floodgates of his wisdom;
Yea, though he strain after folly, his mental monitor shall check him:
For knowledge and ignorance alike have laws essential to their being,—
The sage studieth amusements, and the simple laugheth in his studies.
Few, but full of understanding, are the books of the library of God,
And fitting for all seasons are the gain and the gladness they bestow:
The volume of mystery and Grace, for the hour of deep communings,
When the soul considereth intensely the startling marvel of itself:
The book of destiny and Providence for the time of sober study,
When the mind gleaneth wisdom from the olive grove of history:
And the cheerful pages of Nature, to gladden the pleasant holiday,
When the task of duty is complete, and the heart swelleth high with satisfaction.
The soul may not safely dwell too long with the deep things of futurity;
The mind may not always be bent back, like the Parthian, straining at the past: ([16])
And, if thou art wearied with wrestling on the broad arena of science,
Leave awhile thy friendly foe, half vanquished in the dust,
Refresh thy jaded limbs, return with vigour to the strife,—
Thou shalt easier find thyself his master, for the vacant interval of leisure.

That which may profit and amuse is gathered from the volume of creation,

For every chapter therein teemeth with the playfulness of wisdom.
The elements of all things are the same, though nature hath mixed them with a difference,
And Learning delighteth to discover the affinity of seeming opposites:
So out of great things and small draweth he the secrets of the universe,
And argueth the cycles of the stars, from a pebble flung by a a child.
It is pleasant to note all plants, from the rush to the spreading cedar,
From the giant king of palms, (17) to the lichen that staineth its stem:
To watch the workings of instinct, that grosser reason of brutes,—
The river-horse browsing in the jungle, the plover screaming on the moor,
The cayman, basking on a mud-bank, and the walrus anchored to an iceberg,
The dog at his master's feet, and the milk-kine lowing in the meadow;
To trace the consummate skill that hath modelled the anatomy of insects,
Small fowls that sun their wings on the petals of wild flowers;
To learn a use in the beetle, and more than a beauty in the butterfly;
To recognize affection in a moth, and look with admiration on a spider.
It is glorious to gaze upon the firmament, and see from far the mansions of the blest,
Each distant shining world, a kingdom for one of the redeemed;
To read the antique history of earth, stamped upon those medals in the rocks
Which Design hath rescued from decay, to tell of the green infancy of time;
To gather from the unconsidered shingle mottled star-like agates,
Full of unstoried flowers in the bubbling bloom-chalcedony:
Or gay and curious shells, fretted with microscopic carving,
Corallines, and fresh seaweeds, spreading forth their delicate branches
It is an admirable lore, to learn the cause in the change,
To study the chemistry of Nature, her grand, but simple secrets.
To search out all her wonders, to track the resources of her skill,
To note her kind compensations, her unobtrusive excellence.
In all it is wise happiness to see the well-ordained laws of Jehovah,
The harmony that filleth all his mind, the justice that tempereth his bounty,
The wonderful all-prevalent analogy that testifieth one Creator,
The broad arrow of the Great King, carved on all the stores of his arsenal.
But beware, O worshipper of God, thou forget not him in his dealings,

Though the bright emanations of his power hide him in created glory;
For if, on the sea of knowledge, thou regardest not the pole-star of religion,
Thy bark will miss her port, and run upon the sandbar of folly:
And if, enamoured of the means, thou considerest not the scope to which they tend,
Wherein art thou wiser than the child, that is pleased with toys and baubles?
Verily, a trifling scholar, thou heedest but the letter of instruction:
For as motive is spirit unto action, as memory endeareth place,
As the sun doth fertilize the earth, as affection quickeneth the heart,
So is the remembrance of God in the varied wonders of creation.

Man hath found out inventions, to cheat him of the weariness of life,
To help him to forget realities, and hide the misery of guilt.
For love of praise, and hope of gain, for passion and delusive happiness,
He joineth the circle of folly, and heapeth on the fire of excitement;
Oftentimes sadly out of heart at the tiresome insipidity of pleasure,
Oftentimes labouring in vain, convinced of the palpable deceit;
Yet a man speaketh to his brother, in the voice of glad congratulation,
And thinketh others happy, though he himself be wretched:
And hand joineth hand to help in the toil of amusement,
While the secret aching heart is vacant of all but disappointment.
The cheapest pleasures are the best; and nothing is more costly than sin;
Yet we mortgage futurity, counting it but little loss;
Neither can a man delight in that which breedeth sorrow,
Yet do we hunt for joy even in the fires that consume it.
Whoso would find gladness may meet her in the hovel of poverty,
Where benevolence hath scattered around the gleanings of the horn of plenty;
Whoso would sun himself in peace, may be seen of her in deeds of mercy,
When the pale lean cheek of the destitute is wet with grateful tears.
If the mind is wearied by study, or the body worn with sickness,
It is well to lie fallow fot a while, in the vacancy of sheer amusement;
But when thou prosperest in health, and thine intellect can soar untired,
To seek uninstructive pleasure is to slumber on the couch of indolence.

THE TRAIN OF RELIGION.

Stay awhile, thou blessed band, be entreated, daughters of heaven!
While the chance-met scholar of Wisdom learneth your sacred names:
He is resting a little from his toil, yet a little on the borders of earth,
And fain would he have you his friends, to bid him glad welcome hereafter.
Who among the glorious art thou, that walkest a Goddess and a Queen,
Thy crown of living stars, and a golden cross thy sceptre?
Who among flowers of loveliness is she, thy seeming herald,
Yet she boasteth not thee nor herself, and her garments are plain in their neatness?
Wherefore is there one among the train, whose eyes are red with weeping,
Yet is her open forehead beaming with the sun of ecstasy?
And who is that blood-stained warrior, with glory sitting on his crest?
And who that solemn sage, calm in majestic dignity?
Also, in the lengthening troop see I some clad in robes of triumph,
Whose fair and sunny faces I have known and loved on earth:
Welcome, ye glorified Loves, Graces, and Sciences, and Muses,
That, like sisters of charity, tended in this world's hospital;
Welcome, for verily I knew, ye could not but be children of the light,
Though earth hath soiled your robes, and robbed you of half your glory;
Welcome, chiefly welcome, for I find I have friends in heaven,
And some I might scarce have looked for, as thou, light-hearted Mirth;
Thou, also, star-robed Urania; and thou, with the curious glass,
That rejoicedst in tracking wisdom where the eye was too dull to note it;
And art thou too among the blessed, mild, much injured Poetry?
Who quickenest with light and beauty the leaden face of matter,
Who not unheard, though silent, fillest earth's gardens with music,
And not unseen, though a spirit, dost look down upon us from the stars,—
That hast been to me for oil and for wine, to cheer and uphold my soul,
When wearied, battling with the surge, the stunning surge of life:
Of thee, for well have I loved thee, of thee may I ask in hope,
Who among the glorious is she, that walketh a Goddess and a Queen?
And who that fair-haired herald, and who that weeping saint?
And who that mighty warrior, and who that solemn sage?

Son, happy art thou that Wisdom hath led thee hitherward;

For, otherwise never hadst thou known the joy-giving name of our Queen.
Behold her, the life of men, the anchor of their shipwrecked hopes:
Behold her, the shepherdess of souls, who bringeth back the wanderers to God.
And for that modest herald, she is named on earth, Humility:
And hast thou not known, my son, the tearful face of Repentance?
Faith is yon time-scarred hero, walking in the shade of his laurels;
And Reason, the serious sage, who followeth the footsteps of Faith:
And we, all we, are but handmaids, ministers of minor bliss,
Who rejoice to be counted servants in the train of a Queen so glorious.
But for her name, son of man, it is strange to the language of heaven,
For those who have never fallen need not and may not learn it:
Liegeance we sware to our God, and liegeance well have we kept;
It is only the band of the redeemed who can tell thee the fullness of that name; ([18])
Yet will I comfort thee, my son, for the love wherewith thou hast loved me,
And thou shalt touch for thyself the golden sceptre of Religion.

So that blessed train passed by me; but the vision was sealed upon my soul;
And its memory is shrined in fragrance, for the promise of the Spirit was true:
I learn from the silent poem of all creation round me,
How beautiful their feet, who follow in that train.

OF A TRINITY. ([19])

Despise not, shrewd reckoner, the God of a good man's worship,
Neither let thy calculating folly gainsay the unity of three;
Nor scorn another's creed, although he cannot solve thy doubts;
Reason is the follower of faith, where he may not be precursor:
It is written, and so we believe, waiting not for outward proof,
Inasmuch as mysteries inscrutable are the clear prerogatives of Godhead.
Reason hath nothing positive, faith hath nothing doubtful;
And the height of unbelieving wisdom is to question all things.

When there is marvel in a doctrine, faith is joyful and adoreth;
But when all is clear, what place is left for faith?
Tell me the sum of thy knowledge,—is it yet assured of any thing?
Despise not what is wonderful, when all things are wonderful around thee.
From the multitude of like effects, thou sayest, behold a law:
And the matter thou art baffled in unmaking, is to thy mind an element.
Then look abroad, I pray thee, for analogy holdeth every where,
And the Maker hath stamped his name on every creature of his hand:
I know not of a matter or a spirit, that is not three in one,
And truly should account it for a marvel, a coin without the image of its Cæsar.

Man talketh of himself as ignorant, but judgeth by himself as wise:
His own guess counteth he truth, but the notions of another are his scorn.
But bear thou yet with a brother, whose thought may be less subtle than thine own,
And suffer the passing speculation suggested by analogies to faith.
Like begetteth like, and the great sea of Existence
In each of its uncounted waves holdeth up a mirror to its Maker:
Like begetteth like, and the spreading tree of being
With each of its trefoil leaves pointeth at the trinity of God.
Let him whose eyes have been unfilmed, read this homily in all things,
And thou, of duller sight, despise not him that readeth:
There be three grand principles; life, generation, and obedience;
Shadowing in every creature, the Spirit, and the Father, and the Son.
There be three grand unities, variously mixed in trinities,
Three catholic divisors of the million sums of matter:
Yea, though science hath not seen it, climbing the ladder of experiment,
Let faith, in the presence of her God, promulgate the mighty truth.
Of three sole elements all nature's works consist:
The pine, and the rock to which it clingeth, and the eagle sailing around it:
The lion, and the northern whale, and the deeps wherein he sporteth;
The lizard sleeping in the sun; the lightning flashing from a cloud;
The rose, and the ruby, and the pearl; each one is made of three;
And the three be the like ingredients, mingled in diverse measures.
Thyself hast within thyself body, and life, and mind:
Matter, and breath, and instinct, unite in all beasts of the field;
Substance, coherence and weight, fashion the fabrics of the earth;
The will, the doing, and the deed, combine to frame a fact:

The stem, the leaf, and the flower; beginning, middle, and end;
Cause, circumstance, consequent; and every three is one.
Yea, the very breath of man's life consisteth of a trinity of vapours,
And the noonday light is a compound, the triune shadow of Jehovah. ([2])

Shall all things else be in mystery, and God alone be understood?
Shall finite fathom infinity, though it sound not the shallows of creation?
Shall a man comprehend his Maker, being yet a riddle to himself?
Or time teach the lesson that eternity cannot master?
If God be nothing more than one, a child can compass the thought;
But seraphs fail to unravel the wondrous unity of three.
One verily He is, for there can be but one who is all-mighty;
Yet the oracles of nature and religion proclaim Him three in one.
And where were the value to thy soul, O miserable denizen of earth,
Of the idle pageant of the cross, where hung no sacrifice for thee?
Where the worth to thine impotent heart, of that stirred Bethesda,
All numbed and palsied as it is by the scorpion stings of sin?
No, thy trinity of nature, enchained by treble death,
Helplessly craveth of its God, himself for three salvations:
The soul to be reconciled in love, the mind to be glorified in light,
While this poor dying body leapeth into life.
And if indeed for us all the costly ransom hath been paid,
Bethink thee, could less than Deity have owned so vast a treasure?
Could a man contend with God, and stand against the bosses of His buckler,
Rendering the balance for guilt, atonement to the uttermost?
Thou art subtle to thine own thinking, but wisdom judgeth thee a fool,
Resolving thou wilt not bow the knee to a Being thou canst not comprehend:
The mind that could compass perfection were itself perfection's equal;
And reason refuseth its homage to a God who can be fully understood.

Thou that despisest mystery, yet canst expound nothing,
Wherefore rejectest thou the fact that solveth the enigma of all things?
Wherefore veilest thou thine eyes, lest the light of revelation sun them,
And puttest aside the key that would open the casket of truth?
The mind and the nature of God is shadowed in all his works,
And none could have guessed of his essence, had He not uttered it himself.
Therefore, thou child of folly, that scornest the record of his wisdom,
Learn from the consistencies of nature the needful miracle of Godhead;

Yea, let the heathen be thy teacher, who adoreth many gods,
For there is no wide-spread error that hath not truth for its beginning.
Be content; thine eye cannot see all the sides of a cube at one view,
Nor thy mind in the self-same moment follow two ideas:
There are now many marvels in thy creed, believing what thou seest,
Then let not the conceit of intellect hinder thee from worshipping mystery.

OF THINKING.

Reflection is a flower of the mind, giving out wholesome fragrance,
But reverie is the same flower, when rank and running to seed.
Better to read little with thought, than much with levity and quickness
For mind is not as merchandise, which decreaseth in the using,
But liker to the passions of man, which rejoice and expand in exertion:
Yet live not wholly on thine own ideas, lest they lead thee astray;
For in spirit, as in substance, thou art a social creature;
And if thou leanest on thyself, thou rejectest the guidance of thy betters,
Yea, thou contemnest all men,—Am I not wiser than they?
Foolish vanity hath blinded thee, and warped thy weak judgment;
For, though new ideas flow from new springs, and enrich the treasury of knowledge,
Yet listen often, ere thou think much; and look around thee ere thou judgest.
Memory, the daugter of Attention, is the teeming mother of Wisdom,
And safer is he that storeth knowledge, than he that would make it for himself.

Imagination is not thought, neither is fancy reflection:
Thought paceth like a hoary sage, but imagination hath wings as an eagle:
Reflection sternly considereth, nor is sparing to condemn evil,
But fancy lightly laugheth, in the sun-clad garden of amusement.
For the shy game of the fowler the quickest shot is the surest;
But with slow care and measured aim the gunner pointeth his cannon:
So for all less occasions, the surface thought is best,
But to be master of the great take thou heavier metal.
It is a good thing, and a wholesome, to search out bosom sins,

But to be the hero of selfish imaginings, is the subtle poison of pride:
At night, in the stillness of thy chamber, guard and curb thy thoughts,
And in recounting the doings of the day, beware that thou do it with prayer,
Or thinking will be an idle pleasure, and retrospect yield no fruit.
Steer the bark of thy mind from the syren isle of reverie,
And let a watchful spirit mingle with the glance of recollection:
Also, in examining thine heart, in sounding the fountain of thine actions,
Be more careful of the evil than of the good; and humble thyself in thy sin.

The root of all wholesome thought is knowledge of thyself,
For thus only canst thou learn the character of God toward thee.
He made thee, and thou art; he redeemed thee, and thou wilt be:
Thou art evil, yet he loveth thee: thou sinnest, yet he pardoneth thee.
Though thou canst not perceive him, yet is he in all his works,
Infinite in grand outline, infinite in minute perfection;
Nature is the chart of God, mapping out all his attributes;
Art is the shadow of his wisdom, and copieth his resources.
Thou knowest the laws of matter to be emanations of his will,
And thy best reason for aught is this,—thou, Lord, would have it so.
Yea, what is any law but an absolute decree of God?
Or the properties of matter and mind, but the arbitrary fiats of Jehovah?
He made and ordained necessity; he forged the chain of reason;
And holdeth in his own right hand the first of the golden links.
A fool regardeth mind as the spiritual essence of matter,
And not rather matter as the gross accident of mind.
Can finite govern infinite, or a part exceed the whole,
Or the wisdom of God sit down at the feet of innate necessity?
Necessity is a creature of his hand: for He can never change;
And chance hath no existence where every thing is needful.

Canst thou measure Omnipotence, canst thou conceive Ubiquity,
Which guideth the meanest reptile, and quickeneth the brightest seraph,
Which steereth the particles of dust, and commandeth the path of the comet?
To Him all things are equal, for all things are necessary.
The smith is weary at his forge, and weldeth the metal carelessly,
And the anchor breaketh in its bed, and the vessel foundereth with her crew:
A word of anger is muttered, engendering the midnight murder:

The sun bursteth from a cloud, and maddeneth the toiling husbandman.
Shall these things be, and God not know it?
Shall he know, and not be in them? shall he see, and not be among them?
And how can they be otherwise than as he knoweth?
Truly, the Lord is in all things; verily, he worketh in all.
Think thus, and thy thoughts are firm, ascribing each circumstance to Him;
Yet know surely, and believe the truth, that God willeth not evil:
For adversities are blessings in disguise, and wickedness the Lord abhorreth:
That he is in all things is an axiom, and that he is righteous in all;
Ascribe holiness to Him, while thou musest on the mystery of sin,
For infinite can grasp that which finite cannot compass.

In works of art, think justly: what praise canst thou render unto man?
For he made not his own mind, nor is he the scource of contrivance.
If a cunning workman maketh an engine that fashioneth curious works,
Which hath the praise, the machine or its maker,—the engine, or he that framed it?
And could he frame it so subtly as to give it a will and freedom,
Endow it with complicated powers, and a glorious living soul,
Who, while he admireth the wondrous understanding creature,
Will not pay deeper homage to the Maker of master minds?
Otherwise, thou art senseless as the pagan, that adoreth his own handiwork;
Yea, while thou boastest of thy wisdom, thy mind is as the mind of the savage,
For he boweth down to his idols, and thou art a worshipper of self,
Giving to the reasoning machine the credit due to its Creator.

The keystone of thy mind, to give thy thoughts solidity,
To bind them as in an arch, to fix them as a world in its sphere,
Is to learn from the book of the Lord, to drink from the well of his wisdom.
Who can condense the sun, or analyze the fullness of the Bible,
So that its ideas be gathered, and the harvest of its wisdom be brought in?
That book is easy to the man who setteth his heart to understand it,
But to the careless and profane it shall seem the foolishness of God;
And it is a delicate test to prove thy moral state;
To the humble disciple it is bread, but a stone to the proud and unbelieving:

A scorner shall find nothing but the husks, wherewith to feed his hunger
But for the soul of the simple, it is plenty of full-ripe wheat.
The Scripture abideth the same in the sober majesty of truth;
And the differing aspects of its teaching proceed from diversity in minds.
He that would learn to think may gain that knowledge there;
For the living word, as an angel, standeth at the gate of wisdom,
And publisheth, This is the way, walk ye surely in it.
Religion taketh by the hand the humble pupil of repentance,
And teacheth him lessons of mystery, solving the questions of doubt;
She maketh man worthy of himself, of his high prerogative of reason,
Threadeth all the labyrinths of thought, and leadeth him to his God.

Come hither, child of meditation, upon whose high fair forehead
Glittereth the star of mind in its unearthly lustre,
Hast thou nought to tell us of thine airy joys,—
When borne on sinewy pinions, strong as the western condor,
The soul, after soaring for a while round the cloud-capped Andes of reflection,
Glad in its conscious immortality, leaveth a world behind,
To dare at one bold flight the broad Atlantic to another?
Hast thou no secret pangs to whisper common men,
No dread of thine own energies, still active, day and night,
Lest too ecstatic heat sublime thyself away,
Or vivid horrors, sharp and clear, madden thy tense fibres?
In half-shaped visions of sleep hast thou not feared thy flittings,
Lest reason, like a raking hawk, return not to thy call;
Nor waked to work-day life with throbbing head and heart,
Nor welcomed early dawn to save thee from unrest?
For the wearied spirit lieth as a fainting maiden,
Captive and borne away on the warrior's foam-covered steed,
And sinketh down wounded as a gladiator on the sand,
While the keen falchion of Intellect is cutting through the scabbard of the brain.
Imagination, like a shadowy giant looming on the twilight of the Hartz,
Shall overwhelm Judgment with affright, and scare him from his throne:
In a dream thou mayst be mad, and feel the fire within thee;
In a dream thou mayst travel out of self, and see thee with the eyes of another;
Or sleep in thine own corpse; or wake as in many bodies:

Or swell, as expanded to infinity; or shrink, as imprisoned to a point;
Or among moss-grown ruins may wander with the sullen disembodied,
And gaze upon their glassy eyes until thy heart-blood freeze.

Alone must thou stand, O man! alone at the bar of judgment;
Alone must thou bear thy sentence, alone must thou answer for thy deeds:
Therefore it is well thou retirest often to secrecy and solitude,
To feel that thou art accountable separately from thy fellows:
For a crowd hideth truth from the eyes, society drowneth thought,
And, being but one among many, stifleth the chidings of conscience.
Solitude bringeth woe to the wicked, for his crimes are told out in his ear;
But addeth peace to the good, for the mercies of his God are numbered.
Thou mayst know if it be well with a man,—loveth he gayety or solitude?
For the troubled river rusheth to the sea, but the calm lake slumbereth among the mountains.
How dear to the mind of the sage are the thoughts that are bred in loneliness,
For there is as it were music at his heart, and he talketh within him as with friends:
But guilt maddeneth the brain, and terror glareth in the eye,
Where, in his solitary cell, the malefactor wrestleth with remorse.
Give me but a lodge in the wilderness, drop me on an island in the desert,
And thought shall yield me happiness, though I may not increase it by imparting:
For the soul never slumbereth, but is as the eye of the Eternal,
And, mind, the breath of God, knoweth not ideal vacuity:
At night, after weariness and watching, the body sinketh into sleep,
But the mental eye is awake, and thou reasonest in thy dreams:
In a dream thou mayst live a lifetime, and all be forgotten in the morning:
Even such is life, and so soon perisheth its memory.

OF SPEAKING.

Speech is the golden harvest that followeth the flowering of thought;
Yet oftentimes runneth it to husk, and the grains be withered and scanty.
Speech is reason's brother and a kingly prerogative of man,

That likeneth him to his Maker, who spake, and it was done:
Spirit may mingle with spirit, but sense requireth a symbol;
And speech is the body of a thought, without which it were not seen.
When thou walkest, musing with thyself, in the green aisles of the forest,
Utter thy thinkings aloud, that they take a shape and being;
For he that pondereth in silence crowdeth the storehouse of his mind,
And though he have heaped great riches, yet is he hindered in the using.
A man that speaketh too little, and thinketh much and deeply,
Corrodeth his own heart-strings, and keepeth back good from his fellows?
A man that speaketh too much, and museth but little and lightly,
Wasteth his mind in words, and is counted a fool among men:
But thou, when thou hast thought, weave charily the web of meditation,
And clothe the ideal spirit in the suitable garments of speech.

Uttered out of time, or concealed in its season, good savoureth of evil;
To be secret looketh like guilt, to speak out may breed contention;
Often have I known the honest heart, flaming with indignant virtue,
Provoke unneeded war by its rash ambassador, the tongue:
Often have I seen the charitable man go so slyly on his mission,
That those who met him in the twilight, took him for a skulking thief:
I have heard the zealous youth telling out his holy secrets
Before a swinish throng, who mocked him as he spake;
And I considered, his openness was hardening them that mocked,
Whereas, a judicious keeping-back might have won their sympathy;
I have judged rashly and harshly the hand liberal in the dark,
Because in the broad daylight it hath holden it a virtue to be close;
And the silent tongue have I condemned, because reserve hath chained it,
That it hid, yea from a brother, the kindness it had done by comforting.
No need to sound a trumpet, but less to hush a footfall:
Do thou thy good openly, not as though the doing were a crime.
Secrecy goeth cowled, and Honesty demandeth, Wherefore?
For he judgeth,—judgeth he not well?—that nothing need be hid but guilt;
Why should thy good be evil spoken of through thine unrighteous silence?
If thou art challenged, speak, and prove the good thou doest.
The free example of benevolence, unobtruded, yet unbidden,
Soundeth in the ears of sloth, Go, and do thou likewise:
And I wot the hypocrite's sin to be of darker dye,
Because the good man, fearing, thereby hideth his light:

But neither God nor man hath bid thee cloak thy good,
When a seasonable word would set thee in thy sphere, that all might see thy brightness.
Ascribe the honour to thy Lord, but be thou jealous of that honour,
Nor think it light and worthless, because thou mayst not wear it for thyself:
Remember thy grand prerogative is free unshackled utterance,
And suffer not the floodgates of secrecy to lock the full river of thy speech.

Come, I will show thee an affliction, unnumbered among this world's sorrows,
Yet real, and wearisome, and constant, embittering the cup of life.
There be, who can think within themselves, and the fire burneth at their heart,
And eloquence waiteth at their lips, yet they speak not with their tongue:
There be, whom zeal quickeneth, or slander stirreth to reply,
Or need constraineth to ask, or pity sendeth as her messengers,
But nervous dread and sensitive shame freeze the current of their speech:
The mouth is sealed as with lead, a cold weight presseth on the heart,
The mocking promise of power is once more broken in performance,
And they stand impotent of words, travailing with unborn thoughts:
Courage is cowed at the portal: wisdom is widowed of utterance;
He that went to comfort is pitied; he that should rebuke, is silent.
And fools who might listen and learn, stand by to look and laugh;
While friends, with kinder eyes, wound deeper by compassion,
And thought, finding not a vent, smouldereth, gnawing at the heart,
And the man sinketh in his sphere, for lack of empty sounds.
There be many cares and sorrows thou hast not yet considered,
And well may thy soul rejoice in the fair privilege of speech;
For at every turn to want a word,—thou canst not guess that want;
It is as lack of breath or bread: life hath no grief more galling.

Come, I will tell thee of a joy, which the parasites of pleasure have not known,
Though earth, and air, and sea, have gorged all the appetites of sense.
Behold, what fire is in his eye, what fervour on his cheek!
That glorious burst of winged words!—how bound they from his tongue!
The full expression of the mighty thought, the strong triumphant argument,

The rush of native eloquence, resistless as Niagara,
The keen demand, the clear reply, the fine poetic image,
The nice analogy, the clenching fact, the metaphor bold and free,
The grasp of concentrated intellect, wielding the omnipotence of truth,
The grandeur of his speech, in his majesty of mind!
Champion of the right,—patriot, or priest, or pleader of the innocent cause,
Upon whose lips the mystic bee hath droped the honey of persuasion, ([21])
Whose heart and tongue have been touched, as of old, by the live coal from the altar,
How wide the spreading of thy peace, how deep the draught of thy pleasures!
To hold the multitude as one, breathing in measured cadence,
A thousand men with flashing eyes, waiting upon thy will;
A thousand hearts kindled by thee with consecrated fire,
Ten flaming spiritual hecatombs offered on the mount of God:
And now a pause, a thrilling pause,—they live but in thy words,—
Thou hast broken the bounds of self, as the Nile at its rising,
Thou art expanded into them, one faith, one hope, one spirit,
They breathe but in thy breath, their minds are passive unto thine,
Thou turnest the key of their love, bending their affections to thy purpose,
And all, in sympathy with thee, tremble with tumultuous emotions.
Verily, O man, with truth for thy theme, eloquence shall throne thee with archangels.

OF READING.

One drachma for a good book, and a thousand talents for a true friend:—
So standeth the market where scarce is ever costly:
Yea, were the diamonds of Golconda common as shingles on the shore,
A ripe apple would ransom kings before a shining stone:
And so, were a wholesome book as rare as an honest friend,
To choose the book be mine: the friend let another take.
For altered looks and jealousies and fears have none entrance there:
The silent volume listeneth well, and speaketh when thou listest:

It praiseth thy good without envy, it chideth thine evil without malice,
It is to thee thy waiting slave, and thine unbending teacher.
Need to humour no caprice, need to bear with no infirmity;
Thy sin, thy slander, or neglect, chilleth not, quencheth not, its love;
Unalterably speaketh it the truth, warped not by error nor interest;
For a good book is the best of friends, the same to-day and for ever.

To draw thee out of self, thy petty plans and cautions,
To teach thee what thou lackest, to tell thee how largely thou art blest,
To lure thy thought from sorrow, to feed thy famished mind,
To graft another's wisdom on thee, pruning thine own folly;
Choose discreetly, and well digest the volume most suited to thy case,
Touching not religion with levity, nor deep things when thou art wearied.
Thy mind is freshened by morning air, grapple with science and philosophy;
Noon hath unnerved thy thoughts, dream for a while on fictions;
Gray evening sobereth thy spirit, walk thou then with worshippers;
But reason shall dig deepest in the night, and fancy fly most free.
O books, ye monuments of mind, concrete wisdom of the wisest;
Sweet solaces of daily life; proofs and results of immortality;
Trees yielding all fruits, whose leaves are for the healing of the nations.
Groves of knowledge, where all may eat, nor fear a flaming sword;
Gentle comrades, kind advisers; friends, comforts, treasures;
Helps, governments, diversities of tongues; who can weigh your worth?—
To walk no longer with the just; to be driven from the porch of science;
To bid long adieu to those intimate ones, poets, philosophers, and teachers;
To see no record of the sympathies which bind thee in communion with the good;
To be thrust from the feet of Him, who spake as never man spake;
To have no avenue to heaven but the dim aisle of superstition;
To live as an Esquimaux, in lethargy; to die as the Mohawk, in ignorance:
O what were life, but a blank? what were death, but a terror?
What were man, but a burden to himself? what were mind, but misery?
Yea, let another Omar burn the full library of knowledge, ([22])
And the broad world may perish in the flames, offered on the ashes of its wisdom!

OF WRITING.

THE pen of a ready writer, whereunto shall it be likened?
Ask of the scholar, he shall know,—to the chains that bind a Proteus:
Ask of the poet, he shall say,—to the sun, the lamp of heaven;
Ask of thy neighbour, he can answer, to the friend that telleth my thought:
The merchant considereth it well, as a ship freighted with wares;
The divine holdeth it a miracle, giving utterance to the dumb.
It fixeth, expoundeth, and disseminateth sentiment;
Chaining up a thought, clearing it of mystery, and sending it bright into the world.
To think rightly, is of knowledge; to speak fluently, is of nature;
To read with profit, is of care; but to write aptly, is of practice.
No talent among men hath more scholars and fewer masters:
For to write is to speak beyond hearing, and none stand by to explain.
To be accurate, write; to remember, write; to know thine own mind, write:
And a written prayer is a prayer of faith; special, sure, and to be answered.
Hast thou a thought upon thy brain, catch it while thou canst;
Or other thoughts shall settle there, and this shall soon take wing:
Thine uncompounded unity of soul, which argueth and maketh it immortal,
Yieldeth up its momentary self to every single thought;
Therefore, to husband thine ideas, and give them stability and substance
Write often for thy secret eye: so shalt thou grow wiser.
The commonest mind is full of thoughts; some worthy of the rarest;
And could it see them fairly writ, would wonder at its wealth.
O precious compensation to the dumb, to write his wants and wishes!
O dear amends to the stammering tongue, to pen his burning thoughts!
To be of the college of Eloquence, through these silent symbols;
To pour out all the flowing mind without the toil of speech;
To show the babbling world how it might discourse more sweetly;
To prove that merchandise of words bringeth no monopoly of wisdom;
To take sweet vengeance on a prating crew, for the tongue's dishonour,
By the large triumph of the pen, the homage rendered to a writing.
With such, that telegraph of mind is dearer than wealth or wisdom,
Enabling to please without pain, to impart without humiliation.

Fair girl, whose eye hath caught the rustic penmanship of love,

Let thy bright bow and blushing cheek confess in this sweet hour,—
Let thy full heart, poor guilty one, whom the scroll of pardon hath just reached,—
Thy wet glad face, O mother, with news of a far-off child,—
Thy strong and manly delight, pilgrim of other shores,
When the dear voice of thy betrothed speaketh in the letter of affection.—
Let the young poet exulting in his lay, and hope (how false) of fame,
While, watching at deep midnight, he buildeth up the verse,—
Let the calm child of genius, whose name shall never die,
For that the transcript of his mind hath made his thoughts immortal,—
Let these, let all, with no faint praise, with no light gratitude, confess
The blessings poured upon the earth from the pen of a ready writer.

Moreover, their preciousness in absence is proved by the desire of their presence:
When the despairing lover waiteth day after day,
Looking for a word in reply, one word writ by that hand,
And cursing bitterly the morn ushered in by blank disappointment:
Or when the long-looked-for answer argueth a cooling friend,
And the mind is plied suspiciously with dark inexplicable doubts,
While thy wounded heart counteth its imaginary scars,
And thou art the innocent and injured, that friend the capricious and in fault:
Or when the earnest petition, that craveth for thy needs
Unheeded, yea, unopened, tortureth with starving delay:
Or when the silence of a son, who would have written of his welfare,
Racketh a father's bosom with sharp-cutting fears:
For a letter, timely writ, is a rivet to the chain of affection.
And a letter untimely delayed, is as rust to the solder.
The pen, flowing with love, or dipped black in hate,
Or tipped with delicate courtesies, or harshly edged with censure,
Hath quickened more good than the sun, more evil than the sword,
More joy than woman's smile, more woe than frowning fortune;
And shouldst thou ask my judgment of that which hath most profit in the world,
For answer take thou this, The prudent penning of a letter.

Thou hast not lost an hour, whereof there is a record;
A written thought at midnight shall redeem the livelong day.

Idea is a shadow that departeth, speech is fleeting as the wind,
Reading is an unremembered pastime; but a writing is eternal:
For therein the dead heart liveth, the clay-cold tongue is eloquent,
And the quick eye of the reader is cleared by the reed of the scribe.
As a fossil in the rock, or a coin in the mortar of a ruin,
So the symbolled thoughts tell of a departed soul:
The plastic hand hath its witness in a statue, and exactitude of vision in a picture,
And so, the mind, that was among us, in its writings is embalmed.

OF WEALTH.

Prodigality hath a sister Meanness, his fixed antagonist heart-fellow,
Who often outliveth the short career of the brother she despiseth:
She hath lean lips and a sharp look, and her eyes are red and hungry;
But she sloucheth at his gait, and his mouth speaketh loosely and maudlin.
Let a spendthrift grow to be old, he will set his heart on saving,
And labour to build up by penury that which extravagance threw down:
Even so, with most men, do riches earn themselves a double curse;
They are ill-got by tight dealing: they are ill-spent by loose squandering.
Give me enough, saith Wisdom;—for he feareth to ask for more;
And that by the sweat of my brow, addeth stout-hearted Independence:
Give me enough, and not less, for want is leagued with the tempter;
Poverty shall make a man desperate, and hurry him ruthless into crime;
Give me enough, and not more, saving for the children of distress;
Wealth ofttimes killeth, where want but hindereth the budding:
There is green glad summer near the pole, though brief and after long winter,
But the burnt breasts of the torrid zone yield never kindly nourishment.
Wouldst thou be poor, scatter to the rich,—and reap the tares of ingratitude;
Wouldst thou be rich, give unto the poor;—thou shalt have thine own with usury:
For the secret hand of Providence prospereth the charitable all ways,
Good luck shall he have in his pursuits, and his heart shall be glad within him;

Yet perchance he never shall perceive, that even as to earthly gains,
The cause of his weal, as of his joy, hath been small givings to the poor.

In the plain of Benares is there found a root that fathereth a forest,
Where round the parent banian-tree drop its living scions;
Thirstily they strain to the earth, like stalactites in a grotto,
And strike broad roots, and branch again, lengthening their cool arcades.
And the dervish madly danceth there, and the faquir is torturing his flesh,
And the calm Brahmin worshippeth the sleek and pampered bull;
At the base lean jackalls coil, while from above depending
With dull malignant stare watcheth the branch-like boa.
Even so, in man's heart is a sin that is the root of all evil;
Whose fibres strangle the affections, whose branches overgrow the mind:
And oftenest beneath its shadow thou shalt meet distorted piety,—
The clenched and rigid fist, with the eyes upturned to heaven,
Fanatic zeal with miserly severity, a mixture of gain with godliness,
And him, against whom passion hath no power, kneeling to a golden calf:
The hungry hounds of extortion are there, the bond, and the mortgage, and the writ,
While the appetite for gold, unslumbering, watcheth to glut its maw:—
And the heart, so tenanted and shaded, is cold to all things else;
It seeth not the sunshine of heaven, nor is warmed by the light of charity.

For covetousness disbelieveth God, and laugheth at the rights of men;
Spurring unto theft and lying, and tempting to the poison and the knife;
It sundereth the bonds of love, and quickeneth the flames of hate;
A curse that shall wither the brain, and case the heart with iron.
Content is the true riches, for without it there is no satisfying,
But a ravenous all-devouring hunger gnaweth the vitals of the soul.
The wise man knoweth where to stop, as he runneth in the race of fortune,
For experience of old hath taught him that happiness lingereth midway;
And many in hot pursuit have hasted to the goal of wealth,
But have lost, as they ran, those apples of gold,—the mind and the power to enjoy it.

There is no greater evil among men than a testament framed with injustice;
Where caprice hath guided the boon, or dishonesty refused what was due.
Generous is the robber on the highway, in the open daring of his guilt,
To the secret coward, whose malice liveth and harmeth after him:

Who smoothly sank into the tomb with the smile of fraud upon his face,
And the last black deed of his existence was injury without redress;
For deaf is the ear of the dead, and can hear no palliating reasons;
The smiter is not among the living, and Right pleadeth but in vain.
Yet shall the curse of the oppressed be as blight upon the grave of the unjust;
Yea, bitterly shall that handwriting testify against him at the judgment.
I saw the humble relation that tended the peevishness of wealth,
And ministered with kind hand to the wailings of disease and discontent;
I noted how watchfulness and care were feeding on the marrow of her youth;
How heavy was the yoke of dependence, loaded by petty tyranny;
Yet I heard the frequent suggestion,—it can be but a little longer,
Patience and mute submission shall one day reap a rich reward.
So, tacitly enduring much, waited that humble friend,
Putting off the lover of her youth until the dawn of wealth;
And it came, that day of release, and the freed heart could not sorrow,
For now were the years of promise to yield their golden harvest:
Hope, so long deferred, sickly sparkled in her eye,
The miserable past was forgotten, as she looked for the happier future,
And she checked, as unworthy and ungrateful, the dark, suspicious thought,
That perchance her right had been the safer, if not left alone with honour:
But, alas, the sad knowledge soon came, that her stern task-master's will
Hath rewarded her toil with a jibe, her patience with utter destitution!—
Shall not the scourge of justice lash that cruel coward,
Who mingled the gall of ingratitude with the bitterness of disappointment.
Shall not the hate of men, and vengeance, fiercely pursuing,
Hunt down the wretched being that sinneth in his grave?
He fancied his idol self safe from the wrath of his fellows,
But Hades rose as he came in, to point at him the finger of scorn;
And again must he meet that orphan-maid to answer her, face to face,
And her wrongs shall cling around his neck, to hinder him from rising with the just:
For his last most solemn act hath linked his name with liar,
And the crime of Ananias is branded on his brow!

A good man commendeth his cause to the one great Patron of innocence,
Convinced of justice at the last, and sure of good meanwhile.

He knoweth he hath a Guardian, wise and kind and strong,
And can thank Him for giving, or refusing, the trust or the curse of riches:
His confidence standeth as a rock; he dreadeth not malice nor caprice,
Nor the whisperings of artful men, nor envious secret influence;
He scorneth servile compromise, and the pliant mouthings of deceit;
He maketh not a show of love, where he cannot concede esteem;
He regardeth ill-got wealth, as the root most fruitful of wretchedness,
So he walketh in strict integrity, leaning on God and his right.

No gain, but by its price; labour, for the poor man's meal,
Ofttimes heart-sickening toil, to win him a morsel for his hunger:
Labour, for the chapman at his trade, a dull unvaried round,
Year after year, unto death; yea, what a weariness is it!
Labour for the pale-faced scribe, drudging at his hated desk,
Who bartereth for needful pittance the untold gold of health;
Labour, with fear, for the merchant, whose hopes are ventured on the sea;
Labour, with care, for the man of law, responsible in his gains;
Labour, with envy and annoyance, where strangers will thee wealth;
Labour, with indolence and gloom, where wealth falleth from a father;
Labour, unto all, whether aching thews, or aching head, or spirit,—
The curse on the sons of men, in all their states, is labour.
Nevertheless, to the diligent, labour bringeth blessing;
The thought of duty sweeteneth toil, and travail is as pleasure;
And time spent in doing hath a comfort that is not for the idle;
The hardship is transmuted into joy, by the dear alchemy of Mercy.
Labour is good for a man, bracing up his energies to conquest,
And without it life is dull, the man perceiving himself useless:
For wearily the body groaneth, like a door on rusty hinges,
And the grasp of the mind is weakened, as the talons of a caged vulture.
Wealth hath never given happiness, but often hastened misery:
Enough hath never caused misery, but often quickened happiness:
Enough is less than thy thought, O pampered creature of society,
And he that hath more than enough, is a thief of the rights his brother.

OF INVENTION.

MAN is proud of his mind, boasting that it giveth him divinity,
Yet with all its powers can it originate nothing:
For the great God into all his works hath largely poured out himself,
Saving one special property, the grand prerogative,—Creation.
To improve and expand is ours, as well as to limit and defeat:
But to create a thought or a thing is hopeless and impossible.
Can a man make matter?—and yet this would-be god
Thinketh to make mind, and form original idea:
The potter must have his clay, and the mason his quarry,
And mind must drain ideas from every thing around it.
Doth the soil generate herbs, or the torrid air breed flies,
Or the water frame its monads, or the mist its swarming blight?—
Mediately, through thousand generations, having seeds within themselves,
All things, rare or gross, own one common Father.
Truly spake Wisdom, There is nothing new under the sun:
We only arrange and combine the ancient elements of all things.
Invention is activity of mind, as fire is air in motion.
A sharpening of the spiritual sight, to discern hidden aptitudes;
From the basket and acanthus, is modelled the graceful capital:
The shadowed profile on the wall helpeth the limner to his likeness:
The footmarks stamped in clay, lead on the thoughts to printing;
The strange skin garments cast upon the shore suggest another hemisphere: (23)
A falling apple taught the sage pervading gravitation;
The Huron is certain of his prey, from tracks upon the grass;
And shrewdness, guessing on the hint, followeth on the trail;
But the hint must be given, the trail must be there, or the keenest sight is as blindness.

Behold the barren reef, which an earthquake hath just left dry;
It hath no beauty to boast of, no harvest of fair fruits:
But soon the lichen fixeth there, and, dying, diggeth its own grave, (24)
And softening suns and splitting frosts crumble the reluctant surface;
And cormorants roost there, and the snail addeth its slime,
And efts, with muddy feet, bring their welcome tribute;

And the sea casteth out her dead, wrapped in a shroud of weeds;
And orderly nature arrangeth again the disunited atoms:
Anon, the cold smooth stone is warm with feathery grass,
And the light sporules of the fern are dropt by the passing wind.
The wood-pigeon, on swift wing, leaveth its crop-full of grain;
The squirrel's jealous care planteth the fir-cone and the filbert;
Years pass, and the sterile rock is rank with tangled herbage;
The wild vine clingeth to the brier, and ivy runneth green among the corn,
Lordly beeches are studded on the down, and willows crowd around the rivulet;
And the tall pine and hazel thicket shade the rambling hunter.
Shall the rock boast of its fertility? shall it lift the head in pride?—
Shall the mind of man be vain of the harvest of its thoughts?
The savage is that rock: and a million chances from without,
By little and little acting on the mind, heap up the hotbed of society;
And the soul, fed and fattened on the thoughts and things around it,
Groweth to perfection, full of fruit, the fruit of foreign seeds.
For we learn upon a hint, we find upon a clue,
We yield an hundred-fold; but the great sower is Analogy.
There must be an acrid sloe before a luscious peach,
A boll of rotting flax before the bridal veil,
An egg before an eagle, a thought before a thing,
A spark struck into tinder, to light the lamp of knowledge,
A slight suggestive nod to guide the watching mind,
A half-seen hand upon the wall, pointing to the balance of Comparison.
By culture man may do all things, short of the miracle,—Creation:
Here is the limit of thy power,—here let thy pride be stayed:
The soil may be rich, and the mind may be active, but neither yield unsown;
The eye cannot make light, nor the mind make spirit:
Therefore it is wise in man to name all novelty invention:
For it is to find out things that are, not to create the unexisting:
It is to cling to contiguities, to be keen in catching likeness,
And with energetic elasticity to leap the gulfs of contrast.
The globe kneweth not increase, either of matter or spirit;
Atoms and thoughts are used again, mixing in varied combinations;
And though, by moulding them anew, thou makest them thine own,
Yet have they served thousands, and all their merit is of God.

OF RIDICULE.

SEAMS of thought for the sage's brow, and laughing lines for the fool's face;
For all things leave their track in the mind; and the glass of the mind is faithful.
Seest thou much mirth upon the cheek? there is then little exercise of virtue;
For he that looketh on the world cannot be glad and good:
Seest thou much gravity in the eye? be not assured of finding wisdom,
For she hath too great praise, not to get many mimics.
There is a grave-faced folly; and verily a laughter-loving wisdom;
And what, if surface-judges account it vain frivolity?
There is indeed an evil in excess, and a field may lie fallow too long;
Yet merriment is often as a froth, that mantleth on the strong mind:
And note thou this for a verity,—the subtlest thinker when alone,
From ease of thoughts unbent, will laugh the loudest with his fellows:
And well is the loveliness of wisdom mirrored in a cheerful countenance;
Justly the deepest pools are proved by dimpling eddies;
For that a true philosophy commandeth an innocent life,
And the unguilty spirit is lighter than a linnet's heart:
Yea, there is no cosmetic like a holy conscience:
The eye is bright with trust, the cheek bloomed over with affection,
The brow unwrinkled by a care, and the lip triumphant in its gladness.

And for your grave-faced folly, need not far to look for her;
How seriously on trifles dote those leaden eyes,
How ruefully she sigheth after chances long gone by,
How sulkily she moaneth over evils without cure!
I have known a true-born mirth, the child of innocence and wisdom,
I have seen a base-born gravity, mingled of ignorance and guilt:
And again, a base-born mirth, springing out of carelessness and folly,
And again, a true-born gravity, the product of reflection and right fear.
The wounded partridge hideth in a furrow, and a stricken conscience would be left alone;
But when its breast is healed, it runneth gladly with its fellows:
Whereas the solitary heron, standing in the sedgy fen,

Holdeth aloof from the social world, intent on wiles and death.
Need but of light philosophy to dare the world's dread laugh;
For a little mind courteth notoriety, to illustrate its puny self:
But the sneer of a man's own comrades trieth the muscles of courage,
And to be derided in his home is as a viper in the nest:
The laugh of a hooting world hath in it a notion of sublimity,
But the tittering private circle stingeth as a hive of wasps.
Some have commended ridicule, counting it the test of truth, ([25])
But neither wittily nor wisely; for truth must prove ridicule:
Otherwise a blunt bulrush is to pierce the proof armour of argument,
Because the stolidity of ignorance took it for a barbed shaft.
Softer is the hide of the rhinoceros than the heart of deriding unbelief,
And truth is idler there than the Bushman's feathered reed:
A droll conceit parrieth a thrust that should have hit the conscience,
And the leering looks of humour tickle the childish mind;
For that the matter of a man is mingled most with folly,
Neither can he long endure the searching gaze of wisdom.
It is pleasanter to see a laughing cheek than a serious forehead,
And there liveth not one among a thousand whose idol is not pleasure.
Ridicule is a weak weapon, when levelled at a strong mind;
But common men are cowards, and dread an empty laugh.
Fear a nettle, and touch it tenderly,—its poison shall burn thee to the shoulder;
But grasp it with bold hand, is it not a bundle of myrrh?
Betray mean terror of ridicule, thou shalt find fools enough to mock thee;
But answer thou their laughter with contempt, and the scoffers will lick thy feet.

OF COMMENDATION.

The praise of holy men is a promise of praise from their Master;
A forerunning earnest of thy welcome,—Well done, faithful servant;
A rich preludious note, that droppeth softly on thine ear,
To tell thee the chords of thy heart are in tune with the choirs of heaven.
Yet is it a dangerous hearing, for the sweetness may lull thee into slumber.
And the cordial quaffed with thirst may generate the fumes of presumption.
So seek it not for itself, but taste, and go gladly on thy way,

For the mariner slacketh not his sail, though the sandal-groves of Araby allure him;
And the fragrance of that incense would harm thee, as when, on a summer evening,
The honied yellow flowers of the broom oppress thy charmed sense:
And a man hath too much of praise, for he praiseth himself continually;
Neither lacketh he at any time self-commendation or excuse.

Praise a fool, and slay him: for the canvas of his vanity is spread;
His bark is shallow in the water, and a sudden gust shall sink it:
Praise a wise man, and speed him on his way; for he carrieth the ballast of humility,
And is glad when his course is cheered by the sympathy of brethren ashore.
The praise of a good man is good, for he holdeth up the mirror of Truth,
That Virtue may see her own beauty, and delight in her own fair face:
The praise of a bad man is evil, for he hideth the deformity of Vice,
Casting the mantle of a queen around the limbs of a leper.
Praise is rebuke to the man whose conscience alloweth it not:
And where conscience feeleth it her due, no praise is better than a little.
He that despiseth the outward appearance, despiseth the esteem of his fellows;
And he that overmuch regardeth it, shall earn only their contempt:
The honest commendation of an equal no one can scorn, and be blameless
Yet even that fair fame no one can hunt for and be honoured:
If it come, accept it and be thankful, and be thou humble in accepting;
If it tarry, be not thou cast down; the bee can gather honey out of rue:
And is thine aim so low, that the breath of those around thee
Can speed thy feathered arrow, or retard its flight?
The child shooteth at a butterfly, but the man's mark is an eagle;
And while his fellows talk, he hath conquered in the clouds.
Ally thee to truth and godliness, and use the talents in thy charge:
So shalt thou walk in peace, deserving, if not having.
With a friend, praise him when thou canst; for many a friendship hath decayed,
Like a plant in a crowded corner, for want of sunshine on its leaves:
With another, praise him not often—otherwise he shall despise thee;
But be thou frugal in commending; so will he give honour to thy judgment:
For thou that dost so zealously commend, art acknowledging thine own inferiority,

And he, thou so highly hast exalted, shall proudly look down on thy esteem.

Wilt thou that one remember a thing?—praise him in the midst of thy advice;
Never yet forgat man the word whereby he hath been praised.
Better to be censured by a thousand fools, than reproved but by one man that is wise;
For the pious are slower to help right, than the profane to hinder it:
So, where the world rebuketh, there look thou for the excellent,
And be suspicious of the good, which wicked men can praise.
The captain bindeth his troop, not more by severity than kindness,
And justly, should recompense well-doing, as well as be strict with an offender;
The laurel is cheap to the giver, but precious in his sight who hath won it,
And the heart of the soldier rejoiceth in the approving glance of his chief.
Timely given praise is even better than the merited rebuke of censure,
For the sun is more needful to the plant than the knife that cutteth out a canker;
Many a father hath erred, in that he hath withheld reproof,
But more have mostly sinned, in withholding praise where it was due:
There be many such as Eli among men; but these be more culpable than Eli,
Who chill the fountain of exertion by the freezing looks of indifference:
Ye call a man easy and good, yet he is as a two-edged sword;
He rebuketh not vice, and it is strong: he comforteth not virtue, and it fainteth.
There is nothing more potent among men than a gift timely bestowed;
And a gift kept back where it was hoped, separateth chief friends:
For what is a gift but a symbol, giving substance to praise and esteem?
And where is a sharper arrow than the sting of unmerited neglect?

Expect not praise from the mean, neither gratitude from the selfish;
And to keep the proud thy friend, see thou do him not a service:
For, behold, he will hate thee for his debt: thou hast humbled him by giving;
And his stubbornness never shall acknowledge the good he hath taken from thy hand:
Yea, rather will he turn and be thy foe, lest thou gather from his friendship

That he doth account thee creditor, and standeth in the second place;
Still, O kindly feeling heart, be not thou chilled by the thankless,
Neither let the breath of gratitude fan thee into momentary heat.
Do good for good's own sake, looking not to worthiness nor love;
Fling thy grain among the rocks, cast thy bread upon the waters,
His claim be strongest to thy help who is thrown most helplessly upon thee,—
So shalt thou have a better praise, and reap a richer harvest of reward.

If a man hold fast to thy creed, and fit his thinking to thy notions,
Thou shalt take him for a man right-minded, yea, and excuse his evil:
But seest thou not, O bigot, that thy zeal is but a hunting after praise,
And the full pleasure of a proselyte lieth in the flattering of self?
A man of many praises meeteth many welcomes,
But he who blameth often, shall not keep a friend;
The velvet-coated apricot is one thing, and the spiked horse-chestnut is another;
A handle of smooth amber is pleasanter than rough buck-horn.
Show me a popular man; I can tell thee the secret of his power;
He hath soothed them with glozing words, lulling their ears with flattery;
The smile of seeming approbation is ever the companion of his presence,
And courteous looks, and warm regards, earn him all their hearts.

Nothing but may be better, and every better might be best;
The blind may discern, and the simple prove, fault or want in all things;
And a little mind looketh on the lily with a microscopic eye,
Eager and glad to pry out specks on its robe of purity;
But a great mind gazeth on the sun, glorying in his brightness,
And taking large knowledge of his good, in the broad prairie of creation:
What, though he hatch basilisks? what, though spots are on the sun?
In fullness is his worth, in fullness be his praise!

OF SELF-ACQUAINTANCE.

Knowledge holdeth by the hilt, and heweth out a road to conquest;
Ignorance graspeth the blade, and is wounded by its own good sword:

Knowledge distilleth health from the virulence of opposite poisons;
Ignorance mixeth wholesomes unto the breeding of disease:
Knowledge is leagued with the universe, and findeth a friend in all things;
But ignorance is every where a stranger; unwelcome; ill at ease, and out of place.
A man is helpless and unsafe up to the measure of his ignorance,
For he lacketh perception of the aptitudes commending such a matter to his use,
Clutching at the horn of danger, while he judgeth it the handle of security,
Or casting his anchor so widely, that the granite reef is just within the tether.
Untaught in science he is but half alive, stupidly taking note of nothing,
Or listening with dull wonder to the crafty saws of an empiric;
Simple in the world, he trusteth unto knaves; and then to make amends for folly,
Dealeth so shrewdly with the honest, they cannot but suspect him for a thief;
With an unknown God, he maketh mock of reason, fathering contrivance on chance,
Or doting with superstitious dread on some crooked image of his fancy:
But ignorant of self, he is weakness at heart; the keystone crumbleth into sand,
There is panic in the general's tent, the oak is hollow as hemlock;
Though the warm sap creepeth up its bark, filling out the sheaf of leaves,
Though knowledge of all things beside add proofs of seeming vigour,
Though the master-mind of the royal sage feast on the mysteries of wisdom,
Yet ignorance of self shall bow down the spirit of a Solomon to idols;
The storm of temptation, sweeping by, shall snap that oak like a reed,
And the proud luxuriance of its tufted crown drag it the sooner to the dust.

Youth, confident in self, tampereth with dangerous dalliance,
Till the vice his heart once hated hath locked him in her foul embrace:
Manhood, through zeal of doing good, seeketh high place for its occasions,
Unwitting that the bleak mountain-air will nip the tender budding of his motives;
Or painfully, for love of truth, he climbeth the ladder of science,
Till pride of intellect, heating his heart, warpeth it aside to delusion:
The maiden, to give shadow to her fairness, plaiteth her raven hair,

Heedlessly weaving for her soul the silken net of vanity:
The gray-beard looketh on his gold, till he loveth its yellow smile,
Unconscious of the bright decoy which is luring his heart unto avarice:
Wrath avoideth no quarrel, jealousy counteth its suspicions,
Pining envy gazeth still, and melancholy seeketh solitude:
The sensitive broodeth on his slights, the fearful poreth over horrors,
The train of wantonness is fired, the nerves of indecision are unstrung;
Each special proneness unto harm is pampered by ignorant indulgence,
And the man, for want of warning, yieldeth to the apt temptation.

A smith at the loom, and a weaver at the forge, were but sorry craftsmen,
And a ship that saileth on every wind never shall reach her port:
Yet there be thousands among men who heed not the leaning of their talents,
But, cutting against the grain, toil on to no good end;
And the light of a thoughtful spirit is quenched beneath the bushel of commerce,
While meaner plodding minds are driven up the mountain of philosophy:
The cedar withereth on a wall, while the house-leek is fattening in a hot-bed,
And the dock with its rank leaves hideth the sun from violets.
To every thing a fitting place, a proper honourable use;
The humblest measure of mind is bright in its humble sphere:
The glowworm, creeping in the hedge, lighteth her evening torch,
And her far-off mate, on gossamer sail, steereth his course by that star:
But ignorance mocketh at proprieties, bringing out the glowworm at noon,
And setteth the faults of mediocrity in the full blaze of wisdom.
Ravens croaking in darkness, and a skylark trilling to the sun,
The voice of a screech-owl from a ruin, and the blackbird's whistle in a wood,
A cushion-footed camel for the sands, and a swift reindeer for the snows,
A naked skin for Ethiopia, and rich soft furs for the Pole:
In all things is there a fitness: discord with discord hath its music;
And the harmony of nature is preserved by each one knowing his place.

The blind at an easel, the palsied with a graver, the halt making for the goal,
The deaf ear tuning psaltery, the stammerer discoursing eloquence,—
What wonder if all fail? the shaft flieth wide of the mark,

Alike if itself be crooked, or the bow be strung awry;
And the mind which were excellent in one way, but foolishly toileth in another,
What is it but an ill-strung bow, and its aim a crooked arrow?
By knowledge of self, thou provest thy powers; put not the racer to the plough,
Nor goad the toilsome ox to wager his slowness with the fleet:
Consider thy failings, heed thy propensities, search out thy latent virtues,
Analyze the doubtful, cultivate the good, and crush the head of evil;
So shalt thou catch with quick hand the golden ball of opportunity;
The warrior armed shall be ready for the fray, beside his bridled steed;
Thou shalt ward off special harms, and have the sway of circumstance,
And turn to thy special good the common current of events;
Choosing from the wardrobe of the world, thou shalt suitably clothe thy spirit,
Nor thrust the white hand of peace into the gauntlet of defiance:
The shepherd shall go with a staff, and conquer by sling and stone;
The soldier shall let alone the distaff, and the scribe lay down the sword,
The man unlearned shall keep silence, and learn one attribute of wisdom;
The sage be sparing of his lessons before unhearing ears:
Calm shalt thou be, as a lion in repose, conscious of passive strength,
And the shock that splitteth the globe, shall not unthrone thy self-possession.

Acquaint thee with thyself, O man! so shalt thou be humble:
The hard hot desert of thy heart shall blossom with the lily and the rose;
The frozen cliffs of pride shall melt as an iceberg in the tropics;
The bitter fountains of self-seeking be sweeter than the waters of the Nile.
But if thou lack that wisdom,—thy frail skiff is doomed,
On stronger eddy whirling to the dreadful gorge;
Untaught in that grand lore,—thou standest, cased in steel,
To dare with mocking unbelief the thunderbolts of heaven.
For look now around thee on the universe, behold how all things serve thee;
The teeming soil, and the buoyant sea, and undulating air,
Golden crops, and bloomy fruits, and flowers, and precious gems,
Choice perfumes, and fair sights, soft touches, and sweet music:
For thee, shoaling up the bay, crowd the finny nations,
For thee, the cattle on a thousand hills live, and labour, and die:

Light is thy daily slave, darkness inviteth thee to slumber;
Thou art served by the hands of Beauty, and Sublimity kneeleth at thy feet:
Arise, thou sovereign of creation, and behold thy glory!
Yet more, thou hast a mind; intellect wingeth thee to heaven,
Tendeth thy state on earth, and by it thou divest down to hell;
Thou hast measured the belt of Saturn, thou hast weighed the moons of Jupiter,
And seen, by reason's eye, the centre of thy globe;
Subtly hast thou numbered by billions the leagues between sun and sun,
And noted in thy book the coming of their shadows:
With marvellous unerring truth thou knowest to an inch and to an instant,
The where and the when of the comet's path that shall seem to rush by at thy command:
Arise, thou king of mind, and survey thy dignity!
Yet more,—for once believe religion's flattering tale;
Thou hast a soul, aye, and a God,—but be not therefore humbled:
Thy Maker's self was glad to live and die—a man;
The brightest jewel in his crown is voluntary manhood:
By deep dishonour and great price, bought he that envied freedom,
But thou wast born an heir of all, thy Master scarce could earn.
O climax unto pride, O triumph of humanity,
O triple crown upon thy brow, most high and mighty Self!
Arise thou Lord of all, thou greater than a God!—
How saidst thou, wretched being?—cast thy glance within;
Regard that painted sepulchre, the hovel of thy heart.
Ha! with what fearful imagery swarmeth that small chamber;
The horrid eye of murder scowling in the dark,
The bony hand of avarice filching from the poor,
The lurid fires of lust, the idiot face of folly,
The sickening deed of cruelty, the foul, fierce orgies of the drunken,
Weak contemptible vanity, stubborn stolid unbelief,
Envy's devilish sneer, and the vile features of ingratitude,—
Man, hast thou seen enough? or are these full proof
That thou art a miracle of mercy, and all thy dignity is dross?

Well said the wisdom of earth, O mortal, know thyself;
But better the wisdom of heaven, O man, learn thou thy God:
By knowledge of self thou art conusant of evil, and mailed in panoply to meet it:

By knowledge of God cometh knowledge of good, and universal love is at thy heart.
Every creature knoweth its capacities, running in the road of instinct,
And reason must not lag behind, but serve itself of all proprieties:
The swift to the race, and the strong to the burden, and the wise for right direction;
For self-knowledge filleth with acceptance its niche in the temple of utility:
But vainly wilt thou look for that knowledge, till the clue of all truth is in thy hand,
For the labyrinth of man's heart windeth in complicate deceivings:
Thou canst not sound its depths with the shallow plumb-line of reason,
Till religion, the pilot of the soul, have lent thee her unfathomable coil:
Therefore, for this grand knowledge, and knowledge is the parent of dominion,
Learn God, thou shalt know thyself; yea, and shalt have mastery of all things.

OF CRUELTY TO ANIMALS.

Shame upon thee, savage monarch-man, proud monopolist of reason;
Shame upon creation's lord, the fierce ensanguined despot:
What, man! are there not enough, hunger, and diseases, and fatigue,—
And yet must thy goad or thy thong add another sorrow to existence?
What! art thou not content thy sin hath dragged down suffering and death
On the poor dumb servants of thy comfort, and yet thou must rack them with thy spite?
The prodigal heir of creation hath gambled away his all,—
Shall he add torment to the bondage, that is galling his forfeit serfs?
The leader in nature's pæan himself hath marred her psaltery,
Shall he multiply the din of discord by overstraining all the strings?
The rebel hath fortified his stronghold, shutting in his vassals with him—
Shall he aggravate the woes of the besieged by oppression from within?
Thou twice deformed image of thy Maker, thou hateful representative of Love,
For very shame be merciful, be kind unto the creatures thou hast ruined;
Earth and her million tribes are cursed for thy sake;

Earth and her million tribes still writhe beneath thy cruelty:
Liveth there but one among the million that shall not bear witness against thee?
A pensioner of land or air or sea, that hath not whereof it will accuse thee?
From the elephant toiling at a launch, to the shrew-mouse in the harvest-field,
From the whale which the harpooner hath stricken, to the minnow caught upon a pin,
From the albatross wearied in its flight, to the wren in her covered nest,
From the death-moth and lace-winged dragon-fly, to the lady-bird and the gnat,
The verdict of all things is unanimous, finding their master cruel:
The dog, thy humble friend, thy trusting, honest friend;
The ass, thine uncomplaining slave, drudging from morn to even;
The lamb, and the timorous hare, and the laboring ox at plough;
The speckled trout, basking in the shallow, and the partridge, gleaning in the stubble,
And the stag at bay, and the worm in thy path, and the wild bird pining in captivity,
And all things that minister alike to thy life and thy comfort and thy pride,
Testify with one sad voice that man is a cruel master.

Verily, they are all thine, freely mayst thou serve thee of them all;
They are thine by gift for thy needs, to be used in all gratitude and kind ness:
Gratitude to their God and thine,—their Father and thy Father,
Kindness to them who toil for thee, and help thee with their all:
For meat, but not by wantonness of slaying; for burden, but with limits of humanity;
For luxury, but not through torture; for draught, but according to the strength:
For a dog cannot plead his own right nor render a reason for exemption,
Nor give a soft answer unto wrath, to turn aside the undeserved lash;
The galled ox cannot complain, nor supplicate a moment's respite;
The spent horse hideth his distress, till he panteth out his spirit at the goal;
Also, in the winter of life, when worn by constant toil,
If ingratitude forget his services, he cannot bring them to remembrance:

Behold, he is faint with hunger; the big tear standeth in his eye;
His skin is sore with stripes, and he tottereth beneath his burden;
Hig limbs are stiff with age, his sinews have lost their vigour,
And pain is stamped upon his face, while he wrestleth unequally with toil;
Yet once more mutely and meekly endureth he the crushing blow;
That struggle hath cracked his heart-strings,—the generous brute is dead!
Liveth there no advocate for him? no judge to avenge his wrongs?
No voice that shall be heard in his defence? no sentence to be passed on his oppressor?
Yea, the sad eye of the tortured pleadeth pathetically for him:
Yea, all the justice in heaven is roused in indignation at his woes:
Yea, all the pity upon earth shall call down a curse upon the cruel:
Yea, the burning malice of the wicked is their own exceeding punishment.
The Angel of Mercy stoppeth not to comfort, but passeth by on the other side,
And hath no tear to shed when a cruel man is damned.

OF FRIENDSHIP.

As frost to the bud, and blight to the blossom, even such is self-interest to friendship:
For Confidence cannot dwell where Selfishness is porter at the gate.
If thou see thy friend to be selfish, thou canst not be sure of his honesty;
And in seeking thine own weal, thou hast wronged the reliance of thy friend.
Flattery hideth her varnished face when Friendship sitteth at his board;
And the door is shut upon Suspicion, but Candour is bid glad welcome.
For Friendship abhorreth doubt, its life is in mutual trust,
And perisheth, when artful praise proveth it is sought for a purpose.
A man may be good to thee at times, and render thee mighty service,
Whom yet thy secret soul could not desire as a friend;
For the sum of life is in trifles, and though, in the weightier masses,
A man refuse thee not his purse, nay, his all in thine utmost need,
Yet, if thou canst not feel that his character agreeth with thine own,
Thou never wilt call him friend, though thou render him a heart full of gratitude.
A coarse man grindeth harshly the finer feelings of his brother;

A common mind will soon depart from the dull companionship of wisdom;
A weak soul dareth not to follow in the track of vigour and decision;
And the worldly regardeth with scorn the seeming foolishness of faith.
A mountain is made up of atoms, and friendship of little matters,
And if the atoms hold not together, the mountain is crumbled into dust.

Come, I will show thee a friend; I will paint one worthy of thy trust:
Thine heart shall not weary of him: thou shalt not secretly despise him.
Thou art long in learning him, in unravelling all his worth;
And he dazzleth not thine eyes at first, to be darkened in thy sight afterward,
But riseth from small beginnings, and reacheth the height of thy esteem.
He remembereth that thou art only man; he expecteth not great things from thee;
And his forbearance toward thee silently teacheth thee to be considerate unto him.
He despiseth not courtesy of manner, nor neglecteth the decencies of life:
Nor mocketh the failings of others, nor is harsh in his censures before thee;
For so, how couldst thou tell, if he talketh not of thee in ridicule?
He withholdeth no secret from thee, and rejecteth not thine in turn;
He shareth his joys with thee, and is glad to bear part in thy sorrows.
Yet one thing, he loveth thee too well to show thee the corruptions of his heart:
For as an ill example strengtheneth the hands of the wicked,
So to put forward thy guilt is a secret poison to thy friend:
For the evil in his nature is comforted, and he warreth more weakly against it,
If he find that the friend whom he honoureth, is a man more sinful than himself.
I hear the communing of friends; ye speak out the fullness of your souls,
And being but men, as men, ye own to all the sympathies of manhood: ([26])
Confidence openeth the lips, indulgence beameth from the eye,
The tongue loveth not boasting, the heart is made glad with kindness:
And one standeth not as on a hill, beckoning to the other to follow,
But ye toil up hand in hand, and carry each other's burdens.
Ye commune of hopes and aspirations, the fervent breathings of the heart,
Ye speak with pleasant interchange the treasured secrets of affection,
Ye listen to the voice of complaint, and whisper the language of comfort,
And as in a double solitude, ye think in each other's hearing.

Choose thy friend discreetly, and see thou consider his station,

For the graduated scale of ranks accordeth with the ordinance of heaven:
If a low companion ripen to a friend, in the full sunshine of thy confidence,
Know, that for old age thou hast heaped up sorrow:
For thou sinkest to that level, and thy kin shall scorn thee.
Yea, and the menial thou hast pampered haply shall neglect thee in thy death:
And if thou reachest up to high estates, thinking to herd with princes,
What art thou but a footstool, though so near a throne?
O rush among the lilies, be taught thou art a weed;
O brier among the cedars, hot contempt shall burn thee.
But thou, friend and scholar, select from thine own caste,
And make not an intimate of one, thy servant or thy master;
For only friendship among men is the true republic,
Where all have equality of service, and all have freedom of command.
And yet, if thou wilt take my judgment, be shy of too much openness with any,
Lest thou repent hereafter, should he turn and rend thee:
For many an apostate friend hath abused unguarded confidence,
And bent to selfish ends the secret of the soul.

Absence strengtheneth friendship, where the last recollections were kindly;
But it must be good wine at the last, or absence shall weaken it daily.
A rare thing is faith, and friendship is a marvel among men,
Yet strange faces call they friends, and say they believe, when they doubt.
Those hours are not lost that are spent in cementing affection;
For a friend is above gold, precious as the stores of the mind.
Be sparing of advice by words, but teach thy lesson by example;
For the vanity of man may be wounded, and retort unkindly upon thee.
There be some that never had a friend, because they were gross and selfish;
Worldliness, and apathy, and pride, leave not many that are worthy:
But one who meriteth esteem, need never lack a friend;
For as thistle-down flieth abroad, and casteth its anchor in the soil,
So philanthropy yearneth for a heart, where it may take root and blossom.

Yet I hear the child of sensibility moaning at the wintry cold,
Wherein the mists of selfishness have wrapped the society of men:
He grieveth, and hath deep reasons; for falsehood hath wronged his trust,
And the breaches in his bleeding heart have been filled with the briers of suspicion.

For, alas, how few be friends, of whom charity hath hoped well!
How few there be among men who forget themselves for others!
Each one seeketh his own, and looketh on his brethren as rivals,
Masking envy with friendship, to serve his secret ends.
And the world, that corrupteth all good, hath wronged that sacred name,
For it calleth any man friend, who is not known for an enemy;
And such be as the flies of summer, while plenty sitteth at thy board;
But who can wonder at their flight from the cold denials of want?
Such be as vultures round a carcass, assembled together for the feast:
But a sudden noise scareth them, and forthwith are they specks among the clouds.
There be few, O child of sensibility, who deserve to have thy confidence;
Yet weep not, for there are some, and such some live for thee:
To them is the chilling world a drear and barren scene,
And gladly seek they such as thou art, for seldom find they the occasion:
For, though no man excludeth himself from the high capability of friendship,
Yet verily is the man a marvel whom truth can write a friend.

OF LOVE.

There is a fragrant blossom, that maketh glad the garden of the heart:
Its root lieth deep; it is delicate, yet lasting, as the lilac crocus of autumn;
Loneliness and thought are the dews that water it morn and even;
Memory and Absence cherish it, as the balmy breathings of the south:
Its sun is the brightness of affection, and it bloometh in the borders of Hope;
Its companions are gentle flowers, and the brier withereth by its side.
I saw it budding in beauty; I felt the magic of its smile;
The violet rejoiced beneath it, the rose stooped down and kissed it;
And I thought some cherub had planted there a truant flower of Eden,
As a bird bringeth foreign seeds, that they may flourish in a kindly soil
I saw, and asked not its name; I knew no language was so wealthy,
Though every heart of every clime findeth its echo within.
And yet what shall I say? Is a sordid man capable of—Love?

Hath a seducer known it? Can an adulterer perceive it?
Or he that seeketh strange women, can he feel its purity?
Or he that changeth often, can he know its truth?
Longing for another's happiness, yet often destroying its own;
Chaste, and looking up to God, as the fountain of tenderness and joy;
Quiet, yet flowing deep, as the Rhine among rivers;
Lasting, and knowing not change—it walketh with Truth and Sincerity.

Love:—what a volume in a word, an ocean in a tear,
A seventh heaven in a glance, a whirlwind in a sigh,
The lightning in a touch, a millennium in a moment:
What consecrated joy or woe in blest or blighted love!
For it is that native poetry springing up indigenous to Mind,
The heart's own-country music thrilling all its chords,
The story without an end that angels throng to hear,
The word, the king of words, carved on Jehovah's heart!
Oh! call thou snake-eyed malice mercy, call envy honest praise,
Count selfish craft for wisdom, and coward treachery for prudence,
Do homage to blaspheming unbelief as to bold and free philosophy,
And estimate the recklessness of license as the right attribute of liberty,—
But with the world, thou friend and scholar, stain not this pure name;
Nor suffer the majesty of Love to be likened to the meanness of desire:
For Love is no more such, than seraphs' hymns are discord,
And such is no more Love, than Ætna's breath is summer.

Love is a sweet idolatry, enslaving all the soul,
A mighty spiritual force, warring with the dullness of matter,
An angel-mind breathed into a mortal, though fallen, yet how beautiful!
All the devotion of the heart in all its depth and grandeur.
Behold that pale geranium, pent within the cottage window;
How yearningly it stretcheth to the light its sickly long-stalked leaves,
How it straineth upward to the sun, coveting his sweet influences,
How real a living sacrifice to the God of all its worship!
Such is the soul that loveth; and so the rose-tree of affection
Bendeth its every leaf to look on those dear eyes,
Its every blushing petal basketh in their light,
And all its gladness, all its life, is hanging on their love.

If the love of the heart is blighted, it buddeth not again;

If that pleasant song is forgotten, it is to be learnt no more:
Yet often will thought look back, and weep over early affection;
And the dim notes of that pleasant song will be heard as a reproachful spirit,
Moaning in Æolian strains over the desert of the heart,
Where the hot siroccos of the world have withered its one oasis.

OF MARRIAGE.

Seek a good wife of thy God, for she is the best gift of his providence;
Yet ask not in bold confidence that which he hath not promised.
Thou knowest not his good-will:—be thy prayer then submissive thereunto;
And leave thy petition to his mercy, assured that he will deal well with thee.
If thou art to have a wife of thy youth, she is now living on the earth;
Therefore think of her, and pray for her weal; yea, though thou hast not seen her.
They that love early become like-minded, and the tempter touches them not:
They grow up leaning on each other, as the olive and vine.
Youth longeth for a kindred spirit, and yearneth for a heart that can commune with his own;
He meditateth night and day, doting on the image of his fancy.
Take heed that what charmeth thee is real, nor springeth of thine own imagination;
And suffer not trifles to win thy love; for a wife is thine unto death.
The harp and the voice may thrill thee,—sound may enchant thine ear,
But consider thou, the hand will wither, and the sweet notes turn to discord:
The eye, so brilliant at even, may be red with sorrow in the morning;
And the sylph-like form of elegance must writhe in the crampings of pain.

O happy lot, and hallowed, even as the joy of angels,
Where the golden chain of godliness is entwined with the roses of love:
But beware, thou seem not to be holy, to win favour in the eyes of a creature,

For the guilt of the hypocrite is deadly, and winneth thee wrath elsewhere.
The idol of thy heart is, as thou, a probationary sojourner on earth;
Therefore be chary of her soul, for that is a jewel in her casket.
Let her be a child of God, that she bring with her a blessing to thy house,—
A blessing above riches, and leading contentment in its train:
Let her be an heir of heaven; so shall she help thee on thy way;
For those who are one in faith, fight double-handed against evil.
Take heed lest she love thee before God; that she be not an idolater:
Yet see thou that she love thee well: for her heart is the heart of woman:
And the triple nature of humanity must be bound by a triple chain,
For soul and mind and body—godliness, esteem, and affection.

How beautiful is modesty! it winneth upon all beholders:
But a word or a glance may destroy the pure love that should have been for thee.
Affect not to despise beauty; no one is freed from its dominion:
But regard it not a pearl of price:—it is fleeting as the bow in the clouds.
If the character within be gentle, it often hath its index in the countenance:
The soft smile of a loving face is better than splendour that fadeth quickly.
When thou choosest a wife, think not only of thyself,
But of those God may give thee of her, that they reproach thee not for their being;
See that he hath given her health, lest thou lose her early and weep;
See that she springeth of a wholesome stock, that thy little ones perish not before thee:
For many a fair skin hath covered a mining disease,
And many a laughing cheek been bright with the glare of madness.

Mark the converse of one thou lovest, that it be simple and sincere;
For an artful or false woman shall set thy pillow with thorns.
Observe her deportment with others, when she thinketh not that thou art nigh,
For with thee will the blushes of love conceal the true colour of her mind
Hath she learning? it is good, so that modesty go with it:
Hath she wisdom? it is precious, but beware that thou exceed;
For woman must be subject, and the true mastery is of the mind.
Be joined to thine equal in rank, or the foot of pride will kick at thee:
And look not only for riches, lest thou be mated with misery:
Marry not without means; for so shouldst thou tempt Providence;

But wait not for more than enough; for marriage is the duty of most men;
Grievous indeed must be the burden that shall outweigh innocence and health,
And a well-assorted marriage hath not many cares.
In the day of thy joy consider the poor; thou shalt reap a rich harvest of blessing;
For these be the pensioners of One who filleth thy cup with pleasures;
In the day of thy joy be thankful; He hath well deserved thy praise;
Mean and selfish is the heart that seeketh him only in sorrow.
For her sake, who leaneth on thine arm, court not the notice of the world,
And remember that sober privacy is comelier than public display.
If thou marriest, thou art allied unto strangers: see they be not such as shame thee:
If thou marriest, thou leavest thine own; see that it be not done in anger.

Bride and bridegroom, pilgrims of life, henceforward to travel together,
In this the beginning of your journey, neglect not the favour of Heaven:
And at eventide kneel ye together, that your joy be not unhallowed:
Angels that are round you shall be glad, those loving ministers of mercy,
And the richest blessings of your God shall be poured on his favoured children.
Marriage is a figure and an earnest of holier things unseen,
And reverence well becometh the symbol of dignity and glory.
Keep thy heart pure, lest thou do dishonour to thy state;
Selfishness is base and hateful; but love considereth not itself.
The wicked turneth good into evil, for his mind is warped within him:
But the heart of the righteous is chaste; his conscience casteth off sin.
If thou wilt be loved, render implicit confidence;
If thou wouldst not suspect, receive full confidence in turn:
For where trust is not reciprocal, the love that trusted withereth.
Hide not your grief nor your gladness; be open one with the other,
Let bitterness be strange unto your tongues, but sympathy a dweller in your hearts:
Imparting halveth the evils, while it doubleth the pleasures of life,
But sorrows breed and thicken in the gloomy bosom of Reserve.

Young wife, be not forward, nor forget that modesty becometh thee:
If it be discarded now, who will not hold it feigned before?
But be not as a timid girl,—there is honour due to thine estate;

A matron's modesty is dignified: she blusheth not, neither is she bold.
Be kind to the friends of thine husband, for the love they have to him:
And gently bear with his infirmities; hast thou no need of his forbearance?
Be not always in each other's company; it is often good to be alone;
And if there be too much sameness, ye cannot but grow weary of each other:
Ye have each a soul to be nourished, and a mind to be taught in wisdom,
Therefore, as accountable for time, help one another to improve it.
If ye feel love to decline, track out quickly the secret cause;
Let it not rankle for a day, but confess and bewail it together:
Speedily seek to be reconciled, for love is the life of marriage;
And be ye co-partners in triumph, conquering the peevishness of self.

Let no one have thy confidence, O wife, saving thy husband:
Have not a friend more intimate, O husband, than thy wife.
In the joy of a well-ordered home, be warned that this is not your rest;
For the substance to come may be forgotten in the present beauty of the shadow.
If ye are blessed with children, ye have a fearful pleasure,
A deeper care and a higher joy, and the range of your existence is widened.
If God in wisdom refuse them, thank him for an unknown mercy:
For how can ye tell if they might be a blessing or a curse?
Yet ye may pray, like Hannah, simply dependent on his will:
Resignation sweeteneth the cup, but impatience dasheth it with vinegar.
Now this is the sum of the matter:—if ye will be happy in marriage,
Confide, love, and be patient: be faithful, firm, and holy.

OF EDUCATION.

A BABE in a house is a well-spring of pleasure, a messenger of peace and love:
A resting-place for innocence on earth; a link between angels and men:
Yet is it a talent of trust, a loan to be rendered back with interest;
A delight, but redolent of care; honey-sweet, but lacking not the bitter.
For character groweth day by day, and all things aid it in unfolding,

And the bent unto good or evil may be given in the hours of infancy:
Scratch the green rind of a sapling, or wantonly twist it in the soil,
The scarred and crooked oak will tell of thee for centuries to come;
Even so mayst thou guide the mind to good, or lead it to the marrings of evil,
For disposition is builded up by the fashioning of first impressions:
Wherefore, though the voice of Instruction waiteth for the ear of reason,
Yet with his mother's milk the young child drinketh Education.
Patiencce is the first great lesson; he may learn it at the breast;
And the habit of obedience and trust may be grafted on his mind in the cradle:
Hold the little hands in prayer, teach the weak knees their kneeling;
Let him see thee speaking to thy God; he will not forget it afterward:
When old and gray will he feelingly remember a mother's tender piety,
And the touching recollection of her prayers shall arrest the strong man in his sin.

Select not to nurse thy darling one that may taint his innocence,
For example is a constant monitor, and good seed will die among the tares.
The arts of a strange servant have spoiled a gentle disposition:
Mother, let him learn of thy lips, and be nourished at thy breast.
Character is mainly moulded by the cast of the minds that surround it:
Let then the playmates of thy little one be not other than thy judgment shall approve;
For a child is in a new world, and learneth somewhat every moment,
His eye is quick to observe, his memory storeth in secret,
His ear is greedy of knowledge, and his mind is plastic as soft wax.
Beware then that he heareth what is good, that he feedeth not on evil maxims,
For the seeds of first instructions are dropped into the deepest furrows.
That which immemorial use hath sanctioned, seemeth to be right and true;
Therefore, let him never have to recollect the time when good things were strangers to his thought.
Strive not to centre in thyself, fond mother, all his love;
Nay, do not thou so selfishly, but enlarge his heart for others;
Use him to sympathy betimes, that he learn to be sad with the afflicted;
And check not a child in his merriment,—should not his morning be sunny?
Give him not all his desire, so shalt thou strengthen him in hope;
Neither stop with indulgence the fountain of his tears, so shall he fear thy firmness.

Above all things graft on him subjection, yea, in the veriest trifle;
Courtesy to all, reverence to some, and to thee unanswering obedience.

Read thou first, and well approve, the books thou givest to thy child;
But remember the weakness of his thought, and that wisdom for him must be diluted;
In the honied waters of infant tales, let him taste the strong wine of truth:
Pathetic stories soften the heart; but legends of terror breed midnight misery;
Fairy fictions cram the mind with folly, and knowledge of evil tempteth to like evil:
Be not loth to curb imagination, nor be fearful that truths will depress it;
And for evil, he will learn it soon enough; be not thou the devil's envoy.
Induce not precocity of intellect, for so shouldst thou nourish vanity;
Neither can a plant, forced in the hot-bed, stand against the frozen breath of winter.
The mind is made wealthy by ideas, but the multitude of words is a clogging weight:
Therefore be understood in thy teaching, and instruct to the measure of capacity.
Analogy is milk for babes, but abstract truths are strong meat;
Precepts and rules are repulsive to a child, but happy illustration winneth him:
In vain shalt thou preach of industry and prudence, till he learn of the bee and the ant;
Dimly will he think of his soul, till the acorn and chrysalis have taught him;
He will fear God in thunder, and worship his loveliness in flowers;
And parables shall charm his heart, while doctrines seem dead mystery;
Faith shall he learn of the husbandman casting good corn into the soil;
And if thou train him to trust thee, he will not withhold his reliance from the Lord.
Fearest thou the dark, poor child? I would not have thee left to thy terrors;
Darkness is the semblance of evil, and nature regardeth it with dread:
Yet know thy father's God is with thee still, to guard thee:
It is a simple lesson of dependence, let thy tost mind anchor upon Him.
Did a sudden noise affright thee? lo, this or that hath caused it:
Things undefined are full of dread, and stagger stouter nerves.

The seeds of misery and madness have been sowed in the nights of infancy:
Therefore be careful that ghastly fears be not the night companions of thy child.

Lo, thou art a land-mark on a hill; thy little ones copy thee in all things.
Let, then, thy religion be perfect: so shalt thou be honoured in thy house.
Be instructed in all wisdom, and communicate that thou knowest,
Otherwise thy learning is hidden, and thus thou seemest unwise.
A sluggard hath no respect; an epicure commandeth not reverence;
Meanness is always despicable, and folly provoketh contempt.
Those parents are best honoured whose characters best deserve it;
Show me a shild undutiful, I shall know where to look for a foolish father.
Never hath a father done his duty, and lived to be despised of his son.
But how can that son reverence an example he dare not follow?
Should he imitate thee in thine evil? his scorn is thy rebuke.
Nay, but bring him up aright, in obedience to God and to thee;
Begin betimes, lest thou fail of his fear; and with judgment, that thou lose not his love:
Herein use good discretion, and govern not all alike,
Yet, perhaps, the fault will be in thee, if kindness prove not all-sufficient.
By kindness, the wolf and the zebra become docile as the spaniel and the horse:
The kite feedeth with the starling, under the law of kindness:
That law shall tame the fiercest, bring down the battlements of pride,
Cherish the weak, control the strong, and win the fearful spirit.
Be obeyed when thou commandest; but command not often:
Let thy carriage be the gentleness of love, not the stern front of tyranny.
Make not one child a warning to another; but chide the offender apart:
For self-conceit and wounded pride rankle like poisons in the soul.
A mild rebuke in the season of calmness, is better than a rod in the heat of passion,
Nevertheless spare not, if thy word hath passed for punishment;
Let not thy child see thee humbled, nor learn to think thee false;
Suffer none to reprove thee before him, and reprove not thine own purposes by change;
Yet speedily turn thou again, and reward him where thou canst,
For kind encouragement in good cutteth at the roots of evil.

Drive not a timid infant from his home, in the early spring-time of his life,
Commit not that treasure to an hireling, nor wrench the young heart's fibres :
In his helplessness leave him not alone, a stranger among strange children,
Where affection longeth for thy love, counting the dreary hours;
Where religion is made a terror, and innocence weepeth unheard;
Where oppression grindeth without remedy, and cruelty delighteth in smiting.
Wherefore comply with an evil fashion ? Is it not to spare thee trouble ?
Can he gather no knowledge at thy mouth ? Wilt thou yield thine honour to another ?
What can he gain in learning, to equal what he loseth in innocence ?
Alas! for the price above gold, by which such learning cometh!
For emulative pride and envy are the specious idols of the diligent,
Oaths and foul-mouthed sin burn in the language of the idle:
Bolder in that mimic world of boys stareth brazen-fronted vice,
Than thereafter in the haunts of men, where society doth shame her into corners.
My soul, look well around thee, ere thou give thy timid infant unto sorrows.
There be many that say, We were happiest in days long past,
When our deepest care was an ill-conned book,
And when we sported in that merry sunshine of our life,
Sadness a stranger to the heart, and cheerfulness its gay inhabitant.
True, ye are now less pure, and therefore are more wretched:
But have ye quite forgotten how sorely ye travailed at your tasks,
How childish griefs and disappointments bowed down the childish mind ?
How sorrow sat upon your pillow, and terror hath waked thee up betimes,
Dreading the strict hand of justice, that will not wait for a reason,
Or the whims of petty tyrants, children like yourselves,
Or the pestilent extract of evil poured into the ear of innocence ?
Behold the coral island, fresh from the floor of the Atlantic,
It is dinted by every ripple, and a soft wave can smooth its surface;
But soon its substance hardeneth in the winds and tropic sun,
And weakly the foaming billows break against its adamantine wall;
Even thus, though sin and care dash upon the firmness of manhood,
The timid child is wasted most by his petty troubles;
And seldom, when life is mature, and the strength proportioned to the burden,
Will the feeling mind, that can remember acknowledge to deeper anguish,

Than when, as a stranger and a little one, the heart first ached with anxiety,
And the sprouting buds of sensibility were bruised by the harshness of a school.
My soul, look well around thee, ere thou give thine infant unto sorrows.
Yet there be boisterous tempers, stout nerves, and stubborn hearts,
And there is a riper season, when the mind is well disciplined in good,
And a time, when youth may be bettered by the wholesome occasions of knowledge,
Which rarely will it meet with so well as among the congregation of his fellows.
Only for infancy, fond mother, rend not those first affections;
Only for the sensitive and timorous, consign not thy darling unto misery.

A man looketh on his little one, as a being of better hope;
In himself ambition is dead, but it hath a resurrection in his son;
That vein is yet untried,—and who can tell if it be not golden?
While his, well-nigh worked out, never yielded aught but lead:
And thus is he hurt more sorely, if his wishes are defeated there;
He has staked his all upon a throw, and lo! the dice have foiled him.
All ways, and at all times, men follow on in flocks,
And the rife epidemic of the day shall tincture the stream of education;
Fashion is a foolish watcher posted at the tree of knowledge,
Who plucketh its unripe fruit to pelt away the birds:
But for its golden apples,—they dry upon the boughs,
And few have the courage or the wisdom to eat in spite of fashion:
One while, the fever is to learn, what none will be wiser for knowing,
Exploded errors in extinct tongues, and occasions for their use are small;
And the bright morning of life, for years of misspent time,
Wasted in following sounds, hath tracked up little sense,
Till at noon a man is thrown upon the world, with a mind expert in trifles,
Having yet every thing to learn, that can make him good or useful:
The curious spirit of youth is crammed with unwholesome garbage,
While starving for the mother's milk the breasts of nature yield;
And high-coloured fables of depravity lure with their classic varnish,
While truth is holding out in vain her mirror much despised.

Of olden time, the fashion was for arms, to make an accomplished slayer,
And set gregarious man a-tilting with his fellows;

Thereafter, occult sciences, and mystic arts, and symbols,
How to exorcise a wizard, and how to lay a ghost;
Anon, all for gallantry and presence, the minuet, the palfrey, and the foil,
And the grand aim of education was to produce a coxcomb;
Soon came scholastical dispute with hydra-headed argument,
And the true philosophy of mind confounded in a labyrinth of words:
Then, the Pantheon, and its orgies, initiating docile childhood,
While diligent youth strove hard to render his all unto Cæsar;
And now is seen the passion for utility, when all things are accounted by their price,
And the wisdom of the wise is busied in hatching golden eggs.
Perchance, not many moons to come, and all will again be for abstrusity,
Unravelling the figured veil that hideth Egypt's gods;
Or in those strange Avatars seeking benignant Vishnu,
Kali and Kamala the fair, and much-invoked Ganesa. ([27])

The mines of knowledge are oft laid bare through the forked hazel wand of chance,
And in a mountain of quartz we find a grain of gold.
Of a truth it were well to know all things, and to learn them all at once,
And what, though mortal insufficiency attain to small knowledge of any?
Man loveth exclusions, delighting in the sterile trodden path,
While the broad green meadow is jewelled with wild flowers:
And whether, is it better with the many to follow a beaten track,
Or by eccentric wanderings to cull unheeded sweets?

When his reason yieldeth fruit, make thy child thy friend;
For a filial friend is a double gain, a diamond set in gold.
As an infant, thy mandate was enough, but now let him see thy reasons;
Confide in him, but with discretion; and bend a willing ear to his questions.
More to thee than to all beside, let him owe good counsel and good guidance:
Let him feel his pursuits have an interest, more to thee than to all beside.
Watch his native capacities; nourish that which suiteth him the readiest;
And cultivate early those good inclinations wherein thou fearest he is most lacking:
Is he phlegmatic and desponding? let small successes comfort his hope;
Is he obstinate and sanguine? let petty crosses accustom him to life.
Showeth he a sordid spirit? be quick, and teach him generosity;

Inclineth he to liberal excess? prove to him how hard it is to earn.
Gather to thy hearth such friends as are worthy of honour and attention,
For the company a man chooseth is a visible index of his heart:
But let not the pastor whom thou hearest be too much a familiar in thy house,
For thy children may see his infirmities, and learn to cavil at his teaching.
It is well to take hold on occasions, and render indirect instruction;
It is better to teach upon a system, and reap the wisdom of books:
The history of nations yieldeth grand outlines: of persons, minute details:
Poetry is polish to the mind, and high abstractions cleanse it.
Consider the station of thy son, and breed him to his fortune with judgment:
The rich may profit in much which would bring small advantage to the poor.
But with all thy care for thy son, with all thy strivings for his welfare,
Expect disappointment, and look for pain: for he is of an evil stock, and will grieve thee.

OF TOLERANCE.

A WISE man in a crowded street winneth his way with gentleness,
Nor rudely pusheth aside the stranger that standeth in his path;
He knoweth that blind hurry will but hinder, stirring up contention against him,
Yet holdeth he steadily right on, with his face to the scope of his pursuit:
Even so, in the congress of opinions, the bustling highway of intelligence,
Each man should ask of his neighbour, and yield to him again concession.
Terms ill defined, and forms misunderstood, and customs, where their reasons are unknown,
Have stirred up many zealous souls to fight against imaginary giants:
But wisdom will hear the matter out, and often, by keenness of perception,
Will find in strange disguise the precious truth he seeketh:
So he leaveth unto prejudice or taste the garb and the manner of her presence,
Content to see so nigh the mistress of his love.
There is no similitude in nature that owneth not also to a difference,

Yea, no two berries are alike, though twins upon one stem;
No drop in the ocean, no pebble on the beach, no leaf in the forest, hath its counterpart,
No mind in its dwelling of mortality, no spirit in the world unseen:
And therefore, since capacity and essence differ alike with accident,
None but a bigot partisan will hope for impossible unity.
Wilt thou ensue peace, nor buffet with the waters of contention,
Wilt thou be counted wise and gain the love of men,
Let unobtruded error escape the frown of censure,
Nor lift the glass of truth alway before thy fellows:
I say not, compromise the right, I would not have thee countenance the wrong,
But hear with charitable heart the reasons of an honest judgment;
For thou also hast erred, and knowest not when thou art most right;
Nor whether to-morrow's wisdom may not prove thee simple to-day:
Perchance thou art chiding in another what once thou wast thyself;
Perchance thou sharply reprovest what thou wilt be hereafter.
A man that can render a reason, is a man worthy of an answer;
But he that argueth for victory, deserveth not the tenderness of Truth.

Whiles a man liveth he may mend: count not thy brother reprobate;
When he is dead his chance is gone: remember not his faults in bitterness.
A man, till he dieth, is immortal in thy sight; and then he is as nothing;
Make not the living thy foe, nor take weak vengeance of the dead;
For life is as a game of chess, where least causeth greatest,
And an ill move bringeth loss, and a pawn may insure victory.
Dost thou suspect? seek out certainty: for now, by self-inflicted pain,
Or ill-directed wrath, thou wrongest thyself or thy neighbour:
Suspicion is an early leason, taught in the school of experience,
Neither shalt thou easily unlearn it, though charity ply thee with her preaching;
Yet look thou well for reasons, or ever mistrust hath marred thee,
Or fear curdled thy blood, or jealousy goaded thee to madness:
For a look, or a word, or an act, may be taken well or ill,
As construed by the latitude of love, or the closeness of cold suspicion.

Better is the wrong with sincerity, rather than the right with falsehood:
And a prudent man will not lay siege to the stronghold of ignorant bigotry.
To unsettle a weak mind were an easy inglorious triumph,

And a strong cause taketh little count of the worthless suffrage of a fool:
Lightly he held to the wrong, loosely will he cling to the right;
Weakness is the essence of his mind, and the reed cannot yield an acorn.
Dogged obstinacy is oftentimes the buttress that proppeth an unstable spirit,
But a candid man blusheth not to own he is wiser to-day than yesterday.
A man of little wisdom is a sage among fools;
But himself is chief among the fools, if he look for admiration from them.
A heresy is an evil thing, for its shame is its pride:
Its necessary difference of error is the character it most esteemeth:
Give a man all things short of liberty, thou shalt have no thanks,
And little wilt thou speed with thine opponent, by proving points he will concede.
The tost sand darkeneth the waves; and clear had been the pages of truth,
Had not the glosses of men obscured the simplicity of faith.
In all things consider thine own ignorance, and gladly take occasion to be taught;
But suffer not excess of liberality to neutralize thy mental independence.
The faults and follies of most men make their deaths a gain;
But thou also art a man, full of faults and follies;
Therefore sorrow for the dead, or none shall weep for thee,
For the measure of charity thou dealest, shall be poured into thine own bosom.
That which vexeth thee now, provoking thee to hate thy brother,
Bear with it; the annoyance passeth, and may not return for ever:
The same combinations and results which aggravate thy soul to-day,
May not meet again for centuries in the kaleidoscope of circumstance;
For men and matters change, new elements mixing in continually,
And, as with chemical magic, the sour is transmuted into sweetness,
A little explained, a little endured, a little passed over as a foible,
And, lo, the jagged atoms fit like smooth mosaic.
Thou canst not shape another's mind to suit thine own body,
Think not, then, to be furnishing his brain with thy special notions.
Charity walketh with a high step, and stumbleth not at a trifle:
Charity hath keen eyes, but the lashes half conceal them:
Charity is praised of all, and fear not thou that praise,
God will not love thee less because men love thee more.([23])

OF SORROW.

I SAID, I will seek out sorrow, and minister the balm of pity:
So I sought her in the house of mourning: but peace followed in her train.
Then I marked her brooding silently in the gloomy cavern of Regret;
But a sunbeam of heavenly hope gleamed on her folded wing.
So I turned to the cabin of the poor, where famine dwelt with disease;
But the bed of the sick was smoothed, and the ploughman whistled at his labour.
So I stopped, and mused within myself, to remember where sorrow dwelt,
For I sought to see her alone, uncomforted, uncompanioned.
I went to the prison, but penitence was there, and promise of better times;
I listened at the madman's cell, but it echoed with deluded laughter.
Then I turned me to the rich and noble: I noted the sons of fashion:
A smile was on the languid cheek, that had no commerce with the heart;
Unhallowed thoughts, like fires, gleamed from the window of the eye,
And sorrow lived with those whose pleasures add unto their sins.

His infancy wanted not guilt; his life was continued evil:
He drew in pride with his mother's milk. and a father's lips taught him cursing.
I marked him as the wayward boy; I traced the dissolute youth:
I saw him betray the innocent, and sarifice affection to his lust.
I saw him the companion of knaves, and a squanderer of ill-got gain;
I heard him curse his own misery, while he hugged the chains that galled him:
For well had experience declared the bitterness of guilty pleasure,
But habit, with its iron net, involved him in its folds.
Behind him lowered the thunder-storm, which the caldron of his wickedness had brewed;
Before him was the smooth steep cliff whose base is ruin and despair.
So he madly rushed on, and tried to forget his being:
The noisy revel and the low debauch, and fierce excitement of play,
With dreary interchange of palling pleasures, filled the dull round of existence:
Memory was to him as a foe, so he flew for false solace to the wine-cup,
And stunned his enemy at even, but she rent him as a giant in the morning.

I turned aside to weep; I lost him a little while:
I looked, and years had past: he was hoar with the winter of his age.
And what was now his hope? where was the balm for his sadness?
The memory of the past was guilt: the feeling of the present, remorse.
Then he set his affections on gold, he worshipped the shrine of Mammon,
And to lay richer gifts before his idol, he starved his own bowels;
So, the youth spent in profligacy ended in the gripings of want:
The miser grudged himself husks, to take deeper vengeance of the prodigal.
And I said, this is sorrow; but pity cannot reach it.
This is to be wretched indeed, to be guilty without repentance.

OF JOY.

My soul was sickened within me, so I sought the dwelling-place of Joy.
And I met it not in laughter; I found it not in wealth or power;
But I saw it in the pleasant home, where religion smiled upon content,
And the satisfied ambition of the heart rejoiced in the favour of its God.
Behold the happy man, his face is rayed with pleasure,
His thoughts are of calm delight, and none can know his blessedness;
I have watched him from his infancy, and seen him in the grasp of death,
Yet never have I noted on his brow the cloud of desponding sorrow.
He hath knelt beside his cradle; his mother's hymn lulled him to sleep:
In childhood he hath loved holiness, and drank from that fountain-head of peace.
Wisdom took him for her scholar, guiding his steps in purity:
He lived unpolluted by the world; and his young heart hated sin.
But he owned not the spurious religion engendered of faction and moroseness,
Neither were the sproutings of his soul seared by the brand of superstition.
His love is pure and single, sincere, and knoweth not change:
For his manhood hath been blest with the pleasant choice of his youth:
Behold his one beloved, she leaneth on his arm,

And he looketh on the years that are past, to review the dawn of her affection.
Memory is sweet unto him as a perfect landscape to the sight;
Each object is lovely in itself, but the whole is the harmony of nature.
Behold his little ones around him, they bask in the sunshine of his smile;
And infant innocence and joy lighten their happy faces;
He is holy, and they honour him; he is loving, and they love him;
He is consistent, and they esteem him; he is firm, and they fear him.
His friends are the excellent among men; and the bands of their friendship are strong;
His house is the palace of peace: for the Prince of Peace is there.
As the wearied man to his couch, as the thoughtful man to his musings,
Even so, from the bustle of life, he goeth to his well-ordered home.
And though he often sin, he returneth with weeping eyes:
For he feeleth the mercies of forgiveness, and gloweth with warmer gratitude.

Thus did he walk in happiness, and sorrow was a stranger to his soul;
The light of affection sunned his heart, the tear of the grateful bedewed his feet,
He put his hand with constancy to good, and angels knew him as a brother,
And the busy satellites of evil trembled as at God's ally:
He used his wealth as a wise steward, making him friends for futurity;
He bent his learning to religion, and religion was with him at the last:
For I saw him after many days, when the time of his release was come.
And I longed for a congregated world, to behold that dying saint.
As the aloe is green and well-liking, till the last best summer of its age,
And then hangeth out its golden bells to mingle glory with corruption;
As a meteor travelleth in splendour, but bursteth in dazzling light;
Such was the end of the righteous: his death was the sun at his setting.

Look on this picture of joy, and remember that portrait of sorrow:
Behold the beauty of holiness, behold the deformity of sin!
How long, ye sons of men, will ye scorn the words of wisdom?
How long will ye hunt for happiness in the caverns that breed despair?
Will ye comfort yourselves in misery, by denying the existence of delight,
And from experience in woe, will ve reason that none are happy?

Joy is not in your path, for it loveth not that bleak broad road,
But its flowers are hung upon the hedges that line a narrower way;
And there the faint travellers of earth may wander and gather for themselves,
To soothe their wounded hearts with balm from the amaranths of heaven.

ΘΕΩ ΔΟΞΑ

NOTES.

(FIRST SERIES.)

([1]) "*And thine enfranchised fellows hail thy white victorious sails.*"
Page 12.

See the story of Theseus, as detailed in Dryden's translation of Plutarch Life I.

([2]) "*Who hath companioned a vision from the horn or ivory gate?*"
Page 14.

Virg. Æn. VI. 894–897.

> "Sunt geminæ somni portæ; quarum altera fertur
> Cornea; qua veris facilis datur exitus umbris;
> Altera candenti perfecta nitens elephanto;
> Sed falsa ad cœlum mittunt insomnia Manes."

([3]) "*The sea-wort floating on the waves,*" *&c.* Page 16.

The common sea-weeds on the shores of Europe, the algæ and fuci, after having, for ages, been considered as synonymous with every thing vile and worthless, have, in modern times, been found to be abundant in iodine, the only known cure for scrofula, and kelp, so useful in many manufactures. Horace has signalized his ignorance of this fact in Od. III. 17, 10, "algâ inutili," &c.; and, in II. Sat. 5, 8, ironically saying, that, "—— virtus, nisi cum re, vilior algâ est." Virgil also has put into the mouth of Thyrsis, in Ecl. VII. 42,

"—— Projecta vilior algâ."

([4]) "*Hath the crocus yielded up its bulb,*" *&c.* Page 16.

The autumnal crocus, or colchicum, which consists of little more than a deep bulbous root, and a delicate lilac flower, produces a substance which is called veratrin, and has been used with signal success in the cure of gout and similar diseases. A few lines lower down, with reference to the elm, I would remark, that no use has yet been discovered in the principle called "ulmine."

"The boon of far Peru" is the potato.

([5]) "*When acorns give out fragrant drink,*" *&c.* Page 17.

At a meeting of the Medico-Botanical Society, (in 1837,) the President introduced to the notice of the members a new beverage which very much resembled coffee, and was made from acorns peeled, chopped, and roasted. Bread made from sawdust is certainly not very palatable, but no one can doubt that it is far more sweet and wholesome than "no bread;" in a famine, this discovery, which has passed almost sub silentio, would prove to be of the highest importance. The darnel, it may be observed, in passing, is highly poisonous, and a proper opposite to the lotus.

([6]) "*He, who seeming old in youth,*" *&c.* Page 22.

Compare Isa. lii. 14, "His visage was so marred more than any man, and his form more than the sons of men," with the idea implied in the observation, John viii. 57, "Thou art not yet *fifty years* old, and hast thou seen Abraham? Our Lord was then thirty-three, or, according to some chronologists, even younger.

([7]) "*A sentence hath formed a character, and a character subdued a kingdom.*" Page 25.

A better instance of this could scarcely be found than in the late Lord Exmouth, who first directed his thoughts to the sea from a casual remark made by a groom. See his Life.

([8]) "*That small cavern,*" *&c.* Page 26.

The pineal gland, a small oval about the size of a pea, situated nearly in the centre of the brain, and generally found to contain, even in children, some particles of gravel. Galen, and after him Des Cartes, imagined it the seat of the soul.

([9]) "*The Greek hath surnamed,* ORDER." Page 31.

Κόσμος. The Latins also, who rarely can show a beautiful idea which they have not borrowed from Greece, have made a similar application of the term "mundus" to the fabric of the world.

([10]) "*To this our day the Rechabite wanteth not a man,*" *&c.* Page 37.

I have heard it related of Wolfe, the missionary, that when in Arabia, he fell in with a small wandering tribe, who refused to drink wine, not on Mohammedan principles, but because it had in olden time been "forbidden by Jonadab, the son of Rechab, their father." Compare Jeremiah xxxv. 19, "Jonadab, the son of Rechab, shall not want a man to stand before me for ever." It will be found in Mr. Wolfe's Journal,

([11]) "*Of Rest.*" Page 37.

A very obvious objection to the views of Rest here given has probably occurred to more than one religious reader of the English Bible; "there remaineth a rest for the people of God;" doubtless intending the heavenly inheritance. If the Greek Testament is referred to (Heb. iv. 9), the word translated "rest" will be found to be σαββατισμός; a sabbatism, or perpetual Sabbath, a rest indeed from evil, but very far from being a rest from good: an eternal act of ecstatic intellectual worship, or temporary acts in infinite series. It is true that another word, κατάπαυσις, implying complete cessation, occurs in the context; but this is used of the earthly image, Joshua's rest in Canaan; the material rest of earth becomes in the skies a spiritual Sabbath; although I am ready to admit that the apostle goes on to argue from the word of the type. In passing, let us observe, by way of showing the uncertainty of trusting to any isolated expression of the present scriptural version, that there are no less than six several words of various meaning which in our New Testament are all indifferently rendered rest: as in Matt. xii. 53, ἀνάπαυσις; in John xi. 13, κοίμησις; in Heb. iii. 11, κατάπαυσις; in Acts xi. 31, εἰρήνη; in 2 Thess. i. 7, ἄνεσις; and in Heb. iv. 9, σαββατισμός. The κοίμησις is, I apprehend, what is generally meant by rest; so wishes Byron's Giaour to "sleep without the dream of what he was;" so he who in life "loathed the languor of repose," avows that he "would not, if he might, be blest, and sought no Paradise but Rest." Such, at least, is not the Christian's Sabbath, which indeed fully agrees, as might be expected, with metaphysical inquiries: a good spirit cannot rest from activity in good, nor an evil one from activity in evil. Rest, in its common slothful acceptation, is not possible, or is, at any rate very improbable, in the case of spiritual creatures.

([12]) "*Calm night that breedeth thoughts.*" Page 37.

Εὐφρόνη. Another delicate example of the Greek elegance in mind and language.

([13]) "*Proteus,*" *&c.* Page 43.

Compare Virgil, Geor. IV. 406, 412.

"Tum variæ eludent species atque ora ferarum.
Fiet enim subito sus horridus, atraque tigris,
Squamosusque draco, et fulvâ cervice leæna;
Aut acrem flammæ sonitum dabit, atque ita vinclis
Excidet; aut in aquas tenues dilapsus abibit.
Sed, quanto ille magis formas se vertet in omnes,
Tanto, nate, magis contende tenacia vincla."

([14]) "*We wait, like the sage of Salamis, to see what the end will be.*" Page 45.

In allusion to the well-known anecdote of Solon at the court of Crœsus.

([15]) "*Crowded with a rainbow of emerald, the green memorial of earth.*" Page 58.

See Rev. iv. 3, "There was a rainbow round about the throne, in sight like unto an emerald:" it may be a fanciful but it is a pleasing idea, that this emerald rainbow was, as it were, a reflection of the earth, which "God so loved,'. and whose universal robe is green.

([16]) "*Like the Parthian.*" Page 64.

Compare Horace, Od. I. 19, 12, "Versis animosum equis Parthum," and Virg. Geo. III. 21, "Parthus fidens fugâ, versisque sagittis,', with Psalm lxxviii. 9, "The children of Ephraim carrying bows, who turned themselves back in the day of battle."

([17]) "*The giant king of palms.*" Page 65.

The magnificent Talipat palm, the column of which frequently exceeds one hundred feet in height, whose leaves are each thirty feet in breadth, and whose single crop of fruits feasts a whole country.

([18]) "*It is only the band of the redeemed who can tell thee the fullness of that name.*" Page 68.

Strictly speaking, only a fallen being is capable of religion, a bringing or binding *back* of the affections to their proper object. An angel or other pure intelligence, can have no sympathies with the fallen, as such, and therefore can know nothing of *re-ligion*, as such; his worship is allegiance or liegeance.

([19]) "*Of a Trinity.*" Page 68.

The candid reader who dissents from the doctrine of the Trinity, will have the goodness to remember, that the question itself stands on far other and higher grounds than those of mere analogy: this observation is made in case the slight argument here urged should seem weak and unsatisfactory to a reflective mind: it is nothing more than an addition *pro lucro*. It does not at all affect the argument that the three elements of all things should be now unknown, or unsuspected. The idea thrown out may one day be found to be correct; and in fact it will be very difficult to prove the contrary, inasmuch as to an assertion of its falsity, "ready answer cometh,"—wait until we know more.

([20]) "*The noonday light is a compound, the triune shadow of Jehovah.*" Page 70.

The rainbow, which is light analyzed, is but three colours, blue, yellow, and red, with their intermediate shades. I think no one of these can be mixed or made of others, and in their union they produce colourless light.

([21]) "*Upon whose lips the mystic bee,*" *&c.* Page 78.

The classical reader will not need to be reminded of the omen that happened to the infant Pindar.

([22]) "*Let another Omar burn the full library of knowledge.*" Page 79.

The Alexandrian library, compiled by Ptolemy Euergetes, contained 700,000 manuscripts, all of which were burnt by the fanatical calif Omar.

([23]) "*The strange skin garments cast upon the shore suggest another hemisphere.*" Page 86.

An anecdote I have somewhere heard of Columbus, who, having sailed as far as Flores, one of the Western Islands, was induced to proceed further from hearing that savage robes and weapons had been cast up by the sea, after the prevalence of westerly gales. It will probably be met with in Washington Irving's Life of Columbus.

([24]) "*The lichen . . . dying, diggeth its own grave.*" Page 86.

One of the great uses of these pioneers of vegetation is to corrode and fret the smooth surface of the rocks, by an acid which they generate during decomposition.

([25]) "*Ridicule—the test of truth.* Page 89.

One of the weakest points in the Shaftesbury philosophy, which would weigh principles against puns.

([26]) "*And being but men, as men, ye own to all the sympathies of manhood.*" Page 100.

The noble and masculine sentiment of Terence, which of old electrified the whole theatre

" Homo sum, humani nihil a me alienem puto."

([27]) "*Ganesa.*" Page 113.

The elephant-headed god of prudence who is invoked on every occasion by the Hindoos. Kali, called also Durga, is a destroying power. Kamala signifies "lotus-like," a type of beauty, and one of the names of Lakshmi. Vishnu is the great Preserver in the Brahmin triad: his incarnations are called avatars.

([28]) "*God will not love thee less, because men love thee more.*" Page 116.

It may be scarcely necessary to remark, that the gist of the argument in Matt. v. 11, "Blessed are ye, when men shall revile you and persecute you, and shall say all manner of evil against you," lies in the "falsely, for my sake." This verse has all the characteristics of an epigram,—paradox, brevity, and final satisfaction.

PROVERBIAL PHILOSOPHY

SECOND SERIES.

PROVERBIAL PHILOSOPHY.

INTRODUCTORY.

COME again, and greet me as a friend, fellow-pilgrim upon life's highway:
Leave awhile the hot and dusty road, to loiter in the greenwood of Reflection.
Come, unto my cool dim grotto, that is watered by the rivulet of truth,
And over whose time-stained rock climb the fairy flowers of content;
Here, upon this mossy bank of leisure fling thy load of cares,
Taste my simple store, and rest one soothing hour.

Behold, I would count thee for a brother, and commune with thy charitable soul;
Though wrapt within the mantle of a prophet, I stand mine own weak scholar.
Heed no disciple for a teacher, if knowledge be not found upon his tongue;
For vanity and folly were the lessons these lips untaught could give:
The precious staple of my merchandise cometh from a better country
The harvest of my reaping sprang of foreign seed:
And this poor pensioner of Mercy—should he boast of merit?
The grafted stock,—should that be proud of apples not its own?
Into the bubbling brook I dip my hermit shell;
Man receiveth as a cup, but Wisdom is the river.

Moreover, for this fillagree of fancy, this Oriental garnish of similitude,
Alas, the world is old,—and all things old within it:
I walk a trodden path, I love the good old ways:
Prophets, and priests, and kings have tuned the harp I faintly touch.

Truth in a garment of the past, is my choice and simple theme;
No truth is new to-day; and the mantle was another's.

Still, there is an insect swarm, the buzzing cloud of imagery,
Mote-like steaming on my sight, and thronging my reluctant mind;
The memories of studious culling, and multiplied analogies of nature,
Fresh feelings unrepressed, welling from the heart spontaneous,
Facts, and comparisons, and meditative atoms, gathered on the heap of combination,
Mingle in the fashion of my speech with gossamer dreams of Reverie.
I need not beat the underwood for game; my pheasants flock upon the lawn,
And gamboling hares disport fearless in my dewy field;
I roam no heath-empurpled hills, wearily watching for a covey,
But thoughts fly swift to my decoy, eager to be caught;
I sit no quiet angler, lingering patiently for sport,
But spread my nets for a draught, and take the glittering shoal;
I chase no solitary stag, tracking it with breathless toil,
But hunt with Aurung-zebe, and spear surrounded thousands! (1)

What then,—count ye this a boast?—sweet charity, think it other,
For the dog-fish and poisonous ray are captured in the mullet-haul:
The crane and the kite are of my thoughts, alike with the partridge and the quail,
And unclean meats as of the clean hang upon my Seric shambles.
—How, saith he? shall a man deceive, dressing up his jackal as a lion?
Or colour in staid hues of fact the changing vest of falsehood?—
Brother, unwittingly he may; doubtless, unwillingly he doth:
For men are full of fault, and how should he be righteous?
Carefully my garden hath been weeded, yet shall it be foul with thistle;
My grapery is diligently thinned, and yet many berries will be sour:
From my nets have I flung the bad away, to my small skill and caution;
Yet may some slimy snake have counted for an eel;
The rudder of man's best hope cannot always steer himself from error;
The arrow of man's straightest aim flieth short of truth.
Thus, the confession of sincerity visit not as if it were presumption;
Nor own me for a leader, where thy reason is not guide.

OF CHEERFULNESS.

TAKE courage, prisoner of time, for there be many comforts,
Cease thy labour in the pit, and bask awhile with truants in the sun;
Be cheerful, man of care, for great is the multitude of chances,
Burst thy fetters of anxiety, and walk among the citizens of ease.
Wherefore dost thou doubt? if present good is round thee,
It may be well to look for change, but to trust in a continuance is better;
Whilst, at the crisis of adversity, to hope for some amends were wisdom,
And cheerfully to bear thy cross in patient strength is duty.
I speak of common troubles, and the petty plagues of life,
The phantom-spies of Unbelief, that lurk about his outposts:
Sharp suspicion, dull distrust, and sullen stern moroseness,
Are captains in that locust swarm to lead the cloudy host.
Thou hast need of fortitude and faith, for the adversaries come on thickly,
And he that fled hath added wings to his pursuing foes;
Fight them, and the cravens flee; thy boldness is their panic;
Fear them, and thy treacherous heart hath lent the ranks a legion:
Among their shouts of victory resoundeth the wail of Heraclitus,
While Democrite, confident and cheerful, hath plucked up the standard of their camp. ([a])

Not few nor light are the burdens of life; then load it not with heaviness of spirit;
Sickness, and penury, and travail,—there be real ills enow:
We are wandering benighted, with a waning moon; plunge not rashly into jungles,
Where cold and poisonous damps will quench the torch of hope:
The tide is strong against us; good oarsmen pull or perish,—
If your arms be slack for fear, ye shall not stem the torrent.
A wise traveller goeth on cheerily, through fair weather or foul;
He knoweth that his journey must be sped, so he carrieth his sunshine with him.
Calamities come not as a curse,—nor prosperity for other than a trial;
Struggle,—thou art better for the strife, and the very energy shall hearten thee.
Good is taught in a Spartan school,—hard lessons and a rough discipline,

But evil cometh idly of itself, in the luxury of Capuan holidays;
And wisdom will go bravely forth to meet the chastening scourge,
Enduring with a thankful heart that punishment of Love.

There be three chief rivers of despondency; sin, sorrow, fear;
Sin is the deepest, sorrow hath its shallows, and fear is a noisy rapid:
But even to the darkest holes in guilt's profoundest river
Hope can pierce with quickening ray, and all those depths are lightened.
So long as there is mercy in a God, hope is the privilege of creatures,
And so soon as there is penitence in creatures, that hope is exalted into duty.
Verily, consider this for courage; that the fearful and the unbelieving
Are classed with idolaters and liars, because they trusted not in God: (*)
For it is no other than selfish sin, a hard and proud ingratitude,
Where seeming repentance is herald of despair, instead of hope's forerunner.

Moreover, in thy day of Grief,—for friends, or fame, or fortune,
Well I wot the heart shall ache, and mind be numbed in torpor:
Let nature weep; leave her alone; the freshet of her sorrow must run off;
And sooner will the lake be clear, relieved of turbid floodings.
Yet see that her license hath a limit; with the novelty her agony is over;
Hasten in that earliest calm, to tie her in the leash with Reason.
For regrets are an enervating folly, and the season for energy is come,
Yea rather, that the future may repair with diligence the ruins of the past.

Again, for empty fears, the harassings of possible calamity;
Pray, and thou shalt prosper; trust in God, and tread them down.
Yield to the phantasy,—thou sinnest; resist it, He will aid thee.
Out of him there is no help, nor any sober courage.
Feeble is the comfort of the faithless, a man without a God;
Who dare counsel such an one to fling away his fears?
Fear is the heritage of him, a portion wise and merciful,
To drive the trembler into safety, if haply he may turn and flee:
Nevertheless, let him reckon if he will, that all he counteth casual
May as well be for him as against him: dice have many sides:
And, even as in ailments of the body, diseases follow closely upon dreads,
So, with infirmities of mind, is fear the pallid harbinger of failure.
It were wise to talk undaunted even in an accidental chaos,

For the brave man is at peace and free to get the mastery of circumstance
The stoutest armour of defence is that which is worn within the bosom,
And the weapon that no enemy can parry, is a bold and cheerful spirit:
Catapults in old war worked like Titans, crushing foes with rocks;
So doth a strong-springed heart throw back every load on its assailants.

I went heavily for cares, and fell into the trance of sorrow:
And behold, a vision in my trance, and my ministering angel brought it:
There stood a mountain huge and steep, the awful Rock of Ages;
The sun upon its summit, and storms midway, and deep ravines at foot;
And, as I looked, a dense black cloud, suddenly dropping from the thunder,
Filled, like a cataract, with yeasty foam, a narrow smiling valley:
Close and hard that vaporous mass seemed to press the ground,
And lamentable sounds came up, as of some that were smothering beneath.
Then, as I walked upon the mountain, clear in summer's noon,
For charity I called aloud, Ho! climb up hither to the sunshine.
And even like a stream of light my voice had pierced the mist:
I saw below two families of men, and knew their names of old:
Courage, struggling through the darkness, stout of heart and gladsome,
Ran up the shining ladder which the voice of hope had made;
And tripping lightly by his side, a sweet-eyed helpmate with him,
I looked upon her face to welcome pleasant Cheerfulness;
And a babe was cradled in her bosom, a laughing little prattler,
The child of Cheerfulness and Courage,—could his name be other than Success?
So, from his happy wife, when they both stood beside me on the mountain,
The fond father took that babe, and set him on his shoulder in the sunshine.

Again I peered into the valley, for I heard a gasping moan,
A desolate weak cry, as muffled in the vapours.
So down that crystal shaft into the poisonous mine
I sped for charity to seek and save,—and those I sought fled from me.
At length, I spied far distant, a trembling withered dwarf,
Who crouched beneath the cloak of a tall and spectral mourner;
Then I knew Cowardice and Gloom, and followed them on in darkness,
Guided by their rustling robes and moans and muffled cries,
Until in a suffocating pit the wretched pair had perished,—
And lo, their whitening bones were shaping out an epitaph of Failure.

So I saw that despondency was death, and flung my burdens from me,
And, lightened by that effort, I was raised above the world;
Yea, in the strangeness of my vision, I seemed to soar on wings,
And the names they called my wings were Cheerfulness and Wisdom.

OF YESTERDAY.

Speak, poor almsman of to-day, whom none can assure of a to-morrow,
Tell out, with honest heart, the price thou settest upon yesterday.
Is it then a writing in the dust, traced by the finger of idleness,
Which Industry, clean housewife, can wipe away for ever?
Is it as a furrow on the sand, fashioned by the toying waves,
Quickly to be trampled then again by the feet of the returning tide?
Is it as the pale blue smoke, rising from a peasant's hovel,
That melteth into limpid air, before it topped the larches?
Is it but a vision, unstable and unreal, which wise men soon forget?
Is it as the stranger of the night,—gone, we heed not whither?
Alas! thou foolish heart, whose thoughts are but as these,
Alas! deluded soul, that hopeth thus of Yesterday.

For, behold,—those temples of Ellora, the Brahmin's rock-built shrine,
Behold,—yon granite cliff, which the North Sea buffeteth in vain,—
That stout old forest fir,—these waking verities of life,—
This guest abiding ever, not strange, nor a servant, but a son,—
Such, O man, are vanity and dreams, transient as a rainbow on the cloud,
Weighed against that solid fact, thine ill-remembered Yesterday.

Come, let me show thee an ensample, where Nature shall instruct us;
Luxuriantly the arguments for truth spring native in her gardens.
Seek we yonder woodman of the plain; he is measuring his axe to the elm,
And anon the sturdy strokes ring upon the wintry air:
Eagerly the village schoolboys cluster on the tightened rope,
Shouting, and bending to the pull, or lifted from the ground elastic;
The huge tree boweth like Sisera, boweth to its foes with faintness,—
Its sinews crack,—deep groans declare the reeling anguish of Goliath,

The wedge is driven home,—and the saw is at its heart,—and lo, with solemn slowness,
The shuddering monarch riseth from his throne, toppled with a crash,—and is fallen!

Now, shall the mangled stump teach proud man a lesson;
Now, can we from that elm-tree's sap distill the wine of Truth.
Heed ye those hundred rings, concentric from the core,
Eddying in various waves to the red bark's shore-like rim?
These be the gathering of yesterdays, present all to-day,
This is the tree's judgment, self-history that cannot be gainsaid:
Seven years agone there was a drought,—and the seventh ring is narrowed;
The fifth from hence was half a deluge,—the fifth is cellular and broad.
Thus, Man, thou art a result, the growth of many yesterdays,
That stamp thy secret soul with marks of weal or woe:
Thou art an almanac of self, the living record of thy deeds;
Spirit hath its scars as well as body, sore and aching in their season:
Here is a knot,—it was a crime; there is a canker,—selfishness;
Lo, here, the heart-wood rotten; lo, there, perchance, the sap-wood sound.
Nature teacheth not in vain; thy works are in thee, of thee;
Some present evil bent hath grown of older errors;
And what if thou be walking now uprightly? Salve not thy wounds with poison,
As if a petty goodness of to-day hath blotted out the sin of yesterday:
It is well, thou hast life and light; and the Hewer showeth mercy,
Dressing the root, pruning the branch, and looking for thy tardy fruits;
But, even here, as thou standest, cheerful belike and careless,
The stains of ancient evil are upon thee, the record of thy wrong is in thee:
For, a curse of many yesterdays is thine, many yesterdays of sin,
That, haply little heeded now, shall blast thy many morrows.

Shall then a man reck nothing, but hurl mad defiance at his Judge,
Knowing that less than an omnipotent cannot make the has been, not been?
He ought,—so Satan spake; he must,—so Atheism urgeth;
He may, it was the libertine's thought; he doth,—the bad world said it.
But thou of humbler heart, thou student wiser for simplicity,
While nature warneth thee betimes, heed the loving counsel of Religion.

True, this change is good, and penitence most precious;
But trust not thou thy change, nor rest upon repentance;
For we all are corrupted at the core, smooth as surface seemeth;
What health can bloom in a beautiful skin, when rottenness hath fed upon the bones?
And guilt is parcel of us all; not thou, sweet nursling of affection,
Art spotless, though so passing fair,—nor thou, mild patriarch of virtue.

Behold then the better Tree of Life, free unto us all for grafting,
Cut thee from the hollow root of self, to be budded on a richer Vine.
Be desperate, O man, as of evil, so of good: tear that tunic from thee;
The past can never be retrieved, be the present what it may.
Vain is the penance and the scourge, vain the fast and vigil;
The fencer's cautious skill to-day, can this erase his scars?
It is Man's to famish as a faquir, it is Man's to die a devotee,
Light is the torture and the toil, balanced with the wages of Eternity:
But, it is God's to yearn in love on the humblest, the poorest, and the worst,
For he giveth freely, as a King, asking only thanks for mercy.
Look upon this noble-hearted Substitute; seeing thy woes, he pitied thee,
Bowed beneath the mountain of thy sin, and perished,—but for Godhead;
There stood the Atlas in his power, and Prometheus in his love is there,
Emptying on wretched man the blessings earned from heaven:
Put them not away, hide them in thy heart, poor and penitent receiver,
Be gratitude thy counsellor to good, and wholesome fear unto obedience:
Remember, the pruning-knife is keen, cutting cankers even from the vine:
Remember, twelve were chosen, and one among them liveth—in perdition.

Yea,—for standing unatoned, the soul is a bison on the prairie,
Hunted by those trooping wolves, the many sinful yesterdays:
And it speedeth a terrified Deucalion, flinging back the pebble in his flight,
The pebble that must add one more to those pursuing ghosts. (1)
O man, there is a storm behind, should drive thy bark to haven;
Thy foe, the foe is on thy track, patient, certain, and avenging;
Day by day, solemnly and silently, followeth the fearful past,—
His step is lame but sure; for he catcheth the present in eternity:
And how to escape that foe, the present-past in future?
How to avert that fate, living consequence of causes unexistent?
Boldly we must overleap his birth, and date above his memories,

Grafted on the living Tree that WAS before a yesterday;
No refuge of a younger birth than one that saw creation,
Can hide the child of time from still condemning yesterday.
There is the Sanctuary-city, mocking at the wrath of thine Avenger,
Close at hand, with its wicket on the latch; haste for thy life, poor hunted one!
The gladiator, Guilt, fighteth as of old, armed with net and dagger;
Snaring in the mesh of yesterdays, stabbing with the poniard of to-day:
Fly, thy sword is broken at the hilt; fly, thy shield is shivered;
Leap the barriers and baffle him; the arena of the past is his.
The bounds of Guilt are the cycles of Time; thou must be safe within Eternity;
The arms of God alone shall rescue thee from Yesterday.

OF TO-DAY.

Now, is the constant syllable ticking from the clock of time,
Now, is the watchword of the wise, Now, is on the banner of the prudent.
Cherish thy to-day and prize it well, or ever it be gulfed into the past,
Husband it, for who can promise if it shall have a morrow?
Behold thou art,—it is enough; that present care be thine;
Leave thou the past to thy Redeemer, intrust the future to thy Friend;
But for to-day, child of man, tend thou charily the minutes,
The harvest of thy yesterday, the seed-corn of thy morrow.

Last night died its day; and the deeds thereof were judged:
Thou didst lay thee down as in a shroud, in darkness and death-like slumber;
But at the trumpet of this morn, waking the world to resurrection,
Thou didst arise, like others, to live a new day's life;
Fear, lest folly give thee cause to mourn its passing presence,
Fear, that to-morrow's sigh be not, would God it had not dawned!

For, To-day the lists are set, and thou must bear thee bravely,
Tilting for honour, duty, life, or death without reproach:
To-day, is the trial of thy fortitude, O dauntless Mandan chief;

To-day, is thy watch, O sentinel; to-day thy reprieve, O captive;
What more? to-day is the golden chance wherewith to snatch fruition,—
Be glad, grateful, temperate: there are asps among the figs.
For the potter's clay is in thy hands,—to mould it or to mar it at thy will,
Or idly to leave it in the sun, an uncouth lump, to harden.

O bright presence of To-day, let me wrestle with thee, gracious angel,
I will not let thee go, except thou bless me; bless me, then, To-day:
O sweet garden of To-day, let me gather of thee, precious Eden,
I have stolen bitter knowledge, give me fruits of life To-day:
O true temple of To-day, let me worship in thee, glorious Zion;
I find none other place nor time, than where I am To-day:
O living rescue of To-day, let me run unto thee, ark of refuge;
I see none other hope nor chance, but standeth in To-day:
O rich banquet of To-day, let me feast upon thee, saving manna;
I have none other food nor store, but daily bread To-day!

Behold, thou art pilot of the ship, and owner of that freighted galleon.
Competent, with all thy weakness, to steer into safety or be lost:
Compass and chart are in thy hand: roadstead and rocks thou knowest;
Thou art warned of reefs and shallows; thou beholdest the harbour and its lights.
What? shall thy wantonness or sloth drive the gallant vessel on the breakers?
What? shall the helmsman's hand wear upon the black lee shore?
Vain is that excuse; thou canst escape: thy mind is responsible for wrong:
Vain that murmur; thou may'st live: thy soul is debtor for the right.
To-day, in the voyage of thy life down the dark tide of time,
Stand boldly to thy tiller, guide thee by the pole-star, and be safe;
To-day, passing near the sunken-rocks, the quicksands and whirlpools of probation,
Leave awhile the rudder to swing round, give the wind its heading, and be wrecked.

The crisis of man's destiny is Now, a still recurring danger:
Who can tell the trials and temptations coming with the coming hour?
Thou standest a target-like Sebastian, and the arrows whistle near thee:
Who knoweth when he may be hit? for great is the company of archers.

Each breath is burdened with a bidding, and every minute hath its mission;
For spirits, good and bad, cluster on the thickly peopled air:
Sin may blast thee, grace may bless thee, good or ill this hour:
Chance, and change, and doubt, and fear, are parasites of all.
A man's life is a tower, with a staircase of many steps,
That, as he toileth upward, crumble successively behind him:
No going back, the past is an abyss; no stopping, for the present perisheth;
But ever hasting on, precarious on the foothold of To-day.
Our cares are all To-day; our joys are all To-day;
And in one little word, our life, what is it, but—To-day?

OF TO-MORROW.

There is a floating island, forward, on the stream of time,
Buoyant with fermenting air, and borne along the rapids;
And on that island is a siren, singing sweetly as she goeth,
Her eyes are bright with invitation, and allurement lurketh in her cheeks;
Many lovers vainly pursuing, follow her beckoning finger,
Many lovers seek her still, even to the cataract of death.
To-morrow is that island, a vain and foolish heritage,
And, laughing with seductive lips, Delusion hideth there.
Often, the precious present is wasted in visions of the future,
And coy To-morrow cometh not with prophecies fulfilled.

There is a fairy skiff, plying on the sea of life,
And charitably toiling still to save the shipwrecked crews;
Within, kindly patient, sitteth a gentle mariner,
Piloting, through surf and strait, the fragile barks of men:
How cheering is her voice, how skilfully she guideth,
How nobly leading onward yet, defying even death!
To-morrow is that skiff, a wise and welcome rescue,
And, full of gladdening words and looks, that mariner is Hope.
Often, the painful present is comforted by flattering the future
And kind To-morrow beareth half the burdens of To-day.

To-morrow, whispereth weakness; and To-morrow findeth him the weaker:
To-morrow, promiseth conscience; and behold, no to-day for a fulfilment.
O name of happy omen unto youth, O bitter word of terror to the dotard,
Goal of folly's lazy wish, and sorrow's ever-coming friend,
Fraud's loophole,—caution's hint,—and trap to catch the honest,—
Thou wealth to many poor, disgrace to many noble,
Thou hope and fear, thou weal and woe, thou remedy, thou ruin,
How thickly swarms of thought are clustering round To-morrow.
The hive of memory increaseth, to every day its cell;
There is the labour stored, the honey or corruption:
Each morn the bees fly forth, to fill the growing comb,
And levy golden tribute of the uncomplaining flowers:
To-morrow is their care; they toil for rest To-morrow;
But man deferreth duty's task, and loveth ease to-day.

To-morrow is that lamp upon the marsh, which a traveller never reacheth;
To-morrow, the rainbow's cup, coveted prize of ignorance;
To-morrow, the shifting anchorage, dangerous trust of mariners;
To-morrow, the wrecker's beacon, wily snare of the destroyer.
Reconcile conviction with delay, and To-morrow is a fatal lie;
Frighten resolutions into action, To-morrow is a wholesome truth:
I must, for I fear To-morrow; this is the Cassava's food;
Why should I? let me trust To-morrow,—this is the Cassava's poison.

Lo, it is the even of To-day,—a day so lately a To-morrow;
Where are those high resolves, those hopes of yesternight?
O faint heart, still shall thy whisper be, To-morrow,
And must the growing avalanche of sin roll down that easy slope?
Alas, it is ponderous, and moving on in might, that a Sisyphus may not stop it;
But haste thee with the lever of a prayer, and stem its strength To-day:
For its race may speedily be run, and this poor nut, thyself,
Be whelmed in death and suffocating guilt, that dreary Alpine snow-wreath.

Pensioner of life, be wise, and heed a brother's counsel,
I also am a beadsman, with scrip and staff as thou:
Wouldest thou be bold against the past, and all its evil memories,
Wouldest thou be safe amid the present, its dangers and temptations,
Wouldest thou be hopeful of the future, vague though it be and endless?

Haste thee, repent, believe, obey! thou standest in the courage of a legion;
Commend the Past to God, with all its irrevocable harm,
Humbly, but in cheerful trust, and banish vain regrets;
Come to him, continually come, casting all the Present at his feet,
Boldly, but in prayerful love, and fling off selfish cares;
Commit the Future to his will, the viewless fated Future;
Zealously go forward with integrity, and God will bless thy faith.
For that, feeble as thou art, there is with thee a mighty Conqueror,
Thy friend, the same for ever, yesterday, to-day, and to-morrow;
That friend, changeless as eternity, himself shall make thee friends
Of those thy foes transformed, yesterday, to-day, and to-morrow.

OF AUTHORSHIP.

GREAT is the dignity of Authorship: I magnify mine office;
Albeit in much feebleness I hold it thus unworthily.
For it is to be one of a noble band, the welfare of the world,
Whose haunt is on the lips of men, whose dwelling in their hearts
Who are precious in the retrospect of Memory, and walk among the visions of Hope,
Who commune with the good for everlasting, and call the wisest, brother,
Whose voice hath burst the Silence, and whose light is flung upon the Darkness,
—Flashing jewels on a robe of black, and harmony bounding out of chaos,—
Who gladden empires with their wisdom, and bless to the farthest generation,
Doers of illimitable good, gainers of inestimable glory!
We speak but of the Magnates, we heed none humbler than the highest,
We take no count of sorry scribes, nor waste one thought upon the groundlings;
Our eyes are lifted from the multitude, groping in the dark with candles,
To gaze upon that firmament of praise, the constellated lamps of learning.
Everduring witnesses of Mind, undisputed evidence of Power,
Goodly volumes, living stones, build up their author's temple;
Though of low estate, his rank is above princes,—though needy, he hath worship of the rich,

When Genius unfurleth on the winds his banner as a mighty leader.
Just in purpose, and self-possessed in soul, lord of many talents,
The mental Crœsus goeth forth, rejoicing in his wealth;
Keen and clear perception gloweth on his forehead like a sunbeam,
He readeth men at a glance, and mists roll away before him;
The wise have set him as their captain, the foolish are rebuked at his presence,
The excellent bless him with their prayers, and the wicked praise him by their curses;
His voice, mighty in operation, stirreth up the world as a trumpet,
And kings account it honour to be numbered of his friends.

Rare is the worthiness of Authorship: I justify mine office;
Albeit fancies weak as mine credit not the calling.
For it addeth immortality to dying facts, that are ready to vanish away,
Embalming as in amber the poor insects of an hour;
Shedding upon stocks and stones the tender light of interest,
And illumining dark places of the earth, with radiance of classic lustre.
It hath power to make past things present, and availeth for the present in the future,
Delivering thoughts, and words, and deeds, from the outer darkness of oblivion:
Where are the sages and the heroes, giants of old time?—
Where are the mighty kings that reigned before Agamemnon?—
Alas, they lie unwept, unhonoured, hidden in the midnight:
Alas, for they died unchronicled: their memorial perished with them.
Where are the nobles of Nineveh, and mitred rulers of Babylon?
Where are the lords of Edom, and the royal pontiffs of Thebais?
The golden Satrap, and the Tetrarch,—the Hun, and the Druid, and the Celt?
The merchant princes of Phœnicia, and the minds that fashioned Elephanta?
Alas, for the poet hath forgotten them; and lo! they are outcasts of Memory;
Alas, that they are withered leaves, sapless and fallen from the chaplet of fame.
Speak, Etruria, whose bones be these, entombed with costly care,—
Tell out, Herculaneum, the titles that have sounded in those thy palaces,—
Lycian Zanthus, thy citadels are mute, and the honour of their architects hath died;

Copan and Palenque, dreamy ruins in the West, the forest hath swallowed up your sculptures; (5)
Syracuse,—how silent of the past!—Carthage, thou art blotted from remembrance!
Egypt, wondrous shores, ye are buried in the sandhills of forgetfulness!
Alas,—for in your glorious youth, Time himself was young,
And none durst wrestle with that Angel, iron-sinewed bridegroom of Space;
So he flew by, strong upon the wing, nor dropped one falling feather,
Wherewith some hoary scribe might register their honour and renown.
Beyond the broad Atlantic, in the regions of the setting sun,
Ask of the plume-crowned Incas, that ruled in old Peru,—
Ask of grand Caziques, and priests of the pyramids of Mexico,—
Ask of a thousand painted tribes, high nobility of Nature,
Who, once, could roam their own Elysian plains, free, generous, and happy,
Who, now, degraded and in exile, having sold their fatherland for nought,
Sink and are extinguished in the western seas, even as the sun they follow,—
Where is the record of their deeds, their prowess worthy of Achilles,
Nestor's wisdom, the chivalry of Manlius, the native eloquence of Cicero,
The skill of Xenophon, the spirit of Alcibiades, the firmness of a Maccabæan mother,
Brotherly love that Antigone might envy, the honour and the fortitude of Regulus?
Alas! their glory and their praise have vanished like a summer-cloud;
Alas! that they are dead indeed; they are not written down in the Book of the living.

High is the privilege of Authorship: I purify mine office;
Albeit earthly stains pollute it in my hands.
For it is to the world a teacher and a guide, Mentor of that gay Telemachus;
Warning, comforting, and helping,—a lover and a friend of Man.
Heaven's almoner, Earth's health, patient minister of goodness,
With kind and zealous pen, the wise religious blesseth:
Nature's worshipper, and neophyte of grace, rich in tender sympathies,
With kindled soul and flashing eye the poet poureth out his heartful:
Priest of truth, champion of innocence, warder of the gates of praise,
Carefully with sifting search laboureth the pale historian:

Error's enemy, and acolyte of science, firm in sober argument,
The calm philosopher marshalleth his facts, noting on his page their principles.
These pour mercies upon men; and others, little less in honour,
By cheerful wit and graphic tale refreshening the harassed spirit.
But, there be other some beside, buyers and sellers in the temple,
Who shame their high vocation, greedy of inglorious gain;
There be, who, fabricating books, heed of them meanly as of merchandise
And seek nor use, nor truth, nor fame, but sell their minds for lucre:
O false brethren! ye wot indeed the labour, but are witless of the love;
O lying prophets, chilled in soul, unquickened by the life of inspiration!—
And there be, who, frivolous and vain, seek to make others foolish,
Snaring Youth by loose sweet song, and Age by selfish maxim;
Cleverly heartless, and wittily profane, they swell the river of corruption,
Brilliant satellites of sin,—my soul, be not found among their company.
And there be, who, haters of religion, toil to prove it priestcraft,
Owning none other aim nor hope, but to confound the good:
Woe unto them! for their works shall live; yea, to their utter condemnation:
Woe! for their own handwriting shall testify against them for ever.

Pure is the happiness of Authorship: I glorify mine office;
Albeit lightly having sipped the cup of its lower pleasures.
For it is to feel with a father's heart, when he yearneth on the child of his affections;
To rejoice in a man's own miniature world, gladdened by its rare arrangement.
The poem, is it not a fabric of mind? we love what we create:
That choice and musical order,—how pleasant is the toil of composition!
Yea, when the volume of the universe was blazoned out in beauty by its Author,
God was glad, and blessed his work; for it was very good.
And shall not the image of his Maker be happy in his own mind's doing,
Looking on the structure he hath reared, gratefully, with sweet complacence?
Shall not the Miverva of his brain, panoplied and perfect in proportions,
Gladden the soul and give light unto the eyes of him the travailing parent?
Go to the sculptor, and ask him of his dreams,—wherefore are his nights so moonlit?

Angel faces, and beautiful shapes, fascinate the pale Pygmalion:
Go to the painter, and trace his reveries,—wherefore are his days so sunny?
Choice design and skilful colouring charm the flitting hours of Parrhasius:
Even so, walking in his buoyancy, intoxicate with fairy fancies,
The young enthusiast of authorship goeth on his way rejoicing:
Behold,—he is gallantly attended; legions of thrilling thoughts
Throng about the standard of his mind, and call his Will their captain;
Behold,—his court is as a monarch's; ideas, and grand imaginations
Swell, with gorgeous cavalcade, the splendour of his Spiritual State;
Behold,—he is delicately served; for oftentimes, in solitary calmness,
Some mental fair Egeria smileth on her Numa's worship;
Behold,—he is happy; there is gladness in his eye, and his heart is a sealed fountain,
Bounding secretly with joys unseen, and keeping down its ecstasy of pleasure!

Yea; how dignified, and worthy, full of privilege and happiness,
Standeth in majestic independence the self-ennobled Author!
For God hath blessed him with a mind, and cherished it in tenderness and purity,
Hath taught it in the whisperings of wisdom, and added all the riches of content:
Therefore, leaning on his God, a pensioner for soul and body,
His spirit is the subject of none other, calling no man Master.
His hopes are mighty and eternal, scorning small ambitions:
He hideth from the pettiness of praise, and pitieth the feebleness of envy.
If he meet honours, well; it may be his humility to take them:
If he be rebuked, better; his veriest enemy shall teach him.
For the master-mind hath a birthright of eminence; his cradle is an eagle's eyrie:
Need but to wait till his wings are grown, and genius soareth to the sun:
To creeping things upon the mountain leaveth he the gradual ascent,
Resting his swiftness on the summit only for a higher flight.
Glad in clear good-conscience, lightly doth he look for commendation;
What, if the prophet lacketh honour? for he can spare that praise:
The honest giant careth not to be patted on the back by pigmies:
Flatter greatness, he brooketh it good-humouredly: blame him,—thou tiltest at a pyramid:
Yet, just censure of the good never can he hear without contrition;

Neither would he miss one wise man's praise, for scarce is that jewel and costly.
Only for the herd of common minds, and the vulgar trumpetings of fame,
If aught he heedeth in the matter, his honour is sought in their neglect.
Slender is the marvel, and little is the glory, when round his luscious fruits
The worm and the wasp and the multitude of flies are gathered as to banquet;
Fashion's freak, and the critical sting, and the flood of flatteries, he scorneth;
Cheerfully asking of the crowd the favour to forget him:
The while his blooming fruits ripen in richer fragrance,
A feast for the few,—and the many yet unborn,—who still shall love their savour.

So then, humbly with his God, and proudly independent of his fellows,
Walketh, in pleasures multitudinous, the man ennobled by his pen:
He hath built up, glorious architect, a monument more durable than brass;
His children's children shall talk of him in love, and teach their sons his honour:
His dignity hath set him among princes, the universe is debtor to his worth,
His privilege is blessing for ever, his happiness shineth now,
For he standeth of that grand Election, each man one among a thousand,
Whose sound is gone out into all lands, and their words to the end of the world!

OF MYSTERY.

All things being are in mystery; we expound mysteries by mysteries;
And yet the secret of them all is one in simple grandeur:
All intricate, yet each path plain, to those who know the way;
All unapproachable, yet easy of access, to them that hold the key:
We walk among labyrinths of wonder, but thread the mazes with a clue;
We sail in chartless seas, but behold! the pole-star is above us.
For, counting down from God's good-will, thou meltest every riddle into him,
The axiom of reason is an undiscovered God, and all things live in his ubiquity;

There is only one great secret; but that one hideth every where;
How should the infinite be understood in Time, when it stretcheth on ungrasped for ever;
Can a halting Œdipus of earth guess that enigma of the universe?
Not one: the sword of faith must cut the Gordian knot of nature.

God, pervading all, is in all things the mystery of each;
The wherefore of its character and essence, the fountain of its virtues and its beauties.
The child asketh of its mother,—Wherefore is the violet so sweet?
The mother answereth her babe,—Darling, God hath willed it.
And sages, diving into science, have but a profundity of words,
They track, for some few links, the circling chain of consequence,
And then, after doubts and disputations, are left where they began.
At the bald conclusion of a clown, things are because they are.
Wherefore are the meadows green, is it not to gratify the eye?
But why should greenness charm the eye? such is God's good will.
Wherefore is the ear attuned to a pleasure in musical sounds,
And who set a number to those sounds, and fixed the laws of harmony?
Who taught the bird to build its nest, or lent the shrub its life,
Or poised in the balances of order the power to attract and to repel?
Who continueth the worlds, and the sea, and the heart in motion?
Who commanded gravitation to tie down all upon its sphere?—
For even as a limestone cliff is an aggregate of countless shells,
One riddle concrete of many, a mystery compact of mysteries,
So God, cloudcapped in immensity, standeth the cohesion of all things
And secrets, sublimely indistinct, permeate that Universe, Himself:
As is the whole, so are the parts, whether they be mighty or minute:
The sun is not more unexplained than the tissue of an emmet's wing

Thus, then, omnipresent Deity worketh his unbiassed mind,
A mind, one in moral, but infinitely multiplied in means:
And the uniform prudence of his will cometh to be counted law,
Till mutable man fancieth volition, stirring in the potter's clay:
God, a wise father, showeth not his reasons to his babes;
But willeth in secrecy and goodness; for causes generate dispute:
Then we, his darkling children, watch that invariable purpose,
And invest the passive creature with its Maker's energy and skill.
Therefore, they of old time stopped short of God in idols;

Therefore, in these latter days, we heed not the Jehovah in his works.
Mystery is God's great name; He is the mystery of goodness:
Some other, from the hierarchs of heaven, usurped the mystery of sin.
God is the King, yea, even of himself; he crowned himself with holiness;
The burning circlet of iniquity another found and wore.
God is separate, even from his attributes; but he willed eternally the good;
Therefore freely, though unchangeably, is wise, righteous, and loving:
But ambition, open unto angels, saw the evil, flung aside from everlasting:
It was Lucifer that saw, and nothing loathed those black unclaimed regalia,
So he coveted and stole, to be counted for a king, antagonist of God:
But when he touched the leprous robes, behold, a cheated traitor.

For self-existence, charactered with love, with power, wisdom, and ubiquity,
Could not dwell alone, but willed and worked creation.
Thus in continual exhalation, darkening the void with matter,
Sprang from prolific Deity the creatures of his skill;
And beings, living on his breath, were needfully less perfect than himself,
Therefore less capable of bliss, whereat his benevolence was bounded;
So to make the capability expand, intensely progressive to eternity,
He suffered darkness to illustrate the light, and pain to heighten pleasure;
To heap up happiness on souls he loved, allowed he sin and sorrow,
And then to guilt and grief and shame, he brought unbidden amnesty:
Sinless, none had been redeemed, nor wrapt again in God:
Sorrowless, no conflict had been known, and heaven had been mulcted of its comfort:
Yea, with evil unexhibited, probationary toils unfelt,
Men had not appreciated good, nor angels valued their security.
Herein, to reason's eye, is revealed the mystery of goodness,
Blessing through permitted woe, and teaching by the mystery of sin.

O Chhristian, whose chastened curiosity loveth things mysterious,
Accounting them shadows and eclipses of Him the one great light,
Look now, satisfied with faith, on minds that judge by sense,
And dull from contemplating matter, take small heed of spirit.
Toiling feebly upward, their argument tracketh from below,
They catch the latest consequent, and prove the nearest cause:

What is this? that a seed produced a seed, and so for a thousand seasons.
Ascend a thousand steps, thy ladder leaveth thee in air:
Thou canst not climb to God, and short of Him is nothing;
There is no cause for aught we see, but in his present will.
Begin from the Maker, thou carriest down his attributes to reptiles,
The sharded beetle and the lizard live and move in Him:
Begin from the creature, corruption and infirmity mar thy foolish toil:
Heap Ossa on Olympus,—how much art thou nearer to the stars?
It is easy running from a mountain's top down to the valleys at its foot,
But difficult and steep the laborious ascent, and feebly shalt thou reach it;
Yet man, beginning from himself, that first deluding mystery,
Hopeth from the pit of lies to struggle up to truth;
So, taxing knowledge to its strength, he pusheth one step further,
And fancieth complacently that much is done by reaching a remote effect
Then he maketh answer to himself, as a silly nurse to her little one,
Evading, in a mist of words, hard things he cannot solve;
Till, like an ostrich in the desert, he burieth his head in atoms,
Hoping that, if he is blind, no sun can shine in heaven.

Therefore cometh it to pass, that an atheist is ever the most credulous,
Snatching at any foolish cause, that may dispel his doubts;
And, even as it were for ridicule, a spectacle to men and angels,
The captious and cautious unbeliever is of all men weakest to believe:
Cut from the anchorage of God, his bark is a plaything of the billows;
The compass of his principle is broken, the rudder of his faith unshipped:
Chance and Fate, in a stultified antagonism, govern all for him;
Truth sprang from the conflict of falsities, and the multitude of accidents
hath bred design!
Where is the imposture so gross that shall not entrap his curiosity?
What superstition is so abject that it doth not blanch his cheek?
Whereof can he be sure, with whom Chaos is substitute for Order?
How should his silly structure stand, a pyramid built upon its apex?
Yea, I have seen gray-headed men, the bastard slips of science,
Go for light to glowworms, while they scorn the sun at noon;
Men, who fear no God, trembling at a gipsy's curse,
Men, who jest at a revelation, clinging to a madman's prophecy!

There is a pleasing dread in the fashion of all mysteries,
For hope is mixed therein and fear; who shall divine their issue?

Even the orphan, wandering by night, lost on dreary moors,
Is sensible of some vague bliss amidst his shapeless terrors;
The buoyancy of instant expectation, spurring on the mind to venture
Overbeareth, in its energy, the cramp and the chill of apprehension.
There is a solitary pride, when the heart, in new importance,
Writeth gladly on its archives, the secrets none other men have seen:
And there is a caged terror, evermore wrestling with the mind,
When crime hath whispered his confession, and the secrets are written there in blood:
The village maiden is elated at a tenderly confided tale;
The bandit's wife with sickening fear guessed the premeditated murder;
The sage, with triumph on his brow, hideth his deep discovery;
The idlest clown shall delve all day to find a hidden treasure.

For mystery is man's life; we wake to the whisperings of novelty:
And what, though we lie down disappointed? we sleep, to wake in hope.
The letter, or the news, the chances and the changes, matters that may happen,
Sweeten or embitter daily life with the honey-gall of mystery.
For we walk blindfold,—and a minute may be much,—a step may reach the precipice;
What earthly loss, what heavenly gain, may not this day produce?
Levelled of Alps and Andes, without its valleys and ravines,
How dull the face of earth, unfeatured of both beauty and sublimity:
And so, shorn of mystery, beggared in its hopes and fears,
How flat the prospect of existence, mapped by intuitive foreknowledge?
Praise God, creature of earth, for the mercies linked with secrecy,
That spices of uncertainty enrich thy cup of life:
Praise God, his hosts on high, for the mysteries that make all joy;
What were intelligence, with nothing more to learn, or heaven, in eternity of sameness?

To number every mystery were to sum the sum of all things:
None can exhaust a theme, whereof God is example and similitude.
Nevertheless, take a garland from the garden, a handful from the harvest,
Some scattered drops of spray from the ceaseless mighty cataract.
Whence are we,—whither do we tend,—how do we feel and reason?
How strange a thing is man, a spirit saturating clay!
When doth soul make embryos immortal,—how do they rank hereafter,—
And will the unconscious idiot be quenched in death as nothing?

In essence immaterial, are these minds, as it were thinking machines?
For, to understand may but rightly be to use a mechanism all possess,
So that in reading or hearing of another, a man shall seem unto himself
To be recollecting images or arguments, native and congenial to his mind:
And yet, what shall we say,—who can aread the riddle?
The brain may be clockwork, and mind its spring, mechanism quickened
by a spirit.

Who so shrewd as rightly to divide life, instinct, reason;
Trees, zoophytes, creatures of the plain, and savage man among them?
Hath the mimosa instinct,—or the scallop more than life,—
Or the dog less than reason,—or the brute man more than instinct?
What is the cause of health,—and the gendering of disease?
Why should arsenic kill,—and whence is the potency of antidotes?
Behold, a morsel,—eat and die; the term of thy probation is expired:
Behold, a potion—drink and be alive; the limit of thy trial is enlarged.
Who can expound beauty? or explain the character of nations?
Who will furnish a cause for the epidemic force of fashion?
Is there a moral magnetism living in the light of example?
Is practice electricity?—Yet all these are but names.
Doth normal Art imprison, in its works, spirit translated into substance,
So that the statue, the picture, or the poem, are crystals of the mind?
And doth Philosophy with sublimating skill shred away the matter,
Till rarefied intelligence exudeth even out of stocks and stones?

O mysteries, ye all are one, the mind of an inexplicable Architect
Dwelleth alike in each, quickening and moving in them all.
Fields, and forests, and cities of men, their woes, and wealth, and works,
And customs, and contrivances of life, with all we see and know,
For a little way, a little while, ye hang dependent on each other,
But all are held in one right hand, and by His will ye are.
Here is answer unto mystery, an unintelligible God,
This is the end and the beginning, it is reason that He be not understood.
Therefore it were probable and just, even to a man's weak thinking,
To have one for God who always may be learnt, yet never fully known:
That He, from whom all mysteries spring, in whom they all converge,
Throned in his sublimity beyond the grovellings of lower intellect,
Should claim to be truer than man's truest, the boasted certainty of numbers,
Should baffle his arithmetic, confound his demonstrations, and paralyze the
might of his necessity,

Standing supreme as the mystery of mysteries, every where, yet impersonate,
Essential one in three, essential three in one!

OF GIFTS.

I HAD a seeming friend;—I gave him gifts, and he was gone;
I had an open enemy;—I gave him gifts, and won him;
Common friendship standeth on equalities, and cannot bear a debt;
But the very heart of hate melteth at a good man's love:
Go to, then, thou that sayest,—I will give and rivet the links:
For pride shall kick at obligation, and push the giver from him.
The covetous spirit may rejoice, revelling in thy largess,
But chilling selfishness will mutter,—I must give again:
The vain heart may be glad, in this new proof of man's esteem,
But the same idolatry of self abhorreth thoughts of thanking.

Nevertheless, give; for it shall be a discriminative test,
Separating honesty from falsehood, weeding insincerity from friendship
Give, it is like God; thou weariest the bad with benefits:
Give, it is like God; thou gladdenest the good by gratitude.
Give to thy near of kin, for Providence hath stationed thee his helper:
Yet see that he claim not as his right, thy freewill offering of duty.
Give to the young, they love it; neither hath the poison of suspicion
Spoilt the flavour of their thanks, to look for latent motives.
Give to merit, largely give; his conscious heart will bless thee:
It is not flattery, but love,—the sympathy of men his brethren.
Give, for encouragement in good; the weak desponding mind
Hath many foes, and much to do, and leaneth on its friends.
Yet heed thou wisely these; give seldom to thy better;
For such obtrusive boon shall savour of presumption;
Or, if his courteous bearing greet thy proffered kindness,
Shall not thine independent honesty be vexed at the semblance of a bribe?
Moreover, heed thou this; give to thine equal charily,
The occasion fair and fitting, the gift well chosen and desired:

Hath he been prosperous and blest? a flower may show thy gladness;
Is he in need? with liberal love, tender him the well-filled purse:
Disease shall welcome friendly care in grapes and precious unguents;
And where a darling child hath died, give praise, and hope, and sympathy,
Yet once more, heed thou this; give to the poor discreetly,
Nor suffer idle sloth to lean upon thy charitable arm:
To diligence give, as to an equal, on just and fit occasion;
Or he bartereth his hard-earned self-reliance for the casual lottery of gifts;
The timely loan hath added nerve, where easy liberality would palsy;
Work and wages make a light heart: but the mendicant asketh with a heavy spirit.
A man's own self respect is worth unto him more than money,
And evil is the charity that humbleth, and maketh man less happy.

There are who sow liberalities, to reap the like again;
But men accept his boon, scorning the shallow usurer;
I have known many such a fisherman lose his golden baits;
And oftentimes the tame decoy escapeth with the flock.
Yea, there are who give unto the poor, to gain large interest of God:
Fool,—to think His wealth is money, and not mind:
And haply after thine alms, thy calculated givings,
The hurricane shall blast thy crops, and sink the homeward ship;
Then shall thy worldly soul murmur that the balances were false,
Thy trader's mind shall think of God,—He stood not to his bargain!

Give, saith the preacher, be large in liberality, yield to the holy impulse,
Tarry not for cold consideration, but cheerfully and freely scatter;
So, for complacency of conscience, in a gush of counterfeited charity,
He that hath not wherewith to be just, selfishly presumeth to be generous;
The debtor, and the rich by wrong, are known among the band of the benevolent;
And men extol the noble hearts, who rob that they may give.
Receivers are but little prone to challenge rights of giving,
Nor stop to test, for conscience-sake, the righteousness of mammon:
And the zealot in a cause is a receiver, at the hand which bettereth his cause;
And thus an unsuspected bribe shall blind the good man's judgment:
It is easy to excuse greatness, and the rich are readily forgiven:
What, if his gains were evil, sanctified by using them aright?

O shallow flatterer, self-interest is thy thought,
Hopeless of partaking in the like, thou too wouldest scorn the giver.

Money hath its value; and the scatterer thereof his thanks:
Few men, drinking at a rivulet, stop to consider its source.
The hand that closeth on an alm, be it for necessities or zeal,
Hath small scruple whence it came: Vespasian rejoiceth in his tribute;
Therefore have colleges and hospitals risen upon orphans' wrongs,
Chapels and cathedrals have thriven on the welcome wages of iniquity,
And fraud, in evil compensation, hath salved his guilty conscience,
Not by restoring to the cheated, but by ostentatious giving to the grateful.

So, those who reap rejoice; and reaping, bless the sower:
No one is eager to discover, where discovery tendeth unto loss;
Yet, if knowledge of a theft make gainers thereby guilty,
Can he be altogether innocent who never asked the honesty of gain?
Therefore, O preacher, zealous for charity, temper thy warm appeal,—
Warning the debtor and unjustly rich, they may not dare to give:
To do good is a privilege and guerdon: how shouldest thou rejoice
If ill-got gifts of presumptuous fraud be offered on the altar?
The question is not of degrees; unhallowed alms are evil:
Discourage and reject alike the obolus or talent of iniquity.,

Yet more, be careful that, unworthily, thou gain not an advantage over weakness,
Unstable souls, fervent and profuse, fluttered by the feeling of the moment:
For eloquence swayeth to its will the feeble and the conscious of defect:
Rashly give they, and afterwards are sad,—a gift that doubly erred.
It was the worldliness of priestcraft that accounted almsgiving for charity;
And many a father's penitence hath steeped his son in penury:
Yet, considered he lightly the guilt of a deathbed selfishness
That strove to take with him, for gain, the gold no longer his;
So he died in a false peace, and dying robbed his kindred;
The cunning friar at his side having cheated both the living and the dead.

Charity sitteth on a fair hill-top, blessing far and near,
But her garments drop ambrosia, chiefly on the violets around her:
She gladdeneth indeed the maplike scene, stretching to the verge of the horizon,

For her angel face is lustrous and beloved, even as the moon in heaven.
But the light of that beatific vision gloweth in serener concentration,
The nearer to her heart, and nearer to her home,—that hill-top where she sitteth:
Therefore is she kind unto her kin, yearning in affection on her neighbours,
Giving Gifts to those around who know and love her well.
But the counterfeit of charity, an hypocrite of earth, not a grace of heaven,
Seeketh not to bless at home, for her nearer aspect is ill-favoured:
Therefore hideth she for shame, counting that pride humility,
And none of those around her hearth are gladdened by her gifts:
Rather, with an overreaching zeal, flingeth she her bounty to the stranger,
And scattered prodigalities abroad compensate for meanness in her home;
For benefits showered on the distant shine in unmixed beauty,
So that even she may reap their undiscerning praise:
Therefore native want hath pined, where foreign need was fattened;
Woman been crushed by the tyrannous hand that upheld the flag of liberality;
Poverty been prisoned up and starved by hearts that are maudlin upon crime
And freeborn babes been manacled by men who liberate the sturdy slave.

Policy counselleth a gift, given wisely and in season,
And policy afterward approveth it, for great is the influence of gifts.
The lover, unsmiled upon before, is welcomed for his jewelled bauble;
The righteous cause without a fee must yield to bounteous guilt:
How fair is a man in thine esteem whose just discrimination seeketh thee,
And so, discerning merit, honoureth it with gifts!
Yea, let the cause appear sufficient, and the motive clear and unsuspicious,
As given unto one who cannot help, or proving honest thanks,
There liveth not one among a million who is proof against the charm of liberality,
And flattery, that boon of praise, hath power with the wisest.

Man is of three natures, craving all for charity:
It is not enough to give him meats, withholding other comfort;
For the mind starveth, and the soul is scorned, and so the human animal
Eateth its unsatisfying pittance, a thankless, heartless pauper:
Yet would he bless thee and be grateful, didst thou feed his spirit,
And teach him that thine almsgivings are charities, are loves.
—I saw a beggar in the street, and another beggar pitied him;

Sympathy sank into his soul, and the pitied one felt happier:
Anon passed by a cavalcade, children of wealth and gayety;
They laughed and looked upon the beggar, and the gallants flung him gold;
He, poor spirit-humbled wretch, gathered up their givings with a curse
And went—to share it with his brother, the beggar who had pitied him!

OF BEAUTY.

Thou mightier than Manoah's son, whence is thy great strength,
And wherein the secret of thy craft, O charmer charming wisely?—
For thou art strong in weakness, and in artlessness well-skilled,
Constant in the multitudes of change, and simple amidst intricate complexity.
Folly's shallow lip can ask the deepest question,
And many wise in many words should answer, what is beauty?
Who shall separate the hues that flicker on a dying dolphin,
Or analyze the jewelled lights that deck the peacock's train,
Or shrewdly mix upon a pallette the tints of an iridescent spar
Or set in rank the wandering shades about a watered silk?

For beauty is intangible, vague, ill to be defined:
She hath the coat of a chameleon, changing while we watch it.
Strangely woven is the web, disorderly yet harmonious,
A glistening robe of mingled mesh, that may not be unravelled.
It is shot with heaven's blue, the soul of summer skies,
And twisted strings of light, the mind of noonday suns,
And ruddy gleams of life, that roll along the veins,
A coat of many colours, running curiously together.
There is threefold beauty for man; twofold beauty for the animal;
And the beauty of inanimates is single: body, temper, spirit.
Multiplied in endless combination, issue the changeable results;
Each class verging on the other twain, with imperceptible gradation,
And every individual in each having his propriety of difference,
So that the meanest of creation bringeth in a tribute of the beautiful.

Yea, from the worst in favour shineth out a fitness of design,
The patent mark of beauty, its Maker's name imprest.
For the great Creator's seal is set to all his works;
Its quarterings are Attributes of praise, and all the shield is beauty.
So, that heraldic blazon is Creation's common signet;
And the universal family of life goeth in the colours of its Lord;
But each one, as a several son, shall bear those arms with a difference:
Beauty, various in phase, and similar in seeming oppositions.
The coins of old Rome were struck with a diversity for each,
Barely two be found alike in every Cæsar's image:
So, note thou the seals, ranged around the charters of the Universe,
The finger of God is the stamp upon them all, but each hath its separate variety.

Beauty, theme of innocence, how may guilt discourse thee?
Let holy angels sing thy praise, for man hath marred thy visage.
Still, the maimed torso of a Theseus can gladden taste with its proportions•
Though sin hath shattered every limb, how comely are the fragments!
And music leaveth on the ear a memory of sweet sounds;
And broken arches charm the sight with hints of fair completeness.
So, while humbled at the ruin, be thou grateful for the relics;
Go forth, and look on all around with kind uncaptious eye:
Freely let us wander through these unfrequented ways,
And talk of glorious beauty filling all the world.

For beauty hideth every where, that Reason's child may seek her,
And having found the gem of price, may set it in God's crown.
Beauty nestleth in the rosebud, or walketh the firmament with planets,
She is heard in the beetle's evening hymn, and shouteth in the matins of the sun;
The cheek of the peach is glowing with her smile, her splendour blazeth in the lightning,
She is the dryad of the woods, the naiad of the streams;
Her golden hair hath tapestried the silkworm's silent chamber,
And to her measured harmonies the wild waves beat in time:
With tinkling feet at eventide she danceth in the meadow,
Or, like a Titan, lieth stretched athwart the ridgy Alps;
She is rising in her veil of mist a Venus from the waters,—
Men gaze upon the loveliness,—and lo, it is beautiful exceedingly;

She, with the might of a Briareus, is dragging down the clouds upon the mountain,—
Men look upon the grandeur,—and lo, it is excellent in glory.
For I judge that beauty and sublimity be but the lesser and the great,
Sublime, as magnified to giants, and beautiful, diminished into fairies.
It were a false fancy to solve all beauty by desire,
It were a lowering thought to expound sublimity by dread.
Cowardly men with trembling hearts have feared the furious storm,
Nor felt its thrilling beauty: but is it then not beautiful?
And careless men, at summer's eve, have loved the dimpled waves;
O that smile upon the seas,—hath it no sublimity?
Dost thou nothing know of this,—to be awed at woman's beauty?
Nor, with exhilarated heart, to hail the crashing thunder?
Thou hast much to learn, that never found a fearfulness in flowers,
Thou hast missed of joy, that never basked in beauties of the terrible.

Show me an enthusiast in aught; he hath noted one thing narrowly;
And lo, his keenness hath detected the one dear hiding-place of beauty.
Then he boasteth, simple soul, flattered by discovery,
Fancying that no science else can show so fair and precious:
He hath found a ray of light, and cherisheth the treasure in his closet,
Mocking at those larger minds, that bathe in flooods of noon;
Lo, what a jewel hath he gotten,—this is the monopolist of beauty,—
And lightly heeding all beside, he poured his yearnings thitherward:
Be it for love, or for learning, habit, art, or nature,
Exclusive thought is all the cause of this particular zeal.
But the like intensity of fitness, kind and skilful beauty,
So pleasant to his mind in one thing, filleth all beside:
From the waking minute of a chrysalis to the perfect cycle of chronology,
From the centipede's jointed armour to the mammoth's fossil ribs,
From the kingfisher's shrill note to the cataract's thundering bass,
From the greensward's grateful hues to the fascinating eye of woman,
Beauty, various in all things, setteth up her home in each,
Shedding graciously around an omnipresent smile.

There is beauty in the rolling clouds, and placid shingle beach,
In feathery snows, and whistling winds, and dun electric skies;
There is beauty in the rounded woods, dank with heavy foliage,
In laughing fields, and dinted hills, the valley and its lake;

There is beauty in the gullies, beauty on the cliffs, beauty in sun and shade,
In rocks and rivers, seas and plains,—the earth is drowned in beauty.

Beauty coileth with the water-snake, and is cradled in the shrewmouse's nest,
She flitteth out with evening bats, and the soft mole hid her in his tunnel;
The limpet is encamped upon the shore, and beauty not a stranger to his tent;
The silvery dace and golden carp thread the rushes with her:
She saileth into clouds with an eagle, she fluttereth into tulips with a humming-bird;
The pasturing kine are of her company, and she prowleth with the leopard in his jungle.

Moreover, for the reasonable world, its words, and acts, and speculation,
For frail and fallen manhood, in every work and way
Beauty, wrecked and stricken, lingereth still among us,
And morsels of that shattered sun are dropt upon the darkness.
Yea, with savages and boors, the mean, the cruel, and besotted,
Ever in extenuating grace hide some relics of the beautiful.
Gleams of kindness, deeds of courage, patience, justice, generosity,
Truth welcomed, knowledge prized, rebukes taken with contrition,
All in various measure, have been blest with some of these,
And never yet hath lived the man utterly beggared of the beautiful.

Beauty is as crystal in the torchlight, sparkling on the poet's page;
Virgin honey of Hymettus, distilled from the lips of the orator;
A savour of sweet spikenard, anointing the hands of liberality;
A feast of angels' food set upon the tables of religion.
She is seen in the tear of sorrow, and heard in the exuberance of mirth;
She goeth out early with the huntsman, and watcheth at the pillow of disease.
Science, in his secret laws, hath found out latent beauty,
Sphere and square, and cone and curve, are fashioned by her rules:
Mechanism met her in his forces, fancy caught her in its flittings,
Day is lightened by her eyes, and her eyelids close upon the night.

Beauty is dependence in the babe, a toothless tender nursling;

Beauty is boldness in the boy, a curly rosy truant;
Beauty is modesty and grace in fair retiring girlhood,
Beauty is openness and strength in pure high-minded youth;
Man, the noble and intelligent, gladdeneth earth in beauty,
And woman's beauty sunneth him, as with a smile from heaven.

There is none enchantment against beauty, Magician for all time,
Whose potent spells of sympathy have charmed the passive world:
Verily, she reigneth a Semiramis; there is no might against her;
The lords of every land are harnessed to her triumph.
Beauty is conqueror of all, nor ever yet was found among the nations
That iron-moulded mind, full proof against her power.
Beauty, like a summer's day, subdueth by sweet influences;
Who can wrestle against Sleep?—yet is that giant very gentleness.

Ajax may rout a phalanx, but beauty shall enslave him single-handed:
Pericles ruled Athens, yet is he the servant of Aspasia:
Light were the labour, and often-told the tale, to count the victories of beauty,—
Helen, and Judith, and Omphale, and Thais, many a trophied name,
At a glance the misanthrope was softened, and repented of his vows:
When beauty asked, he gave, and banned her—with a blessing;
The cold ascetic loved the smile that lit his dismal cell,
And kindly stayed her step, and wept when she departed;
The bigot abbess felt her heart gush with a mother's feeling,
When looking on some lovely face beneath the cloister's shade;
Usury freed her without ransom: the buccaneer was gentle in her presence:
Madness kissed her on the cheeek, and Idiocy brightened at her coming:
Yea, the very cattle in the field, and hungry prowlers of the forest,
With fawning homage greeted her, as beauty glided by.
A welcome guest, unbidden, she is dear to every hearth;
A glad spontaneous growth of friends are springing round her rest:
Learning sitteth at her feet, and Idleness laboureth to please her;
Folly hath flung aside his bells, and leaden Dullness gloweth;
Prudence is rash in her defence; Frugality filleth her with riches;
Despair came to her for counsel; and Bereavement was glad when she consoled;
Justice putteth up his sword at the tear of supplicating beauty,
And Mercy, with indulgent haste, hath pardoned beauty's sin.

For beauty is the substitute for all things, satisfying every absence,
The rich delirious cup, to make all else forgotten;
She also is the zest unto all things, enhancing every presence,
The rare and precious ambergris, to quicken each perfume.
O beauty, thou art eloquent; yea, though slow of tongue,
Thy breast, fair Phryne, pleaded well before the dazzled judge;
O beauty, thou art wise; yea, though teaching falsely,
Sages listen, sweet Corinna, to commend thy lips; ([6])
O beauty, thou art ruler; yea, though lowly as a slave,
Myrrha, that imperial brow is monarch of thy lord;
O beauty, thou art winner; yea, though halting in the race,
Hippodame, Camilla, Atalanta,—in gracefulness ye fascinate your umpires;
O beauty, thou art rich; yea, though clad in russet,
Attalus cannot boast his gold against the wealth of beauty;
O beauty. thou art noble; yea, though Esther be an exile,
Set her up on high, ye kings, and bow before the majesty of beauty!

Friend and scholar, who, in charity, hast walked with me thus far,
We have wandered in a wilderness of sweets, tracking beauty's footsteps:
And ever as we rambled on among the tangled thicket,
Many a startled thought hath tempted further roaming;
Passion, sympathetic influence, might of imaginary halos,—
Many the like would lure aside, to hunt their wayward themes.
And, look you!—from his ferny bed in yonder hazel coppice,
A dappled hart hath flung aside the boughs and broke away;
He is fleet and capricious as the zephyr, and with exulting bounds
Hieth down a turfy lane between the sounding woods;
His neck is garlanded with flowers, his antlers hung with chaplets,
And rainbow-coloured ribbons stream adown his mottled flanks:
Should we follow?—foolish hunters thus to chase afoot,—
Who can track the airy speed and doubling wiles of Taste?

For the estimates of human beauty, dependent upon time and clime,
Manifold and changeable, are multiplied the more by strange gregarious fashion:
And notable ensamples in the great turn to epidemics in the lower,
So that a nation's taste shall vary with its rulers.
Stern Egypt, humbled to the Greek, fancied softer idols;

Greece, the Roman province, nigh forgat her classic sculpture;
Rome, crushed beneath the Goth, loved his barbarian habits;
And Alaric, with his ruffian horde, is tamed by silken Rome.
Columbia's flattened head, and China's crumpled feet,—
The civilized tapering waist,—and the pendulous ears of the savage,—
The swollen throat among the mountains, and an ebon skin beneath the tropics,—
These shall all be reckoned beauty; and for weighty cause:
First, for the latter; Providence in mercy tempereth taste by circumstance,
So that Nature's must shall hit her creature's liking;
Second, for the middle; though the foolishness of vanity seek to mar proportion,
Still, defects in those we love shall soon be counted praise;
Third, for the first; a chief and a princess, maimed or distorted from the cradle,
Shall coax the flattery of slaves to imitate the great in their deformity;
Hence groweth habit; and habits make a taste,
And so shall servile zeal deface the types of beauty.
Whiles Alexander conquered, crookedness was comely;
And followers learn to praise the scars upon their leader's brow.
Youth hath sought to flatter Age by mimicking gray hairs;
Age plastereth her wrinkles, and is painted in the ruddiness of Youth.
Fashion, the parasite of Rank, apeth faults and failings,
Until the general Taste depraved hath warped its sense of beauty.

Each man hath a measure for himself, yet all shall coincide in much;
A perfect form of human grace would captivate the world;
Be it manhood's lustre, or the loveliness of woman, all would own its beauty,
The Caffre and Circassian, Russians and Hindoos, the Briton, the Turk and Japanese.
Not all alike, nor all at once, but each in proportion to intelligence,
His purer state in morals, and a lesser grade in guilt:
For the high standard of the beautiful is fixed in Reason's forum,
And sins, and customs, and caprice, have failed to break it down:
And reason's standard for the creature pointeth three perfections,
Frame, knowledge, and the feeling heart, well and kindly mingled:
A fair dwelling, furnished wisely, with a gentle tenant in it,—
This is the glory of humanity: thou hast seen it seldom.

There is a beauty of the body; the superficial polish of a statue,
The symmetry of form and feature, delicately carved and painted.
How bright in early bloom the Georgian sitteth at her lattice,
How softened off in graceful curves her young and gentle shape:
Those dark eyes, lit by curiosity, flash beneath the lashes,
And still her velvet cheek is dimpled with a smile.
Dost thou count her beautiful?—even as a mere fair figure,
A plastic image, little more,—the outer garb of woman:
Yea,—and thus far it is well; but Reason's hopes are higher,—
Can he sate his soul on a scantling third of beauty?

Yet is this the pleasing trickery, that cheateth half the world,
Nature's wise deceit, to make up waste in life:
And few be they that rest uncaught, for many a twig is limed;
Where is the wise among a million, that took not form for beauty?
But watch it well; for vanity and sin, malice, hate, suspicion,
Lowering as clouds upon the countenance, will disenchant its charms.
The needful complexity of beauty claimeth mind and soul,
Though many coins of foul alloy pass current for the true:
And albeit fairness in the creature shall often co-exist with excellence,
Yet hath many an angel shape been tenanted by fiends.
A man, spiritually keen, shall detect in surface beauty
Those marring specks of evil, which the sensual cannot see;
Therefore is he proof against a face, unlovely to his likings,
And common minds shall scorn the taste, that shrunk from sin's distortion.

There is a beauty of the reason: grandly independent of externals,
It looketh from the windows of the house, shining in the man triumphant.
I have seen the broad blank face of some misshapen dwarf
Lit on a sudden as with glory, the brilliant light of mind:
Who then imagined him deformed? intelligence is blazing on his forehead,
There is empire in his eye, and sweetness on his lip, and his brown cheek glittereth with beauty:
And I have known some Nireus of the camp, a varnished paragon of chamberers, (7)
Fine, elegant, and shapely, moulded as the master-piece of Phidias,—
Such an one, with intellects abased, have I noted crouching to the dwarf,
Whilst his lovers scorn the fool whose beauty hath departed!

And there is a beauty for the spirit; mind in its perfect flowering,
Fragrant, expanded into soul, full of love and blessed.
Go to some squalid couch, some famishing death-bed of the poor;
He is shrunken, cadaverous, diseased;—there is here no beauty of the body.
Never hath he fed on knowledge, nor drank at the streams of science,
He is of the common herd, illiterate;—there is here no beauty of the reason.
But lo! his filming eye is bright with love from heaven,
In every look it beameth praise, as worshipping with seraphs;
What honeycomb is hived upon his lips, eloquent of gratitude and prayer,—
What triumph shrined serene upon that clammy brow,
What glory flickering transparent under those thin cheeks,—
What beauty in his face!—Is it not the face of an angel?

Now, of these three, infinitely mingled and combined,
Consisteth human beauty, in all the marvels of its mightiness:
And forth from human beauty springeth the intensity of Love;
Feeling, thought, desire, the three deep fountains of affection.
Son of Adam, or daughter of Eve, art thou trapped by nature,
And is thy young eye dazzled with the pleasant form of beauty?
This is but a lower love: still it hath its honour;
What God hath made and meant to charm, let not man depise.
Nevertheless, as reason's child, look thou wisely farther,
For age, disease, and care, and sin, shall tarnish all the surface;
Reach a loftier love; be lured by the comeliness of mind,—
Gentle, kind, and calm, or lustrous in the livery of knowledge.
And more, there is a higher grade; force the mind to its perfection,—
Win those golden trophies of consummate love:
Add unto riches of the reason, and a beauty moulded to thy liking,
The precious things of nobler gaace that well adorn a soul;
Thus, be thou owner of a treasure, great in earth and heaven,
Beauty, wisdom, goodness,—in a creature like its God.

So then, draw we to an end; with feeble step and faltering.
I follow beauty through the universe, and find her home Ubiquity:
In all that God hath made, in all that man hath marred,
Lingereth beauty or its wreck, a broken mould and castings.
And now, having wandered long time, freely and with desultory feet,
To gather in the garden of the world a few fair sample flowers,

With patient scrutinizing care let us cull the conclusion of their essence,
And answer to the riddle of Zorobabel, Whence the might of beauty. (8)

Ugliness is native unto nothing, but possible abstract evil:
In every thing created, at its worst, lurk the dregs of loveliness.
We be fallen into utter depths, yet once we stood sublime,
For man was made in perfect praise, his Maker's comely image:
And so his new-born ill is spiced with older good,
He carrieth with him, yea, to crime, the withered limbs of beauty.
Passions may be crooked generosities; the robber stealeth for his children;
Murder was avenger of the innocent, or wiped out shame with blood.
Many virtues, weighted by excess, sink among the vices;
Many vices, amicably buoyed, float among the virtues.
For, albeit sin is hate, a foul and bitter turpitude,
As hurling back against the Giver all his gifts with insult;
Still, when concrete in the sinner it will seem to partake of his attractions,
And in seductive masquerade shall cloak its leprous skin;
His broken lights of beauty shall illume its utter black,
And those refracted rays glitter on the hunch of its deformity.

Verily the fancy may be false, yet hath it met me ir my musings,
(As expounding the pleasantness of pleasure, but no ways extenuating license,)
That even those yearnings after beauty, in wayward wanton youth,
When guileless of ulterior end, it craveth but to look upon the lovely,
Seem like struggles of the soul, dimly remembering pre-existence,
And feeling in its blindness for a long-lost god, to satisfy its longing;
As if the sucking babe, tenderly mindful of his mother,
Should pull a dragon's dugs, and drain the teats of poison.
Our primal source was beauty, and we pant for it ever and again;
But sin hath stopped the way with thorns: we turn aside, wander, and are lost.

God, the undiluted good, is root and stock of beauty,
And every child of reason drew his essence from that stem.
Therefore, it is of intuition, an innate hankering for home,
A sweet returning to the well, from which our spirit flowed,
That we, unconscious of a cause, should bask these darkened souls
In some poor relics of the light that blazed in primal beauty,

And, even like as exiles of idolatry, should quaff from the cisterns of creation
Stagnant draughts, for those fresh springs that rise in the Creator.

Only, being burthened with the body, spiritual appetite is warped,
And sensual man, with taste corrupted, drinketh of pollutions:
Impulse is left, but indiscriminate; his hunger feasteth upon carrion;
His natural love of beauty doteth over beauty in decay.
He still thirsteth for the beautiful; but his delicate ideal hath grown gross,
And the very sense of thirst hath been fevered from affection into passion.
He remembereth the blessedness of light, but it is with an old man's memory,
A blind old man from infancy, that once hath seen the sun,
Whom long experience of night hath darkened in his cradle recollections,
Until his brightest thought of noon is but a shade of black.

This then is thy charm, O beauty, all pervading;
And this thy wondrous strength, O beauty, conqueror of all:
The outline of our shadowy best, the pure and comely creature,
That winneth on the conscience with a saddening admiration:
And some untutored thirst for God, the root of every pleasure,
Native to creatures, yea in ruin, and dating from the birthday of the soul.
For God sealeth up the sum, confirmed exemplar of proportions,
Rich in love, full of wisdom, and perfect in the plentitude of Beauty. (*)

OF FAME.

Blow the trumpet, spread the wing, fling thy scroll upon the sky,
Rouse the slumbering world, O Fame, and fill the sphere with echo:
—Beneath thy blast they wake, and murmurs come hoarsely on the wind,
And flashing eyes and bristling hands proclaim they hear thy message:
Rolling and surging as a sea, that upturned flood of faces
Hasteneth with its million tongues to spread the wondrous tale;

The hum of added voices groweth to the roaring of a cataract,
And rapidly from wave to wave is tossed that exaggerated story,
Until those stunning clamours, gradually diluted in the distance,
Sink ashamed, and shrink afraid of noise, and die away.
Then brooding Silence, forth from his hollow caverns,
Cloaked and cowled, and gliding along, a cold and stealthy shadow,
Once more is mingled with the multitude, whispering as he walketh,
And hushing all their eager ears to hear some newer Fame.

So all is still again; but nothing of the past hath been forgotten;
A stirring recollection of the trumpet ringeth in the hearts of men:
And each one, either envious or admiring, hath wished the chance were his
To fill, as thus, the startled world with fame, or fear, or wonder.
This lit thy torch of sacrilege, Ephesian Eratostratus; ([10])
This dug thy living grave, Pythagoras, the traveller from Hades;
For this, dived Empedocles into Ætna's fiery whirlpool;
For this conquerors, regicides, and rebels, have dared their perilous crimes.
In all men, from the monarch to the menial, lurketh lust of fame;
The savage and the sage alike regard their labours proudly:
Yea, in death, the glazing eye is illumined by the hope of reputation,
And the stricken warrior is glad, that his wounds are salved with glory.

For fame is a sweet self-homage, an offering grateful to the idol,
A spiritual nectar for the spiritual thirst, a mental food for mind,
A pregnant evidence to all of an after immaterial existence,
A proof that soul is scatheless, when its dwelling is dissolved.
And the manifold pleasures of fame are sought by the guilty and the good;
Pleasures, various in kind, and spiced to every palate;
The thoughtful loveth fame as an earnest of better immortality,
The industrious and deserving, as a symbol of just appreciation,
The selfish, as a promise of advancement, at least to a man's own kin,
And common minds as a flattering fact that men have been told of their existence.

There is a blameless love of fame, springing from desire of justice,
When a man hath featly won and fairly claimed his honours:

And then fame cometh as encouragement to the inward consciousness of merit,
Gladdening by the kindliness and thanks, wherewithal his labours are rewarded.
But there is a sordid imitation, a feverish thirst for notoriety,
Waiting upon vanity and sloth, and utterly regardless of deserving:
And then fame cometh as a curse; the fire-damp is gathered in the mine:
The soul is swelled with poisonous air, and a spark of temptation shall explode it.

Idle causes, noised awhile, shall yield most active consequents,
And therefore it were ill upon occasion, to scorn the voice of rumour.
Ye have seen the chemist in his art mingle invisible gases;
And lo, the product is a substance, a heavy dark precipitate;
Even so fame, hurtling on the quiet with many meeting tongues,
Can out of nothing bring forth fruits, and blossom on a nourishment of air.
For many have earned honour, and thereby rank and riches,
From false and fleeting tales, some casual mere mistake;
And many have been wrecked upon disgrace, and have struggled with poverty and scorn,
From envious hints and ill reports, the slanders cast on innocence.
Whom may not scandal hit? those shafts are shot at a venture:
Who standeth not in danger of suspicion? that net hath caught the noblest.
Cæsar's wife was spotless, but a martyr to false fame; ([11])
And Rumour, in temporary things, is gigantic as a ruin or a remedy:
Many poor and many rich have testified its popular omnipotence,
And many a panic-stricken army hath perished with the host of the Assyrians.

Nevertheless, if opportunity be nought, let a man bide his time;
So the matter be not merchandise nor conquest, fear thou less for character.
If a liar accuseth thee of evil, be not swift to answer;
Yea, rather give him license for a while; it shall help thine honour afterward:
Never yet was calumny engendered, but good men speedily discerned it,
And innocence hath burst from its injustice, as the green world rolling out of Chaos.

What, though still the wicked scoff, this also turneth to his praise;
Did ye never hear that censure of the bad is buttress to a good man's glory?
What, if the ignorant still hold out, obstinate in unkind judgment,—
Ignorance and calumny are paired; we affirm by two negations;
Let them stand round about, pushing at the column in a circle,
For all their toil and wasted strength, the foolish do but prop it.
And note thou this; in the secret of their hearts, they feel the taunt is false,
And cannot help but reverence the courage that walketh amid calumnies unanswering:
He standeth as a gallant chief, unheeding shot or shell;
He trusted in God his Judge; neither arrows nor the pestilence shall harm him.

A high heart is a sacrifice to heaven; should it stoop among the creepers in the dust,
To tell them that what God approved is worthy of their praise!
Never shall it heed the thought; but flaming on in triumph to the skies,
And quite forgetting fame, shall find it added as a trophy.
A great mind is an altar on a hill; should the priest descend from his altitude
To canvass offerings and worship from dwellers on the plain?
Rather with majestic perseverance, will he minister in solitary grandeur,
Confident the time will come when pilgrims shall be flocking to the shrine.
For fame is the birthright of genius; and he recketh not how long it be delayed:
The heir need not hasten to his heritage, when he knoweth that his tenure is eternal.
The careless poet of Avon, was he troubled for his fame?
Or the deep-mouthed chronicler of Paradise, heeded he the suffrage of his equals?
Mæonides took no thought, commiting all his honours to the future,
And Flaccus, standing on his watch-tower, spied the praise of ages.

Smoking flax will breed a flame, and the flame may illuminate a world:
Where is he who scorned that smoke as foul and murky vapour?
The village stream swelled to a river, and the river was a kingdom's wealth;

Where is he who boasted he could step across that stream?
Such are the beginnings of the famous: little in the judgment of their peers,
The juster verdict of posterity shall fix them in the orbits of the Great.
Therefore dull Zoilus, clamouring ascendant of the hour,
Will soon be fain to hide his hate, and bury up his bitterness for shame:
Therefore mocking Monus, offended at the steps of Beauty, ([12])
Shall win the prize of his presumption, and be hooted from his throne among the stars.
For, as the shadow of a mountain lengtheneth before the setting sun,
Until that screening Alp have darkened all the canton,—
So Fame groweth to its great ones; their images loom larger in departing:
But the shadow of mind is light, and earth is filled with its glory.

And thou, student of the truth, commended to the praise of God,
Wouldst thou find applause with men?—seek it not, nor shun it.
Ancient fame is roofed in cedar, and her walls are marble:
Modern fame lodgeth in a hut, a slight and temporary dwelling;
Lay not up the treasures of thy soul within so damp a chamber,
For the moth of detraction shall fret thy robe, and drop its eggs upon thy motive;
Or the rust of disheartening reserve shall spoil the lustre of thy gold,
Until its burnished beauty shall be dim as tarnished brass;
Or thieves, breaking through to steal, shall claim thy jewelled thoughts,
And turn to charge the theft on thee, a pilferer from them!

There is a magnanimity in recklessness of fame, so fame be well deserving,
That rusheth on in fearless might, the conscious sense of merit;
And there is a littleness in jealousy of fame, looking as aware of weakness,
That creepeth cautiously along, afraid that its title will be challenged.
The wild boar, full of beech-mast, flingeth him down among the brambles
Secure in bristly strength, without a watch he sleepeth:
But the hare, afraid to feed, croucheth in its own soft form;
Wakefully with timid eyes, and quivering ears, he listeneth.
Even so, a giant's might is bound up in the soul of Genius,
His neck is strong with confidence, and he goeth tusked with power
Sturdily he roameth in the forest, or sunneth him in fen and field,

And scareth from his marshy lair a host of fearful foes.
But there is a mimic talent, whose safety lieth in its quickness,
A timorous thing of doubting guile, that scarce can face a friend:
This one is captious of reproof, provident to snatch occasion,
Greedy of applause, and vexed to lose one tittle of the glory.
He is a poor warder of his fame, who is ever on the watch to keep it spotless;
Such care argueth debility, a garrison relying on its sentinel.
Passive strength shall scorn excuses, patiently waiting a reaction,
He wotteth well that truth is great, and must prevail at last:
But fretful weakness hasteth to explain, anxiously dreading prejudice,
And ignorant that perishable falsehood dieth as a branch cut off.

Purity of motive and nobility of mind shall rarely condescend
To prove its rights, and prate of wrongs, or evidence its worth to others;
And it shall be small care to the high and happy conscience
What jealous friends, or envious foes, or common fools may judge.
Should the lion turn and rend every snarling jackal,
Or an eagle be stopped in his career to punish the petulance of sparrows?
Should the palm-tree bend his crown to chide the brier at his feet,
Nor kindly help its climbing, if it hope, and be ambitious?
Should the nightingale account it worth her pains to vindicate her music,
Before some sorry finches, that affect to judge of song?
No: many an injustice, many a sneer, and slur,
Is passed aside with noble scorn by lovers of true fame:
For well they wot that glory shall be tinctured good or evil,
By the character of those who give it, as wine is flavoured by the wine-skin:
So that worthy fame floweth only from a worthy fountain,
But from an ill-conditioned troop, the best report is worthless.
And if the sensibility of genius count his injuries in secret,
Wisely will he hide the pains a hardened herd would mock;
For the great mind well may be sad to note such littleness in brethren,
The while he is comforted and happy in the firmest assurance of desert.

Cease awhile, gentle scholar;—seek other thoughts and themes;
Or dazzling fame with wildfire light will lure us on for ever.
For look, all subjects of the mind may range beneath its banner,
And time would fail and patience droop, to count that numerous host.
The mine is deep, and branching wide,—and who can work it out?

Years of thought would leave untold the boundless topic, Fame.
Every matter in the universe is linked in suchwise unto others,
That a deep full treatise upon one thing might reach to the history of all things:
And before some single thesis had been followed out in all its branches,
The wandering thinker would be lost in the pathless forest of existence.
What were the matter or the spirit, that hath no part in Fame?
Where were the fact irrelevant, or the fancy out of place?
For the handling of that mighty theme should stretch from past to future,
Catching up the present on its way, as a traveller burdened with time.
All manner of men, their deeds, hopes, fortunes, and ambitions,
All manner of events and things, climate, circumstance, and custom,
Wealth and war, fear and hope, contentment, jealousy, devotion,
Skill and learning, truth, falsehood, knowledge of things gone and things to come,
Pride and praise, honour and dishonour, warnings, ensamples, emulations
The excellent in virtues, and the reprobate in vice, with the cloud of in different spectators,—
Wave on wave with flooding force throng the shoals of thought,
Filling that immeasurable theme, the height and depth of Fame.
With soul unsatisfied and mind dismayed, my feet have touched the threshold,
Fain to pour these flowers and fruits an offering on that altar:
Lo, how vast the temple,—there are clouds within the dome!
Yet might the huge expanse be filled with volumes writ on Fame.

OF FLATTERY.

MUSIC is commended of the deaf;—but is that praise despised?
I trow not: with flattered soul, the musician heard him gladly.
Beauty is commended of the blind;—but is that compliment misliking?
I trow not; though false and insincere, woman listened greedily.
Vacant Folly talketh high of Learning's deepest reason;
Is she hated for her hollowness?—learning held her wiser for the nonce.
The worldly and the sensual, to gain some end, did homage to religion:

And the good man gave thanks as for a convert, where others saw the hypocrite.

Yet none of these were cheated at the heart, nor steadily believed those flatteries;
They feared the core was rotten, while they hoped the skin was sound:
But the fruits have so sweet fragrance, and are verily so pleasant to the eyes,
It were an ungracious disenchantment to find them apples of Sodom.
So they laboured to think all honest, winking hard with both their eyes;
And hushed up every whisper that could prove that praise absurd;
They willingly regard not the infirmities that make such worship vain,
And palliate to their own fond hearts the faults they will not see.
For the idol rejoiceth in his incense, and loveth not to shame his suppliants,
Should he seek to find them false, his honours die with theirs:
An offering is welcome for its own sake, set aside the giver,
And praise is precious to a man, though uttered by the parrot or the mocking-bird.

The world is full of fools; and sycophancy liveth on the foolish:
So he groweth great and rich, that fawning supple parasite.
Sometimes he boweth like a reed, cringing to the pompousness of pride,
Sometimes he strutteth as a gallant, pampering the fickleness of vanity:
I have known him listen with the humble, enacting, silent marveller,
To hear some purse-proud dunce expound his poverty of mind;
I have heard him wrangle with the obstinate, vowing that he will not be convinced,
When some weak youth hath wisely feared the chance of ill success:
Now, he will barely be a winner,—to magnify thy triumphs afterward;
Now, he will hardly be a loser,—but cannot cease to wonder at thy skill:
He laudeth his own worth, that the leader may have glory in his follower;
He meekly confesseth his unworthiness, that the leader may have glory in himself.
Many wiles hath he, and many modes of catching,
But every trap is selfishness, and every bait is praise.

Come, I would forewarn thee and forearm thee; for keen are the weapons of his warfare;
And, while my soul hath scorned him, I have watched his skill from far.
His thoughts are full of guile, deceitfully combining contrarieties,

And when he doeth battle in a man, he is leagued with traitorous Self-love;
Strange things have I noted, and opposite to common fancy;
We leave the open surface, and would plumb the secret depths.
For he will magnify a lover even to disparaging his mistress;
So much wisdom, goodness, grace,—and all to be enslaved?
Till the Narcissus, self-enamoured, whelmed in floods of flattery,
Is cheated from the constancy and fervency of love by friendship's subtle praise.
Moreover, he will glorify a parent, even to the censure of his child,—
O degenerate scion, of a stock so excellent and noble!
Scant will be in well-earned praise of a son before his father;
And rarely commendeth to a mother her daughter's budding beauty:
Yet shall he extol the daughter to her father, and be warm about the son before his mother;
Knowing that self-love entereth not, to resist applause with jealousies.
Wisely is he sparing of hyperbole where vehemence of praise would humble,
For many a father liketh ill to be counted second to his son:
And shrewdly the flatterer hath reckoned on a self still lurking in the mother,
When his tongue was slow to speak of graces in the daughter.
But if he descend a generation, to the grandsire his talk is of the grandson,
Because in such high praise he hideth the honours of the son;
And the daughter of a daughter may well exceed, in beauty, love, and learning,
For unconsciously old age perceived—she cannot be my rival.
These are of the deep things of flattery: and many a shallow sycophant
Hath marvelled ill that praise of children seldom won their parents.
This therefore note, unto detection; flattery can sneer as well as smile;
And a master in the craft wotteth well that his oblique thrust is surest.

Flattery sticketh like a burr, holding to the soil with anchors,
A vital, natural, subtle seed, every where hardy and indigenous.
Go to the storehouse of thy memory, and take what is readiest to thy hand,—
The noble deed, the clever phrase, for which thy pride was flattered:
Oh, it hath been dwelt upon in solitude, and comforted thy heart in crowds,
It hath made thee walk as in a dream, and lifted the head above thy fellows;
It hath compensated months of gloom, that minute of sweet sunshine,
Drying up the pools of apathy, and kindling the fire of ambition:

Yea, the flavour of that spice, mingled in the cup of life,
Shall linger even to the dregs, and still be tasted with a welcome;
The dame shall tell her grandchild of her coy and courted youth,
And the graybeard prateth of a stranger, that praised his task at school.

Ofttimes to the sluggard and the dull, flattery hath done good service,
Quickening the mind to emulation, and encouraging the heart that failed.
Even so, a stimulating poison, wisely tendered by the leech,
Shall speed the pulse, and rally life, and cheat astonished death.
For, as a timid swimmer ventureth afloat with bladders,
Until self-confidence and growth of skill have made him spurn their aid,
Thus commendation may be prudent, where a child hath ill deserved it;
But praise unmerited is flattery, and the cure will bring its cares:
For thy son may find thee out, and thou shalt rue the remedy:
Yea rather, where thou canst not praise, be honest in rebuke.

I have seen the objects of a flatterer mirrored clearly on the surface,
Where self-love scattereth praise to gather praise again.
This is a commodity of merchandise, words put out at interest;
A scheme for canvassing opinions, and tinging them all with partiality.
He is but a harmless fool; humour him with pitiful good-nature:
If a poetaster quote thy song, be thou tender to his poem:
Did the painter praise thy sketch? be kind, commend his picture,
He looketh for a like return; then thank him with thy praise.
In these small things, with these small minds, count thou the sycophant a courtier,
And pay back, as blindly as ye may, the too transparent honour.

Also, where the flattery is delicate, coming unobtrusive and in season,
Though thou be suspicious of its truth, be generous at least to its gentility.
The skilful thief of Lacedæmon had praise before his judges,
As many caitiffs win applause for genius in their calling.
Moreover, his meaning may be kind,—and thou art a debtor to his tongue;
Hasten well to pay the debt, with charity and shrewdness:
He must not think thee caught, nor feel himself discovered,
Nor find thine answering compliment as hollow as his own.
Though he be a smiling enemy, let him heed thee as the fearless and the friendly;
A searching look, a poignant word, may prove thou art aware:

Still, with compassion to the frail, though keen to see his soul,
Let him not fear for thy discretion: see thou keep his secret, and thine own.

However, where the flattery is gross, a falsehood clear and fulsome,
Crush the venomous toad, and spare not for a jewel in his head.
Tell the presumptuous in flattery, that or ever he bespatter thee with praise,
It might be well to stop and ask how little it were worth:
Thou hast not solicited his suffrage,—let him not force thee to refuse it;
Look to it, man, thy fence is foiled,—and thus we spoil the plot.
Self-knowledge goeth armed, girt with many waapons,
But carrieth whip for flattery, to lash it like a slave:
But the dunce in that great science goeth as a greedy tunny,
To gorge both bait and hook, unheeding all but appetite:
He smelleth praise and swalloweth,—yea, though it be palpable and plain;
Say unto him, Folly thou art Wisdom,—he will bless thee for thy lie.

Flatterer, thou shalt rue thy trade, though it hath many present gains;
Those varnished wares may sell apace, yet shall they spoil thy credit.
Thine is the intoxicating cup, which whoso drinketh it shall nauseate;
Thine is trickery and cheating; but deception never pleased for long.
And though, while fresh, thy fragrance seemed even as the dews of charity,
Yet afterward it fouled thy censer, as with savour of stale smoke.
For the great mind detected thee at once, answering thine emptiness with pity,
He saw thy self-interested zeal, and was not cozened by vain-glory:
And the little mind is bloated with the praise, scorning him who gave it,
A fool shall turn to be thy tyrant, if thou hast dubbed him great:
And the medium mind of common men, loving first thy music,
After, when the harmonies are done, shall feel small comfort in their echoes;
For either he shall know thee false, conscious of contrary deservings,
And, hating thee for falsehood, soon will scorn himself for truth;
Or, if in aught to toilsome merit honest praise be due,
Though for a season, belike, his weakness hath been raptured at thy witching,
Shall he not speedily perceive, to the vexing of his disappointed spirit,
That thine exaggerative tongue had robbed him of fair fame?
Thou hast paid in forger's coins, and he hath earned true money:

For the substance of just praise thou hast put him off with shadows of the sycophant.
Thou art all things to all men, for ends false and selfish,
Therefore shalt be nothing unto any one, when those thine ends are seen

Turn aside, young scholar, turn from the song of Flattery!
She hath the Siren's musical voice, to ravish and betray.
Her tongue droppeth honey, but it is the honey of Anticyra;
Her face is a mask of facination, but there hideth deformity behind;
Her coming is the presence of a queen, heralded by courtesy and beauty,
But, going away, her train is held by the hideous dwarf, Disgust.

Know thyself, thy evil as thy good, and flattery shall not harm thee:
Yea, her speech shall be a warning, a humbling, and a guide.
For wherein thou lackest most, there chiefly will the sycophant commend thee,
And then most warmly will congratulate, when a man hath least deserved
Behold, she is doubly a traitor; and will underrate her victim's best,
That, to the comforting of conscience, she may plead his worse for better.

Therefore is she dangerous,—as every lie is dangerous:
Believe her tales, and perish; if thou act upon such counsel.
Her aims are thine, not thee; thy wealth, and not thy welfare;
Thy suffrage, not thy safety; thine aid, and not thine honour.
Moreover, with those aims insured, ceaseth all her glozing;
She hath used thee as a handle,—but her hand was wise to turn it:
Thus will she glorify her skill, that it deftly caught thy kindness,
Thus will she scorn thy kindness, so pliable and easy to her skill.
And then, the flatterer will turn to be thy foe, the bitterest and hottest,
Because he oweth thee much hate to pay off many humblings.
Thinkest thou now that he is high, he loveth the remembrance of his lowliness,
The servile manner, the dependent smile, the conscience self-abased?
No, this hour is his own, and the flatterer will be found a busy mocker;
He that hath salved thee with his tongue shall now gnash upon thee with his teeth,
Yea, he will be leader in the laugh,—silly one, to listen to thy loss,
We scarce had hoped to lime and take another of the fools of flattery.

At the last; have charity, young scholar,—yea, to the sycophant convicted;
Be not a Brutus to thyself, nor stern in thine own cause.
Pardon exaggerated praise; for there is a natural impulse
Spurring on the nobler mind, to colour facts by feelings:
Take an indulgent view of each man's interest in self,
Be large and liberal in excuses; is not that infirmity thine own?
Search thy soul and be humble; and mercy abideth with humility;
So that, yea, the insincere, may find the pitiful, and love thee.
Mildly put aside, without rudeness of repulse, the pampering hand of flattery,
For courtesy and kindness have gone beneath its guise, and ill shouldst thou rebuke them.

Thou art incapable of theft: but flowers in the garden of a friend
Are thine to pluck with confidence, and it were unfriendliness to hesitate;
Thou abhorrest flattery: but a generous excess in praise
Is thine to yield with honest heart, and false were the charity to doubt it;
The difference lieth in thine aim; kindliness and good are of charity,
But selfish, harmful, vile, and bad, is flattery's evil end.

OF NEGLECT.

Generous and righteous is thy grief, slighted child of sensibility;
For kindliness enkindleth love, but the waters of indifference quench it;
Thy soul is athrist for sympathy, and hungereth to find affection.
The tender scions of thy heart yearn for the sunshine of good feeling;
And it is an evil thing and bitter, when the cheerful face of Charity,
Going forth gayly in the morning to woo the world with smiles,
Is met by those wayfaring men with coldness, suspicion, and repulse,
And turneth into hard dead stone at the Gorgon visage of Neglect.
O brother, warm and young, covetous of others' favour,
I see thee checked and chilled, sorrowing for censure or forgetfulness.
Let coarse and common minds despise—that wounding of thy vanity,
Alas, I note a sorer cause, the blighting of thy love;
Let the callous sensual deride thee,—disappointed of thy praise,

Alas, thou nast a juster grief, defrauded of their kindness:
It is a theme for tears to feel the soft heart hardening,
The frozen breath of apathy sealing up the fountain of affection;
It is a pang keen only to the best, to be injured well-deserving,
And slumbering Neglect is injury,—could ye not watch one hour?
When God himself complained, it was that none regarded,
And indifference bowed to the rebuke, Thou gavest Me no kiss when I came in.

Moreover, praise is good; honour is a treasure to be hoarded;
A good man's praise foreshadoweth God's, and in His smile is heaven:
But men walk on in hardihood, steeling their sinfulness to censure,
And where rebuke is ridiculed, the love of praise were an infirmity;
The judge thou heedest not in fear, cannot have deep homage of thy hope,
And who then is the wise of this world, that will own he trembleth at his fellows?
Calm, careless, and insensible, he mocketh blame or calumny,
Neither should his dignity be humbled to some pittance of their praise:
The rather, let false pride affect to trample on the treasure
Which evermore in secret strength unconquered Nature prizeth;
Rather, shall he stifle now the rising bliss of triumph,
Lest after, in the world's Neglect, he must acknowledge bitterness.

For lo, that world is wide, a huge and crowded continent,
Its brazen sun is mammon, and its iron soil is care,
A world full of men, where each man clingeth to his idol;
A world full of men, where each man cherisheth his sorrow;
A world full of men, multitude shoaling upon multitude;
A surging sea, where every wave is burdened with an argosy of self;
A boundless beach, where every stone is a separate microscopic world;
A forest of innumerable trees, where every root is independent.

What then is the marvel or the shame, if units be lost among the million?
Canst thou reasonably murmur, if a leaf drop off unnoticed?
Wondrous in architecture, intricate and beautiful, delicately tinged and scented,
Exquisite of feeling and mysterious in life, none cared for its growth, or its decay:
None? yea,—no one of its fellows,—nor cedar, palm, nor bramble—

None? its twinborn brother scarcely missed it from the spray:
None?—if none indeed, then man's neglect were bitterness;
And life a land without a sun, a globe without a God!
Yea, flowers in the desert, there be that love your beauty;
Yea, jewels in the sea, there be that prize your brightness;
Children of unmerited oblivion, there be that watch and woo you,
And many tend your sweets, with gentle ministering care:
Thronging spirits of the happy, and the ever present Good One,
Yearning seek those precious things man hath not heart to love;
Gems of the humblest or the highest, pure and patient in their kind,
The souls unhardened by ill-usage, and uncorrupt by luxury.

And ye, poor desolates unsunned, toilers in the dark damp mine,
Wearied daughters of oppression, crushed beneath the car of avarice,
There be that count your tears,—he hath numbered the hairs of thy head,—
There be that can forgive your ill with kind considerate pity:
Count ye this for comfort, Justice hath her balances,
And yet another world can compensate for all:
The daily martyrdom of patience shall not be wanting of reward;
Duty is a prickly shrub, but its flower will be happiness and glory.

Ye too, the friendless, yet dependent, that find nor home nor lover,
Sad imprisoned hearts, captive to the net of circumstance,—
And ye, too harshly judged, noble unappreciated intellects,
Who, capable of highest, lowlier fix your just ambition in content,
And chiefest, ye famished infants of the poor, toiling for your parents' bread,
Tired, and sore, and uncomforted the while, for want of love and learning,
Who struggle with the pitiless machine in dull continuous conflict,
Tasked by iron men, who care for nothing but your labour,—
Be ye long-suffering and courageous; abide the will of Heaven·
God is on your side; all things are tenderly remembered:
His servants here shall help you; and where those fail you through Neglect,
His kingdom still hath time and space for ample discriminative Justice:
Yea, though utterly on this bad earth ye lose both right and mercy,
The tears that we forgat to note, our God shall wipe away.

Nevertheless, kind spirit, susceptible and guileless,

Meek uncherished dove, in a carrion flock of fowls,
Sensitive mimosa, shrinking from the winds that help to root the fir,
Fragile nautilus, shipwrecked in the gale whereat the conch is glad,
Thy sharp peculiar grief is uncomforted by hope of compensation,
For it is a delicate and spiritual wound, which the probe of pity bruiseth;
Yet hear how many thoughts extenuate its pain;
Even while a kindred heart can sorrow for its presence.
For the sting of neglect is in this,—that such as we are, all forget us,
That men and women, kith and kin, so lightly heed of other:
Sympathy is lacking from the guilty such as we, even where angels minister,
And souls of fine accord must prize a fellow-sinner's love:
For the worst love those who love them, and the best claim heart for heart,
And it is a holy thirst to long for love's requital:
Hard it will be, hard and sad, to love and be unloved,
And many a thorn is thrust into the side of him that is forgotten.
The oppressive silence of reserve, the frost of failing friendship,
Affection blighted by repulse, or chilled by shallow courtesy,
The unaided struggle, the unconsidered grief, the unesteemed self-sacrifice,
The gift, dear evidence of kindness, long due, but never offered,
The glance estranged, the letter flung aside, the greeting ill received,
The services of unobtrusive care unthanked, perchance unheeded,
These things, which hard men mock at, rend the feelings of the tender,
For the delicate tissue of a spiritual mind is torn by those sharp barbs;
The coldness of a trusted friend, a plentitude ending in vacuity,
Is as if the stable world had burst a hollow bubble.

But, consider child of sensibility; the lot of men is labour,
Labour for the mouth, or labour in the spirit, labour stern and individual.
Worldly cares and worldly hopes exact the thoughts of all,
And there is a necessary selfishness rooted in each mortal breast.
The plans of prudence, or the whisperings of pride, or all-absorbing reveries of love,
Ambition, grief, or fear, or joy, set each man for himself:
Therefore, the centre of a cycle, whereunto all the universe convergeth,
Is seen in fallen solitude, the naked selfish heart:
Stripped of conventional deceptions, untrammelled from the harness of society,
We all may read one little word engraved on all we do;

Other men, what are they unto us? the age, the mass, the million,—
We segregate distinct from generalities, that isolated particle, a self:
It is the very law of our life, a law for soul and body,
An earthly law for earthly men, toiling in responsible probation.
For each is the all unto himself, disguise it as we may,
Each infinite, each most precious; yet even as a nothing to his neighbour.
O consider, we be crowding up an avenue, trapped in the decoy of time,
Behind us the irrevocable past, before us the illimitable future,
What wonder is there, if the traveller, wayworn, hopeful, fearful,
Burdened himself, so lightly heed the burden of his brother?
How shouldst thou marvel and be sad that the pilgrims trouble not to learn thee,
When each hath to master for himself the lessons of life and immortality?

Moreover, what art thou,—so vainly impatient of neglect,
Where then is thy worthiness, that so thou claimest honour?
Let the true judgment of humility reckon up thine ill deserts,
How little is there to be loved, how much to stir up scorn?
The double heart, the bitter tongue, the rash and erring spirit,
Be these, ye purest among men, your passports into favour?
It is mercy in the Merciful, and justice in the Just, to be jealous of his creature's love,
But how should evil or duplicity arrogate affection to itself?
Where love is happiness and duty, to be jealous of that love is godlike,
But who can reverence the guilty? who findeth pleasure in the mean?
Check the presumption of thy hopes: thankfully take refuge in obscurity
Or, if thou claimest merit, thy sin shall be proclaimed upon the housetops.

Yet again: consider them of old, the good, the great, the learned,
Who have blessed the world by wisdom, and glorified their God by purity
Did those speed in favour? were they the loved and the admired?
Was every prophet had in honour? and every deserving one remembered to his praise?
What shall I say of yonder band, a glorious cloud of witnesses,
The scorned, defamed, insulted,—but the excellent of earth?
It were weariness to count up noble names, neglected in their lives,
Whom none esteemed, nor cared to love, till death had sealed them his.
For good men are the health of the world, valued only when it perisheth,
Like water, light, and air, all precious in their absence.

Who hath considered the blessing of his breath, till the poison of an asthma struck him?
Who hath regarded the just pulses of his heart, till spasm or paralysis have stopped them?
Even thus, an unobserved routine of daily grace and wisdom,
When no more here, had worship of a world, whose penitence atoned for its neglect.
And living genius is seen among infirmities, wherefrom the commoner are free;
And other rival men of mind crowd this arena of contention;
And there be many cares; and a man knoweth little of his brother;
Feebly we appreciate a motive, and slowly keep pace with a feeling;
And social difference is much; and experience teacheth sadly,
How great the treachery of friends, how dangerous the courtesy of enemies
So, the sum of all these things operateth largely upon all men,
Hedging us about with thorns, to cramp our yearning sympathies,
And we grow materialized in mind, forgetting what we see not,
But, immersed in perceptions of the present, keep things absent out of thought:
Thus, where ingratitude, and guilt, and labour, and selfishness would harden,
Humbly will the good man bow, unmurmuring, to Neglect.

Yet once more, griever at Neglect, hear me to thy comfort, or rebuke:
For, after all thy just complaint, the world is full of love.
O heart of childhood, tender, trusting, and affectionate,
O youth, warm youth, full of generous attentions,
O woman, self-forgetting woman, poetry of human life;
And not less thou, O man, so often the disinterested brother,
Many a smile of love, many a tear of pity,
Many a word of comfort, many a deed of magnanimity,
Many a stream of milk and honey pour ye freely on the earth,
And many a rosebud of love rejoiceth in the dew of your affection.
Neglect? O liberal world, for thine are many prizes:
Neglect? O charitable world, where thousands feed on bounty;
Neglect? O just world, for thy judgments err not often;
Neglect? O libel on a world, where half that world is woman!
Where is the afflicted, whose voice, once heard, stirreth not a host of comforters?

Where is the sick untended, or in prison, and they visited him not?
The hungry is fed, and the thirsty satisfied, till ability set limits to the will,
And those who did it unto them, have done it unto God!
For human benevolence is large, though many matters dwarf it,
Prudence, ignorance, imposture, and the straitenings of circumstance and time.
And if to the body, so to the mind, the mass of men are generous:
Their estimate who know us best, is seldom seen to err:
Be sure the fault is thine, as pride, or shallowness, or vanity,
If all around thee, good and bad, neglect thy seeming merit:
No man yet deserved, who found not some to love him;
And he that never kept a friend need only blame himself:
Many for unworthiness will droop and die, but all are not unworthy;
It must indeed be cold clay soil that killeth every seed.
Therefore examine thy state, O self-accounted martyr of Neglect,
It may be, thy merit is a cubit, and thy measure thereof a furlong:
But grant it greater than thy thoughts, and grant that men thy fellows
For pleasure, business, or interest, misuse, forget, neglect thee,—
Still be thou conqueror in this, the consciousness of high deservings;
Let it suffice thee to be worthy; faint not thou for praise;
For that thou art, be grateful; go humbly even in thy confidence;
And set thy foot on the neck of an enemy so harmless as Neglect.

OF CONTENTMENT.

Godliness with Contentment,—these be the pillars of felicity,
Jachin, wherewithal it is established, and Boaz, in the which is strength: ([13])
And upon their capitals is lily-work, the lotus fruit and flower,
Those fair and fragrant types of holiness, innocence, and beauty;
Great gain pertaineth to the pillars, nets and chains of wreathen gold,
And they stand up straight in the temple porch, the house where Glory dwelleth.

The body craveth meats, and the spirit is athirst for peacefulness;
He that hath these, hath enough; for all beyond is vanity.

Surfeit vaulteth over pleasure, to light upon the hither side of pain;
And great store is great care, the rather if it mightily increaseth.
Albeit too little is a trouble, yet too much shall swell into an evil,
If wisdom stand not nigh to moderate the wishes:
For covetousness never had enough, but moaneth at its wants for ever,
And rich men have commonly more need to be taught contentment than
the poor.
That hungry chasm in their market-place gapeth still unsatisfied,
Yea, fling in all the wealth of Rome,—it asketh higher victims;
So, when the miser's gold cannot fill the measure of his lust,
Curtius must leap into the pit, and avarice shall close upon his life. ([14])

Behold Independence in his rags, all too easily contented,
Careful for nothing, thankful for much, and uncomplaining in his poverty;
Such an one have I somewhile seen earn his crust with gladness:
He is a gatherer of simples, culling wild herbs upon the hills:
And now, as he sitteth on the beach, with his mortherless child beside him,
To rest them in the cheerful sun, and sort their mints and horehound,—
Tell me, can ye find upon his forehead the cloud of covetous anxiety,
Or note the dull unkindled eyes of sated sons of pleasure?—
For there is more joy of life with that poor picker of the ditches,
Than among the multitude of wealthy who wed their gains to discontent.

I have seen many rich, burdened with the fear of poverty;
I have seen many poor, buoyed with all the carelessness of wealth;
For the rich had the spirit of a pauper, and the moneyless a liberal heart;
The first enjoyeth not for having, and the latter hath nothing but enjoy
ment.
None is poor but the mean in mind, the timorous, the weak, and unbe-
lieving;
None is wealthy but the affluent in soul, who is satisfied and floweth over.
The poor-rich is attenuate for fears, the rich-poor is fattened upon hopes;
Cheerfulness is one man's welcome, and the other warneth from him by
his gloom.
Many poor have the pleasures of the rich, even in their own possessions;
And many rich miss the poor man's comforts, and yet feel all his cares.
Liberty is affluence, and the Helots of anxiety never can be counted weal-
thy;
But he that is disenthralled from fear, goeth for the time a king;

He is royal, great, and opulent, living free of fortune,
And looking on the world as owner of its good, the Maker's child and heir
Whereas the covetous is slavish, a very Midas in his avarice.
Full of dismal dreams, and starved amongst his treasures:
The ceaseless spur of discontent goaded him with instant apprehension,
And his thirst for gold could never be quenched, for he drank with the throat of Crassus. ([15])

Vanity and dreary disappointment, care, and weariness and envy;
Vanity is graven upon all things; wisely spake the preacher.
For ambition is a burning mountain, thrown up amid the turbid sea,
A Stromboli in sullen pride above the hissing waves:
And the statesman climbing there, forgetful of his patriot intentions,
Shall hate the strife of each rough step, or ever he hath toiled midway;
And every truant from his home, the happy home of duty,
Shall live to loathe his eminence of cares, that seething smoke and lava.
Contentment is the temperate repast, flowing with milk and honey;
Ambition is the drunken orgy, fed by liquid flames;
A black and bitter frown is stamped upon the forehead of Ambition,
But fair Contentment's angel-face is rayed with winning smiles.

There was in Tyre a merchant, the favourite child of fortune,
An opulent man with many ships, to trade in many climes;
And he rose up early to his merchandise, after feverish dreaming,
And lay down late to his hot unrest, overwhelmed with calculated cares.
So, day by day, and month by month, and year by year, he gained;
And grew gray, and waxed great; for money brought him all things.
All things?—verily not all; the kernel of the nut is lacking,—
His mind was a stranger to content, and as for Peace, he knew her not:
Luxuries palled upon his palate, and his eyes were satiate with purple;
He could coin much gold, but buy no happiness with it.
And on a day, a day of dread, in the heat of inordinate ambition,
When he threw with a gambler's hand, to lose or to double his possessions,
The chance hit him,—he had speculated ill,—and men began to whisper;—
Those he trusted, failed; and their usuries had bribed him deeply:
One ship foundered out at sea,—and another met the pirate,—
And so, with broken fortunes, men discreetly shunned him.
He was a stricken stag, and went to hide away in solitude,

And there in humility, he thought,—he resolved, and promptly acted:
From the wreck of all his splendours, from the dregs of the goblet of affluence,
He saved with management a morsel and a drop, for his daily cup and platter:
And lo, that little was enough, and in enough was competence:
His cares were gone,—he slept by night, and lived at peace by day:
Cured of his guilty selfishness,—money's love, envy, competition,—
He lived to be thankful in a cottage that he had lost a palace:
For he found in his abasement, what he vainly had sought in high estate,
Both mind and body well at ease, though robed in the russet of the lowly.

Once more; a certain priest, happy in his high vocation,
With faith, and hope, and charity, well served his village altar;
As men count riches, he was poor; but great were his treasures in heaven,
And great his joys on earth, for God's sake doing good:
He had few cares and many consolations, one of the welcome every where;
The labourer accounted him his friend, and magnates did him honour at their table:
With a large heart and little means he still made many grateful,
And felt as the centre of a circle, of comfort, calmness, and content.
But on a weaker Sabbath,—for he preached both well and wisely,—
Some casual hearer loudly praised his great neglected talents:
Why should he be buried in obscurity, and throw these pearls to swine?
Could he not still be doing good,—the whilst he pushed his fortunes?
Then came temptation, even on the spark of discontent;
The neighbouring town had a pulpit to be filled; hotly did he canvass and won it:
Now was he popular and courted, and listened to the spell of admiration,
And toiled to please the taste, rather than to pierce the conscience.
Greedily he sought, and seeking found, the patronizing notice of the great;
He thirsted for emoluments and honours, and counted rich men happy:
So he flattered, so he preached; and gold and fame flowed in;
They flowed in,—he was reaping his reward,—and he felt himself a fool.
Alas, what a shadow was he following,—how precious was the substance he had left!
Man for God, gold for good, this was his miserable bargain.
The village church, its humble flock, and humbler parish priest,
Zeal, devotion, and approving heaven,—his books, and simple life,

His little farm and flower-beds,—his recreative rambles with a friend,
And haply at the eventide the leaping trouts, to help their humble fare,—
All these wretchedly exchanged for what the world called fortune,
With the harrowing conscience of a state relapsed to vain ambitions.
Then, for God was gracious to his soul, his better thoughts returned,
And better aims with better thoughts, his holy walk of old.
Sickened of style, and ostentation, and the dissipative fashions of society,
He deserted from the ranks of Mammon, and renewed his allegiance to God:
For he found that the praises of men, and all that gold can give,
Are not worthy to be named against godliness and calm contentment.

OF LIFE.

A CHILD was playing in a garden, a merry little child,
Bounding with triumphant health, and full of happy fancies;
His kite was floating in the sunshine,—but he tied the string to a twig,
And ran among the roses to catch a new-born butterfly;
His horn-book lay upon a bank, but the pretty truant hid it,
Buried up in gathered grass, and moss, and sweet wild-thyme;
He launched a paper boat upon the fountain,—then wayward turned aside,
To twine some vagrant jessamines about the dripping marble:
So, in various pastime, shadowing the schemes of manhood,
That curly-headed boy consumed the golden hours:
And I blessed his glowing face, envying the merry little child,
As he shouted with the ecstasy of being, clapping his hands for joyfulness:
For I said, Surely, O Life, thy name is happiness and hope,
Thy days are bright, thy flowers are sweet, and pleasure the condition of thy gift.

A youth was walking in the moonlight, walking not alone,
For a fair and gentle maid leant on his trembling arm:
Their whispering was still of beauty, and the light of love was in their eyes,
Their twin young hearts had not a thought unvowed to love and beauty:

The stars, and the sleeping world, and the guardian eye of God,
The murmur of the distant waterfall, and nightingales warbling in the thicket,
Sweet speech of years to come, and promises of fondest hope,
And more, a present gladness in each other's trust;
All these fed their souls with the hidden manna of affection,
While their faces shone beatified in the radiance of reflected Eden:
I gazed on that fond youth, and coveted his heart,
Attuned to holiest symphonies, with music in its strings;
For I said, Surely, O Life, thy name is love and beauty;
Thy joys are full, thy looks most fair, thy feelings pure and sensitive.

A man sat beside his merchandise, a careworn altered man,
His waking hope, his nightly fear, were money and its losses:
Rarely was the laugh upon the cheek, except in bitter scorn,
For his foolishness of heart, and the lie of its romance, counting Love a treasure.
His talk is of stern Reality, chilling unimaginative facts,
The dull material accidents of this sensual body;
Lucreless honour were contemptible, impoverished affection but a pauper's riches,
Duty, struggling unrewarded, the bargain of a cheated fool;
The market-value of a fancy must be measured by the gain it bringeth,
No man is fed, or clothed by fame, or love, or duty:—
So toiled he day by day, that cold and joyless man;
I gazed upon his haggard face, and sorrowed for the change:
For I said, Surely, O Life, thy name is care and weariness,
Thy soul is parched, thy winds are fierce, and the suns above thee hardening.

A withered elder lay upon his bed, a desolate man and feeble;
His thoughts were of the past, the early past, the bygone days of youth:
Bitterly repented he the years stolen by the god of this world:
Remembering the maiden of his love, and the heart-stricken wife of his selfishness.
For the sunshiny morning of life came again to him a vivid truth,
But the years of toil as a long dim dream, a cloudy blighted noon:
He saw the nutting schoolboy, but forgat the speculative merchant;
The callous calculating husband was shamed by the generous lover:

He knew that the weeds of worldliness, and the smoky breath of Mammon
Had choked and killed those tender shoots, his yearnings after honour and affection:
So was he sick at heart, and my pity strove to cheer him,
But a deep and dismal gulf lay between comfort and his soul.
Then I said, Surely, O Life, thy name is vanity and sorrow,
Thy storms at noon are many, and thine eventide is clouded by remorse.

Now, when I thought upon these things, my heart was grieved within me:
I wept with bitterness of speech, and these were the words of my complaining:
"Wherefore then must happiness and love wither into care and vanity,—
Wherefore is the bud so beautiful, but flower and fruit so blighted?
Hard is the lot of man; to be lured by the meteor of romance,
Only to be snared, and to sink, in the turbid mud-pool of reality."

Suddenly, a light,—and a rushing presence,—and a consciousness of something near me,—
I trembled, and listened, and prayed: then I knew the Angel of Life:
Vague, and dimly visible, mine eye could not behold him,
As, calmly unimpassioned, he looked upon an erring creature:
Unseen, my spirit apprehended him; though he spake not, yet I heard;
For a sympathetic communing with Him flashed upon my mind electric.

Pensioner of God, be grateful; the gift of Life is good:
The life of heart, and life of soul, mingled with life for the body.
Gladness and beauty are its just inheritance,—the beauty thou hast counted for romance:
And guardian spirits weep that selfishness and sorrow should destroy it.
Thou hast seen the natural blessing marred into a curse by man;
Come then, in favour will I show thee the proper excellence of life.
Keep thou purity, and watch against suspicion,—love shall never perish;
Guard thine innocency spotless, and the buoyancy of childhood shall remain.
Sweet ideals feed the soul, thoughts of loveliness delight it;
The chivalrous affection of uncalculating youth lacketh not honourable wisdom.
Charge not folly on invisibles, that render thee happier and purer:
The fair frail visions of Romance have a use beyond the maxims of the Real.

Behold, a patriarch of years, who leaneth on the staff of religion;
His heart is fresh, quick to feel, a bursting fount of generosity;
He, playful in his wisdom, is gladdened in his children's gladness:
He, pure in his experience, loveth in his son's first love:
Lofty aspirations, deep affections, holy hopes are his delight;
His abhorrence is to strip from Life its charitable garment of Ideal.
The cold and callous sneerer, who heedeth of the merely practical,
And mocketh at good uses in imaginary things, that man is his scorn;
The hard unsympathizing modern, filled with facts and figures,
Cautious and coarse, and materialized in mind, that man is his pity.
Passionate thirst for gain never hath burnt within his bosom;
The leaden chains of that dull lust have not bound him prisoner:
The shrewd world laughed at him for honesty, the vain world mouthed at him for honour,
The false world hated him for truth, the cold world despised him for affection:
Still, he kept his treasure, the warm and noble heart,
And in that happy wise old man survive the child and lover.
For human Life is as Chian wine, flavoured unto him who drinketh it,
Delicate fragrance comforting the soul, as needful substance for the body:
Therefore, see thou art pure and guileless; so shall thy Realities of Life
Be sweetened, and tempered, and gladdened by the wholesome spirit of Romance.

Dost thou live, man, dost thou live,—or only breathe and labour?
Art thou free, or enslaved to a routine, the daily machinery of habit?
For one man is quickened into Life, where thousands exist as in a torpor,
Feeding, toiling, sleeping, an insensate weary round:
The plough, or the ledger, or the trade, with animal cares and indolence,
Make the mass of vital years a heavy lump unleavened.
Drowsily lie down in thy dullness, fettered with the irons of circumstance,
Thou wilt not wake to think and feel a minute in a month.
The epitome of common life is seen in the common epitaph,
Born on such a day, and dead on such another, with an interval of three-score years.
For time hath been wasted on the senses, to the hourly diminishing of spirit;
Lean is the soul and pineth, in the midst of abundance for the body:
He forgat the world to which he tended, and a creature's true nobility,

Nor wished that hope and wholesome fear should stir him from his hardened satisfaction.
And this is death in life; to be sunk beneath the waters of the Actual,
Without one feebly-struggling sense of an airier spiritual realm:
Affection, fancy, feeling—dead; imagination, conscience, faith,
All wilfully expunged, till they leave the man mere carcass.
See thou livest, whiles thou art: for heart must live, and soul,
But care and sloth and sin and self, combine to kill that life.
A man will grow to an automaton, an appendage to the counter or the desk,
If mind and spirit be not roused to raise the plodding groveller:
Then praise God for Sabbaths, for books, and dreams, and pains,
For the recreative face of nature, and the kindling charities of home;
And remember, thou that labourest,—thy leisure is not loss,
If it help to expose and undermine that solid falsehood, the Material.

Life is a strange avenue of various trees and flowers;
Lightsome at commencement, but darkening to its end in a distant massy portal.
It beginneth as a little path, edged with the violet and primrose,
A little path of lawny grass, and soft to tiny feet:
Soon, spring thistles in the way, those early griefs of school,
And fruit-trees ranged on either hand show holiday delights:
Anon, the rose and the mimosa hint at sensitive affection,
And vipers hide among the grass, and briers are woven in tne hedges:
Shortly, staked along in order, stand the slender saplings,
While hollow hemlock and tall ferns fill the frequent interval:
So advancing, quaintly mixed, majestic line the way
Sturdy oaks, and vigorous elms, the beech and forest-pine:
And here the road is rough with rocks, wide, and scant of herbage,
The sun is hot in heaven, and the ground is cleft and parched:
And many-times a hollow-trunk, decayed or lightning-scathed,
Or in its deadly solitude, the melancholy upas:
But soon, with closer ranks, are set the sentinel trees,
And darker shadows hover amongst Autumn's mellow tints;
Ever and anon, a holly,—junipers, and cypresses, and yews;
The soil is damp; the air is chill; night cometh on apace:
Speed to the portal, traveller,—lo, there is a moon,
With smiling light to guide thee safely through the dreadful shade:

Hark,—that hollow knock,—behold, the warder openeth,
The gate is gaping, and for thee;—those are the jaws of Death!

OF DEATH.

KEEP silence, daughter of frivolity,—for Death is in that chamber!
Startle not with echoing sound the strangely solemn peace.
Death is here in spirit, watcher of a marble corpse,—
That eye is fixed, that heart is still,—how dreadful in its stillness!
Death, new tenant of the house, pervadeth all the fabric;
He waiteth at the head, and he standeth at the feet, and hideth in the caverns of the breast:
Death, subtle leech, hath anatomized soul from body,
Dissecting well in every nerve its spirit from its substance:
Death, rigid lord, hath claimed the heriot clay,
While joyously the youthful soul hath gone to take his heritage;
Death, cold usurer, hath seized his bonded debtor;
Death, savage despot, hath caught his forfeit serf;
Death, blind foe, wreaketh petty vengeance on the flesh;
Death, fell cannibal, gloateth on his victim,
And carrieth it with him to the grave, that dismal banquet-hall,
Where in foul state the Royal Goul holdeth secret orgies.

Hide it up, hide it up, draw the decent curtain:
Hence! curious fool, and pry not on corruption:
For the fearful mysteries of change are being there enacted,
And many actors play their part on that small stage, the tomb.
Leave the clay, that leprous thing, touch not the fleshly garment:
Dust to dust, it mingleth well among the sacred soil:
It is scattered by the winds, it is wafted by the waves, it mixeth with herbs and cattle,
But God hath watched those morsels, and hath guided them in care:
Each waiting soul must claim his own, when the archangel soundeth,
And all the fields, and all the hills, shall move a mass of life;
Bodies numberless, crowding on the land, and covering the trampled sea,

Darkening the air precipitate, and gathered scatheless from the fire;
The Himalayan peaks shall yield their charge, and the desolate steppes of
Siberia,
The Maelström disengulf its spoil, and the iceberg manumit its captive:
All shall teem with life, the converging fragments of humanity,
Till every conscious essence greet his individual frame;
For in some dignified similitude, alike, yet different in glory,
This body shall be shaped anew, fit dwelling for the soul:
The hovel hath grown to a palace, the bulb hath burst into the flower,
Matter hath put on incorruption, and is at peace with spirit.

Amen,—and so it shall be:—but now, the scene is drear,—
Yea, though promises and hope strive to cheat its sadness;
Full of grief, though faith herself is strong to speed the soul,
For the partner of its toil is left behind to endure an ordeal of change.
Dear partner, dear and frail, my loved though humble home,—
Should I cast thee off without a pang, as a garment flung aside?
Many years, for joy and sorrow, have I dwelt in thee,
How shall I be reckless of thy weal, nor hope for thy perfection?
This also, He that lent thee for my uses in mortality,
Shall well fulfill with boundless praise on that returning day.
Behold, thou shalt be glorified; thou, mine abject friend,—
And should I meanly scorn thy state, until it rise to greatness?
Far be it, O my soul, from thine expectant essence,
To be heedless, if indignity or folly desecrate those thine ashes:
Keep them safe with careful love; and let the mound be holy;
And, thou that passest by, revere the waiting dead.

Naples sitteth by the sea, keystone of an arch of azure,
Crowned by consenting nations peerless queen of gayety:
She laugheth at the wrath of Ocean, she mocketh the fury of Vesuvius,
She spurneth disease and misery and famine, that crowd her sunny street:
The giddy dance, the merry song, the festal glad procession,
The noonday slumber and the midnight serenade,—all these make up her
Life;
Her Life?—and what her Death?—look we to the end of life,—
Solon, and Tellus the Athenian, wisely have ye pointed to the grave.
For behold yon dreary precinct,—those hundreds of stone wells,—([16])
A pit for a day, a pit for a day,—a pit to be sealed for a year:

And in the gloom of night, they raised the year-closed lid,—
Look in,—for gnawing lime hath half consumed the carcasses;
Thus, they hurl the daily dead into that horrible pit,
The dead that only died this day,—as unconsidered offal!
There, a stark white heap, unwept, unloved, uncared for,
Old men and maidens, young men and infants, mingle in hideous corruption:
Fling in the gnawing lime,—seal up the charnel for a year;
For lo, a morrow's dawn hath tinged the mountain summit.
O fair false city, thou gay and gilded harlot,
Woe, for thy wanton heart; woe, for thy wicked hardness:
Woe unto thee, that the lightsomeness of Life, beneath Italian suns,
Should meet the solemnity of Death in a sepulchre so foul and fearful.

For that, even to the best, the wise and pure and pious,
Death, repulsive king, thine iron rule is terrible:
Yea, and even at the best, in company of buried kindred,
With hallowing rites, and friendly tears, and the dear old country church,
Death, cold and lonely, thy frigid face is hateful,
The bravest look on thee with dread, the humblest curse thy coming.
Still, ye unwise among mankind, your foolishness hath added fears;
The crowded cemetery, the catacomb of bones, the pestilential vault,
With fancy's gliding ghost at eve, her moans and flaky footfalls,
And the gibbering train of terror to fright your coward hearts.
We speak not here of sin, nor the phantoms of a bloody conscience,
Nor of solaces, and merciful pardon; we heed but the inevitable grave;
The grave, that wage of guilt, that due return to dust,
The grave, that goal of earth, and starting-post for heaven.

Plant it with laurels, sprinkle it with lilies, set it upon yonder dewy hill,
Midst holy prayers, and generous grief, and consecrating blessings:
Let Sophocles sleep among his ivy, green perennial garlands, ([17])
Let olives shade their Virgil, and roses bloom above Corinne;
To his foster-mother, Ocean, intrust the mariner in hope,
The warrior's spirit, let it rise on high, from the flaming fragrant pyre.
But heap not coffins and corruption to infect the mass of living,
Nor steal from odious realities the charitable poetry of Death:
It is wise to gild uncomeliness, it is wise to mask necessity,
It is wise from cheerful sights and sounds to draw their gent.e uses;

Hide the facts, the bitter facts, the foul and fearful facts,
Tend the body well in hope, this were praise and wisdom;
But to plunge in gloom the parting soul, that hath loved its clay tenement so long,
This were vanity and folly, the counsel of moroseness and despair.
Not thus the Scythian of old time welcomed Death with songs;
Not thus the shrewd Egyptian decorated Death with braveries;
Not thus on his funeral tower sleepeth the sun-worshipping Parsee;
Not thus the Moslem saint lieth in his arabesque mausoleum;
Not thus the wild red Indian, hunter of the far Missouri,
In flowering trees hath nested up his forest-loving ancestry; ([18])
Not thus the Switzer mountaineer scattereth ribboned garlands
About the rustic cross that halloweth the bed of his beloved;
Not thus the village maiden wisheth she may die in spring,
With store of violets and cowslips to be sprinkled on her snow-white shroud;
Not thus the dying poet asketh a cheerful grave,—
Lay him in the sunshine, friends, nor sorrow that a Christian hath departed!

Yea, it is the poetry of Death, an Orpheus gladdening Hades,
To care with mindful love for all so dear—and dead;
To think of them in hope, to look for them in joy, and—but for its simple vanity,—
To pray with all the earnestness of nature for souls who cannot change.
For the tree is felled, and boughed, and bare, and the Measurer standeth with his line;
The chance is gone for ever, and is past the reach of prayer:
For men and angels, good and ill, have rendered all their witness;
The trial is over, the jury are gone in, and none can now be heard;
Well are they agreed upon the verdict, just, and fixed, and final,
And the sentence showeth clear before the Judge hath spoken:
Now—while resting matter is at peace within the tomb,
The conscious spirit watcheth in unspeakable suspense;
Racked with a fearful looking forward, or blissfully feeding on the foretaste,
Waiting souls in eager expectation pass the solemn interval;
They slumber not in death, but awaken, quickened to the terror of the judgment;

They lie not insensate among darkness, but exult, looking to the light.
Idiocy, brightening on the instant, when that veil is torn,
Is grateful that his torpor here hath left him as an innocent ;
The young child, stricken as he played, and guileless babes unborn,
Freed from fetters of the flesh, burst into mind immediate:
Madness judgeth wisely, and the visions of the lunatic are gone,
And each hasteneth to praise the mercy that made him irresponsible.
For soul is one, though manifold in act, working the machinery of brain,
Reason, fancy, conscience, passion, are but varying phases ;
If, in God's wise purpose, the machine were shattered or confused,
Still is soul the same, though it exhibit with a difference :
Therefore, dissipate the brain, and set its inmate free,
Behold, the maniacs and embryos stand in their place intelligent.
That solvent eateth away all dross, leaving the gold intact :
Matter lingereth in the retort, spirit hath flown to the receiver :
And lo, that recipient of the spirits, it is some aerial world,
An oasis midway on the desert space, separating earth from heaven,
A prison-house for essences incorporate, a limbus vague and wild,
Tartarus for evil, and Paradise for good, that intermediate Hades.

O Death, what art thou ? a Lawgiver that never altereth.
Fixing the consummating seal, whereby the deeds of life become established ;
O Death, what art thou ? a stern and silent usher,
Leading to the judgment for Eternity, after the trial scene of time ;
O Death, what art thou ? an husbandman, that reapeth always,
Out of season, as in season, with the sickle in his hand :
O Death, what art thou ? the shadow unto every substance,
In the bower as in the battle, haunting night and day :
O Death, what art thou ? nurse of dreamless slumbers
Freshening the fevered flesh to a wakefulness eternal :
O Death, what art thou ? strange and solemn Alchymist,
Elaborating life's elixir from these clayey crucibles :
O Death, what art thou ? antitype of nature's marvels,
The seed and dormant chrysalis bursting into energy and glory.
Thou calm, safe anchorage for the shattered hulls of men,—
Thou spot of gelid shade, after the hot-breathed desert,—
Thou silent waiting-hall, where Adam meeteth with his children,—
How full of dread, how full of hope, loometh inevitable Death :

Of dread, for all have sinned; of hope, for One hath saved;
The dread is drowned in joy, the hope is filled with immortality!
—Pass along, pilgrim of life, go to thy grave unfearing,
The terrors are but shadows now that haunt the vale of Death.

OF IMMORTALITY.

Gird up thy mind to contemplation, trembling inhabitant of earth:
Tenant of a hovel for a day,—thou art heir of the universe for ever!
For, neither congealing of the grave, nor gulfing waters of the firmament,
Nor expansive airs of heaven, nor dissipative fires of Gehenna,
Nor rust of rest, nor wear, nor waste, nor loss, nor chance, nor change,
Shall avail to quench or overwhelm the spark of soul within thee!

Thou art an imperishable leaf on the evergreen bay-tree of Existence;
A word from Wisdom's mouth, that cannot be unspoken;
A ray of Love's own light; a drop in Mercy's sea;
A creature, marvellous and fearful, begotten by the fiat of Omnipotence.
I, that speak in weakness, and ye, that hear in charity,
Shall not cease to live and feel, though flesh must see corruption;
For the prison-gates of matter shall be broken, and the shackled soul go free,
Free, for good or ill, to satisfy its appetence for ever:
For ever,—dreadful doom, to be hurried on eternally to evil,—
For ever,—happy fate, to ripen into perfectness—for ever!

And is there a thought within thy heart, O slave of sin and fear,
A black and harmful hope, that erring spirit dieth!
That primal disobedience hath ensured the death of soul,
And separate evil sealed it thine—thy curse, Annihilation?
Heed thou this; there is a Sacrifice; the Maker is Redeemer of his creature;
Freely unto each, universally to all, is restored the privilege of essence:
Whether unto grace or guilt, all must live through Him,
Live in vital joy, or live in dying woe:
Death in Adam, life in Christ; the curse hung upon the cross:

Who art thou that heedest of redemption, as narrower than the fall ?
All were dead,—He died for all; that living, they might love;
If living souls withhold their love,—still, He hath died for them.
Eve stole the knowledge; Christ gave the life:
Knowledge and life are the perquisites of soul, the privilege of man:
Mercy stepped between, and stayed the double theft;
God gave; and giving, bought; and buying, asketh love:
And in such asking rendereth bliss, to all that hear and answer,
For love with life is heaven; and life unloving, hell.
Creature of God, his will is for thy weal, eternally progressing;
Fear not to trust a Maker's love, nor a Saviour's ransom:
He drank for all,—for thee and me,—the poison of our deeds;
We shall not die, but live,—and of his grace, we love.
For in the mysteries of Mercy, the One fore-knowing Spirit
Outstrippeth reason's halting choice, and winneth men to Him:
Who shall sound the depths ? who shall reach the heights ?
Freedom, in the gyves of fate; and sovereignty, reconciled with justice.

If then, as annihilate by sin, the soul was ever forfeit,
Godhead paid the mighty price, the pledge hath been redeemed;
He, from the waters of Oblivion raised the drowning race,
Lifting them even to Himself, the baseless Rock of Ages.
None can escape from Adam's guilt, or second Adam's guerdon:
Sin and death are thine; thine also is interminable being:
Let it be even as thou wilt, still are we ransomed from nonentity,
The worlds of bliss and woe are peopled with immortals:
And ruin is thy blame; for thou, the worst, art free
To take from Heaven the grace of love, as the gift of life:
Yet is not remedy thy praise; for thou, the best, art bound
In self, and sin, and darkling sloth, until He break the chain:
None can tell, without a struggle, if that chain be broken;
Strive to-day,—one effort more may prove that thou art free!
Here is faith and prayer, here is the Grace and the Atonement,
Here is the creature feeling for its God, and the prodigal returning to his Father.
But, behold, his reasonable children, standing in just probation,
With ears to hear, neglect; with eyes to see, refuse:
They will not have the blessing with the life, the blessing that enricheth immortality;

And look for pleasures out of God, for heaven in life alone:
So they snatch that awful prize, existence void of love,
And in their darkening exile make a needful hell of self.

Therefore fear, thou sinner, lest the huge blessing, Immortality,
Be blighted in thine evil to a curse,—it were better he had not been born;
Therefore hope, thou saint, for the gift of immortality is free;
Take and live, and live in love: fear not, thou art redeemed!
The happy life, that height of hope, the knowledge of all good,
This is the blessing on obedience, obedience the child of faith:
The miserable life, that depth of all despair, the knowledge of all evil,
This is the curse upon impenitence, impenitence that sprung of unbelief.
God, from a beautiful necessity, is Love in all he doeth,
Love, a brilliant fire, to gladden or consume:
The wicked work their woe by looking upon love, and hating it:
The righteous find their joys in yearning on its loveliness for ever.

Who shall imagine Immortality, or picture its illimitable prospect?
How feebly can a faltering tongue express the vast idea!
For consider the primeval woods that bristle over broad Australia,
And count their autumn leaves, millions multiplied by millions;
Thence look up to a moonless sky from a sleeping isle of the Ægæan,
And add to those leaves yon starry host, sparkling on the midnight, numberless;
Thence traverse an Arabia, some continent of eddying sand,
Gather each grain, let none escape, add them to the leaves and to the stars,
Afterwards gaze upon the sea, the thousand leagues of an Atlantic,
Take drop by drop, and add their sum to the grains, and leaves, and stars;
The drops of ocean, the desert sands, the leaves, and stars innumerable,
(Albeit, in that multitude of multitudes, each small unit were an age,)
All might reckon for an instant, a transient flash of Time,
Compared with this intolerable blaze, the measureless enduring of Eternity!

O grandest gift of the Creator,—O largess worthy of a God,—
Who shall grasp that thrilling thought, life and joy for ever?
For the sun in heaven's heaven is Love that cannot change,
And the shining of that sun is life, to all beneath its beams:
Who shall arrest it in the firmament,—or drag it from its sphere?

Or bid its beauty smile no more, but be extinct for ever?
Yea, where God hath given, none shall take away,
Nor build up limits to his love, nor bid his bounty cease;
Wide, as space is peopled, endless as the empire of heaven,
The river of the water of life floweth on in majesty for ever!

Why should it seem a thing impossible to thee, O man of many doubts,
That God shall wake the dead, and give this mortal immortality?
Is it that such riches are unsearchable, the bounty too profuse?
And yet what gift, to cease or change, is worthy of the King Almighty?
For remember the moment thou art not, thou mightest as well not have been;
A millennium and an hour are equal in the gulf of that desolate abyss, annihilation:
If Adam had existed till to-day, and to-day had perished utterly,
What were his gain in the length of a life, that hath passed away for ever?
No tribute of thanks can exhale from the empty censer of nonentity;
The Giver, with his gift reclaimed, is mulcted of all praise.

Tell me, ye that strive in vain to cramp and dwarf the soul,
Wherefore should it cease to be, and when shall essence die?
It is,—and therefore shall be,—till just obstacle opposeth:
Show no cause for change, and reason leaneth to continuance.
The body verily shall change; this curious house we live in
Never had continuing stay, but changeth every instant:
But the spiritnal tenant of the house abideth in unalterable consciousness;
He may fly to many lands, but cannot flee himself:
The soil wherein ye drop the seed, by suns or rains may vary:
But the seed is the same; and soul is the seed; and flesh but its anchorage to earth.

The machine may be broken, and rust corrode the springs: but can rust feed on motion?
Worms may batten on the brain: but can worms gnaw the mind?
Dynamics are, and dwell apart, though matter be not made;
Spirit is, and can be separate, though a body were not:
Power is one, be it lever, screw, or wedge; but it needeth these for illustration:

Mind is one, be it casual or ideal; but it is shown in these.
The creature is constructed individual, for trial of his reasonable will,
Clay and soul commingled wisely, mingled, not confused:
As power is not in the spring, till somewhat give it action,
So until spirit be infused, the organism lieth inergetic.

Or shalt thou say that mind is the delicate offspring of matter,
The bright consummate flower that must perish with its leaf?
Go to: doth weight breed lightness? is freedom the atmosphere of prisons?
When did the body elevate, expand, and bud the mind?
Lo, a red-hot cinder flung from the furnaces of Ætna,—
There is fire in that ash; but did the pumice make it?
Nay, cold clod, never canst thou generate a flame,
Nay, most exquisite machinery, nevermore elaborate a mind;
Rather do ye battle and contend, opposite the one to the other;
Till God shall stop the strife, and call the body colleague.

Garment of flesh, and art thou then a vest, so tinged with subtle poison,
(Maddening tunic of the centaur,) as to kill the soul?
Not so: fruit of disobedience, rot in dissolution, as thou must,—
The seed is in the core, its germ is safe, and life is in that germ:
Moreover, Marah shall be sweetened; and a Good Physician
Yet shall heal those gangrene wounds, the spotted plague of sin:
He, through worldly trials, and the separative cleansing of the grave,
Shall change its corruptible to glory, and wash that garment white.

Still, is the whisper in thy heart, that oftenest the bed of death
Seemeth but a sluggish ebb, of sinking soul and body?
Mind dwelling long-time sensual in the chambers of the flesh,
May slumber on in conscious sloth, and wilfully be dulled:
But is it therefore nigh to dissolution, even as the body of this death?
Ask the stricken conscience, gasping out its terrors;
Ask the dying miser, loth to leave his gold;
Ask the widowed poor, confiding her fatherless to strangers;
Ask the martyr-maid, a broken reed so strong,
That weak and tortured frame, with triumph on its brow!—
O thou gainsayer, the finger of disease may seem to reach the soul,
But it is a spiritual touch, sympathy with that which aileth:
Pain or fear may dislocate and shatter this delicate machinery of nerves;

But madness proveth mind: the fault is in the engine, not the impetus:
Dissipate the mists of matter, lo, the soul is clear:
Timour's cage bowed it in the dust, but now it goeth forth a freeman.

Yet more, there is reason in moralities, that the soul must live;
If God be king in heaven, or have care for earth,
Can wickedness have triumphed with impunity, or virtue toiled unseen?
Shall cruelty torture unavenged, and the innocent complain unheard?
Is there no recompense for woe,—must there be no other world for justice,—
No hope in setting suns of good, nor terror for the evil at its zenith?
How shall ye make answer unto this, a just God prospering iniquity,
Wisdom encouraging the foolish, and Goodness abetting the depraved?

Yet again; mine erring brother, pardon this abundance of my speech,
Yield me thy candour and thy charity, listening with a welcome:
For, even now, a thousand thoughts are trooping to my theme;
O mighty theme, O feeble thoughts! Alas, who is sufficient?
Judge not so high a cause by these poor words alone,
For lo, the advocate hath little skill: pardon, and pass on:
Certify thyself with surer proofs; fledge thine own mind for flight;
Think, and pray; those better proofs shall follow on with holy aspiration.
Yet, in my humbler grade to help thy weal and comfort,
Thy weal for this and higher worlds, and comfort in thy sickness,
Suffer the multitude of fancies, walking with me still in love;
But tread in fear, it is holy ground,—remember Immortality!

Wilt thou argue from infirmities, thine abject evil state,
As how should stricken wretched man indeed exist for ever:
The brutal and besotted, the savage and the slave, the sucking infant and the idiot,
The mass of mean and common minds, and all to be immortal?
Consider every beginning, how small it is and feeble:
Ganges, and the rolling Mississippi, sprung of brooks among the mountains;
That yew-tree of a thousand years was once a little seed;
And Nero's marble Rome, a shepherd's mud-built hovel:
A speck is on the tropic sky, and it groweth to the terrible tornado;
An apple, all too fair to see, destroyed a world of souls·

A tender babe is born,—it is Attila, scourge of the nations!
A seeming malefactor dieth,—it is Jesus, the Saviour of men!

And hive not in thy thoughts the vain and wordy notion,
That nothing which was born in time, can tire out the footsteps of Infinity.
Reckon up a sum in numbers; where shall progression stop?
The starting-post is definite and fixed, but what is the goal of numeration?
So begin upon a moment, and when shall being end?
Souls emanate from God, to travel with him equally for ever.
Moreover, thou that objectest the unenterable circle of eternity,
That none but He from everlasting can endure, as to a future everlasting,
Consider, may it be impossible that creatures were counted in their Maker,
And so, that the confines of eternity are filled by God alone?
Trust not thy soul upon a fancy: who would freight a bubble with a diamond,
And launch that priceless gem on the boiling rapids of a cataract?

If then we perish not at death, but walk in spirit through the darkness,
Waiting for a mansion incorruptible, whereof this body is the seed,
Tell me, when shall be the period? time and its ordeals are done;
The storms are passed, the night is at an end, behold the Sabbath morning.
Is Death to be conqueror again, and claim once more the victory,—
Can the enemy's corpse awaken into life, and bruise the Champion's head?
Evil, terrible ensample, that foil to the attributes of Good,
Is banished to its own black world, weeded out of earth and heaven:
Shall that great gulf be passed, and sin be sown again?—
We know but this, the book of truth proclaimeth gladly, Never!

There remaineth the will of our God: when he repenteth of his creature,
Made by self-suggested mercy, ransomed by self-sacrificing justice,—
When Truth, that swore unto his neighbour, disappointeth him, and cleaveth to a lie,—
When the counsels of Wisdom are confounded, and Love warreth with itself,
When the Unchangeable is changed, and the arm of Omnipotence is broken,
Then,—thy quenchless soul shall have reached the goal of its existence.

But it seemeth to thy notions of the merciful and just, a false and fearful thing,

To lay such a burden upon time, that eternity be built on its foundation:
As if so casual good or ill should colour all the future,
And the vanity of accident, or sternness of necessity, save or wreck a soul.
Were it casual, vain, or stern, this might pass for truth:
But all things are marshalled by Design, and carefully tended by Benevolence.
O man, thy Judge is righteous,—noting, remembering, and weighing;
Want, ignorance, diversities of state, are cast into the balance of advantage:
The poisonous example of a parent asketh for allowance in a child;
Care, diseases, toils, and frailties,—all things are considered.
And again, a mysterious Omniscience knoweth the spirits that are his,
While the delicate tissues of Event are woven by the fingers of Ubiquity.
Should Providence be taken by surprise from the possible impinging of an accident,
One fortuitous grain might dislocate the banded universe:
The merest seeming trifle is ordered as the morning light;
And he that rideth on the hurricane, is pilot of the bubble on the breaker.

Once more, consider Matter,—how small a thing is father to the greatest:
Thou that lightly hast regarded the results of so called accident.
A blade of grass took fire in the sun,—and the prairies are burnt to the horizon:
A grain of sand may blind the eye, and madden the brain to murder:
A careful fly deposited its egg in the swelling bud of an acorn,—
The sapling grew,—cankrous and gnarled,—it is yonder hollow oak:
A child touched a spring, and the spring closed a valve, and the labouring engine burst,—
A thousand lives were in that ship,—wrecked by an infant's finger!
Shall nature preach in vain?—thy casualty, guided in its orbit,
Though less than a mote upon the sunbeam, saileth in a fleet of worlds;
That trivial cause, watered and observed of the Husbandman day by day,
In calm undeviating strength doth work its large effect.
Thus, in the pettiness of life note thou seeds of grandeur,
And watch the hour-glass of Time with the eyes of an heir of Immortality.

There still be clouds of witnesses,—if thou art not weary of my speech,—
Flocks of thoughts adding lustre to the light, and pointing on to Life.
For reflect how Truth and Goodness, well and wisely put,
Commend themselves to every mind with wondrous intuition:

What is this? the recognition of a standard, unwritten, natural, uniform;
Telling of one common source, the root of Good and True.
And if thus present soul can trace descent from Deity,
Being, as it standeth, individual, a separate reasonable thing,
What should hinder that its hope may not trace gladly forward,
And, in astounding parallel, like Enoch, walk with God?
Yea, the genealogy of soul, that vivifying breath of a Creator,
Breath, no transient air, but essence, energy, and reason,
Is looming on the past, and shadowing the future, sublimely as Melchisedek of old,
Having not beginning, nor end of days, but present in the majesty of Peace!

O false scholar, credulous in vanities, and only skeptical of truth,
Wherefore toil to cheat thy soul of its birthright, Immortality?
Is it for thy guilt? He pardoneth: is it for thy frailty? He will help:
Though thou fearest, He is Love; and Mercy shall be deeper than Despair;
Even for thy full-blown pride, is it much to be receiver of a God?
And lo, thy rights, He made thee; thy claims, He hath redeemed.
Hath the fair aspect of affection no beauty that thou shouldst desire it?
And are those sorrows nothing to thee that passest by?
For it is a fact, immutable, that God hath dwelt in Man?
With gentle, generous love ennobling while He bought us.
What, though thou art false, ignorant, weak, and daring,—
Can the sun be quenched in heaven—or only Belisarius be blind?

But, even stooping to thy folly, grant all these hopes are vain;
Stultify reason, wrestle against conscience, and wither up the heart,
Where is thy vast advantage?—I have all that thou hast,
The buoyancy of life as strong, and term of days no shorter;
My cup is full with gladness,—my griefs are not more galling:
And thus, we walk together, even to the gates of death:
There, (if not also on my journey, blessing every step,
Gladdening with light, and quickening with love, and killing all my cares,)
There,—while thou art quailing, or sullenly expecting to be nothing,—
There,—is found my gain,—I triumph, where thou tremblest.
Grant all my solace is a lie, yet it is a fountain of delight,
A spice in every pleasure, and a balm for every pain:
O precious wise delusion, scattering both misery and sin,—
O vile and silly truth, depraving while it curseth!

Darkling child of knowledge, commune with Socrates and Cicero:
They had no prejudice of birth, no dull parental warpings;
See, those lustrous minds anticipate the dawning day,—
Whilst thou, poor mole, art burrowing back to darkness from the light.
I will not urge a revelation, mercies, miracles, and martyrs,
But, after twice a thousand years, go learn thou of the pagan;
It were happier and wiser even among fools, to cling to the shadow of a hope,
Than, in the company of sages, to win the substance of despair:
But here, the sages hope;—despair is with the fools,
The base bad hearts, the stolid heads, the sensual, and the selfish.

And wilt thou, sorry scorner, mock the phrase, despair?
Despair for those who die and live,—for me, I live and die;
What have I to do with dread? my taper must go out?—
I nurse no silly hopes, and therefore feel no fears:
I am hastening to an End.—O false and feeble answer:
For hope is in thee still, and fear,—a racking deep anxiety
Erring brother, listen; and take thine answer from the ancients:
Consider every end, that it is but the end of a beginning.
All things work in circles: weariness induceth unto rest,
Rest invigorateth labour, and labour causeth weariness:
War produceth peace, and peace is wanton unto war;
Light dieth into darkness, and night dawneth into day;
The rotting jungle reeds scatter fertility around;
The buffalo's dead carcass hath quickened life in millions;
The end of toil is gain, the end of gain is pleasure,
Pleasure tendeth unto waste, and waste commandeth toil.

So, is death an end,—but it breedeth an infinite beginning;
Limits are for time, and death killed time; Eternity's beginning is for ever.
Ambition, hath it any goal indeed? is not all fruition, disappointment?
A step upon the ladder, and another, and another,—we start from every end:
Look to the eras of mortality; babe, student, man,
The husband, the father, the deathbead of a saint,—and is it then an end?
That common climax, Death, shall it lead to nothing?
How strong a root of causes, flowering a consequence of vapour:
That solid chain of facts, is it snapped for ever?
How stout a show of figures, weakly summing to nonentity.

Or haply, Death, in the doublings of thy thought, shall seem continuous ending:
A dull eternal slumber, not an end abrupt.
O most futile chrysalis, wherefore dost thou sleep?
Dreamless, unconscious, never to awake,—what object in such slumber?
If thou art still to live, it may as well be wakefully as sleeping:
How grovelling must that spirit be, to need eternal sleep;
Or was indeed the toil of life so heavy and so long,
That nevermore can rest refresh thine overburdened soul?
Sleep is a recreance to body, but when was mind asleep?
Even in a swoon it dreameth, though all be forgotten afterwards:
The muscles seek relaxing, and the irritable nerves ask peace:
But life is a constant force, spirit an unquietable impetus;
The eye may wear out as a telescope, and the brain work slow as a machine,
But soul, unwearied, and for ever, is capable of effort unimpaired.

I live, move am conscious: what shall bar my being?
Where is the rude hand, to rend this tissue of existence?
Not thine, shadowy Death, what art thou but a phantom?
Not thine, foul Corruption, what art thou but a fear?
For death is merely absent life, as darkness absent light:
Not even a suspension, for the life hath sailed away, steering gladly somewhere.
And corruption, closely noted, is but a dissolving of the parts,
The parts remain, and nothing lost, to build a better whole.
Moreover, mind is unity, however versatile and rapid;
Thou canst not entertain two coincident ideas, although they quickly follow:
And Unity hath no parts, so that there is nothing to dissolve;
And element is still unchanged in every searching solvent.
Who then shall bid me be annulled,—He that gave me being?
Amen, if God so will; I know that will is love:
But love hath promised life, and therefore I shall live;
So long as He is God, I shall be his Creature!

And here, shrewd reasoner, so eager to prove that thou must perish,
I note a sneer upon thy lip, and ridicule is haply on thy tongue:
How, said he,—creature of a God, and are not all his creatures,—

The lion, and the gnat,—yea, the mushroom, and the crystal,—have all these a soul?
Thy fancies tend to prove too much, and overshoot the mark:
If I die not with brutes, then brutes must live with me?—
I dare not tell thee that they will, for the word is not in my commission:
But of the twain it is the likelier; continuance is the chance:
Men, dying in their sins, are likened unto beasts that perish:
They are dark, animal, insensate, but have they not a lurking soul?
The spirit of a man goeth upward, reasonable, apprehending God;
The spirit of a beast goeth downward, sensual, doting on the creature:
Who told thee they die at dissolution? boldly think it out,—
The multitude of flies, and the multitude of herbs, the world with all its beings:
Is Infinity too narrow, Omnipotence too weak, and Love so anxious to destroy?
Doth Wisdom change its plan, and a Maker cancel his created?
God's will may compass all things, to fashion and to nullify at pleasure:
Yet are there many thoughts of hope, that all which are shall live.
True, there is no conscience in the brute, beyond some educated habit,
They lay them down without a fear, and wake without a hope:
Hunger and pain is of the animal; but when did they reckon or compare?
They live, idealess, in instinct; and while they breathe they gain:
The master is an idol to his dog, who cannot rise beyond him;
And void of capability for God, there would seem small cause for an infinity.
Therefore, caviller, my poor thoughts dare not grant they live;
But is it not a great thing to assume their annihilation—and thine own?
Would it be much if a speck on space, this globe with all its millions,
Verily, after its pollution, were suffered to exist in purity?
Or much, if guiltless creatures, that were cruelly entreated upon earth,
Found some commensurate reward in lower joys hereafter?
Or much, if a Creator, prodigal of life, and filled with the profundity of love,
Rejoice in all creatures of his skill, and lead them to perfection in their kind?
O man, there are many marvels; yet life is more a mystery than death:
For death may be some stagnant life,—but life is present God!

Many are the lurking holes of evil; who shall search them out?

Who so skilled to cut away the cancer with its fibres?
For wily minds with sinuous ease escape from lie to lie;
And cowards driven from the trench steal back to hide again.
Vain were the battle, if a warrior, having slain his foes,
Shall turn and find them vital still, unharmed, yea unashamed:
For Error, dark magician, daily cast out killed,
Quickeneth animate anew beneath the midnight moon:
Once and again, once and again, hath reason answered wisely;
But not the less with brazen front doth folly urge her questions.
It were but unprofitable toil, a stand-up fight with unbelief:
When was there candour in a caviller, and who can satisfy the faithless?
Too long, O truant from the fold, have I tracked thy devious paths:
Too long, treacherous deserter, fought thee as a noble foeman:
Haply, my small art, and an arm too weakly for its weapon,
Hath failed to pierce thine iron coat, and reach thy stricken soul:
Haply, the fervour of my speech, and too patient sifting of thy fancies,
Shall tend to make thee prize them more, as worthier and wiser:
Go to: be mine the gain: we measure swords no more:
Go,—and a word go with thee,—Man, thou ART Immortal!

Child of light, and student in the truth, too long have I forgotten thee:
Lo, after parley with an alien, let me hold sweet converse with a brother.
Glorious hopes, and ineffable imaginings, crowd our holy theme,
Fear hath been slaughtered on the portal, and Doubt driven back to darkness:
For Christ hath died, and we in Him; by faith His all is ours,—
Cross and crown, and love, and life; and we shall reign in Him!
Yea, there is a fitness and a beauty in ascribing immortality to mind,
That its energies and lofty aspirations may have scope for indefinite expansion.
To learn all things is privilege of reason, and that with a growing capability,
But in this age of toil and time we scarce attain to alphabets:
How hardly in the midst of our hurry, and jostled by the cares of life,
Shall a man turn and stop to consider mighty secrets;
With barely hours, and barely powers, to fill up daily duties,
How small the glimpse of knowledge his wondering eye can catch.
And knowledge is a noting of the order wherein God's attributes evolve,
Therefore worthy of the creature, worthy of an angel's seeking;

Yea, and human knowledge, meagre though the harvest,
Hath its roots, both deep and strong; but the plants are exotic to the climate;
All we seem to know demand a longer learning,
History, and science, and prophecy, and art, are workings all of God:
And there are galaxies of globes, millions of unimagined beings,
Other senses, wondrous sounds, and thoughts of thrilling fire,
Powers of strange might, quickening unknown elements,
And attributes and energies of God, which man may never guess.

Not in vain, O brother, hath soul the spurs of enterprise,
Nor aimlessly panteth for adventure, waiting at the cave of mystery:
Not in vain the cup of curiosity, sweet and richly spiced,
Is ruby to the sight, and ambrosia to the taste, and redolent with all fragrance:
Thou shalt drink, and deeply, filling the mind with marvels;
Thou shalt watch no more, lingering, disappointed of thy hope:
Thou shalt roam where road is none, a traveller untrammelled,
Speeding at a wish, emancipate, to where the stars are suns!

Count, count your hopes, heirs of immortality and love;
And hear my kindred faith, and turn again to bless me.
For lo, my trust is strong to dwell in many worlds,
And cull of many brethren there, sweet knowledge ever new:
I yearn for realms where fancy shall be filled, and the ecstasies of freedom shall be felt,
And the soul reign gloriously, risen to its royal destinies:
I look to recognize again, through the beautiful mask of their perfection,
The dear familiar faces I have somewhile loved on earth:
I long to talk with grateful tongue of storms and perils past,
And praise the mighty Pilot that hath steered us through the rapids:
He shall be the focus of it all, the very heart of gladness,—
My soul is athirst for God, the God who dwelt in Man!
Prophet, priest, and king, the sacrifice, the substitute, the Saviour,
Rapture of the blessed in the hunted one of earth, the pardoner in the victim:
How many centuries of joy concentrate in that theme;
How often a Methuselah might count his thousand years, and leave it unexhausted.
And lo, the heavenly Jerusalem, with all its gates one pearl,

That pearl of countless price, the door by which we entered,—
Come, tread the golden streets, and join that glorious throng,
The happy ones of heaven and earth, ten thousand times ten thousand:
Hark, they sing that song,—and cast their crowns before Him;
Their souls alight with Love,—Glory, and Praise, and Immortality!
Veil thine eyes: no son of time may see that holy vision,
And even the seraph at thy side hath covered his face with wings.

Doth he not speak parables?—each one goeth on his way:
Ye that hear, and I that counsel, go on our ways forgetful.
For the terrible realities whereto we tend, are hidden from our eyes,—
We know but heed them not, and walk as if the temporal were all things.
Vanities buzzing on the ear, fill its drowsy chambers,
Slow to dread those coming fears, the thunder and the trumpet;
Motes streaming on the sight, dim our purblind eyes,
Dark to see the ponderous orb of nearing Immortality:
Hemmed in by hostile foes, the trifler is busied on an epigram; ([19])
The dull ox, driven to slaughter, careth but for pasture by the way.
Alas, that the precious things of truth, and the everlasting hills,
The mighty hopes we spake of, and the consciousness we feel,—
Alas, that all the future, and its adamantine facts,
Clouded by the present with intoxicating fumes,—
Should seem even to us, the great expectant heirs,
To us, the responsible and free, fearful sons of reason,
Only as a lovely song, sweet sounds of solemn music,
A pleasant voice, and nothing more,—doth he not speak parables?

Look to thy soul, O man, for none can be surety for his brother:
Behold, for heaven—or for hell,—thou canst not escape from Immortality!

OF IDEAS.

Mind is like a volatile essence, flitting hither and thither,
A solitary sentinel of the fortress body, to show himself every where by turns:
Mind is indivisible and instant, with neither parts nor organs,

That it doeth, it doth quickly, but the whole mind doth it:
An active, versatile agent, untiring in the principle of energy,
Nor space, nor time, nor rest, nor toil, can affect the tenant of the brain;
His dwelling may verily be shattered, and the furniture thereof be dis arranged,
But the particle of Deity in man slumbereth not, neither can be wearied.
However swift to change, even as the field of a kaleidoscope,
It taketh in but one idea at once, moulded for the moment to its likeness
Mind is as the quicksilver, which, poured from vessel to vessel,
Instantly seizeth on a shape, and as instantly again discardeth it;
For it is an apprehensive power, closing on the properties of Matter,
Expanding to enwrap a world, collapsing to prison up an atom:
As, by night, thine irritable eyes may have seen strange changing figures,
Now a wheel, now suddenly a point, a line, a curve, a zigzag,
A maze ever altering, as the dance of gnats upon a sunbeam,
Swift, intricate, neither to be prophesied, nor to be remembered in succession,
So, the mind of a man, single, and perpetually moving,
Flickering about from thought to thought, changed with each idea,
For the passing second metamorphosed to the image of that within its ken,
And throwing its immediate perceptions into each cause of contemplation.
It shall regard a tree; and unconsciously, in separate review,
Embrace its colour, shape, and use, whole and individual conceptions;
It shall read or hear of crime, and cast itself into the commission;
It shall note a generous deed, and glow for a moment as the doer;
It shall imagine pride or pleasure, treading on the edges of temptation;
Or heed of God and of his Christ, and grow transformed to glory.

Wherefore, it is wise and well to guide the mind aright,
That its aptness may be sensitive to good, and shrink with antipathy from evil:
For use will mould and mark it, or non-usage dull and blunt it;—
So to talk of spirit by analogy with substance;
And analogy is a truer guide, than many teachers tell of:
Similitudes are scattered round, to help us, not to hurt us;
Moses, in his every type, and the Greater than a Moses, in his parables,
Preach in terms that all may learn, the philosophic lessons of analogy;
And here, in a topic immaterial, the likeness of analogy is just;
By habits, knit the nerves of mind, and train the gladiator shrewdly:

For thought shall strengthen thinking, and imagery speed imagination
Until thy spiritual inmate shall have swelled to the giant of Otranto.

Nevertheless, heed well, that this Athlete, growing in thy brain,
Be a wholesome Genius, not a cursed Afrite:
And see thou discipline his strength, and point his aim discreetly;
Feed him on humility and holy things, weaned from covetous desires;
Hour by hour, and day by day, ply him with ideas of excellence,
Dragging forth the evil but to loathe, as a Spartan's drunken Helot:
And win, by gradual allurements, the still expanding soul,
To rise from a contemplated universe, even to the Hand that made it.

A common mind perceiveth not beyond his eyes and ears:
The palings of the park of sense enthral this captured roebuck:
And still, though fettered in the flesh, he doth not feel his chains,
Externals are the world to him, and circumstance his atmosphere.
Therefore, tangible pleasures are enough for the animal-man;
He is swift to speak and slow to think, dreading his own dim conscience;
And solitude is terrible, and exile worse than death,
He cannot dwell apart, nor breathe at a distance from the crowd;
But minds of nobler stamp, and chiefest the mint-marked of heaven,
Walk independent by themselves, freely manumitted of externals:
They carry viands with them, and need no refreshment by the way,
Nor drink of other wells than their own inner fountain.
Strange shall it seem how little such a man will lean upon the accidents of life,
He is winged, and needeth not a staff; if it break,—he shall not fall.
And lightly perchance doth he remember the stale trivialities around him,
He liveth in the realm of thought, beyond the world of things:
These are but transient Matter, and himself enduring Spirit:
And worldliness will laugh to scorn that sublimated wisdom.
His eyes may open on a prison-cell, but the bare walls glow with imagery;
His ears may be filled with execration, but are listening to the music of sweet thoughts;
He may dwell in a hovel with a hero's heart, and canopy his penury with peace,
For mind is a kingdom to the man, who gathereth his pleasure from Ideas.

OF NAMES.

ADAM gave the name, when the Lord had made his creature,
For God led them in review, to see what man would call them:
As they struck his senses, he proclaimed their sounds,
A name for the distinguishing of each, a numeral by which it should be known:
He specified the partridge by her cry, and the forest prowler by his roaring,
The tree by its use, and the flower by its beauty, and every thing according to its truth.

There is an arbitrary name, whereunto the idea attacheth;
And there is a reasonable name, linking its fitness to idea:
Yet shall these twain run in parallel courses,
Neither shalt thou readily discern the habit from the nature.
For mind is apt and quick to wed ideas and names together,
Nor stoppeth its perception to be curious of priorities;
And there is but little in the sound, as some have vainly fancied.
The same tone in different tongues shall be suitable to opposite ideas;
Yea, take an ensample in thine own; consider similar words:
How various and contrary the thoughts those kindred names produce:
A house shall seem a fitting word to call a roomy dwelling,
Yet there is a like propriety in the small smooth sound, a mouse:
Mountain, as if of a necessity, is a word both mighty and majestic,—
What heed ye then of fountain?—flowing silver in the sun.

Many a fair flower is burdened with preposterous appellatives,
Which the wiser simplicity of rustics entitled by its beauties:
And often the conceit of science, loving to be thought cosmopolite,
Shall mingle names of every clime, alike obscure to each.
There is wisdom in calling a thing fitly; name should note particulars
Through a character obvious to all men, and worthy of their instant acceptation.
The herbalist had a simple cause for every word upon his catalogue,
But now the mouth of Botany is filled with empty sound;
And many a peasant hath an answer on his tongue, concerning some vexed flower,
Shrewder than the centipede phrase wherewithal philosophers invest it.

For that, the foolishness of pride, and flatteries of cringing homage,
Strew with chaff the threshing-floors of science; names perplex them all:
The entomologist, who hath pried upon an insect, straightway shall endow it with his name;
It had many qualities and marks of note,—but in chief, a vain observer:
The geographer shall journey to the pole, through biting frost and desolation,
And, for some simple patron's sake, shall name that land, the happy:
The fossilist hath found a bone, the rib of some huge lizard,
And forthwith standeth to it sponsor, to tack himself on reptile immortalities:
The sportsman, hunting at the Cape, found some strange-horned antelope,
The spots are new, the fame is cheap, and so his name is added.
Thus, obscurities encumber knowledge, even by the vanity of men,
Who play into each other's hand the game of giving names.

Various are the names of men, and drawn from different wells;
Aspects of body, or characters of mind, the creature's first idea:
And some have sprung of trades, and some of dignities or office;
Other some added to a father's, and yet more growing from a place:
Animal creation, with sciences and things,—their composites, and near associations,
Contributed their symbolings of old, wherewith to title men:
And heraldry set upon its cresture the figured attributes as ensigns
By which, as by a name concrete, its bearer should be known.

Egypt opened on the theme, dressing up her gods in qualities;
Horns of power, feathers of the swift, mitres of catholic dominion,
The sovereign asps, the circle everlasting, the crook and thong of justice,
By many mystic shapes and sounds displayed the idol's name.
Thereafter, high-plumed warriors, the chieftains of Etruria and Troy,
And Xerxes, urging on his millions to the tomb of pride, Thermopylæ,
And Hiero with his bounding ships all figured at the prow,
And Rome's Prætorian standards, piled with strange devices,
And stout crusaders pressing to the battle, locked in shining steel,—
These all in their speaking symbols, earned, or wore, a name.
Eve, the mother of all living, and Abraham, father of a multitude,
Jacob, the supplanter, and David the beloved, and all the worthies of old time,

Noah, who came for consolation, and Benoni, son of sorrow,
Kings and prophets, children of the East, owned each his title of significance.

There be names of high descent, and thereby storied honours;
Names of fair renown, and therein characters of merit:
But to lend the lowborn noble names, is to shed upon them ridicule and evil
Yea, many weeds run rank in pride, if men have dubbed them cedars.
And to herald common mediocrity with the noisy notes of fame,
Tendeth to its deeper scorn; as if it were to call the mole a mammoth.
Yet shall ye find the trader's babe dignified with sounding titles,
And little hath the father guessed the harm he did his child:
For either may they breed him discontent, a peevish repining at his station,
Or point the finger of despite at the mule in the trappings of an elephant:
And it is a kind of theft to filch appellations from the famous,
A soiling of the shrines of praise with folly's vulgar herd.
Prudence hath often gone ashamed for the name they added to his father's,
If minds of mark and great achievements bore it well before;
For he walketh as the jay in the fable, though not by his own folly,
Another's fault hath compassed his misfortune, making him a martyr to his name.

Who would call the tench a whale, or style a torch, Orion?
Yet many a silly parent hath dealt likewise with his nursling.
Give thy child a fit distinguishment, making him sole tenant of a name,
For it were a sore hindrance to hold it in common with a hundred;
In the Babel of confused identities fame is little feasible,
The felon shall detract from the philanthropist, and the sage share honours with the simple:
Still, in thy title of distinguishment, fall not into arrogant assumption,
Steering from caprice and affectations; and for all thou doest, have a reason.
He that is ambitious for his son, should give him untried names,
For those that have served other men, haply may injure by their evils;
Or otherwise may hinder by their glories; therefore set him by himself,
To win for his individual name some clear specific praise.
There were nine Homers, all goodly sons of song; but where is any record of the eight?

One grew to fame, an Aaron's rod, and swallowed up his brethren : ([80])
Who knoweth ? more distinctly titled, those dead eight had lived ;
But the censers were ranged in a circle, to mingle their sweets without a difference.

Art thou named of a common crowd, and sensible of high aspirings ?
It is hard for thee to rise,—yet strive : thou mayst be among them a Musæus.
Art thou named of a family, the same in successive generations ?
It is open to thee still to earn for epithets, such an one, the good or great.
Art thou named foolishly ? show that thou art wiser than thy fathers,
Live to shame their vanity or sin by dutiful devotion to thy sphere.
Art thou named discreetly ? it is well, the course is free ;
No competitor shall claim thy colours, neither fix his faults upon thee :
Hasten to the goal of fame between the posts of duty,
And win a blessing from the world, that men may love thy name;
Yea, that the unction of its praise, in fragrance well deserving,
May float adown the stream of time, like ambergris at sea ;
So thy sons may tell their sons, and those may teach their children,
He died in goodness, as he lived ;—and left us his good name.
And more than these : there is a roll whereon thy name is written ;
See that, on the Book of Doom, that name is fixed in light :
Then, safe within a better home, where time and its titles are not found,
God will give thee his new Name, and write it on thy heart :
A Name, better than of sons, a Name dearer than of daughters,
A Name of union, peace, and praise, as numbered in thy God.

OF THINGS.

Abstracted from all substance, and flying with the feathered flock of thoughts,
The idea of a thing hath the nature of its Soul, a separate seeming essence :
Intimately linked to the idea, suggesting many qualities,
The name of a thing hath the nature of its Mind, an intellectual recorder:
And the matter of a thing, concrete, is a Body to the perfect creature,

Compacted three in one, as all things else within the Universe.
Nothing canst thou add to them, and nothing take away, for all have these proportions,
The thought, the word, the form, combining in the Thing:
All separate, yet harmonizing well, and mingled each with other,
One whole in several parts, yet each part spreading to a whole:
The idea is a whole, and the meaning phrase that spake idea, a whole,
And the matter, as ye see it, is a whole; the mystery of true tri-unity:
Yea, there is even a deeper mystery,—which none, I wot, can fathom,
Matter, different from properties whereby the solid substance is described.
For, size and weight, cohesion and the like, live distinct from matter,
Yet who can image matter, unendowed with size and weight?
As in the spiritual, so in the material, man must rest with patience,
And wait for other eyes wherewith to read the books of God.

Men have talked learnedly of atoms, as if matter could be ever indivisible.
They talk, but ill are skilled to teach, and darken truth by fancies:
An atom by our grosser sense was never yet conceived,
And nothing can be thought so small, as not to be divided:
For an atom runneth to infinity, and never shall be caught in space,
And a molecule is no more indivisible than Saturn's belted orb.
Things intangible, multiplied by multitudes, never will amass to substance,
Neither can a thing which may be touched, be made of impalpable proportions;
The sum of indivisibles must needs be indivisible, as adding many nothings,
And the building up of atoms into matter is but a silly sophism;
Lucretius and keen Anaximander, and many that have followed in their thoughts,
(For error hath a long black shadow, dimming light for ages,)
In the foolishness of men without a God fancied to fashion Matter
Of intangibles, and therefore uncohering, indivisibles and therefore Spirit.

Things breed thoughts; therefore at Thebes and Heliopolis,
In hieroglyphic sculptures are the priestly secrets written;
Things breed thoughts; therefore was the Athens of Idolatry
Set with carved images, frequent as the trees of Academus;
Things breed thoughts; therefore the Brahmin and the Burman
With mythologic shapes adorn their coarse pantheon;
Things breed thoughts; therefore the statue and the picture,

Relics, rosaries, and miracles in act, quicken the Papist in his worship:
Things breed thoughts; therefore the lovers at their parting,
Interchanged with tearful smiles the dear reminding tokens;
Things breed thoughts; therefore, when the clansman met his foe,
The blood-stained claymore in his hand revived the memories of vengeance.

Things teach with double force; through the animal eye, and through the mind,
And the eye catcheth in an instant, what the ear shall not learn within an hour.
Thence is the potency of travel, the precious might of its advantages
To compensate its dissipative harm, its toil and cost and danger.
Ulysses, wandering to many shores, lived in many cities,
And thereby learnt the minds of men, and stored his own more richly:
Herodotus, the accurate and kindly, spake of that he saw,
And reaped his knowledge on the spot, in fertile fields of Egypt:
Lycurgus culled from every clime the golden fruits of justice;
And Plato roamed through foreign lands, to feed on truth in all.
For travel, conversant with Things, bringeth them in contact with the mind;
We breathe the wholesome atmosphere about ungarbled truth:
Pictures of fact are painted on the eye, to decorate the house of intellect,
Rather than visions of fancy, filling all the chambers with a vapour.
For, in ideas, the great mind will exaggerate, and the lesser extenuate truth:
But in Things the one is chastened, and the other quickened, to equality;
And in Names,—though a property be told, rather than an arbitrary accident,
Still shall the thought be vague or false, if none hath seen the Thing;
For in Things the property with accident standeth in a mass concrete,
These cannot cheat the sense, nor elude the vigilance of spirit.
Travel is a ceaseless fount of surface education,
But its wisdom will be simply superficial, if thou add not thoughts to things:
Yet, aided by the varnish of society, things may serve for thoughts,
Till many dullards that have seen the world shall pass for scholars:
Because one single glance will conquer all descriptions,
Though graphic, these left some unsaid, though true, these tended to some error,
And the most witless eye that saw, had a juster notion of its object
Than the shrewdest mind that heard and shaped its gathered thoughts of Things.

OF FAITH.

Confidence was bearer of the palm; for it looked like conviction of desert:
And where the strong is well assured, the weaker soon allow it.
Majesty and beauty are commingled, in moving with immutable decision,
And well may charm the coward hearts that turn and hide for fear.
Faith, firmness, confidence, consistency,—these are well allied;
Yea, let a man press on in aught, he shall not lack of honour:
For such an one seemeth as superior to the native instability of creatures:
That he doeth, he doeth as a god, and men will marvel at his courage.
Even in crimes a partial praise cannot be denied to daring,
And many fearless chiefs have won the friendship of a foe.

Confidence is conqueror of men; victorious both over them and in them;
The iron will of one stout heart shall make a thousand quail:
A feeble dwarf, dauntlessly resolved, will turn the tide of battle,
And rally to a nobler strife the giants that had fled:
The tenderest child, unconscious of a fear, will shame the man to danger,
And when he dared it, danger died, and faith had vanquished fear.
Boldness is akin to power: yea, because ignorance is weakness,
Knowledge with unshrinking might will nerve the vigorous hand:
Boldness hath a startling strength; the mouse may fright a lion,
And oftentimes the horned herd is scared by some brave cur.
Courage hath analogy with faith, for it standeth both in animal and moral;
The true is mindful of a God, the false is stout in self:
But true or false, the twain are faith; and faith worketh wonders:
Never was a marvel done upon the earth, but it had sprung of faith:
Nothing noble, generous, or great, but faith was the root of the achievement;
Nothing comely, nothing famous, but its praise is faith.
Leonidas fought in human faith, as Joshua in divine:
Xenophon trusted to his skill, and the sons of Mattathias to their cause: (21)
In faith Columbus found a path across those untried waters:
The heroines of Arc and Saragossa fought in earthly faith:
Tell was strong, and Alfred great, and Luther wise, by faith;
Margaret by faith was valiant for her son, and Wallace mighty for his people:

Faith in his reason made Socrates sublime, as faith in his science, Galileo:
Ambassadors in faith are bold, and unreproved for boldness:
Faith urged Fabius to delays, and sent forth Hannibal to Cannæ:
Cæsar at the Rubicon, Miltiades at Marathon: both were sped by faith.
I set not all in equal spheres: I number not the martyr with the patriot;
I class not the hero with his horse, because the twain have courage:
But only for ensample and instruction, that all things stand by faith;
Albeit faith of divers kinds, and varying in degrees.
There is faith towards men, and there is faith towards God;
The latter is the gold, and the former is the brass; but both are sturdy metal:
And the brass mingled with the gold floweth into rich Corinthian;
A substance bright and hard and keen, to point Achilles' spear:
So shalt thou stop the way against the foes that hem thee;
Trust in God, to strengthen man;—be bold, for He doth help.

Yet more: for confidence in man, even to the worst and meanest,
Hath power to overcome his ill, by charitable good.
Fling thine unreserving trust, even on the conscience of a culprit,
Soon wilt thou shame him by thy faith, and he will melt and mend:
The nest of thieves will harm thee not, if thou dost bear thee boldly:
Boldly, yea and kindly, as relying on their honour:
For the hand so stout against agression, is quite disarmed by charity;
And that warm sun will thaw the heart case-hardened by long frost.
Treat men gently, trust them strongly, if thou wish their weal;
Or cautious doubts and bitter thoughts will tempt the best to foil thee;
Believe the well in sanguine hope, and thou shalt reap the better;
But if thou deal with men so ill, thy dealings make them worse.
Despair not of some gleams of good still lingering in the darkest,
And among veterans in crime, plead thou as with their children:
So astonied at humanities, the bad heart long estranged,
Shall even weep to feel himself so little worth thy love;
In wholesome sorrow will he bless thee; yea, and in that spirit may repent;
Thus, wilt thou gain a soul, in mercy given to thy faith.

Look aside to lack of faith, the mass of ills it bringeth;
All things treacherous, base, and vile, dissolving the brotherhood of men.
Bonds break; the cement hath lost its hold, and each is separate from other;

That which should be neighbourly and good, is cankered into bitterness and evil.
O thou serpent, fell Suspicion, coiling coldly round the heart,—
O thou asp of subtle Jealousy, stinging hotly to the soul,—
O distrust, reserve, and doubt,—what reptile shapes are here,
Poisoning the garden of a world with death among its flowers!
No need of many words, the tale is easy to be told:
A point will touch the truth, a line suggest the picture.
For if, in thine own home, a cautious man and captious,
Thou hintest at suspicion of a servant, thou soon wilt make a thief;
Or if, too keen in care, thou dost evidently disbelieve thy child,
Thou hast injured the texture of his honour, and smoothed to him the way of lying:
Or if thou observest upon friends, as seeking thee selfishly for interest,
Thou hast hurt their kindliness to thee, and shalt be paid with scorn:
Or if, O silly ones of marriage, your foul and foolish thoughts,
Hashly misinterpreting in each the levity of innocence for sin,
Shall pour upon the lap of home pain where once was pleasure,
And mix contentions in the cup, that mantled once with comforts,
Bitterly and justly shall ye rue the punishment due to unbelief;
Ye trust not each the other, nor the mutual vows of God;
Take heed, for the pit may now be near, a pit of your own digging,—
Faith abused tempteth unto crime, and doubt may make its monster.

Man verily is vile, but more in capability than action;
His sinfulness is deep, but his transgressions may be few, even from the absence of temptation:
He is hanging in a gulf midway, but the air is breathable about him:
Thrust him not from that slight hold, to perish in the vapours underneath,
For, God pleadeth with the deaf, as having ears to hear,
Christ speaketh to the dead, as those that are capable of living;
And an evil teacher is that man, a tempter to much sin,
Who looketh on his hearers with distrust, and hath no confidence in brethren.
All may mend; and sympathies are healing; and reason hath its influence with the worst;
And in those worst is ample hope, if only thou have charity, and faith.

Somewhiles have I watched a man exchanging the sobriety of faith,

Old lamps for new,—even for fanatical excitements.
He gained surface, but lost solidity; heat, in lieu of health;
And still with swelling words and thoughts he scorned his ancient coldness:
But his strength was shorn as Samson's; he walked he knew not whither;
Doubt was on his daily path; and duties showed not certain.
Until, in an hour of enthusiasm, stung with secret fears,
He pinned the safety of his soul on some false prophet's sleeve.
And then, that sure word failed; and with it failed his faith;
It failed, and fell; O deep and dreadful was his fall in faith.
He could not stop, with reason's rein, his coursers on the slope,
And so they dashed him down the cliff of hardened unbelief.
With overreaching grasp he had strained for visionary treasures,
But a fiend had cheated his presumption, and hurled him to despair;
So he lay in his blood, the victim of a credulous false faith,
And many nights, and night-like days, he dwelt in outer darkness,
But, within a while, his variable mind caught a new impression,
A new impression of the good old stamp, that sealed him when a child:
He was softened, and abjured his infidelity; he was wiser, and despised his credulity:
And turned again to simple faith more simply than before.
Experience had declared too well his mind was built of water,
And so renouncing strength in self, he fixed his faith in God.

It is not for me to stipulate for creeds; Bible, Church, and Reason,
These three shall lead the mind, if any can, to truth.
But I must stipulate for faith; both God and man demand it:
Trust is great in either world, if any would be well.
Verily, the skeptical propensity is an universal foe;
Sneering Pyrrho never found, nor cared to find, a friend:
How could he trust another? and himself, whom would he not deceive?
His proper gains were all his aim, and interests clash with kindness.
So, the Bedouin goeth armed, an enemy to all,
The spear is stuck beside his couch, the dagger hid beneath his pillow.
For society, void of mutual trust, of credit, and of faith,
Would fall asunder as a waterspout, snapped from the cloud's attraction.

Faith may rise into miracles of might, as some few wise have shown:
Faith may sink into credulities of weakness, as the mass of fools have witnessed.

Therefore, in the first, saints and martyrs have fulfilled their mission,
Conquering dangers, courting deaths, and triumphing in all.
Therefore, in the last, the magician and the witch, victims of their own delusion,
Have gained the bitter wages of impracticable sins.
They believed in allegiance with Satan; they worked in that belief,
And thereby earned the loss and harm of guilt that might not be,
For, faith hath two hands; with the one it addeth virtue to indifferents;
Yea, it sanctified a Judith and a Jael, for what otherwise were treachery and murder:
With the other hand it heapeth crime even on impossibles or simples,
And many a wizard well deserved the faggot for his faith:
He trusted in his intercourse with evil, he sacrificed heartily to fiends,
He withered up with curses to the limit of his will, and was vile, because he thought himself a villain.

A great mind is ready to believe, for he hungereth to feed on facts,
And the gnawing stomach of his ignorance craveth unceasing to be filled:
A little mind is boastful and incredulous, for he fancieth all knowledge is his own,
So will he cavil at a truth; how should it be true, and he not know it?—
There is an easy scheme, to solve all riddles by the sensual,
And thus, despising mysteries, to feel the more sufficient:
For it comforteth the foul hard heart, to reject the pure unseen,
And relieveth the dull soft head, to hinder one from gazing upon vacancy.
True wisdom, labouring to expound, heareth others readily;
False wisdom, sturdy to deny, closeth up her mind to argument.
The sum of certainties is found so small, their field so wide an universe,
That many things may truly be, which man hath not conceived:
The characters revealed of God are a strong mind's sole assurance
That any strangeness may not stand a sober theme for faith.
Ignorance being light denied, this ought to show the stronger in its view,
But ignorance is commonly a double negative, both of light and morals:
So, adding vanity to blindness, for ease it taketh refuge in a doubt,
And aching soon with ceaseless doubt, it finisheth the strife by misbelieving.

Faith, by its very nature, shall embrace both credence and obedience:
Yea, the word for both is one, and cannot be divided. (**)

For, work void of faith, wherein can it be counted for a duty?
And faith not seen in work,—whereby can the doctrine be discovered?
Faith in religion is an instrument; a handle, and the hand to turn it;
Less a condition than a mean, and more an operation than a virtue.
A moral sickness, like to sin, must have a moral cure;
And faith alone can heal the mind, whose malady is sense.
Ye are told of God's deep love; they that believe will love him;
They that love him, will obey; and obedience hath its blessing.
Ye are taught of the soul's great price: they that believe will prize it,
And, prizing soul, will cherish well the hopes that make it happy.
Effects spring from feelings: and feelings grow of faith:
If a man conceive himself insulted, will not his anger smite?
Thus, let a soul believe his state, his danger, destiny, redemption,
Will he not feel eager to be safe, like him that kept the prison at Philippi?

A mother had an only son, and sent him out to sea:
She was a widow, and in penury; and he must seek his fortunes.
How often in the wintry nights, when waves and winds were howling,
Her heart was torn with sickening dread, and bled to see her boy.
And on one sunny morn, when all around was comfort,
News came that, weeks agone, the vessel had been wrecked;
Yea, wrecked, and he was dead! they had seen him perish in his agony:
Oh then, what agony was like to hers,—for she believed the tale?
She was bowed and broken down with sorrow, and uncomforted in prayer;
Many nights she mourned, and pined, and had no hope but death.
But on a day, while sorely she was weeping, a stranger broke upon her loneliness,—
He had news to tell, that weather-beaten man, and must not be denied:
And what were the wonder-working words that made this mourner joyous,
That swept her heaviness away, and filled her world with praise?
Her son was saved,—is alive,—is near!—O did she stop to question?
No, rushing in the force of faith, she met him at the door!

OF HONESTY.

All is vanity which is not honesty;—thus is it graven on the tomb;—
And there is no wisdom but in piety;—so the dead man preacheth:

For, in a simple village church, among those classic shades
Which sylvan Evelyn loved to rear, (his praise and my delight,)
These, the words of truth, are writ upon his sepulchre
Who learnt much lore, and knew all trees from the cedar to the hyssop on the wall.
A just conjunction, godliness and honesty, ministering to both worlds,
Well wed, and ill to be divided, a pair that God hath joined together.
I touch not now the vulgar thought, as of tricks and cheateries in trade;
I speak of honest purpose, character, speech and action:
For an honest man hath special need of charity, and prudence,
Of a deep and humbling self-acquaintance, and of blessed commerce with his God,
So that the keennesses of truth may be freed from asperities of censure,
And the just but vacillating mind be not made the pendulum of arguments:
For a false reason, shrewdly put, can often not be answered on the instant,
And prudence looketh unto faith, content to wait solutions:
Yea, it looketh, yea, it waiteth, still holding honesty in leash,
Lest, as a hot young hound, it track not game, but vermin.
Many a man of honest heart, but ignorant of self and God,
Hath followed the marsh-fires of pestilence, esteeming them the lights of truth;
He heard a cause, which he had not skill to solve,—and so received it gladly,
And that cause brought its consequence of harm to an unstable soul.
Prudence for a man's own sake, never should be separate from honesty
And charity, for other's good and his, must still be joined therewith:
For the harshly chiding tongue hath neither pleasuring nor profit,
And the cold unsympathizing heart never gained a good.
Sin is a sore, and folly is a fever; touch them tenderly for healing;
The bad chirurgeon's awkward knife harmeth spite of honesty.
Still, a rough diamond is better than the polished paste,—
That courteous, flattering fool, who spake of vice as virtue:
And honesty, even by itself, though making many adversaries,
Whom prudence might have set aside, or charity have softened,
Evermore will prosper at the last, and gain a man great honour
By giving others many goods, to his own cost and hindrance.

Freedom is father of the honest, and sturdy Independence is his brother:
These three, with heart and hand, dwell together in unity.

The blunt yeoman, stout and true, will speak unto princes unabashed:
His mind is loyal, just and free, a crystal in its plain integrity;
What should make such an one ashamed? where courtiers kneel, he standeth;—
I will indeed bow before the king, but knees were knit for God.
And many such there be, of a high and noble conscience,
Honourable, generous, and kind, though blessed with little light:
What should he barter for his freedom? some petty gain of gold?
Free of speech, and free in act, magnates honour him for boldness:
Long may he flourish in his peace, and a stalwart race around him,
Rooted in the soil like oaks, and hardy as the pine upon the mountains!

Yet, there be others, that will truckle to a lie, selling honesty for interest:
And do they gain?—they gain but loss; a little cash, with scorn.
Behold, the sorrowful change wrought upon a fallen nature:
He hath lost his own esteem, and other men's respect;
For the buoyancy of upright faith, he is clothed in the heaviness of cringing;
For plain truth where none could err, he hath chosen tortuous paths;
In lieu of his majesty of countenance—the timorous glances of servility:
Instead of Freedom's honest pride,—the spirit of a slave.

Nevertheless, there is somewhat to be pleaded, even for a necessary guile,
Whilst the world, and all that is therein, lieth deep in evil.
Who can be altogether honest,—a champion never out of mail,
Ready to break a lance for truth with every crowding error?
Who can be altogether honest,—dragging out the secrecies of life,
And risking to be lashed and loathed for each unkind disclosure?
Who can be altogether honest,—living in perpetual contentions,
And prying out the petty cheats that swell the social scheme?
For he must speak his instant mind,—a mind corrupt and sinful,
Exhibiting to other men's disgust its undisguised deformities;
He must utter all the hatred of his heart, and add to it the venom of his tongue;
Shall he feel, and hide his feelings? that were the meanness of a hypocrite.—
Still, O man, such hypocrisy is better than this bold honesty to sin:
Kill the feeling, or conceal it: let shame at least do the work of charity.
O charity, thou livest not in warnings, meddling among men,

Rebuking every foolish word, and censuring small sins;
This is not thy secret,—rather wilt thou hide their multitude,
And silence the condemning tongue, and wearisome exhortation,
But for thee, thy strength and zeal shine in encouragement to good,
Lifting up the lantern of ensample, that wanderers may find the way:
That lantern is not lit to gaze on all the hatefulness of evil,
But set on high for life and light, the loveliness of good.
The hard censorious mind sitteth as a keen anatomist,
Tracking up the fibres in corruption, and prying on a fearful corpse:
But the charitable soul is a young lover, enamoured little wisely,
That saw no fault in her he loved, and sought to see one less;
So, in his kind and genial light, she grew more worthy of his love;
Won to good by gentle suns, and not by frowning tempest.

Verily, infirm thyself,—be slow to chide a brother's imperfections:
For many times the decent veil must hang on faults of nature,
And the rude hands, that rend it, offend against the modesty of right,
While seeming zeal, and its effort to do good, is only feigned self-praise.
Often will the meannesses of life, hidden away in corners,
Prove wisdom; and the generous is glad to leave them unregarded in the shade.
The follies none are found to praise, let them die unblamed:
Thine honest strife will only tend to make some think them wise:
And small conventional deceits, let them live uncensured:
Or if thou war with pigmies, thou shalt haply help the cranes.
Where to be blind was safety, Ovid had been wise for winking: ([23])
And when a tell-tale might do harm, be sure it is prudent to be dumb:
That which is just and fit is often found combating with honesty:
In the cause of good, be wise; and in a case indifferent, keep silence.

Let honesty's unblushing face be shaded by the mantle of humility,
So shall it shine a lamp of love, and not the torch of strife:
Otherwise the lantern of Diogenes, presumptuously thrust before the face,
If it never find an honest man, shall often make an angered.
Let honesty be companied by charity of heart, lest it walk unwelcome,
Or the mouthing censor of others and himself, soon shall sink to scorn.
Let honesty be added unto innocence of life: then a man may only be its martyr:

But if openness of speech be found with secrecy of guilt, the martyr will be seen a malefactor.

There is a cunning scheme, to put on surface bluntness,
And cover still deep water, with the clamorous ripples of a shallow.
For a man, to gain his selfish ends, will make a stalking-horse of honesty;
And hide his poaching limbs behind, that he may cheat the quicker.
Such an one is loud and ostentatious, full of oaths for argument,
Boastful of honour and sincerity, and not to be put down by facts:
He is obstinate, and showeth it for firmness; he is rude, displaying it for truth:
And glorieth in doggedness of temper, as if it were uncompromising justice.
Be aware of such a man; his brawling covereth designs;
This specious show of honesty cometh as the herald of a thief:
His feint is made with awkward clashing on the buckler's boss,
But meanwhile doth his secret skill ensure its fatal aim.
This is the hypocrite of honesty; ye may know him by an overacted part;
Taking pains to turn and twist, where other men walk straight;
Or walking straight, he will not step aside to let another pass,
But roughly pusheth on, provoking opposition on the way;
He is full of disquietude for calmness, full of intriguing for simplicity,
Valorous with those who cannot fight, and humble to the brave;
Where brotherly advice were good, this man rudely blameth,
And on some small occasion, flattereth with coarse praise.
The craven in a lion's skin hath conquer'd by his character for courage;
Sheep's clothing helped the wolf, till he slew by his character for kind ness.

For honesty hath many gains, and well the wise have known
This will prosper to the end, and fill their house with gold.
The phosphorus of cheatery will fade, and all its profit perish,
While honesty, with glowing light, endureth as the moon.
Yea, it would be wise in a world of thieves, where cheating were a virtue,
To dare the vice of honesty, if any would be rich.
For that which by the laws of God is heightened into duty,
Ever, in the practice of a man, will be seen both policy and privilege.

Thank God, ye toilers for your bread, in that, daily labouring,
He hath suffered the bubbles of self-interest to float upon the stream of duty:
For honesty, of every kind, approved by God and man,
Of wealth and better weal is found the richest cornucopia.
Tempered by humbleness and charity, honesty of speech hath honour;
And mingled well with prudence, honesty of purpose hath its praise:
Trust paveth homage unto truth, rewarding honesty of action:
And all men love to lean on him, who never failed nor fainted.
Freedom gloweth in his eyes, and nobleness of nature at his heart,
And Independence took a crown and fixed it on his head:
So, he stood in his intregrity, just and firm of purpose,
Aiding many, fearing none, a spectacle to angels, and to men:
Yea,—when the shattered globe shall rock in the throes of dissolution,
Still, will he stand in his integrity, sublime—an honest man.

OF SOCIETY.

BETTER is the mass of men, Suspicion, than thy fears
Kinder than thy thoughts, O chilling heart of Prudence,
Purer than thy judgments, ascetic tongue of censure,
In all things worthier to love, if not also wiser to esteem.
Yea, let the moralist condemn, there be large extenuations of his verdict,
Let the misanthrope shun men and abjure, the most are rather loveable than hateful.
How many pleasant faces shed their light on every side!
How many angels unawares have crossed thy casual way!
How often, in thy journeyings, hast thou made thee instant friends,
Found, to be loved a little while, and lost, to meet no more;
Friends of happy reminiscence, although so transient in their converse,
Liberal, cheerful, and sincere, a crowd of kindly traits.
I have sped by land and sea, and mingled with much people,
But never yet could find the spot unsunned by human kindness:
Some more and some less,—but, truly, all can claim a little;
And a man may travel through the world, and sow it thick with friendships.

There be indeed, to say it in all sorrow, bad apostate souls,
Deserted of their ministering angels, and given up to liberty of sin,—
And other some, the miserly and mean, whose eyes are keen and greedy,
With stony hearts, and iron fists, to filch, and scrape, and clutch,—
And others yet again, the coarse in mind, selfish, sensual, brutish,
Seeming as incapable of softer thoughts, and dead to better deeds;
Such, no lover of the good, no follower of the generous and gentle,
Can nearer grow to love, than may consist with pity.
Few verily are these among the mass, and cast in fouler moulds,
Few and poor in friends, and well-deserving of their poverty:
Yet, or ever thou hast harshly judged, and linked their presence to disgust,
Consider well the thousand things that made them all they are.
Thou hast not thought upon the causes, ranged in consecutive necessity,
Which tended long to these effects, with sure constraining power.
For each of those unlovely ones, if thou couldst hear his story,
Hath much to urge of just excuse, at least as men count justice:
Foolish education, thwarted opportunities, natural propensities unchecked,—
Thus were they discouraged from all good, and pampered in their evil:
And if thou wilt apprehend them well, tenderly looking on temptations,
Bearing the base indulgently, and liberally dealing with the froward,
Thou shalt discern a few fair fruits even upon trees so withered,
Thou shalt understand how some may praise, and some be found to love them.

Nevertheless for these, my counsel is, Avoid them if thou canst;
For the finer edges of thy virtues will be dulled by attrition with their vice.
And there is an enemy within thee; either to palliate their sin,
Until, for surface sweetness, thou too art drawn adown the vortex;
Or, even unto fatal pride, to glorify thy purity by contrast,
Until the publican and the harlot stand nearer heaven than the Pharisee:
Or daily strife against their ill, in subtleness may irritate thy soul,
And in that struggle thou shalt fail, even through infirmity of goodness;
Or, callous by continuance of injuries, thou wilt cease to pardon,
Cease to feel, and cease to care, a cold case-hardened man.
Beware of their example,—and thine own; beware the hazards of the battle;
But chiefly be thou ware of this, an unforgiving spirit.

Many are the dangers and temptations compassing a bad man's presence:
The upas hath a poisonous shade, and who would slumber there?
Wherefore, avoid them if thou canst; only, under providence and duty,
If thy lot be cast with Kedar, patiently and silently live to their rebuke.

How beautiful thy feet, and full of grace thy coming,
O better, kind companion, that art well for either world!
There is an atmosphere of happiness floating round that man,
Love is throned upon his heart, and light is found within his dwelling,
His eyes are rayed with peacefulness, and wisdom waiteth on his tongue;
Seek him out, cherish him well, walking in the halo of his influence;
For he shall be fragrance to thy soul, as a garden of sweet lilies,
Hedged and apart from the outer world, an island of the blest among the seas.

There is an outer world, and there is an inner centre;
And many varying rings concentric round the self:
For, first, about a man,—after his communion with heaven,—
Is found the helpmate even as himself, the wife of his vows and his affections:
See then that ye love in faith, scorning petty jealousies,
For Satan spoileth too much love, by souring it with doubts;
See that intimacy die not to indifference, nor anxiety sink into moroseness,
And tend ye well the mutual minds bound in a copartnership for life.

Next of those concentric circles, radiating widely in circumference,
Wheel in wheel, and world in world,—come the band of children:
A tender nest of soft young hearts, each to be separately studied,
A curious eager flock of minds, to be severally tamed and tutored.
And a man, blest with these, hath made his own society,
He is independent of the world, hanging on his friends more loosely:
For the little faces round his hearth are friends enow for him,
If he seek others, it is for the sake of these, and less for his own pleasure.
What companionship so sweet, yea, who can teach so well
As these pure budding intellects, and bright unsullied hearts?
What voice so musical as theirs, what visions of elegance so comely,
What thoughts and hopes and holy prayers, can others cause like these?
If ye count society for pastime,—what happier recreation than a nursling,
Its winning ways, its prattling tongue, its innocence and mirth?
If ye count society for good,—how fair a field is here,
To guide these souls to God, and multiply thyself for heaven!

And this sweet social commerce with thy children, groweth as their growth,
Unless thou fail of duty, or have weaned them by thine absence.
Keep them near thee, rear them well, guide, correct, instruct them:
And be the playmate of their games, the judge in their complainings.
So shall the maiden and the youth love thee as their sympathizing friend,
And bring their joys to share with thee, their sorrows for consoling:
Yea, their inmost hopes shall yearn to thee for counsel,
They will not hide their very loves if thou hast won their trust;
But, even as man and woman, shall they gladly seek their father,
Feeling yet as children feel, though void of fear in honour:
And thou shalt be a Nestor in the camp, the just and good old man,
Hearty still, though full of years, and held the friend of all;
No secret shall be kept from thee; for if ill, thy wisdom may repair it;
If well, thy praise is precious; and they would not miss that prize.
O the blessing of a home, where old and young mix kindly,
The young unawed, the old unchilled, in unreserved communion!
O that refuge from the world, when a stricken son or daughter
May seek, with confidence of love, a father's hearth and heart!
Sure of a welcome, though others cast them out; of kindness, though men scorn them;
And finding there the last to blame, the earliest to commend.
Come unto me, my son, if sin shall have tempted thee astray,
I will not chide thee like the rest, but help thee to return;
Come unto me, my son, if men rebuke and mock thee,
There always shall be one to bless,—for I am on thy side!

Alas,—and bitter is their loss, the parents and the children,
Who, loving up and down the world, have missed each other's friendship.
Haply, it had grown of careless life, for years go swiftly by;
Or sprang of too much carefulness, that drank up all the streams:
Haply, sullen disappointment came and quenched the fire;
Haply, sternness or misrule, crushed or warped the feelings.
Then, ill-combined in tempers, they learnt not each the other;
The growing child grew out of love, and drew the breath of fear;
The youth ill-trained renounced his fears, and made a league with cunning;
And so those hardened men were foes, that should have been chief friends.
Where was the cause, the mutual cause! O hunt it out to kill it:

And what the cure, the simple cure ?—A mutual flash of love.
For dull estrangement's daily air froze up those sympathies
By cold continuance in apathy, or cutting winds of censure;
It was a slow process, which any fleeting hour could have melted;
But every hour duly came and passed without the sun.
Caution, care, and dry distrust, obscured each other's mind,
Till both those gardens rich to yield, were rank with many weeds:
And doubt, a hidden worm, gnawed at the root of their Society,
They lacked of mutual confidence, and lived in mutual dread.
Judge me, many fathers; and hearken to my counsel, many sons;
I come with good in either hand, to reconcile contentions:
For better friends can no man have, than those whom God hath given,
And he that hath despised the gift, thought ill of that he knew not.
Be ye wiser,—(I speak unto the sons)—and win paternal friendships,
Cultivate their kindness, seek them out with honour, and be the screening Japheth to their failings:
And be ye wiser,—(I speak unto the fathers,)—gain those filial comrades,
Cherish their reasonable converse, and look not with coldness on your children.
For the friendship of a child is the brightest gem set upon the circlet of Society,
A jewel worth a world of pains,—a jewel seldom seen.

The third cycle on the waters, another of those rings upon the onyx,
A further definite broad zone, holdeth kith and kin;
A motley band of many tribes, and under various banners;
The intimate and strangers, the known and loved, or only seen for loathing:
Some, dear for their deserts, shall honour and have honour of relationship,
Some, despising duties, will add to it both burden and disgrace.
A man's nearest kin are oftentimes far other than his dearest,
Yet in the season of affliction those will haste to help him.
For, note thou this, the providence of God hath bound up families together,
To mutual aid and patient trial; yea, those ties are strong,
Friends are ever dearer in thy wealth, but relations to be trusted in thy need,
For these are God's appointed way, and those the choice of man.

There is lower warmth in the kin, but smaller truth in friends,
The latter show more surface, and the first have more of depth.
Relations rally to the rescue, even in estrangement and neglect,
Where friends will have fled at thy defeat, even after promises and kindness.
For friends come and go, the whim that bound may loose them,
But none can dissever a relationship, and Fate hath tied the knot

Wide, and edged with shadowy bounds, a distant boulevard to the city,
The common crowd of social life is buzzling round about;
That is as the outer court, with all defences levelled,
Ranged around a man's own fortress, and his father's house.
For many friends go in and out, and praise thee, finding pasture,
And some are honey-comb to-day, who turn to gall to-morrow:
And many a garrulous acquaintance with frequent visit
Will spend his leisure to thy cost, selling dullness dearly:
For the idle call is a heavy tax, where time is counted gold,
And even in the day of relaxation, haply he may spare his presence,—
He found himself alone, and came to talk,—till they that hear are tired;
Let the man bethink him of an errand, that his face be not unwelcome.

But many friends there be, both well and wisely greeted,
Gladly are they hailed upon the hills, and are chidden that they come so seldom.
Of such are the early recollections, schoolfriendships that have thriven to gray hairs,
And veteran men are young once more, and talk of boyish pranks;
And such, yet older on the list, are those who loved thy father,
Thy father's friend, and thine, who tendereth thee tried love:
Such also, many gentle hearts, whom thou hast known too lately,
Hastening now to learn their worth, and chary of those minutes;
And such thy faithful pastor, coming to thy home with peace,—
Greet the good man heartily,—and bid thy children bless him!

Many thoughts, many thoughts,—who can catch them all?
The best are ever swiftest-winged, the duller lag behind;
For behold, in these vast themes, my mind is as a forest of the West,
And flocking pigeons come in clouds, and bend the groaning branches;
Here for a rest, then off and away,—they have sped to other climes,

And leave me to my peace once more, a holiday from thoughts.
I dare not lure them back, for the mighty subject of Society
Would tempt to many a hackneyed note in many a weary key:
Sage warmings, stout advice, experiences ever to be learned,
The foolish floatiness of vanity, and solemn trumperies of pride,—
Economy, the poor man's mint,—extravagance, the rich man's pitfall,
Harmful copings with the better, and empty-headed apings of the worse,
Circumstance and custom, sympathies, antipathies, diverse kinds of conversation,
Vapid pleasures, the wearines of gayety, the strife and bustle of the world,
Home comforts, the miseries of style, the cobweb lines of etiquette,
The hollowness of courtesies, and substance of deceits,—idleness, business, and pastime,—
The multitude of matters to be done, the when, and where, and how,
And varying shades of characters, to do, undo, or miss them,—
All these, and many more alike, thick converging fancies,
Flit in throngs about my theme, as honey-bees at even to their hive.
Find an end, or make one; these seeds are dragon's teeth:
Sown thoughts grow to things, and fill that field, the world;
Many wise have gone before, and used the sickle well:
Who can find a corner now, where none have bound the sheaves?
So, other some may reap: I do but glean and gather:
My sorry handful hath been culled after the ripe harvest of Society.

OF SOLITUDE.

Who hath known his brother,—or found him in his freedom unrestrained?
Even he whose hidden glance hath watched his deepest Solitude.
For we walk the world in domino, putting on characters and habits,
And wear a social Janus-mask, while others stand around:
I speak not of the hypocrite, nor dream of meant deceptions,
But of that quick unconscious change, whereof the best know most.
For mind hath its influence on mind; and no man is free but when alone;
Yea, let a dog be watching thee, its eye will tend to thy restraint
Self-possession cannot be so perfect, with another intellect beside thee;
It is not as a natural result, but rather the educated produce.

The presence of a second spirit must control thine own,
And throw it off its equipoise of peace, to balance by an effort.
The common minds of common men know of this but little ;
What then ? they know nothing of themselves : I speak to those who know ;
The consciousness that some are hearing, cometh as a care,
The sense that some are watching near, bindeth thee to caution ;
And the tree of tender nerves shrinketh as a touched mimosa,
Drooping like a plant in drought, with half its strength decayed.
There are antipathies warning from the many, and sympathies drawing to the some,
But merchant-minds have crushed the first, and cannot feel the latter :
Whereas to the quickened apprehension of a keen and spiritual intellect,
Antipathies are galling, and sympathies oppress, and solitude is quiet.

He that dwelleth mainly by himself, heedeth most of others,
But they that live in crowds, think chiefly of themselves.
There is indeed a selfish seeming, where the anchorite liveth alone,
But probe his thoughts,—they travel far, dreaming for ever of the world :
And there is an apparent generosity when a man mixeth freely with his fellows,
But prove his mind, by day and night, his thoughts are all of self :
The world, inciting him to pleasures, or relentlessly provoking him to toil,
Is full of anxious rivals, each with a difference of interest ;
So must he plan and practice for himself, even as his own best friend ;
And the gay soul of dissipation never had a thought unselfish.
The hermit standeth out of strife, abiding in a contemplative calmness ;
What shall he contemplate,—himself ? a meagre theme for musing :
He hath cast off follies, and kept aloof from cares ; a man of simple wants.
God and the soul, these are his excuse, a just excuse, for solitude :
But he carried with him to his cell the half-dead feelings of humanity ;
There were they rested and refreshed ; and he yearned once more on men.

Where is the wise, or the learned, or the good, that sought not solitude for thinking,
And from seclusion's secret vale brought forth his precious fruits ?—
Forests of Aricia, your deep shade mellowed Numa's wisdom ;
Peaceful gardens of Vaucluse, ye nourished Petrarch's love ;
Solitude made a Cincinnatus, ripening the hero and the patriot,
And taught De Stael self-knowledge, even in the damp Bastile ; (24)

It fostered the piety of Jerome, matured the labours of Augustine,
And gave imperial Charles religion for ambition:
That which Scipio praised, that which Alfred practised,
Which fired Demosthenes to eloquence, and fed the mind of Milton,
Which quickened zeal, nurtured genius, found out the secret things of science,
Helped repentance, shamed folly, and comforted the good with peace.
By all men just and wise, by all things pure and perfect,
How truly, Solitude, art thou the fostering nurse of greatness!

Enough;—the theme is vast; sear me these necks of Hydra:
What shall drive away the thoughts flocking to this carcass?
Yea,—that all which man may think, hath long been said of Solitude
For many wise have proved and preached its evils and its good.
I cannot add,—I will not steal; enough, for all is spoken:
Yet heed thou these for practice and discernment among men.

There are pompous talkers, solemn, oracular, and dull:
Track them from society to solitude; and there ye find them fools.
There are light-hearted jesters, taking up with company for pastime;
How speed they when alone?—serious, wise, and thoughtful.
And wherefore? both are actors, saving when in solitude,
There they live their truest life, and all things show sincere:
But the fool, by pomposity of speech, striveth to be counted wise,
And the wise, for holiday and pleasance, playeth with the fool's best bauble;
The solemn seemer, as a rule, will be found more ignorant and shallow
Than those who laugh both loud and long, content to hide their knowledge.

For thee; seek thou Solitude, but neither in excess, nor morosely;
Seek her for her precious things, and not of thine own pride.
For there, separate from a crowd, the still small voice will talk with thee,
Truth's whisper, heard and echoed by responding conscience;
There, shalt thou gather up the ravelled skeins of feeling,
And mend the nets of usefulness, and rest awhile for duties;
There, shalt thou hive thy lore, and eat the fruits of study,
For Solitude delighteth well to feed on many thoughts;
There, as thou sittest peaceful, communing with fancy,
The precious poetry of life shall gild its leaden cares;
There, as thou walkest by the sea, beneath the gentle stars,

Many kindling seeds of good will sprout within thy soul;
Thou shalt weep in Solitude,—thou shalt pray in Solitude,
Thou shalt sing for joy of heart, and praise the grace of Solitude.
Pass on, pass on!—for this is the path of Wisdom:
God make thee prosper on the way: I leave thee well with Solitude.

THE END.

Every beginning is shrouded in a mist, those vague ideas beyond,
And the traveller setteth on his journey, oppressed with many thoughts,
Balancing his hopes and fears, and looking for some order in the chaos,
Some secret path between the cliffs, that seem to bar his way:
So, he commenceth at a clue, unravelling its tangled skein,
And boldly speedeth on to thread the labyrinth before him.
Then as he gropeth in the darkness, light is attendant on his steps,
He walketh straight in fervent faith, and difficulties vanish at his presence;
The very flashing of his sword scattereth those shadowy foes;
Confident and sanguine of success, he goeth forth conquering and to conquer.

Every middle is burdened with a weariness,—to have to go as far again,—
And Diligence is sick at heart, and Enterprise foot-sore:
That which began in zeal, bursting as a fresh-dug spring,
Goeth on doggedly in toil, and hath no help of nature:
Then, is need of moral might, to wrestle with the animal reaction.
Still to fight, with few men left, and still, though faint, pursuing.
The middle is a marshy flat, whereon the wheels go heavily,
With clouds of doubt above, and ruts of discouragement below:
Press on, sturdy traveller, yet a league, and yet a league!
While every step is binding wings on thy victorious feet.

Every end is happiness, the glorious consummation of design,
The perils past, the fears annulled, the journey at its close:
And the traveller resteth in complacency, home-returned at last:
Work done may claim its wages, the goal gained hath won its prize.

While the labour lasted, while the race was running,
Many times the sinews ached, and half refused the struggle;
But now, all is quietness, a pleasant hour given to repose;
Calmness in the retrospect of good, and calmness in the prospect of a blessing.
Hope was glad in the beginning, and fear was sad midway,
But sweet fruition cometh in the end, a harvest safe and sure.
That which is, can never not have been: facts are solid as the pyramids:
A thing done is written in the rock, yea, with a pen of iron.
Uncertainty no more can scare, the proof is seen complete,
Nor accident render unaccomplished, for the deed is finished.
Thus the end shall crown the work, with grace, grace, unto the topstone,
And the work shall triumph in its crown, with peace, peace, unto the builder.

I have written, as other some of old, in quaint and meaning phrase,
Of many things for either world, a crowd of facts and fancies:
And will ye judge me, men of mind?—judge in kindly calmness;
For bitter words of haste or hate have often been repented.
Deep dreaming upon surface reading; imagery crowded over argument;
Order less considered in the multitude of thoughts; this witnessing is just.
Scripture gave the holier themes, the well-turned words and wisdom;
While Fancy on her swallow's wing skimmed those deeper waters.
And wilt thou say with shrewdness,—He hath burnished up old truths,
But where he seemed to fashion new, the novelty was false?
Alas, for us in these last days, our elders reaped the harvest;
Alas, for all men in all times, who glean so many tares!
That which is true, how should it be new? for time is old in years:
That which is new, how should it be true? for I am young in wisdom.

Nevertheless, I have spoken at my best, according to the mercies given me,
Of high, and deep, and famous things, of Evil, or of Good. ([25])
I have told of Errors near akin to Truth, and wholesomes linked with poison;
Of subtle Uses in the humblest, and the deep-laid plots of Pride:
I have praised Wisdom, comforted thy Hope, and proved to thee the folly of complainings;
Hinted at the hazard of an influence, and turned thee from the terrors of Ambition.

I have shown thee thy captivity to Law; yet bade thee hide Humilities;
I have lifted the curtains of Memory; and smoothed the soft pillow of Rest.
Experience had his sober hour; and Character its keen appreciation;
And holy Anger stood sublime, where Hatred fell condemned.
Prayer spake the mind of God, even in his own good words;
And Zeal, with kindness warmly mixt, allied him to Discretion.
I taught thee that nothing is a Trifle, even to the laugh of Recreation:
I led thee with the Train of Religion, to be dazzled at the name of the Triune.
Thought confessed his unseen fears; and Speech declared his triumphs;
I sang the blessedness of books; and commended the prudence of a letter;
Riches found their room, either unto honour—or despising;
Inventions took their lower place, for all things come of God.
I scorned Ridicule; nor would humble me for Praise; for I had gained Self-knowledge;
And pleaded fervently for Brutes, who suffer for man's sin.
Then, I rose to Friendship; and bathed in all the tenderness of Love;
Knew the purity of Marriage: and blessed the face of Children.
And whereas by petulance or pride, I had haply said some evil,
Mine after-thought was Tolerance, to bear the faults of all:
Many faults, ill to hear, bred the theme of Sorrow;
Many virtues, dear to see, induced the gush of Joy.

Thus, for a while, as leaving thee in joy, was I loth to break that spell;
I roamed to other things and thoughts, and fashioned other books.
But in a season of reflection, after many days,
A thought stood before me in its garment of the past,—and lo, a legion with it!
They came in thronging bands,—I could not fight nor fly them,—
And so they took me to their tent, the prisoner of thoughts.

Then, I bade thee greet me well, and heed my cheerful counsels;
For every day we have a Friend, who changeth not with time.
Gladly did I speak of my commission, for I felt it graven on my heart,
And could not hold my wiser peace, but magnified mine office.
Mystery had left her echoes in my mind, and I discoursed her secret:
And thence I turned aside to Man, and judged him for his Gifts.
Beauty, noble thesis, had a world of sweets to sing of,

And dated all her praise from God, the birthday of the soul.
Thence grew Fame; and Flattery came like Agag;
But this was as the nauseous dregs of that inspiring cup:
Forth from Flattery sprang in opposition harsh and dull Neglect:
And kind Contentment's gentle face to smile away the sadness.
Life, all buoyancy and light, and Death, that sullen silence,
Sped the soul to Immortality, the final home of man.
Then, in metaphysical review, passed a triple troop,
Swift Ideas, sounding Names, and heavily armed Things;
Faith spake of her achievements even among men her brethren;
And Honesty, with open mouth, would vindicate himself:
The retrospect of social life had many truths to tell of,
And then I left thee to thy Solitude, learning there of Wisdom.

Friend and scholar, lover of the right, mine equal kind companion,—
I prize indeed thy favour, and these sympathies are dear:
Still, if thy heart be little with me, wot thou well, my brother,
I canvass not the smile of praise, nor dread the frowns of censure.
Through many themes in many thoughts, have we held sweet converse;
But God alone be praised for mind: He only is sufficient.
And every thought in every theme by prayer had been established:
Who then should fear the face of man, when God hath answered prayer?
I speak it not in arrogance of heart, but humbly, as of justice,
I think it not in vanity of soul, but tenderly, for gratitude,—
God hath blessed my mind, and taught it many truths;
And I have echoed some to thee, in weakness, yet sincerely:
Yea, though ignorance and error shall have marred those lessons of His teaching,
I stand in mine own Master's praise, or fall to His reproof.
If thou lovest, help me with thy blessing; if otherwise, mine shall be for thee;
If thou approvest, heed my words: if otherwise, in kindness be my teacher
Many mingled thoughts for self have warped my better aim,
Many motives tempted still, to toil for pride or praise:
Alas, I have loved pride and praise, like others worse or worthier;
But hate and fear them now, as snakes that fasten on my hand:
Scævola burnt both hand and crime: but Paul flung the viper on the fire:

He shook it off, and felt no harm: so be it!—I renounce them.
Rebuke then, if thou wilt rebuke,—but neither hastily nor harshly;
Or, if thou wilt commend, be it honestly, of right; I work for God and good.

NOTES.

(SECOND SERIES.)

([1]) "*Hunt with Aureng-zebe,*" *&c.* Page 130.

The great Mogul; who reigned in the seventeenth century; and was famous, amongst other things, for having all but exterminated wild beasts from the region of Hindoostan: he effected this by surrounding the whole country with his army, and then drawing to a focus with the animals in the centre. Somerville, in the end of Book II. of the Chase, gives a spirited account of that mighty hunting:

" Now the loud trumpet sounds a charge. The shouts
Of eager hosts, through all the circling line,
And the wild howlings of the beasts within
Rend wide the welkin: flights of arrows, winged
With death, and javelins launched from every arm,
Gall sore the brutal bands, with many a wound
Gored through and through."——

([2]) Page 131.

Heraclitus, and Democritus, are severally known as the crying and laughing philosophers: they typify opposite kinds of seekers after wisdom: both being prejudiced by excess. Our age of the world seems to have fallen upon the latter, which, with a protest against abuse, is certainly the wiser of the two. " The house of mourning is better than the house of feasting," for this influence, along with others of more weight, viz., that it tends to a cheerful and calm reaction, rather than to feelings of dullness and satiety. A few lines further, " the luxury of Capuan holidays," alludes to Hannibal's fatal rest after the battle of Cannæ.

([3]) *Revelation* xxi. 8. Page 132.

" But the fearful, and the unbelieving, and the abominable, and murderers, and whoremongers, and sorcerers, and idolaters, and all liars, shall have their part in the lake that burneth with fire."

(4) "*Deucalion flinging back the pebble in his flight,*" *&c.* Page 136.

Descendunt; velantque caput, tunicasque recingunt;
Et jussos lapides sua post vestigia mittunt.
Saxa (quis hoc credat, nisi sit pro teste vetustas?)
Ponere duritiem cœpêre, suumque rigorem: &c. &c.
In-que brevi spatio, superorum munere, saxa
Missa viri manibus faciem traxêre virilem.
Ovid Met. lib. i.

(5) "*Copan and Palenque,*" *&c.* Page 143.

The remains of these ancient cities, buried in the forests of Central America, have been recently made known to our wonder in the entertaining travels of Mr. J. L. Stephens. A brief and apt quotation, to illustrate the line, occurs in vol. i. p. 103. " * * Some fragments with most elegant designs, and some in workmanship equal to the finest monuments of the Egyptians; one, displaced from its pedestal by enormous roots; another locked in the close embrace of branches of trees, and almost lifted out of the earth; another, hurled to the ground, and bound down by huge vines and creepers; and one standing, with its altar before it, in a grove of trees which grew around, seemingly to shade and shroud it, as a sacred thing in the solemn stillness of the woods, it seemed a divinity mourning over a fallen people."

(6) Page 161.

Corinna, a Theban lady, was once adjudged to have overcome in verse her countryman, the deep-mouthed Pindar; but she is credibly believed to have owed her success in a great measure to her beauty. Phryne, (not the too-celebrated courtezan of Athens, but a Phryne of fairer fame,) is mentioned as having been accused, like Socrates, of impiety against heathenism, and like him condemned to die; however, the fairer witness of truth was fortunate enough to escape martyrdom by unveiling her bosom to the judges, and thereby influencing their sentence. Quintilian, Orat. lib. ii. c. 15, has this passage to our purpose. "Et Phrynen * * * conspectu corporis, quod illa, speciosissimum alioqui, diducta undaveret tunica, putant periculo liberatam." Athenæus, xiii. 590, tells us that it was by the address and counsel of Hyperides, her advocate, that *προαγαγὼν αὐτὴν εἰς τουμφανές, καὶ περίῤῥηξας τοὺς χιτωνίσκους, γυμνά τε τὰ στέρνα ποιήσας*, he influenced the judges of the Areopagus to acquit her. "Ionian Myrrha" is a character finely drawn by Byron in his tragedy of Sardanapalus.

(7) "*Some Nireus of the camp,*" *&c.* Page 163.

Homer disposes very summarily of a personage who has nothing to recommend him but his beauty. Nireus is mentioned only in one passage of the

Iliad: lib. ii. 673. Νιρεὺς, ὃς κάλλιστος ἀνὴρ, &c.; and it is significantly added, Ἀλλ' ἀλαπαδνὸς ἔην: an epithet of double intention, powerless in troops, and imbecile in mind.

(8) 1 *Esdras* iv. 13, *et seq.* Page 165.

Zorobabel holds argument before Darius, that "Woman is more powerful than wine or the king, but that Truth beareth off the victory from woman." He sets up beauty above all earthly things, v. 32, "O ye men, how can it be but women should be strong, seeing they do thus?" and it is small disparagement, that Truth should overcome her; for "Great is truth, and mighty above all things." v. 41.

(9) *Ezekiel* xxviii. 12. Page 166.

"Thou sealest up the sum," (otherwise to be rendered, "Thou art the standard of measures,") "full of wisdom, and perfect in beauty." It is quite fair, and according to scriptural usage, (compare Hosea xi. 1, with Matt. ii. 15,) to take such a passage as this out of its context, as primarily referable to a King of Tyrus, but in a higher sense applicable to the King of Heaven.

(10) Page 167.

Eratostratus fired the temple of Diana at Ephesus, solely to make himself a name: the incendiary certainly succeeded, for he has come down to our times famous (if in no other way) at least for his criminal and foolish love of notoriety. Pythagoras induced the vulgar to believe in his supernatural qualifications, by immuring himself in a cavernous pit for months, whence returning with a ghastly aspect, he gave out that he had been a visiter in Hadës. As for Empedocles, few cannot have heard, that he leaped into Ætna to make the world imagine that he had vanished from its surface as a god: unluckily, however, the volcano disgorged one of the philosopher's sandals, and proved at once the manner of his death, and the quality of his mind; ex pede Herculem.

(11) "*Cæsar's wife.*" Page 168.

Pompeia, third wife of Julius Cæsar, and divorced from him, according to Plutarch, solely because "he would have the chastity of Cæsar's wife free even from suspicion."

(12) Page 170.

Momus, a typification of the force of ridicule, was once counted among the hierarchs of heathen mythology: but, as he made game of every one, he never found a friend; and when at length, in a gush of hypercriticism, he presumed to censure the peerless Mother of Beauty for awkwardness in walking, the enraged celestials flung him from their sphere, and sent the fallen spirit down to men.

(13) 1 *Kings* vii. 21. Page 184.

"He set the pillars in the porch of the temple; and he set up the right pillar, and called the name thereof Jachin [He shall establish]: and he set up the left pillar; and called the name thereof Boaz [in it is strength]: and upon the top of the pillars was lily-work."

(14) Page 185.

An application of the story of Curtius, (as given by Livy, lib. vii. 6,) who leaped into a gulf, in the forum, because the Auruspices had declared that it should never close until the most precious thing in Rome, "the strength of the city," had been flung into it. We are told that "equo, quàm poterat maximè ornato, insidentem, armatum se in specum immisisse."

(15) Page 186.

To drink with the throat of Crassus, may well be thought to have passed into a proverb for inordinate lust of wealth: for Orodes the Parthian, having overthrown him in battle, cut off his head, and then, to satirize the insatiable nature of his avarice, poured melted gold down his throat. The evil dreams of Midas are as famous as his other well-earned punishments; and we are told that he died, in consequence of taking too violent a remedy for delivering himself from those nightly torments.

(16) Page 194.

Mr. Willis, in "Pencillings by the Way," vol. i. p. 115, gives a graphic account of the public burial-ground of Naples. * * * "There are three hundred and sixty-five pits in this place, one of which is opened every day for the dead of the city. They are thrown in without shroud or coffin, and the pit sealed up at night for a year." * * "And thus are flung into this noisome pit, like beasts, the greater part of the population of this vast city,—the young and old, the vicious and the virtuous together, without the decency even of a rag to keep up the distinctions of life! Can human beings thus be thrown away? men like ourselves, women, children, like our sisters and brothers? I never was so humiliated in my life as by this horrid spectacle. I did not think a man—a felon even, or a leper,—what you will, that is guilty or debased,—I did not think any thing that had been human could be so recklessly abandoned. Pah! It makes one sick at heart! God grant I may never die at Naples!"

Truly this would seem to spoil the proverb, Vedi Napoli, poi mori.

(17) Page 195.

Sophocles lived to be nearly a hundred years old: and to typify the perpetua fame of their "sweet Attic bee," the Athenians used to decorate his tomb wit festoons of flowering ivy.

(18) Page 196.

Mr. Catlin, in his interesting work on the North American tribes, vol. ii. p 10, alludes to "the usual mode of the Omahas, of depositing their dead in th crotches, and on the branches of trees, enveloped in skins," &c.

(19) "*Hemmed in by hostile foes, the trifler is busied on an epigram.* Page 212.

Even in matters temporal, a literal instance of this occurs in the history of Frederick the Great of Prussia, who, during the mortal struggles of the seve years' war, frequently occupied the eve before a battle in the studious compo sition of profane jests, and bad poetry.

(20) "*Nine Homers,*" *&c.* Page 218.

It is true that seven of these have so perished from memory, that we know nothing of their works; we only know they lived: an eighth, however, he of Hierapolis and one of the poetic Pleiades of the age of Philadelphus, is reported to have written no less than five-and-forty plays.

Musæus, a little lower down, is Virgil's tall prophet in the Elysian fields, mentioned Æn. vi. 667.

> "Musæum ante omnes; medium nam plurima turba
> Hunc habet, atque humeris extantem suspicit altis."

(21) "*Sons of Mattathias,*" *&c.* Page 221.

John, Simon, Judas, Eleazar, and Jonathan, who liberated Israel from the domination of the Greeks, about B. C. 160; and who were known by the general name of the Maccabees, from the initial Hebrew letters of the first four words from Ex. xv. 11, being inscribed on their standard.

(22) "*The word for both is one,*" *&c.* Page 225.

πίστις, a derivative from πείθομαι, will almost as readily bear the sense of obedience, as of persuasion, and of credence. I know not whether a similar latent sympathy may be thought to exist between our own old English word "faith," and the Norman "fait," factum, a deed: at any rate, the coincidence is worth a passing notice.

([23]) "*Ovid had been wise for winking.*" Page 229.

The poet Ovid was exiled for life to the shores of the Black Sea for having seen, and indiscreetly divulged, some intrigue in the family of Augustus. He complains frequently o this hard lot; for example,

> "Inscia quod crimen viderunt lumina plector,
> Peccatumque oculos est habuisse meum."

But he might with greater justice have accused his tongue than his eyes.

([24]) Page 238.

Madame de Staël somewhere uses these words: "To enjoy ourselves, we must seek solitude. It was in the Bastile that I first became acquainted with myself."

Scipio is reported to have originated the popular sayings, "I am never less idle than when I have most leisure," and "I am never less alone than when alone."

The Emperor Charles V., with the example of Dioclesian before him, resigned his crown, and retired from the world to the monastery of St. Just, at Plazencia, in Spain: where, as Robertson says, "he buried in solitude and silence his grandeur and his ambition."

([25]) Page 241.

It may be necessary to acquaint the reader that this section takes a retrospective glance at my former series of subjects treated in the proverbial style: a brief recapitulation of the present series follows, finishing the work.

A THOUSAND LINES.

A THOUSAND LINES.

PROLOGUE.

My heart presents her gift; in turn, of thee
 I ask a little time, an idle hour,
Kindly to spend with these my thoughts and me,
 Wooing the fragrance of the Muses' bower;
Not without name or note, yet nameless now
 As one devoid of fame and skill and power,
 Bearing no charge upon mine argent shield,
A candidate unknown with vizored brow,
 Full of young hopes I dare the tented field!—
Not so:—this is no time for measuring swords;
 Thou art no craven though thy spirit yield,
For yonder are fair looks and friendly words:
 Choose a more peaceful image:—here, reveal'd
Shines a small sample of my golden hoards.

SLOTH.

"A LITTLE more sleep, a little more slumber,
A little more folding the hands to sleep,"
For quick-footed dreams, without order or number,
Over my mind are beginning to creep,—
Rare is the happiness thus to be raptured
By your wild whispers, my Fanciful train,
And, like a linnet, be carelessly captured
In the soft nets of my beautiful brain!

Touch not these curtains!—your hand will be tearing
Delicate tissues of thoughts and of things;—
Call me not!—your cruel voice will be scaring
Flocks of young visions on gossamer wings:
Leave me, O leave me,—for in your rude presence
Nothing of all my bright world can remain,—
Thou art a blight to this garden of pleasance,
Thou art a blot on my beautiful brain!

Cease your dull lecture on cares and employment,
Let me forget awhile trouble and strife,
Leave me to peace,—let me husband enjoyment,—
This is the heart and the marrow of life!
For to my feeling the choicest of pleasures
Is to lie thus, without peril or pain,
Lazily listening the musical measures
Of the sweet voice in my beautiful brain!

Hush,—for the halo of calmness is spreading
Over my spirit, as mild as a dove;
Hush,—for the angel of comfort is shedding
Over my body his vial of love;
Hush,—for new slumbers are over me stealing,
Thus would I court them again and again,
Hush,—for my heart is intoxicate,—reeling
In the swift waltz of my beautiful brain!

ACTIVITY.

OPEN the casement, and up with the Sun!
His gallant journey is just begun;
Over the hills his chariot is roll'd,
Banner'd with glory, and burnish'd with gold,—
Over the hills he comes sublime,
Bridegroom of Earth, and brother of Time!

Day hath broken, joyous and fair;
Fragrant and fresh is the morning air,—
Beauteous and bright those orient hues,
Balmy and sweet these early dews;
O, there is health, and wealth, and bliss
In dawning Nature's motherly kiss!

Lo, the wondering world awakes,
With its rosy-tipp'd mountains and gleaming lakes,
With its fields and cities, deserts and trees,
Its calm old cliffs, and its sounding seas,
In all their gratitude blessing HIM
Who dwelleth between the Cherubim!

Break away boldly from Sleep's leaden chain;
Seek not to forge that fetter again;
Rather, with vigour and resolute nerve,
Up, up, to bless man, and thy Master to serve,
Thankful and hopeful, and happy to raise
The offering of prayer, and the incense of praise!

Gird thee, and do thy watching well,
Duty's Christian sentinel!
Sloth and Slumber never had part
In the warrior's will, or the patriot's heart;
Soldier of God on an enemy's shore!
Slumber and sloth thrall *thee* no more.

ADVENTURE.

How gladly would I wander through some strange and savage land,
The lasso at my saddle bow, the rifle in my hand,
A leash of gallant mastiffs bounding by my side,
And for a friend to love, the noble horse on which I ride!

Alone, alone—yet not alone, for God is with me there,
The tender hand of Providence shall guide me every where,
While happy thoughts and holy hopes, as spirits calm and mild,
Shall fan with their sweet wings the hermit-hunter of the wild!

Without a guide,—yet guided well,—young, buoyant, fresh and free
Without a road,—yet all the land a highway unto me,—
Without a care, without a fear, without a grief or pain,
Exultingly I thread the woods, or gallop o'er the plain!

Or, brushing through the copse, from his leafy home I start
The stately elk, or tusky boar, the bison, or the hart,
And then,—with eager spur, to scour away, away,
Nor stop,—until my dogs have brought the glorious brute to bay.

Or, if the gang of hungry wolves come yelling on my track,
I make my ready rifle speak, and scare the cowards back;
Or, if the lurking leopard's eyes among the branches shine,
A touch upon the trigger—and his spotted skin is mine!

And then the hunter's savoury fare at tranquil eventide,—
The dappled deer I shot to-day upon the green hillside;
My feasted hounds are slumbering round beside the water-course,
And plenty of sweet prairie-grass for thee, my noble horse.

Hist! hist! I heard some prowler snarling in the wood;
I seized my knife and trusty gun, and face to face we stood!
The Grizzly Bear came rushing on,—and, as he rush'd, he fell!
Hie at him, dogs! my rifle has done its duty well!

Hie at him, dogs! one bullet cannot kill a foe so grim;
The God of battles nerve a man to grapple now with him,—
And straight between his hugging arms I plunge my whetted knife,
Ha—ha! it splits his iron heart, and drinks the ruddy life!

Frantic he struggles—welling blood—the strife is almost o'er,—
The shaggy monster, feebly panting, wallows in his gore,—
Here, lap it hot, my gallant hounds,—the blood of foes is sweet;
Here, gild withal your dewlapp'd throats, and wash your brawny feet!

So shall we beard those tyrants in their dens another day,
Nor tamely wait, with slavish fear, their coming in the way;
And pleasant thoughts of peace and home shall fill our dreams to-night,
For lo, the God of battles has help'd us in the fight!

THE SONG OF SIXTEEN.

Who shall guess what I may be?
Who can tell my fortune to me?
For, bravest and brightest that ever was sung
May be—and shall be—the lot of the young!

Hope, with her prizes and victories won,
Shines in the blaze of my morning sun,
Conquering Hope, with golden ray,
Blessing my landscape far away;

All my meadows and hills are green,
And rippling waters glance between,—
All my skies are rosy bright,
Laughing in triumph at yester-night:

My heart, my heart within me swells,
Panting, and stirring its hundred wells;—
For youth is a noble seed, that springs
Into the flower of heroes and kings!

Rich in the present, though poor in the past,
I yearn for the future, vague and vast:
And lo! what treasure of glorious things
Giant Futurity sheds from his wings:

Pleasures are there, like dropping balms,
And glory and honour with chaplets and palms,
And mind well at ease, and gladness, and health
A river of peace, and a mine of wealth!

Away with your counsels, and hinder me not,—
On, on let me press to my brilliant lot;
Young and strong, and sanguine and free,
How knowest thou what I may be?

FORTY.

Ah, poor youth! in pitiful truth,
Thy pride must feel a fall, poor youth:
What thou shalt be, well have I seen,—
Thou shalt be only what others have been.

Haply, within a few swift years,
A mind bowed down with troubles and fears,
The commonest druge of men and things,
Instead of your—conquering heroes and kings.

Haply, to follies an early wreck,—
For the cloud of presumption is now like a speck,
And with a whelming, sudden sweep,
The storm of temptation roars over the deep;

Lower the sails of pride, rash youth,
Stand to the lowly tiller of truth;
Quick! or your limber bark shall be
The sport of the winds on a stormy sea.

Care and peril in lieu of joy,—
Guilt and dread may be thine, proud boy:
Lo, thy mantling chalice of life
Is foaming with sorrow, and sickness, and strife;

Cheated by pleasure, and sated with pain,—
Watching for honour, and watching in vain,—
Aching in heart, and ailing in head,
Wearily earning daily bread.

—It is well. I discern a tear on thy cheek:
It is well,—thou art humbled, and silent, and meek:
Now,—courage again! and, with peril to cope,
Gird thee with vigour, and helm thee with hope!

For life, good youth, hath never an ill
Which hope cannot scatter, and faith cannot kill;
And stubborn realities never shall bind
The free-spreading wings of a cheerful mind.

THE SONG OF SEVENTY.

I AM not old,—I cannot be old,
Though threescore years and ten
Have wasted away, like a tale that is told,
The lives of other men:

I am not old; though friends and foes
Alike have gone to their graves,
And left me alone to my joys or my woes,
As a rock in the midst of the waves.

I am not old,—I cannot be old,
Though tottering, wrinkled and gray:
Though my eyes are dim, and my marrow is cold,
Call me not old to-day.

For early memories round me throng,
  Old times, and manners, and men,
As I look behind on my journey so long,
  Of threescore miles and ten;

I look behind, and am once more young,
  Buoyant, and brave, and bold,
And my heart can sing, as of yore it sung,
  Before they called me old.

I do not see her,—the old wife there—
  Shrivelled, and haggard, and gray,
But I look on her blooming, and soft, and fair
  As she was on her wedding day!

I do not see you, daughters and sons,
  In the likeness of women and men,
But I kiss you now as I kissed you once,
  My fond little children then:

And as my own grandson rides on my knee,
  Or plays with his hoop or kite,
I can well recollect I was merry as he—
  The bright-eyed little wight!

'Tis not long since,—it cannot be long,—
  My years so soon were spent,
Since I was a boy, both straight and strong,
  Yet now am I feeble and bent.

A dream, a dream,—it is all a dream!
  A strange, sad dream, good sooth;
For old as I am, and old as I seem,
  My heart is full of youth:

Eye hath not seen, tongue hath not told,
  And ear hath not heard it sung,
How buoyant and bold, though it seem to grow old,
  Is the heart, for ever young;

For ever young,—though life's old age
Hath every nerve unstrung:
The heart, the heart is a heritage
That keeps the old man young!

NATURE'S NOBLEMAN.

Away with false fashion, so calm and so chill,
Where pleasure itself cannot please;
Away with cold breeding, that faithlessly still
Affects to be quite at its ease;
For the deepest in feeling is highest in rank,
The freest is first in the band,
And nature's own Nobleman, friendly and frank,
Is a man with his heart in his hand!

Fearless in honesty, gentle yet just,
He warmly can love,—and can hate,
Nor will he bow down with his face in the dust
To Fashion's intolerant state:
For best in good breeding, and highest in rank,
Though lowly or poor in the land,
Is nature's own Nobleman, friendly and frank,
The man with his heart in his hand!

His fashion is passion, sincere and intense,
His impulses, simple and true,
Yet tempered by judgment, and taught by good sense,
And cordial with me, and with you:
For the finest in manners, as highest in rank,
It is *you*, man! or *you*, man! who stand
Nature's own Nobleman, friendly and frank,—
A man with his heart in his hand!

NEVER GIVE UP.

NEVER give up! it is wiser and better
  Always to hope, than once to despair;
Fling off the load of Doubt's cankering fetter,
  And break the dark spell of tyrannical care:
Never give up! or the burthen may sink you,—
  Providence kindly has mingled the cup,
And in all trials or troubles, bethink you,
  The watchword of life must be, Never give up!

Never give up! there are chances and changes
  Helping the hopeful, a hundred to one,
And through the chaos High Wisdom arranges
  Ever success,—if you'll only hope on:
Never give up! for the wisest is boldest,
  Knowing that Providence mingles the cup,
And of all maxims the best, as the oldest,
  Is the true watchword of Never give up!

Never give up!—though the grape-shot may rattle,
  Or the full thunder-cloud over you burst,
Stand like a rock,—and the storm or the battle
  Little shall harm you, though doing their worst:
Never give up!—if adversity presses,
  Providence wisely has mingled the cup,
And the best counsel, in all your distresses,
  Is the stout watchword of Never give up!

THE SUN.

BLAME not, ye million worshippers of gold—
  Modern idolaters—their works and ways,
When Asia's children, in the times of old,
  Knelt to the sun, outpouring prayer and praise

As to God's central throne; for when the blaze
Of that grand eye is on me, and I stand
Watching its majesty with painful gaze,
I too could kneel among that Persian band,
Had not the Architect of yon bright sphere
Taught me Himself; bidding me look above,
Beneath, around, and still to find Him—here!
King of the heart, dwelling in no fixt globe,
But gladly throned within the spirit of love,
Wearing that light ethereal as a robe.

THE MOON.

I KNOW thee not, O moon,—thou caverned realm,
Sad satellite, a giant ash of death,
Where cold, alternate, and the sulphurous breath
Of ravaging volcanoes, overwhelm
All chance of life like ours,—art thou not
Some fallow world, after a reaping time
Of creatures' judgment, resting in thy lot?
Or haplier must I take thee for the blot
On God's fair firmament, the home of crime,
The prison-house of sin, where damned souls
Feed upon punishment?—O thought sublime,
That, amid Night's black deeds, when evil prowls
Through the broad world, then, watching sinners well,
Glares over all the wakeful eye of—Hell!

THE STARS.

I.

FAR-FLAMING stars, ye sentinels of Space,
Patient and silent ministers around

Your Queen, the moon, whose melancholy face
  Seems ever pale with pity and grief profound
For sinful Earth,—I, a poor groveller here,
  A captive eagle chain'd to this dull ground,
Look up and love your light in hope and fear:
  Hope, that among your myriad host is one,
A kingdom for my spirit, a bright place
  Where I shall reign when this short race is run,
  An heir of joy, and glory's mighty son!
Yet, while I hope, the fear will freeze my brain—
What if indeed for worthless me remain
  No waiting sceptre, no predestined throne?

THE STARS.

II.

HENCE, doubts of darkness! I am not mine own,
  But ransomed by the King of that bright host:
  In Him my just humility shall boast,
And claim through Him that sceptre and that throne.
Yes, world of light,—when by the booming sea
  At eve I loiter on this shingly coast,
In seeming idleness,—I gaze on thee,
(I know not which—but one,) fated to be
  My glorious heritage, my heavenly home,
A temple and a paradise for me,
  Whence my celestial form at will may roam
  To other worlds, unthought and unexplor'd,
Whose atmosphere is bliss and liberty,
  The palaces and gardens of the Lord!

FORGIVE AND FORGET.

WHEN streams of unkindness, as bitter as gall,
  Bubble up from the heart to the tongue,

And Meekness is writhing in torment and thrall,
By the hands of Ingratitude wrung,—
In the heat of injustice, unwept and unfair,
While the anguish is festering yet,
None, none but an angel, or God, can declare
"I now can forgive and forget."

But, if the bad spirit is chased from the heart,
And the lips are in penitence steep'd,
With the wrong so repented the wrath will depart,
Though scorn on injustice were heaped;
For the best compensation is paid for all ill,
When the cheek with contrition is wet,
And every one feels it is possible still,
At once to forgive and forget.

To forget? It is hard for a man with a mind,
However his heart may forgive,
To blot out all perils and dangers behind,
And but for the future to live:
Then how shall it be? for at every turn
Recollection the spirit will fret,
And the ashes of injury smoulder and burn,
Though we strive to forgive and forget.

Oh, hearken! my tongue shall the riddle unseal,
And mind shall be partner with heart,
While thee to thyself I bid conscience reveal,
And show thee how evil thou art:
Remember thy follies, thy sins, and—thy crimes,
How vast is that infinite debt!
Yet Mercy hath seven by seventy times
Been swift to forgive and forget!

Brood not on insults or injuries old,
For thou art injurious too,—
Count not their sum till the total is told,
For thou art unkind and untrue:

And if all thy harms are forgotten, forgiven,
  Now mercy with justice is met,
Oh, who would not gladly take lessons of heaven,
  Nor learn to forgive and forget?

Yes, yes; let a man, when his enemy weeps,
  Be quick to receive him, a friend;
For thus on his head in kindness he heaps
  Hot coals,—to refine and amend;
And hearts that are Christian more eagerly yearn,
  As a nurse on her innocent pet,
Over lips that, once bitter, to penitence turn,
  And whisper, Forgive and forget.

"MY MIND TO ME A KINGDOM IS."

Eureka! this is truth sublime,
Defying change, outwrestling time—
Eureka! well that truth is told,
Wisely spake the bard of old—
Eureka! there is peace and praise
In this short and simple phrase,
A sea of comforts, wide and deep,
Wherein my conscious soul to steep,
A hoard of happy-making wealth
To doat on, miserly, by stealth,
Through Time my reason's ripest fruit,
For all eternity its root,
Earth's harvest, and the seed of heaven,
To me, to me, by mercy given!

Yes, eureka,—I have found it,
And before the world will sound it;
This remains, and still shall stay
When life's gauds have passed away,

This, of old my treasure-truth,
The bosom joy that warm'd my youth,
My happiness in manhood's prime,
My triumph down the stream of time,
Till death shall lull this heart in age,
And deathless glory crown my page,
My grace-born truth and treasure this,—
" My mind to me a kingdom is."

Noble solace, true and strong,
Great reward for human wrong,
With an inward blessing still
To compensate all earthly ill,
To recompense for adverse fates,
Woes, or wants, or scorns, or hates,
To cherish, after man's neglect,
When foes deride, and friends suspect,
To soothe and bless the spirit bow'd
Down by the selfish and the proud,
To lift the soul above this scene
Of petty troubles trite and mean,
O there is mortal might in this,—
" My mind to me a kingdom is."

Carve it deep, with letters bold,
In the imperishable gold,
Grave it on some primal rock
That hath stood the earthquake shock,
Make that word a citizen
Dwelling in the hearts of men,
Sound it in the ears of age,
Stamp it on the printed page,
Gladden sympathizing youth
With the soft music of this truth,
This echoed note of heavenly bliss,
" My mind to me a kingdom is."

Ay, chide or scorn,—I will be proud,—
I am not of a slavish crowd;

No serf is here to outward things,—
He rules with chiefs! he reigns with kings!
Tell out thy secret joys, my mind,
Free and fearless as the wind,
And pour the triumphs of the soul
In words that like a river roll,
Foaming on with vital force
From their ever-gushing source,
Fountains of truth, that overwhelm
With swollen streams this royal realm,
And in Nilotic richness steep
My heart's Thebaïd, rank and deep!

Or bolder, as my thoughts inspire,
Change that water into fire!
From the vext bowels of my soul
Lava currents roar and roll,
Bursting out in torrent wide
Through my crater's ragged side,
Rushing on from field to field,
Till all with boiling stone is seal'd,
And my hot thoughts, in language pent,
Stand their own granite monument!
Yes! all the elements are mine,
To crush, create, dissolve, combine,—
All mine,—the confidence is just,
On God I ground my high-born trust
To stand, when pole is rent from pole,
Calm in my majesty of soul,
Watching the throes of this wreck'd world,
When from their thrones the Alps are hurl'd,
When fire consumes earth, sea, and air,
To stand, unharm'd, undaunted there,
And grateful still to boast in this,
"My mind to me a kingdom is."

Brother poet, dead so long,
Heed these echoes to thy song,
And love me now, where'er thou art,
Yearning with magnetic heart

From thy throne in some bright sphere
On this poor brother grovelling here;
For I, too, I can stoutly sing
I am every inch a king!
A king of Thought, a Potentate
Of glorious spiritual state,
A king of Thought, a king of Mind,
Realms unmapp'd and undefined,—
A king! beneath no man's control,
Invested with a royal soul,
Crown'd by God's imperial hand
Before him as a king to stand,
And by His wisdom train'd and taught
To rule my realm as King of Thought.

O thoughts,—how ill my fellow-men,
O thoughts,—how scanty my poor pen
Can guess or tell the myriad host
Wherewith you crowd my kingdom's coast!
For I am hemm'd and throng'd about
With your triumphant rabble-rout,
Hurried along by that mad flood,
The joy-excited multitud
A conqueror, borne upon the foam,
Of his great people's gladness home,
A monarch in his grandest state,
On whom a thousand thousand wait!
Lo! they come—my Tribes of Thought,
Fierce and flush'd and fever-fraught!
From the horizon all around
I hear with pride their coming sound;
See! their banners circling near,—
Glittering groves of shield and spear,
Flying clouds of troopers gay,
Serried lines in dark array,
Veterans calm with temper'd sword,
And a dishevelled frantic horde,—
On they come with furious force,
Tramping foot and thundering horse,

On they come, converging loud,
With clanging arms, a glorious crowd
Shouting impatient, fierce and free,
For me, their Monarch, yea, for me!

Then, in my majesty and power,
I quell the madness of the hour,
Bid that tumultuous turmoil cease,
And frown my multitudes to peace.
Each to his peril and his post!
All hush'd throughout my mighty host:
Courage clear, and duty stern,—
Heads that freeze and hearts that burn;
Marshalled straight in order due,
Legions! pass in swift review,
Bending to my blazoned will,
Loyal to that standard still,
And hailing me with homage then
King of Thoughts—and thus, of Men!

What? am I powerless to control
Nations, by my single soul?
What? have I not made thousands thrill
By the mere impulse of my will,
When the strong Thought goes forth, and binds
Captive a wandering herd of minds?
And is not this to reign alone
More than the ermine and the throne,
The jewelled state, the gilded rooms,
The mindless man in borrowed plumes?
Yes,—if the inmate soul outweighs
Its dull clay house in power and praise:
Yes,—if Eternity be true,
And Time both false and fleeting too,
Then, humbler kings, my boast be this,
"My mind to me a kingdom is.'

And what, though weak and slow of speech,
Ill to comfort, dull to teach?

What, though hiding from the ken
Of my small prying fellow-men,—
Still within my musing mind,
Wisdom's secret stores I find,
And, little noticed, sweetly feed
On hidden manna, meat indeed,
Blessed thoughts I never told
Unconsidered, uncontroll'd,
Rushing by as thick and fast
As autumn leaves upon the blast:
Or better, like the gracious rain
Dropping on some thirsty plain.
And is not this to be a king,
To carry in my heart a spring
Of ceaseless pleasures, deep and pure,
Wealth cannot buy, nor power procure?
Yea,—by the poet's artless art,
And the sweet searchings of his heart,
By his unknown, unheeded bliss,
"My mind to me a kingdom is."

Place me on some desert shore
Foot of man ne'er wandered o'er;
Lock me in a lonely cell
Beneath some prison citadel;
Still, here or there, within I find
My quiet kingdom of the Mind;
Nay,—mid the tempest fierce and dark,
Float me on peril's frailest bark,
My quenchless soul could sit and think
And smile at danger's dizziest brink:
And wherefore?—God, my God, is still
King of kings in good and ill;
And where He dwelleth—every where—
Safety supreme and peace are there;
And where he reigneth—all around—
Wisdom, and love, and power are found;
And reconciled to Him and bliss,
"My mind to me a kingdom is."

Thus for my days; each waking hour
Grand with majesty and power,
Every minute rich in treasure,
Gems of peace, and pearls of pleasure.
And for my nights—those wondrous nights?
How manifold my Mind's delights,
When the young truant, gladly caught
In its own labyrinths of thought,
Finds there is another realm to range,
The dynasties of Chance and Change.
O dreams,—what know I not of dreams?
Their name, their very essence, seems
A tender light, not dark nor clear,
A sad sweet mystery wild and dear,
A dull soft feeling unexplained,
A lie half true, a truth half feigned:
O dreams,—what know I not of dreams?
When Reason, with inebriate gleams,
Looses from his wise control
The prancing Fancies of the soul,
And sober Judgment, slumbering still,
Sets free Caprice to guide the Will.
Within one night have I not spent
Years of adventurous banishment,
Strangely groping like the blind
In the dark caverns of my mind?
Have I not dwelt, from eve till morn,
Lifetimes in length for praise or scorn,
With fancied joys, ideal woes,
And all sensation's warmest glows,
Wondrously thus expanding Life
Through seeming scenes of peace or strife,
Until I verily reign sublime,
A great creative king of Time?

And there are people, things, and places,
Usual themes, familiar faces,
A second life, that looks as real
As this dull world's own unideal,

Another life of dreams by night,
That, still forgotten wanes in light,
Yet seems itself to wake and sleep,
And in that sleep dreams doubly deep,
While those same dreams may dream anon,
Tangled mazes wandering on!
Yes, I have often, weak and worn,
Feebly waked at earliest morn,
As a shipwreck'd sailor, tost
By the wild waves on some rough coast,
Of perils past remembering nought
But some dim cataracts of thought,
And only roused betimes to know
That yesterday seems years ago!
And I can apprehend full well
What old Pythagoras could tell
Of other scenes, and other climes,
And other Selfs in other times;
For, oft my consciousness has reel'd
With scores of "Richards in the field,"
As, multiform, with no surprise,
I see myself in other guise,
And wonderless walk side by side
With mine own soul, self-multiplied!
If it be royal then to reign
Over an infinite domain,
If it be more than monarch can
To lengthen out the life of man,
Yea, if a godlike thing it be
To revel in ubiquity,
Is there but empty boast in this,
"My mind to me a kingdom is?"
—Peace, rash fool; be proud no more,
Count thy faults and follies o'er,
Turn aside, and note within
Thy secret charnel-house of Sin,
Thy bitter heart, thy covetous mind.
Evil thoughts, and words unkind:

Can so foul and mean a thing
Reign a spiritual King?
Art thou not—yea thou, myself,
In hope a slave to pride and pelf?
Art thou not,—yea, thou, my mind,
Weak and naked, poor and blind?
Yea, be humble; yea, be still;
Meekly bow that rebel Will;
Seek not selfishly for praise;
Go more softly all thy days;
For to thee belongs no power,
Wretched insect of an hour,—
And if God in bounteous dole,
Hath grafted life upon thy soul,
Know thou, there is out of Him
Nor light in mind, nor might in limb;
And, but for One, who from the grave
Of sin and death stood forth to save,
Thy mind, that royal mind of thine,
So great, ambitious and divine,
Would but a root of anguish be,
A madness and a misery,
A bitter fear, a hideous care
All too terrible to bear,
Kingly,—but king of pains and woes,
The sceptred slave to throbs and throes!

Justly then, my God, to thee,
My royal soul shall bend the knee.
My royal soul, Thy glorious breath,
By Thee set free from guilt and death,
Before thy Majesty bows down,
Offering the homage of her crown,
Well pleased to sing in better bliss,
" My God to me a kingdom is."

TARRING CHURCH.

Mother,—beneath fair Tarring's heavenward spire,
Where in old years thy youthful vows were paid,
When God had granted thee thy heart's desire,
And she went forth a wife, who came a maid,
With mindful steps thus wisely have we stray'd,
Full of deep thoughts: for where that sacred fire
Of Love was kindled, in the self-same spot,
Thou, with the dear companion of thy lot,
Thy helpmate all those years, mine honour'd sire,
To-day have found fulfilled before your eyes
The promise of old time;—look round and see
Thy children's children! lo, these babes arise,
And call thee blessed: Blessed both be ye!
And in your blessing bless ye these, and me.

SONNET; ON A BIRTH.

At length,—a dreary length of many years,
God's favour hath shone forth! and blest thee well,
O handmaid of the Lord, for all thy tears,
For all thy prayers, and hope, and faith—and fears,
With that best treasure of consummate joy
A childless wife alone can fully tell
How sorely long withheld—her first-born boy:
This blessing is from heav'n; to heav'n once more,
Another Hannah with her Samuel,
Render thou back the talent yielding ten,
A spirit, trained right early to adore,
A heart to yearn upon its fellow-men,
A being, meant and made for endless heaven,
This give to God: this, God to thee hath given.

DUTY.

Pearls before swine: this is an old complaint;
In very humbleness, and not in pride,
The spirit feels it true; yet makes a feint
To rest with man's neglect well satisfied,
And have its wealth of words, its stores of thought
Despised or unregarded: woe betide
The heart that lives on praise! considering nought
Of Duty's royal edicts, that command
Thy talents to be lent, thy lamp to shine:
Soul, be not faint; nor, body, stay thy hand;
Heed only this,—not whether those be swine
But whether these be pearls, precious and pure;
That so, whatever fate the world make thine,
With God for Judge, thy guerdon be secure.

COUNSEL.

FOR MUSIC.

There is a time for praising,
And a better time for pray'r,—
The heart its anthem raising,
Or uttering its care:
One minute is for smiling,
And another for the tear,—
Hope, by turns, beguiling,
Or her haggard brother, Fear.

But, if in joy thou praisest
The generous Hand that gave,—
And if in woe thou raisest
The prayer that He may save;
Thy griefs shall seem all pleasure,
As the chidings of a Friend,
And thy joys ecstatic measure
A beginning without end!

HOME.

FOR MUSIC.

I NEVER left the place that knew me,
And may never know me more,
Where the chords of kindness drew me,
And have gladdened me of yore,
But my secret soul has smarted
With a feeling full of gloom
For the days that are departed,
And the place I call'd my Home.

I am not of those who wander
Unaffectioned here and there,
But my heart must still be fonder
Of my sites of joy or care;
And I point sad memory's finger
(Though my faithless foot may roam)
Where I've most been made to linger
In the place I call'd my Home.

BYEGONES.

FOR MUSIC.

"LET byegones be byegones,"—they foolishly say,
And bid me be wise and forget them;
But old recollections are active to-day,
And I can do nought but regret them;
Though the present be pleasant, all joyous and gay,
And promising well for the morrow,
I love to look back on the years past away,
Embalming my byegones in sorrow.

If the morning of life has a mantle of gray,
Its noon will be blither and brighter,

If March has its storm, there is sunshine in May,
 And light out of darkness is lighter:
Thus the present is pleasant, a cheerful to-day,
 With a wiser, a soberer gladness,
Because it is tinged with the mellowing ray
 Of a yesterday's sunset of sadness.

RULE, BRITANNIA!

A STIRRING SONG FOR PATRIOTS, IN THE YEAR 1860.

To the tune of "Wha wouldna fight for Charlie?"

Rise! ye gallant youth of Britain,
 Gather to your country's call,
On your hearts her name is written,
 Rise to help her, one and all!
Cast away each feud and faction,
 Brood not over wrong nor ill,—
Rouse your virtues into action,
 For we love our country still,—
Hail, Britannia! hail, Britannia!
 Raise that thrilling shout once more;
Rule, Britannia! Rule, Britannia!
 Conqueror over sea and shore!

France is coming, full of bluster,
 Hot to wipe away her stain,
Therefore, brothers, here we muster
 Just to give it her again!
And if foemen, blind with fury,
 Dare to cross our ocean-gulf,
Wait not then for judge nor jury,—
 Shoot them as you would a wolf!

For Britannia, just Britannia,
  Claims our chorus as before;
Rule, Britannia! Rule, Britannia!
  Conqueror over sea and shore.

They may writhe, for we have galled them
  With our guns in every clime,—
They may hate us, for we called them
  Serfs and subjects in old time!
Boasting Gaul, we calmly scorn you
  As old Æsop's bull the frogs;
Come and welcome! for, we warn you,
  We shall fling you to our dogs!
For Britannia, our Britannia,
  Thunders with a lion's roar;
Rule Britannia! Rule, Britannia!
  Conqueror over sea and shore.

See, uprear'd our holy standard!
  Crowd around it, gallant hearts!
What! should Britain's fame be slandered
  As by fault on *our* parts?
Let the rabid Frenchman threaten,
  Let the mad invader come,
We will hunt them out of Britain,
  Or can die for hearth and home!
For Britannia, dear Britannia,
  Wakes our chorus evermore—
Rule, Britannia! Rule, Britannia!
  Conqueror over sea and shore.

Rise then, patriots! name endearing,
  Flock from Scotland's moors and dales,
From the green, glad fields of Erin,
  From the mountain homes of Wales,—
RISE! for sister England calls you,
  RISE! our common weal to serve,
RISE! while now the song enthralls you,
  Thrilling every vein and nerve,

Hail, Britannia! hail, Britannia!
  Conquer, as thou didst of yore!
Rule, Britannia! Rule, Britannia!
  Over every sea and shore.

THE EMIGRANT SHIP.

FOR MUSIC.

  Far away, far away,
The emigrant ship must sail to-day:
  Cruel ship,—to look so gay
Bearing the exiles far away.

  Sad and sore, sad and sore,
Many a fond heart bleeds at the core,
  Cruel dread,—to meet no more,
Bitter sorrow, sad and sore.

  Many years, many years
At best will they battle with perils and fears;
  Cruel pilot,—for he steers
The exiles away for many years.

  Long ago, long ago!
For the days that are gone their tears shall flow:
  Cruel hour,—to tear them so
From all they cherished long ago.

  Fare ye well, fare ye well!
To joy and to hope it sounds as a knell
  Cruel tale it were to tell
How the emigrant sighs farewell.

  Far away, far away!
Is there indeed no hope to-day?
  Cruel and false it were to say
There are no pleasures far away.

Far away, far away!
Every night and every day
Kind and wise it were to pray,
God be with them far away!

THE ASSURANCE OF HORACE.

I HAVE achieved a tower of fame
More durable than gold,
And loftier than the royal frame
Of Pyramids of old,—
Which none inclemencies of clime,
Nor fiercest winds that blow,
Nor endless change, nor lapse of time,
Shall ever overthrow!

I cannot perish utterly:
The brighter part of me
Must live—and live—and never die,
But baffle Death's decree!
For I shall always grow, and spread
My new-blown honors still,
Long as the priest and vestal tread
The Capitolian hill.

I shall be sung, where thy rough waves,
My native river, foam,—
And where old Daunus scantly laves
And rules his rustic home;
As chief and first I shall be sung,
Though lowly, great in might
To tune my country's heart and tongue,
And tune them both aright.

Thou then, my soul, assume thy state,
And take thine honors due:

Be proud, as thy deserts are great,—
  To thine own praise be true!
Thou too, celestial Muse, come down,
  And with kind haste prepare
The laurel for a Delphic crown
  To weave thy poet's hair.

THE ASSURANCE OF OVID.

Now have I done my work!—which not Jove's ire
Can make undone, nor sword, nor time, nor fire.
Whene'er that day, whose only powers extend
Against this body, my brief life shall end,
Still in my better portion evermore
Above the stars undying shall I soar!
My name shall never die: but through all time,
Wherever Rome shall reach a conquered clime,
There, in that people's tongue, shall this my page
Be read and glorified from age to age;—
Yea, if the bodings of my spirit give
True note of inspiration, I shall live!

POST-LETTERS.

Lottery tickets every day,—
  And ever drawn a blank!
Yet none the less we pant and pray
  For prizes in that bank:
Morn by morn, and week by week,
  They cheat us, or amuse,
Whilst on we fondly hope, and seek
  Some stirring daily news.

The heedless postman on his path
  Is scattering joys and woes;
He bears the seeds of life and death,
  And drops them as he goes!
I never note him trudging near
  Upon his common track,
But all my heart is hope, or fear,
  With visions bright, or black!

I hope—what hope I not?—vague things
  Of wondrous possible good;
I dread—as vague imaginings,
  A very viper's brood:
Fame's sunshine, fortune's golden dews
  May now be hovering o'er,—
Or the pale shadow of ill news
  Be cowering at my door!

O Mystery, master-key to life,
  Thou spring of every hour,
I love to wrestle in thy strife,
  And tempt thy perilous power;
I love to know that none can know
  What this day may bring forth,
What bliss for me, for me what woe
  Is travailing in birth!

See, on my neighbour's threshold stands
  Yon careless common man,
Bearing, perchance, in those coarse hands,
  My Being's altered plan!
My germs of pleasure, or of pain,
  Of trouble, or of peace,
May there lie thick as drops of rain
  Distilled from Gideon's fleece!

Who knoweth? may not loves be dead,—
  Or those we loved laid low,—
Who knoweth? may not wealth be fled,
  And all the world my foe?

Or who can tell if Fortune's hour
  (Which once on all doth shine)
Be not within this morning's dower,
  A prosperous morn of mine?

Ah, cold Reality!—in spite
  Of hopes, and endless chance,
That bitter postman, ruthless wight,
  Has cheated poor Romance;
No letters! O the dreary phrase:
  Another day forlorn:—
And thus I wend upon my ways
  To watch another morn.

Cease, babbler!—let those doubtings cease:
  What! should a son of heaven
With the pure manna of his Peace
  Mix up his faithless leaven?
Not so!—for in the hands of God,
  And in none earthly will,
Abide alike my staff, and rod,
  My good, and seeming ill.

SOCIETY.

ALAS, we do but act; we are not free;
  The presence of another is a chain
  My trammeled spirit strives to break, in vain:
How strangely different myself from me!
  Thoughtful in solitude, serenely blest,
Crown'd and enthroned in mental majesty,
Equal to all things great, and daring all,
  I muse of mysteries, and am at rest;
  But, in the midst, some dull intruded guest
Topples me from my heights, holding in thrall

With his hard eye the traitor in my breast,
  That before humbler intellects is cow'd,
  Silently shrinking from the common crowd,
And only with the highest self-possest.

ON AN INFANT.*

Look on this babe; and let thy pride take heed,
  Thy pride of manhood, intellect, or fame,
That thou despise him not: for he indeed,
  And such as he, in spirit and heart the same,
Are God's own children in that kingdom bright
  Where purity is praise,—and where before
  The Father's throne, triumphant evermore,
The ministering angels, sons of light,
  Stand unreproved; because they offer them
  Mix'd with the Mediator's hallowing pray'r
The innocence of babes in Christ like this:
  O guardian Spirit, be my child thy care,
Lead him to God, obedience and bliss,
To God, O fostering cherub, thine and his!

* William Knighton Tupper, the Author's second son

EPILOGUE.

ARE there no sympathies, no loves between us?
Is my hope vain?—I have not vext thee long,
Nor lent thee thoughts from God and good that wean us,
Nor given thee words that warp from right to wrong:
And if, at times, my too trinmphant song
Hath seem'd self-praise,—doth it indeed demean us
That when a man feels hotly at his heart
The quick spontaneous fire of thoughts and words,
He will not play the hypocrite's ill part,
Flinging aside the meed his Mind affords?
No! with all gratitude and humbleness
I claim mine own; nor can affect to scorn
A gift, of my Creator's goodness born
Which is my grace and glory to possess.

HACTENUS:

SUNDRY OF MY LYRICS HITHERTO

HACTENUS.

THE NEW YEAR.

The old man he is dead, young heir!
  And gone to his long account;
Come! stand on his hearth, and sit in nis chair,
  And into his saddle mount!

The old man's face was a face to be fear'd,
  But thine both loving and gay;
O, who would not choose for that stern white bea
  A bright young cheek alway?

The old man he had outlived them all,
  His friends, he said, were gone;
But hundreds are wassailing now in the hall,
  And true friends every one!

The old man moaned both sore and long
  Of pleasures past, he said;
But pleasures to come are the young heir's song,
  The living, not the dead!

The old man babbled of old regrets,
  Alack! how much he owed;
But the young heir has not a feather of debts
  His heart withal to load!

The old man used to shudder, and seem
  Remembering secret sin;
But the happy young heir is as if in a dream, —
  Paradise all within!

Alas! for the old man, — where is he now?
  And fear for thyself, young heir;
For he was innocent once as thou,
  As ruddy, and blithe, and fair:

Reap wisdom from his furrowed face,
  Cull counsel from his fear;
O, speed thee, young heir, in gifts and in grace,
  And blessings on thee, — New Year!

ALL'S FOR THE BEST.

(*To the same music as "Never Give Up."*)

All's for the best! be sanguine and cheerful,
  Trouble and sorrow are friends in disguise,
Nothing but Folly goes faithless and fearful,
  Courage for ever is happy and wise:
All for the best, — if a man would but know it,
  Providence wishes us all to be blest,
This is no dream of the pundit or poet,
  Heaven is gracious, and — All's for the best!

All for the best. set this on your standard,
  Soldier of sadness, or pilgrim of love,
Who to the shores of Despair may have wander'd,
  A way-wearied swallow, or heart-stricken dove:
All for the best! — be a man but confiding,
  Providence tenderly governs the rest,
And the frail bark of his creature is guiding
  Wisely and warily, all for the best.

All for the best! then fling away terrors,
  Meet all your fears and your foes in the van,
And in the midst of your dangers or errors
  Trust like a child, while you strive like a man
All's for the best! — unbiass'd, unbounded,
  Providence reigns from the East to the West;
And, by both wisdom and mercy surrounded,
  Hope and be happy that All's for the best!

THE RIDDLE READ.

World of sorrow, care, and change,
  Even to myself I seem,
As adown thy vale I range,
  Wandering in a dream:
  All things are so strange.

For, the dead who died this day,
  Fair and young, or great and good,
Though we mourn them, where are they?
  — With those before the flood;
  Equally past away.

Living hearts have scantly time
  To feel some other heart most dear,
Scarce can love the love sublime
  Unselfishly sincere, —
  Death nips it in its prime!

Minds have hardly power to learn
  How much there is to know aright,
Can dimly thro' the mist discern
  Some little glimpse of light, —
  The order is, Return!

Willing hands but just begin
  Wisely to work for God and man,
And some poor wages barely win
  As one who well began, —
  The Master calls, Come in!

Well, — this is well: for well-begun
  Is all the good man here may do;
He cannot hope to see half-done;
  A furlong is crept through,
  And lo, the goal is won!

This is the life of sight and sense,
  And other brighter lives depend
On all we here can just commence
  But long before an end
  God calls his servant hence.

Take courage, courage: not in vain
  The Ruler has appointed thus;
Account it neither grief nor pain
  His mercy spareth us —
  It is the laborer's gain.

Here we begin to love and know;
  And when God's willing grace perceives
The plant of heav'n hath roots to grow,
  He plucks the ranker leaves,
  And doth transplant it so!

OLD HAUNTS.

FOR MUSIC.

I LOVE to linger on my track
  Wherever I have dwelt,
In after years to loiter back,
  And feel as once I felt;
My foot falls lightly on the sward,
  Yet leaves a deathless dint,
With tenderness I still regard
  Its unforgotten print.

Old places have a charm for me
  The new can ne'er attain,
Old faces—how I long to see
  Their kindly looks again!
Yet, these are gone:—while all arouna
  Is changeable as air,
I'll anchor in the solid ground,
  And root my memories there!

THE BATTLE OF ROLEIA.

YE children of the veterans
  Who fought for faithless Spain,
And for ungrateful Portugal
  Pour'd out their blood like rain,—
Come near me, and hear me,
  For I would tell you well
How gallantly your fathers fought,
  Or gloriously they fell!

I sing Roleia's bloody strife,
  The first of many frays
When iron Wellesley led us on
  Invincible always;
Roleia gay and ever green,
  Festooned with vines and flowers,
Roleia, scorch'd and blood-bedew'd,—
  And half that blood was ours!

The seventeenth of August,
  It shone out bright and clear,
And still we press'd the Frenchman's flank,
  And hung upon his rear:
From Brilos and Obidos
  Had we driven the bold Laborde,
And now among the mountain rocks
  We sought him with the sword!

All golden is the plain with wheat,
  All purple are the hills,
With luscious vineyards ripe and sweet,
  And laced with crystal rills;
Yet must the rills run down with gore,
  The corn be trampled red,
Before Roleia's threshing-floor
  Is glutted with her dead!

O cheerily the bugles spoke,
  And all our hearts beat high
When over Monte Junto broke
  The sun upon the sky;
Right early from Obidos
  We gladly sallied, then
A goodly host, in columns three,
  Of fourteen thousand men.

Brave Ferguson led on the left,
  And Trant the flanking right,
With iron Arthur in the midst,

The focus of the fight;
And fast by Wellesley's gallant side
The Craufurd rode amain,
And Hill, the British soldier's pride,
And Nightingale, and Fane.

Crouching like a tiger,
In his high and rocky lair,
The Frenchman howled and showed his teeth,
And — wished he wasn't there;
For Craufurd, Hill, and Nightingale,
Flew at him as he lay,
And up our gallant fellows sprang
As bloodhounds on the prey!

And, look! we hunt the bold Laborde
To Zambugeira's height —
While Trant with Fane and Ferguson
Outflank him left and right;
And then with cheers we charge the front,
With cheers the foe reply, —
No child's play was that battle brunt,
We swore to win or die!

Rattled loud the muskets' roar, —
We struggled man to man, —
The rugged rocks were washed in gore,
With gore the gullies ran!
Fiercely through those mountain paths
Our bloody way we force, —
And find in strength upon the heights
The Frenchman, foot and horse;

Ah, then, my Ninth, and Twenty-ninth,
Your courage was too hot,
For down on your disordered ranks
Secure they pour the shot;
But all their horse and foot and guns
Could never make you fly, —

The losing Frenchman fights and runs,
  But Britons fight — and die!

Up to the rescue, Ferguson!
  And keep the hard-fought hill;
Their chiefs are picked off, one by one,
  And lo, they rally still;
They rally, and rush stoutly on, —
  The bold Laborde gives way, —
The day is lost! the day is won!
  And ours is the day!

Then, well retreating, sage and slow,
  Alternately in mass
With charging horse, the wily foe
  Gains Runa's rocky pass;
And left us thus Roleia's field,
  With other fields in store,
Vimiera, Torres Vedras, —
  And half a hundred more!

RETROSPECT.

How many years are fled, —
How many friends are dead:
    Alas, how fast
    The past hath past, —
How speedily life hath sped!

Places, that knew me of yore,
Know me for their's no more;
    And sore at the change
    Quite strange I range
Where I was at home before.

Thoughts and things each day
Seem to be fading away;
  Yet this is, I wot,
  Their lot to be not
Continuing in one stay.

A mingled mesh it seems
Of facts and fancy's gleams;
  I scarce have power
  From hour to hour
To separate things from dreams.

Darkly, as in a glass,
Like a vain shadow they pass;
  Their ways they wend
  And tend to an end,
The goal of life, alas!

Alas? and wherefere so?—
Be glad for this passing show:
  The world and its lust
  Back must to their dust
Before the soul can grow.

Expand! my willing mind,
Thy nobler life to find,
  Thy childhood leave
  Nor grieve to bereave
Thine age of toys behind.

PEACE AND QUIETNESS.

PEACE is the precious atmosphere I breathe;
  And my calm mind goes to her dewy bower,
A trellis rare of fragrant thoughts to wreathe,
  Mingling the scents and tints of every flower;

For pity, vex her not: those inner joys
  That bless her in this consecrated hour,
Start and away, like plovers, at a noise,
Sensitive, timorous: — O do not scare
  My happy fancies, lest the flock take wing,
Fly to the wilderness and perish there!
  For I have secret luxuries, that bring
Gladness and brightness to mine eyes and heart,
  Memory, and Hope, and keen Imagining,
Sweet thoughts and peaceful, never to depart.

Then give me Silence; for my spirit is rare,
  Of delicate edge and tender: when I think
I rear aloft a mental fabric fair;
But soon as words come hurtling on the air,
  Down to this dust my ruined fancies sink:
  Look you! on yonder Alp's precipitous brink
An avalanche is tottering; — one breath
  Loosens an icy chain; — it falls, — it falls,
Filling the buried glens and glades with death!
Or as, when on the mountain's granite walls
  The hunter spies a chamois, — hush! be calm,
A word will scare it, — even so, my Mind
  Creative, energizing, seeks the balm
Of Quiet: Solitude and Peace combin'd.

THE EARLY GALLOP.

(*Written in the saddle, on the crown of my hat.*)

At five on a dewy morning,
  Before the blazing day,
To be up and off on a high-mettled horse,
  Over the hills away, —
To drink the rich, sweet breath of the gorse,
  And bathe in the breeze of the Downs,

Ha! man, if you can, match bliss like this
  In all the joys of towns!

With glad and grateful tongue to join
  The lark at his matin hymn,
And thence on faith's own wing to spring
  And sing with Cherubim!
To pray from a deep and tender heart,
  With all things praying anew,
The birds and the bees, and the whispering trees,
  And heather bedropt with dew,—
To be one with those early worshippers
  And pour the pæan too!

Then, off again with a slackened rein,
  And a bounding heart within,
To dash at a gallop over the plain,
  Health's golden cup to win!
This, this is the race for gain and grace
  Richer than vases and crowns;
And you that boast your pleasures the most,
  Amid the steam of towns,
Come taste true bliss in a morning like this,
  Galloping over the Downs!

ASCOT: JUNE 3, 1847.—WHEN HERO WON

Modern Olympia! shorn of all their pride—
  The patriot spirit, and unlucred praise—
  Thou art a type of these degenerate days
When love of simple honor all hath died;
Oh dusty, gay, and eager multitude,
  Agape for gold—No! do not thus condemn;
For hundreds here are innocent, and good,
  And young, and fair, among,—but not of—them;

And hundreds more enjoy, with gratitude,
  This well-earned holiday, so bright and green:
  Do not condemn! it *is* a stirring scene,
Though vanity and folly fill it up:
  Look, how the mettled racers please the Queen
Ha, brave John Day — a Hero wins the cup!

LIFE.

Ποία γαρ ἡ ζωὴ ἡμῶν; ἀτμίς.

A BUSY dream, forgotten ere it fades,
  A vapor melting into air away,
Vain hopes, vain fears, a mesh of lights and shades,
  A chequered labyrinth of night and day,
This is our life; a rapid, surgy flood
  Where each wave haunts its fellow; on they press;
To-day is yesterday, and hope's young bud
  Has fruited a to-morrow's nothingness:
Still on they press, and we are borne along,
  Forgetting and forgotten, trampling down
The living and the dead in that fierce throng,
  With little heed of Heaven's smile or frown,
And little care for others' right or wrong,
So we in iron selfishness stand strong.

WATERLOO.

THERMOPYLÆ and Canæ
  Were glorious fields of yore,
Leonidas and Hannibal
  Right famous evermore;

But we can claim a nobler name,
  A field more glorious too,
The chief who thus achieved for us
  Victorious Waterloo.

Let others boast of Cæsar's host
  Led on by Cæsar's skill,
And how fierce Attila could rout,
  And Alaric could kill; —
But we — right well, O hear me tell
  What British troops can do,
When marshalled by a Wellington,
  To win a Waterloo!

O for a Pindar's harp to tune
  The triumphs of that day!
O for a Homer's pictured words
  To paint the fearful fray! —
Alas, my tongue and harp ill-strung
  In feeble tones and few,
Hath little skill — yet right good will
  To sing of Waterloo.

Then gather round, my comrades,
  And hear a soldier tell
How full of honor was the day
  When — every man did well!
And though a soldier's speech be rough,
  His heart is hot and true,
While thus he tells of Wellington,
  At hard-fought Waterloo.

Sublimely calm, our iron Duke,
  A lion in his lair,
Waited and watched with sleepless eye
  To see what France would dare,
Nor deign'd to stir from Brussels
  Until he surely knew

The foe was rushing on his fate
  At chosen Waterloo.

What? should the hunter waste his strength,
  Nor hold his good hounds back
Before he knows they near the foes
  And open on the track?
No: let "surprise" blight Frenchmen's eyes,
  For truly they shall rue
The giant skill that, stern and still,
  Drew them to Waterloo!

Hotly the couriers gallop up
  To Richmond's festive scene, —
Alone, alone the chieftain stood
  Undaunted and serene;
Ready, ready, — staunch and steady, —
  And forth the orders flew
That marched us off to Quatre Bras,
  And whelming Waterloo.

Begin, begin with Quatre Bras,
  That twin-born field of fame
Where many a gallant deed was done
  By many a gallant name,
That battle-field, which seemed to yield
  An earnest and review
Of all that British courage dared
  And did at Waterloo.

We heard from far old Blucher's guns,
  At Ligny's blazing street,
And hurried on to Weimar's aid,
  Right glad the foe to meet;
A score of miles to Quatre Bras;
  But still to arms we stood,
And cheerly rushed without a pause
  To win the Boissy wood ·

Then, just like cowards, three to one,
  Before we could deploy,
To crush us, Ney and Excelmans
  Flew down with fiendish joy;
But stout we stood in hollow squares,
  And fought, and kept the ground,
While lancer spears and cuirassiers
  Were charging us all round:

Aye, aye, my men, we battled then
  Like wolves and bears at bay,
And thousands there among the dead
  With sable Brunswick lay:
And back to back in that attack
  The Ninety second fought,—
And "steadily" the Twenty-eighth
  Behaved as Britons ought.

Then up came Maitland with the guards,
  Hurrah! they clear the wood;
But still the furious Frenchman charged,
  And still we stoutly stood,
Till gently night drew on, and that
  Drew off the treacherous Ney,
For when the morning dimly broke
  —The fox had stole away!

This much, my lads, for Quatre Bras,
  And now for Waterloo,
Where skill and courage did it all,
  With God's good help in view!
For we were beardless, raw recruits,
  And they, more numerous far,
Were fierce, mustachioed mighty men,
  The veterans of war.

The God of battles help'd us soon,
  As godless France drew nigh,

It was the great eighteenth of June,
  The sun was getting high; —
And suddenly two hundred guns
  At once, with thundering throats,
Peal'd out their dreadful overture
  In deep volcano notes!

Then, by ten thousands, horse and foot,
  Came on the foaming Gaul,
And still with bristling front we stood
  As solid as a wall:
And stout Macdonnell's Hougoumont,
  The centre of the van,
Was storm'd and storm'd and storm'd — in vain,
  — He held it like a man!

O who can count the myriad deeds
  That hundreds did in fight?
Ponsonby falls, and Picton bleeds,
  And — both are quenched in night:
And many a hero subaltern
  And hero private too
Beat Ajax and Achilles both
  In winning Waterloo!

What shall I say on that dread day
  Of Ferrier and his band?
Ten times he chased the foes away,
  And charged them sword in hand;
Six of those ten he led his men
  With blood upon his brow, —
And weakly in the eleventh died
  To live in glory now!

Or, give a stave to Shaw the brave,
  — In death the hero sleeps, —
Hemm'd by a score, he knockd them o'er,
  And hewed them down in heaps;

Till, wearied out, the lion stout
 Beset as by a pack
Of hungry hounds, fell full of wounds,
 But none upon his back!

And Halket then before his men
 Dash'd forward, and made prize
(While both the lines in wonderment
 Could scarce believe their eyes)
Of a gaily-plumed French General
 Haranguing his array;
But Halket caught him, speech and all,
 And bore him right away!

Thee too, De Lancey, generous chief,
 For thee a niche be found,—
Wounded to death, he scorn'd relief
 Whilst others bled around;
And D'Oyley and Fitzgerald died,
 Just as the day was won,—
And Gordon, by his general's side—
 The side of Wellington!

And Somerset and Uxbridge then
 Gave each a limb to death;
Curzon and Canning cheered their men
 With their last dying breath;
And gallant Miller, stricken sore,
 With fainting utterance cries,
"Bring me my colors! wave them o'er
 Your colonel till he dies!"

Then furious waxed the Emperor
 That Britons wouldn't run,
"Les bêtes, pourquoi ne fuient ils pas?
 Et donc, ce Vellington?"
But Vellington still holds his own
 For eight red hours and more,

"Why comes not Marshal Blucher down?
— Ha! — there's his cannons' roar, —

"Up, guards, and at them! charge!" — the word
Like forkéd lightning passes,
And lance, and bayonet, and sword
Rush on in glittering masses!
Back, back, the surging columns roll
In terrified dismay,
And onward shout against the rout
The conquerors of the day!

O now, the tide of battle
Is turn'd to seas of blood,
When case and grape shot rattle
Among the multitude,
And Fates, led on by Furies,
Destroy the flying host,
And Chaos, mated with Despair,
Makes all the lost most lost!

Woe, woe! thou catiff-hero,
Thou Emperor — and slave,
Why didst not thou, too, nobly bleed
With those devoted brave?
No, no, the coward's thought was self,
And "sauve qui peut" his cry,
And verily at Waterloo
Did Great Napoleon die!

And died to fame, while yet his name
Was on ten thousand tongues
That trusted him, and pray'd to him,
And — curs'd him for their wrongs!
O noble souls! Imperial Guard,
Had *your* chief been but true,
Ye would have stood and stopp'd the rout
At crushing Waterloo.

Still as they fled from Wellington
  To Blucher's arms they flew;
These two made up the Quatre Bras
  To clutch a Waterloo!
Ha! Blucher's Prussian vengeance
  Was fully sated then,
When hated France upon the field
  Left forty thousand men.

Thus, comrades, hath a soldier told
  What Wellington's calm skill,
When help'd by troops of British mould
  And God's almighty will,
Against a veteran triple force
  In battle-field can do:—
Then, three times three for Wellington,
  The Prince of Waterloo!

"ARE YOU A GREAT READER?"

I hope to ripen into richer wine
  Than mixed Falernian; those decantered streams
Pour'd from another's chalice into thine
  Make less of wisdom than the scholar dreams;
Precept on precept, tedious line on line,
  That never-thinking, ever-reading plan
  Fashion some patchwork garments for a man,
But starve his mind: it starves of too much meat,
  An undigested surfeit; as for me
I am untamed, a spirit free and fleet
  That cannot brook the studious yoke, nor be
Like some dull grazing ox without a soul,
  But feeling racer's shoes upon my feet,
Before my teacher starts, I touch the goal.

THE VERDICT.

I LEAVE all judgments to that better world
And my more righteous Judge: for He shall tell
In the dread day when from their thrones are hurl'd
Each human tyranny and earthly spell,
That which alone of all He knoweth well—
The heart's own secret; He shall tell it out
With all the feelings and the sorrows there,
The fears within, the foes that hemm'd without,
Neglect, and wrong, and calumny and care:
For He hath saved thine every tearful pray'r
In His own lachrymal; and noted down
Each unconsidered grief with tenderest love:
Look up! beyond the cross behold the crown,
And for all wrongs below all rights above!

GUERNSEY.

GUERNSEY! to me and in my partial eyes
Thou art a holy and enchanted isle,
Where I would linger long, and muse the while
Of ancient thoughts and solemn memories,
Quickening the tender tear or pensive smile:
Guernsey!—for nearly thrice a hundred years
Home of my fathers! refuge from their fears,
And haven to their hope,—when long of yore
Fleeing Imperial Charles and bloody Rome
Protestant martyrs, to thy seagirt shore
They came to seek a temple and a home,
And found thee generous,—I their son would pour
My heart full all of praise and thanks to thee,
Island of welcomes,—friendly, frank, and free!

ALL'S RIGHT.

FOR MUSIC.

O NEVER despair at the troubles of life,
All's right!
In the midst of anxiety, peril, and strife,
All's right!
The cheerful philosophy never was wrong
That ever puts this on the tip of my tongue
And makes it my glory, my strength, and my song,
All's right!

The Pilot beside us is steering us still,
All's right!
The Champion above us is guarding from ill,
All's right!
Let others who know neither Father nor Friend
Go trembling and doubting in fear to the end, —
For me, on this motto I gladly depend,
All's right!

THE COMPLAINT OF AN ANCIENT BRITON

DISINTERRED BY ARCHÆOLOGISTS.

Two thousand years agone
They heaped my battle grave,
And each a tear and each a stone,
My mourning warriors gave;
For I had borne me well,
And fought as patriots fight,
Till, like a British chief, I fell
Contending for the right.

Seamed with many a wound,
  All weakly did I lie;
My foes were dead or dying round,—
  And thus I joyed to die!
For their marauding crew
  Came treacherously to kill,—
The many came against the few
  To storm our sacred hill.
We battled and bled,
  We won, and paid the price,
For I, the chief, lay down with the dead,
  A willing sacrifice!
My liegemen wailed me long,
  And treasured up my bones,
And reared my kist secure and strong
  With tributary stones:
High on the breezy down
  My native hill's own breast
Nigh to the din of mine ancient town,
  They left me to my rest.
I hoped for peace and calm
  Until my judgment hour,
And then to awake for the victor's palm
  And patriot's throne of power!
And lo, till this dark day
  Did men my grave revere:
Two thousand years had passed away,
  And still I slumbered here:
But now, there broke a noise
  Upon my silent home,
'Twas not the Resurrection voice
  That burst my turfy tomb,—
But men of prying mind,
  Alas, my fellow men,
Ravage my grave, my bones to find
  With sacreligious ken!
Mine honor doth abjure
  Your new barbarian race;
Restore, restore my bones secure

To some more secret place!
With mattock and with spade
Ye dare to break my rest;
The pious mound is all unmade
My clan had counted blest:
Take, take, my buckler's boss,
My sword, and spear, and chain, —
Steal all ye can of this world's dross,
But — rest my bones again!
I know your modern boast
Is light, and learning's spread, —
Learn of a Celt to show them most,
In honor to the Dead!

FARLEY HEATH,

NEAR ALBURY.

Many a day have I whiled away
Upon hopeful Farley heath,
In its antique soil digging for spoil
Of possible treasure beneath;
For Celts, and querns, and funeral urns,
And rich red Samian ware,
And sculptured stones, and centurion's bones
May all lie buried there!

How calmly serene, and glad have I been
From morn till eve to stay,
My Surrey serfs turning the turfs
The happy live-long day;
With eye still bright, and hope yet alight,
Wistfully watching the mould
As the spade brings up fragments of things
Fifteen centuries old!

Pleasant and rare it was to be there
  On a joyous day of June,
With the circling scene all gay and green
  Steep'd in the silent noon;
When beauty distils from the calm glad hills,—
  From the downs and dimpling vales
And every grove, lazy with love,
  Whispereth tenderest tales!

O then to look back upon Time's old track,
  And dream of the days long past,
When Rome leant here on his sentinel spear,
  And loud was the clarion's blast—
As wild and shrill from Martyr's hill
  Echoed the patriot shout,
Or rushed pell-mell with a midnight yell
  The rude barbarian rout!

Yes; every stone has a tale of its own—
  A volume of old lore;
And this white sand from many a brand
  Has polished gouts of gore;
When Holmbury-height had its beacon light,
  And Cantii held old Leith,
And Rome stood then with his iron men
  On ancient Farley heath!

How many a group of that exiled troop
  Have here sung songs of home,
Chanting aloud to a wondering crowd
  The glories of old Rome!
Or lying at length have bask'd their strength
  Amid this heather and gorse,
Or down by the well in the larch-grown dell
  Watered the black war-horse!

Look, look! my day-dream right ready would seem
  The past with the present to join,—

For see! I have found in this rare ground
  An eloquent green old coin,
With turquoise rust on its Emperor's bust,—
  Some Cæsar, august Lord;
And the legend terse, and the classic reverse,
  "Victory, valor's reward!—"

Victory,—yes! and happiness,
  Kind comrade, to me and to you,
When such rich spoil has crowned our toil
  And proved the day-dream true;
With hearty acclaim how we hail'd by his name
  The Cæsar of that coin,
And told with a shout his titles out,
  And drank his health in wine!

And then how blest the noon-day rest
  Reclined on a grassy bank,
With hungry cheer and the brave old beer
  Better than Odin drank;
And the secret balm of the spirit at calm,
  And poetry, hope, and health,—
Aye, have I not found in that rare ground
  A mine of more than wealth?

WISDOM.

It is the way we go, the way of life,
  A drop of pleasure in a sea of pain,
A grain of peace amid a load of strife,
  With toil and grief, and grief and toil again:
Yea:—but for this; the firm and faithful breast,
  Bolder than lion's, confident and strong,
That never doubts its birthright to be blest,
  And dreads no evil while it does no wrong:

14

This, this is wisdom, manful and serene,
  Towards God all penitence and prayer and trust,
But to the troubles of this shifting scene
  Simply courageous, and sublimely just:
Be then such wisdom thine, my heart within,—
There is no foe nor woe nor grief but—Sin.

THE HEART'S HUSBAND.

FOR MUSIC.

Go, leave me to weep for the years that are past,
  For my youth, and its friends, and its pleasures all dead,
My spring and my summer are fading too fast,
  And I long to live over the days that are fled;
It is not for sorrows or sins on my track
  That I mournfully cast my fond yearnings behind,—
—Ah, no,—from affection I love to look back,
  It is only my heart that has wedded my Mind.

And still, let the Mind that has married a Heart
  Though loving, be strong as a King in his pride,
And ever command that all weakness depart
  From the realm that he rules in the soul of his bride;
For what, if all time and all pleasures decay?
  My Mind is myself, an invincible chief,—
Like a child's broken toys are the years past away,
  And my Heart, half-ashamed, has forgotten her grief.

PROPHETS.

Prophets at home, — I smile to note your wrongs;
How scantly praised at each ancestral hearth
Are ye, caress'd by million hearts and tongues,
And full of honors over half the earth:
O petty jealousies and paltry strife!
The little minds that chronicle a birth
Stood once for teachers in the task of life;
But, as the child of genius grew apace,
Dismay'd at his gigantic lineaments,
They feared to find his glory their disgrace,
His mind their master: so their worldly aim
Is still to vex him with discouragements,
To check the springtide budding of his fame,
And keep it down to save themselves a name

WHEAT-CORN, AND CHAFF.

My little learning fadeth fast away,
And all the host of words and forms and rules
Bred in my teeming youth of books and schools
Dwindle to less and lighter; night and day
I dream of tasks undone, and lore forgot,
Seeming some sailor in the "ship of fools,"
Some debtor owing what he cannot pay,
Some conner of old themes remembered not.
Despise such small oblivion; 'tis the lot
Of human life, amid its chance and change
To learn, and then unlearn; to seek and find,
And then to lose familiars grown quite strange:
Store up, store wisdom's corn in heart and mind,
But fling the chaff on every winnowing wind.

THE HAPPY MAN.

A MAN of no regrets,
He goes his sunny way
Owing the past no load of debts
The present cannot pay:
He wedded his first love,
Nor loved another since;
He sets his nobler hopes above;
He reigns in joy a Prince!

A man of no regrets,
He hath no cares to vex,
No secret griefs, nor mental nets
Nor troubles to perplex;
Forgiveness to his sin,
And help in every need,
Blessing around, and peace within,
Crown him a King indeed!

A man of no regrets,
Upon his Empire free
The sun of gladness never sets,—
Then who so rich as he?
Yea, GOD upon my heart
Hath poured all blessings down;
Then yield to Him, with all thou art,
The homage of thy crown!

HERALDIC.

High in Battle's antlered hall
Ancient as its Abbey wall,
Hangs a helmet, brown with rust,
Cobweb'd o'er, and thick in dust
High it hangs, 'mid pikes and bows
Scowling still at spectral foes,
Proud and stern, with vizor down,
And fearful in its feudal frown.
When I saw what ail'd thee, heart,
Wherefore should I stop and start?
That old helm, with that old crest,
Is more to me than all the rest;
Battered, broken, though it be,
That old helm is all to me.
Yon black greyhound knoweth well:
Many a tale hath it to tell
How in troublous times of old
Sires of mine, with bearing bold,
Bearing bold, but much mischance,
Sway'd the sword, or poised the lance,—
Much mischance, desponding still,
They fought and fell, foreboding ill:
And their scallop, gules with blood,
Fessed amid the azure flood,
Show'd the pilgrim, slain afar
O'er the sea, in Holy War:
While that faithful greyhound black
Vainly watch'd the wild boar's track;
And the legend and the name
Proved all lost but hope and fame,—
Tout * est *perdu*, fors l'honneur,
Mas "*L'Espoir est ma force*" sans peur.

---

* Corruption, in the course of generations, has converted this piece of chivalrous despondency into the Author's modernized and ineuphonious name.

THE TRUE EPICURE.

How saidst thou? — Pleasure: why, my life is pleasure;
My days are pleasantness, my nights are peace;
I drink of joys which neither cloy nor cease,
A well that gushes blessings without measure.
Ah, thou hast little heed how rich and glad,
How happy is my soul in her full treasure,
How seldom but for honest pity sad,
How constantly at calm! — my very cares
Are sweetness in my cup, as being sent;
And country quiet and retired leisure
Keep me from half the common fears and snares;
And I have learnt the wisdom of content:
Yea, and, to crown the cup of peace with praise,
Both God and man have blest my works and ways.

THRENOS.

VANITY, vanity! dead hopes and fears,
Dim flitting phantoms of departed years,
Unsatisfying shadows, vague and cold,
Of thoughts and things that made my joys of old,
Sad memories of the kindly words and ways
And looks and loves of friends in other days, —
Alas! all gone — a dream, a very dream,
A dream is all you are, and all you seem!

O life, I do forget thee: I look back,
And lo, the desert wind has swept my track:
I stand upon this bare and solid ground,
And, strangely wakened, wonder all around;
How came I here? and whence? and whither tend?

Speak, friend! — if death and time have spared a friend.
Behold, the place that knew me well of yore
Knoweth me not; and that familiar floor
Where all my kith and kin were wont to meet
Is now grown strange, and throng'd by other feet:

O soul, my soul, consider thou that spot,
Root there thy gratitude, and leave it not;
Still let remembrance, with a swimming eye,
Live in those rooms, nor pass them coldly by;
Still let affection cling to those old days,
And yearning fondly paint them bright with praise:
O once my home — with all thy blessings fled,
O forms and faces — gathered to the dead,
O scenes of joy and sorrow — faded fast!
— How hollow sound thy footsteps, ghostlike PAST!
An aching emptiness is all thou art,
A famine hid within the caverned heart.

Thou changeless ONE, — how blest to have no change, --
Only with Thee, my God, I feel not strange;
Thou art the same for ever and for aye,
To-morrow and to-day as yesterday,
Thou art the same, — a tranquil Present still;
There I can hide, and bless Thy sovereign will:
Yes, bless Thee, O my Father, that Thy love
Call'd in an instant to the bliss above,
From ills to come and grief and care and fear,
Thy type to me, most honor'd and most dear!
O true and tender spirit, pure and good,
So vex'd on earth and little understood,
Thy gentle nature was not fit for strife,
But quail'd to meet the waking woes of life;
And therefore God our Father kindly made
Thy sleep a death, lest thou shouldst feel afraid!

THE DEAD.

A DIRGE.

I LOVE the dead!
The precious spirits gone before,
And waiting on that peaceful shore
To meet with welcome looks
and kiss me yet once more

I love the dead!
And fondly doth my fancy paint
Each dear one, wash'd from earthly taint,
By patience and by hope
made a most gentle saint.

O glorious dead!
Without one spot upon the dress
Of your ethereal loveliness,
Ye linger round me still
with earnest will to bless.

Enfranchised dead!
Each fault and failing left behind
And nothing now to chill or bind,
How gloriously ye reign
in majesty of mind!

O royal dead!
The resting, free, unfettered dead,
The yearning, conscious, holy dead,
The hoping, waiting, calm,
the happy, changeless dead!

I love the dead!
And well forget their little ill,
Eager to bask my memory still

In all their best of words
and deeds and ways and will.

I bless the dead!
Their good, half choked by this world's weeds,
Is blooming now in heavenly meads,
And ripening golden fruit,
of all those early seeds.

I trust the dead!
They understand me frankly now,
There are no clouds on heart or brow,
But spirit, reading spirit,
answereth glow for glow.

I praise the dead!
All their tears are wiped away,
Their darkness turned to perfect day,—
How blessed are the dead,
how beautiful be they!

O gracious dead!
That watch me from your paradise
With happy tender starlike eyes,
Let your sweet influence rain
me blessings from the skies.

Yet, helpless dead,
Vainly my yearning nature dares
Such unpremeditated prayers;—
All vain it were for them,
as even for me their's.

Immortal dead!
Ye in your lot are fixed as fate,
And man or angel is too late
To beckon back by prayer
one change upon your state.

O, godlike dead,
Ye that do rest, like Noah's dove,
Fearless I leave you to the love
Of him who gave you peace
to bear with you above.

And ye, the dead
Godless on earth, and gone astray,
Alas, your hour is past away,—
The Judge is just; for you
it now were sin to pray.

Still, all ye dead,
First may be last and last be first,—
Charity counteth no man curst,
But hopeth still in Him
whose love would save the worst.

Therefore, ye dead,
I love you, be ye good or ill,
For God, our God, doth love me still,
And you He loved on earth
with love that naught could chill.

And some, just dead,
To me on earth most deeply dear,
Who loved and nursed and blest me here,
I love you with a love
that casteth out all fear.

Come near me, Dead!
In spirit come to me, and kiss,—
No!—I must wait awhile for this
A few, few years or days
and I too feed on bliss!

TO AMERICA:

I.

COLUMBIA, child of Britain, — noblest child,
  I praise the growing lustre of thy worth,
And fain would see thy great heart reconcil'd
  To love the mother of so blest a birth:
For we are one, Columbia! still the same
In lineage, language, laws, and ancient fame,
  The natural nobility of earth:
Yes, we are one; the glorious days of yore,
When dear old England earn'd her storied name,
Are thine as well as ours for evermore;
  And thou hast rights in Milton, ev'n as we,
Thou too canst claim "sweet Shakspeare's wood-notes wild," —
  And chiefest, brother, we are both made free
Of one Religion, pure and undefil'd!

II.

I blame thee not, as other some have blam'd, —
  The high-born heir had grown to man's estate,
I mock thee not as some who should be shamed,
  Nor ferret out thy faults with envious hate;
Far otherwise, — by generous love inflamed,
  Patriot, I praise my country's foreign son,
Rejoicing in the blaze of good and great
  That diadems thy head! — go on, go on,
Young Hercules, thus travelling in might,
Boy-Plato, filling all the west with light.
  Thou new Themistocles for enterprise,
Go on and prosper, Acolyte of fate!
  And, precious child, dear Ephraim, turn those eyes, —
For thee thy Mother's yearning heart doth wait.

III.

Let aged Britain claim the classic Past,
  A shining track of bright and mighty deeds,
For thee I prophesy the Future vast
  Whereof the Present sows its giant seeds:
Corruption and decay come thick and fast
  O'er poor old England; yet a few dark years
And we must die as nations died of yore!
But, in the millions of thy teeming shore,
  Thy patriots, sages, warriors, saints, and seers,
We live again, Columbia! yea, once more
  Unto a thousand generations live,
    The mother in the child; to all the West
  Through Thee shall We earth's choicest blessings give,
    Ev'n as our Orient world in Us is blest.

IV.

Thou noble scion of an ancient root,
  Born of the forest-king! spread forth, spread forth, —
High to the stars thy tender leaflets shoot,
  Deep dig thy fibres round the ribs of earth!
  From sea to sea, from South to icy North,
    It must ere long be thine, through good or ill,
To stretch thy sinewy boughs: Go, wondrous child!
    The glories of thy destiny fulfil; —
  Remember then thy mother in her age,
Shelter her in the tempest, warring wild,
  Stand thou with us when all the nations rage
So furiously together! — we are one:
  And, through all time, the calm historic page
Shall tell of Britain blest in thee her son.

THE THANKS OF PARLIAMENT TO WELLINGTON AND HIS ARMY.

OUT spake a nation's voice,
  Concentred in her king,
While cannons roar, and hearts rejoice,
  And all the steeples ring:

Out spake old England then
  By prelates and by peers;
By all her best and wisest men,
  Her sages and her seers —

Old England and her pair
  Of sisters, north and west,
The comely graces, fresh and fair,
  Who charm the world to rest.

All honor to the brave! —
  The living and the dead, —
Who only fought to bless and save,
  And crush the hydra's head:

All honor and all thanks
  To every mother's son,
Saxon, or Celt, or Gael, or Manx,
  Who fought with Wellington!

For heroes were they all,
  To conquer or to die,
By Ahmednuggra's bastion'd wall
  Or desperate Assye:

And heroes still, they strive
  Against the dangerous Dane,
When France stirred up the northern hive,
  To sting us on the main:

All heroes, heroes still,
  For Lusitania's right;
Be red Roleia's hard-fought hill,
  And Vimiera's fight:

And stout the heroes stood
  On Talavera's day;
And wrote their conquering names in blood
  At Salamanca's fray;

Still heroes, on they went
  O'er Ciudad's gory fosse,
And stern Sebastian's battlement,
  And thundering Badajoz

And, heroes ever, taught
  Old Soult to fly and yield,
Shouting "Victory" as they fought
  On red Vittoria's field;

And, heroes aye, they flew
  To Orthez, conquering yet;
Until, at whelming Waterloo,
  The Frenchman's sun had set!

Then, thanks! thou glorious chief,
  And thanks! ye gallant band,
Who, under God, to man's relief
  Stretched out the saving band:

All Britain thanks you well,
  By peasant, peer, and king;
To all who fought for us, or fell,
  Immortal honors bring!

Peal fast the merry chime,
  And bid the cannon roar
In praise of heroes, whom all time
  Shall cherish evermore!

PAIN.

Delay not, sinner, till the hour of pain
  To seek repentance; pain is absolute,
Exacting all the body and the brain,
  Humanity's stern king from head to foot:
  How canst thou pray, while fevered arrows shoot
Through this torn targe, — while every bone doth ache,
  And the scared mind raves up and down her cell
Restless, and begging rest for mercy's sake?
  Add not to death the bitter fears of hell;
  Take pity on thy future self, poor man,
  While yet in strength thy timely wisdom can, —
Wrestle to-day with sin; and spare that strife
  Of meeting terrors in the van,
Just at the ebbing agony of life.

THREE VERSIONS OF ADRIAN'S APOSTROPHE.

Animula, vagula, blandule,
Hospes, comesque, corporis,
Quæ nunc abibis in loca?
Pallidula, rigidi, nudula,
Nec, ut soles, dabis jocos?

I.

Pleasant little fluttering sprite,
  Long my bosom's merry guest,
Whither now to wing thy flight?
Ah! thou frozen little wight,
  Pale, and naked, and unblest,
  Never more a jibe or jest?

II.

Soft little butterfly-guest of my heart,
Whither now flittest thou, spirit of mine?
Woe, — for thy merriment must it depart
Naked and frigid and pallid to pine?

III.

Soul, thou tiny truant dear,
Bosom friend for many a year,
Restless little darling, say,
Whither stealest thou away?

Pallid as a fainting maid,
Naked, icy-cold, afraid,
Is then all thy wit in vain, —
Shalt thou never laugh again?

NO SURRENDER.

FOR MUSIC.

Ever constant, ever true,
Let the word be, No surrender;
Boldly dare and greatly do!
This shall bring us bravely through,
No surrender, No surrender;
And though Fortune's smiles be few
Hope is always springing new,
Still inspiring me and you
With a magic — No surrender!

Nail the colors to the mast,
Shouting glad, No surrender!
Troubles near are all but past —

Serve them as you did the last,
  No surrender, No surrender!
Though the skies be overcast
And upon the sleety blast
Disappointments gather fast,
  Beat them off with No Surrender!

Constant and courageous still,
  Mind, the word is No surrender;
Battle, tho' it be uphill,
Stagger not at seeming ill,
  No surrender, No surrender!
Hope, — and thus your hope fulfil, —
There's a way where there's a will,
And the way all cares to kill
  Is to give them — No surrender!

NEVER MIND.

FOR MUSIC.

Soul, be strong, whate'er betide,
God himself is guard and guide, —
With my Father at my side,
    Never mind!

Clouds and darkness hover near,
Men's hearts failing them for fear,
But be thou of right good cheer,
    Never mind!

Come what may, some work is done,
Praise the Father through the Son,
Goals are gain'd and prizes won,
    Never mind!

And if now the skies look black
All the past behind my back,
Is a bright and blessed track;
Never mind!

Stand in patient courage still,
Working out thy Master's will,
Compass good, and conquer ill;
Never mind!

Fight, for all their bullying boast,
Dark temptation's evil host,
This is thy predestined post;
Never mind!

Be then tranquil as a dove;
Through these thunder-clouds above
Shines afar the heaven of love;
Never mind!

THE CROMLECH DU TUS, GUERNSEY.*

Hoary relic, stern and old,
Heaving huge above the mould
Like some mammoth, lull'd to sleep
By the magic-murmuring deep,
Till those grey gigantic bones
Gorgon-time hath frown'd to stones, —
Who shall tell thine awful tale,
Massy Cromlech at "The Vale?"
Ruthless altar, hungry tomb!
Superstition's throne of gloom,
Where, in black sepulchral state,

---

* See an interesting paper by Mr. F. C. Lukis, in the Archæological Journal for April, 1845.

High the hooded Spectre sate,
Terrible and throng'd by fears
Brooding for a thousand years
As a thunder-cloud above
All that wretched men may love,—
Is there no grim witness near
That shall whisper words of fear,
Every brother's heart to thrill,
Every brother's blood to chill,
While thy records are revealed,
And thy mysteries unsealed?
Lift, with Titan toil and pain,
Lift the lid by might and main,—
Lift the lid and look within
On—this charnel house of Sin!
O, twin brethren, how and when
Dwelt ye in this rocky den!
Rise, dread martyrs! for your bones
Chronicle these cromlech-stones!
Rise, ye grisly, ghastly pair,
—Skeletons! how came ye there—
Kneeling starkly side by side
More like life than those who died?
More like life?—O what a spell
Of horror cowers in that cell!
More like life?—Alive they went
Into that stone tenement,
Bound as in religious ease
Meekly kneeling on their knees,
And the cruel thongs confin'd
All but the distracted mind,
That with terror raved to see.
Woe! how slow such death would be:
Woe! how slow and full of dread:
Pining, dying, but not dead—
Pining, dying in the tomb,
Drown'd in gulfs of starving gloom,
With corruption, hideous fear,
Creeping noiselessly more near,

While the victims slowly died,
Link'd together side by side,
Till in manacled mad strife
Both had struggled out of life!

Yea: some idol claim'd the price
Of this living sacrifice;
Some grim demon's dark high priest
Bound these slaves for Odin's feast,
Offering up with rites of hell
Human pangs to Thor or Bel! —

Christians, ponder on these bones;
Kneel around the Cromlech-stones;
Kneel and thank our God above
That His name, His heart is Love,
That His thirst is, — not for blood,
But — for joy and gratitude;
That He bids no soul be sad,
But is glad to make *us* glad;
That He loves not man's despair,
But delights to bless his prayer!

A FAMILY PICTURE.

My little ones, my darling ones, my precious things of earth,
How gladly do I triumph in the blessing of your birth;
How heartily for praises, and how earnestly for prayers,
I yearn upon your loveliness, my dear delightful cares!

O children, happy word of peace, my jewels and my gold,
My truest friends till now, and still my truest friends when old,
I will be every thing to you, your playmate and your guide,
Both Mentor and Telemachus for ever at your side!

I will be every thing to you, your sympathizing friend,
To teach, and help, and lead, and bless, and comfort, and defend;
O come to me and tell me all, and ye shall find me true,
A brother in adversity to fight it out for you!

Yea, sins or follies, griefs or cares, or young affection's thrall,
Fear not, for I am one with you, and I have felt them all;
I will be tender, just, and kind, unwilling to reprove,
I will do all to bless you all by wisdom and by love.

O blessed boon and gain to me, O mercy, praise, and pride!
Ye lack none other heritage your father's name beside:
When I am dead, your little ones shall read my words with glee,
When they are dead, their little ones will still remember me.

My tender babes, delighted I review you as ye stand,
A pretty troop of fairies and young cherubs hand in hand,
And tell out all your names to be a dear familiar sound
Wherever English hearths and hearts about the world abound.

My eldest, of the sparkling eyes, my Ellin, nine years old,
Thou thoughtful good example of the loving little fold,
My Ellin, they shall hear of thee, fair spirit, holy child,
The truthful and the well-resolved, the liberal and the mild.

And thee, my Mary, what of thee? — the beauty of thy face?
The coyly-pretty whims and ways that ray thee round with grace?
— O more than these; a dear warm heart that still must thrill and glow
With pure affection's sunshine, and with feeling's overflow!

Thou too, my gentle five-year-old, fair Margaret the pearl,
A quiet, sick, and suffering child, sweet patient little girl,—
Yet gay withal and frolicsome at times wilt thou appear,
And like a bell thy merry voice rings musical and clear.

And next my Selwyn, precious boy, a glorious young mind,
The sensitive, the passionate, the noble, and the kind,

Whose light-brown locks bedropt with gold, and large eyes full
of love,
And generous nature mingle well the lion and the dove.

The last, an infant toothless one, now prattling on my knee,
Whose bland, benevolent, soft face is shining upon me;
Another silver star upon our calm domestic sky,
Another seed of happy hope, dropt kindly from on high.

This sealeth up the sum to us, my loved and loving wife,
Be these to us the pleasure and the business of life:
And thou to me, what art thou not? through infancy and youth,
And manhood's prime, as now, my all of constancy and truth!

A happy man, — be this my praise, — not riches, rank, or fame,
A happy man, with means enough, — no other lot or name:
A happy man, with you for friends, my children and my wife, —
— Ambition is o'ervaulted here in all that gladdens life!

Yes! leave me to my happy thoughts, and these about me still,
In ancient woods of Albury, or on my fresh Furze Hill;
And, children, teach your children, too, by righteousness to stand,
For so they shall inherit peace and blessings in the land.

POSTSCRIPT.

HENRY DE B. T.

Hail then a sixth! my doubly triple joy,
Another blessing in a third-born boy,
Another soul by generous Favor sent
To teach and train for heaven through content,
Another second-self with hopes like mine
In better worlds beyond the stars to shine,
Another little hostage from above

The pledge and promise of our Father's love!
God guard the babe; and cherish the young child·
And bless the boy with nurture wise and mild;
And lead the lad, and yearn upon the youth;
And make the man a man of trust and truth;
Through life and death uphold him all his days,
And then translate him to Thyself with praise!

ERRATA.

AN AUTHOR'S COMPLAINT.

O FRIENDS and brothers, judge me not unheard;
Make not a man offender for a word:
For often have I noted seeming fault
That harm'd my rhymes, and made my reasons halt,
Whilst all that error was some printer's sloth,
Who, scorning rhyme and reason, slew them both:
Be ye then liberal to your far-off friend,
Where garbled, guess him; and where maim'd, amend
Trust him for wit, when types have marr'd the word,
And wisdom, too, where only blockheads err'd.

IMPROMPTU.

TO ONE WHO SAID THAT SHE DISLIKED POETRY.

LADY, thou lovest high and holy Thought,
  And noble deeds, and hopes sublime or beauteous,
Thou lovest charities in secret wrought,
  And all things pure and generous and duteous;

What then if these be drest in robes of power,
  Triumphant WORDS, that thrill the heart of man,
Conquering for good beyond the flitting hour,
  With stately march, and music in the van?

VENUS:

A REPLY TO LONGFELLOW'S POEM ON MARS, IN "VOICES OF THE NIGHT."

THOU lover of the blaze of Mars,
  Come out with me to-night,
For I have found among the stars
  A name of nobler light:

Thy boast is of the unconquered Mind,
  The strong, the stern, the still;
Mine of the happier Heart, resign'd
  To Wisdom's holy will.

They call my star by Beauty's name,
  The gentle Queen of Love;
And look! how fair its tender flame
  Is flickering above:

O star of peace, O torch of hope,
  I hail thy precious ray,
A diamond on the ebon cope
  To shine the dark away.

Within my heart there is no light
  But cometh from above,
I give the first watch of the night
  To the sweet planet, Love:

The star of Charity and Truth,
  Of cheerful thoughts and sage,
The lamp to guide my steps in youth,
  And gladden mine old age!

O brother, yield: thy fiery Mars,
  For all his mailed might,
Is not so strong among the stars
  As mine, the Queen of night:

A Queen to shine all nights away,
  And make the morn more clear,
Contentment gilding every day,—
  —There is no twilight here!

Yes; in a trial world like this .
  Where all that comes—is sent,
Learn how divine a thing it is
  To smile and be content!

"THE WARM YOUNG HEART."

FOR MUSIC.

A BEAUTIFUL face, and a form of grace
  Were a pleasant sight to see,
And gold, and gems, and diadems,
  Right excellent they be:
But beauty and gold, tho' both be untold,
  Are things of a worldly mart,
The wealth that I prize, above ingots or eyes,
  Is a heart,—a warm young heart!

O face most fair, shall thy beauty compare
  With affection's glowing light?

O riches and pride, how pale ye beside
  Love's wealth, serene and bright!
I spurn thee away, as a cold thing of clay,
  Tho' gilded and carved thou art,
For all that I prize, in its smiles and its sighs,
  Is a heart, — a warm young heart!

A CONSECRATION.

October 29, 1847.

LIKE some fair Nun, the pious and the chaste,
  Shalford, thy new-born temple stands serene,
Modestly deck'd in pure old English taste,
  The village beauty of thy tranquil scene;
And we to-day have made religious haste
  To see thee wedded to thy heavenly Spouse.
  Kneeling in unison of praise and prayer
To help the offering of thy maiden vows:
  Hark! what a thrilling utterance is there,
"Lift up your heads, ye everlasting gates," —
  As GOD's high-priest with apostolic care
To HIM this tent of glory consecrates:
  Good work! to be remembered for all time,
  The seed of mercies endless and sublime!

'Come in, thou King of Glory," yea, come in,
  Rest here awhile, great Conqueror for good!
Bless thou this font to cleanse from Adam's sin,
  Spread thou this table with celestial food!
  And, kindled by Thy grace to gratitude,
May thousands here eternal treasures win,
  As, hither led, from time to time with joy
They seek their Father: lo! before mine eyes
Visions and promises of good arise, —

The tender babe baptized, the stripling boy
 Confirm'd for godliness, the maid and youth
Wedded in love, the man mature made wise,
 The elder taught in righteousness and truth,
And each an heir of life before he dies!

THE THANKSGIVING HYMN AND CHANT.

FOR THE HARVEST HOME OF 1847.

O NATION, Christian nation,
 Lift high the hymn of praise,
The God of our Salvation
 Is love in all his ways;
He blesses us, and feedeth
 Every creature of his hand,
To succor him that needeth,
 And to gladden all the land!

Rejoice, ye happy people,
 And peal the changing chime
From every belfried steeple
 In symphony sublime:
Let cottage and let palace
 Be thankful, and rejoice,
And woods, and hills, and valleys,
 Re-echo the glad voice!

From glen, and plain, and city,
 Let gracious incense rise,
The Lord of life in pity
 Hath heard his creatures' cries;
And where in fierce oppressing
 Stalk'd fever, fear, and dearth,
He pours a triple blessing
 To fill and fatten earth!

Gaze round in deep emotion:
  The rich and ripen'd grain
Is like a golden ocean
  Becalmed upon the plain;
And we who late were weepers,
  Lest judgment should destroy,
Now sing, because the reapers
  Are come again with joy!

O praise the hand that giveth
  — And giveth evermore —
To every soul that liveth
  Abundance flowing o'er!
For every soul He filleth
  With manna from above,
And over all distilleth
  The unction of His love.

Then gather, Christians, gather,
  To praise with heart and voice
The good Almighty Father,
  Who biddeth you rejoice:
For he hath turned the sadness
  Of his children into mirth,
And we will sing with gladness
  The harvest-home of earth!

O BLESS the God of harvest, praise him through the land,
Thank him for his precious gifts, his help, and liberal love:
Praise him for the fields that have rendered up their riches,
And, dressed in sunny stubbles, take their Sabbath after toil;
Praise him for the close-shorn plains, and uplands lying bare,
And meadows, where the sweet-breathed hay was stacked in early summer;
Praise him for the wheat-sheaves, gathered safely into barn,
And scattering now their golden drops beneath the sounding flail;
Praise him for the barley mow, a little hill of sweetness;

Praise him for the clustering hop, to add its fragrant bitter;
Praise him for the wholesome root, that fattened in the furrow;
Praise him for the mellow fruits that bend the groaning bough;
For blessings on thy basket, and for blessings on thy store,
For skill and labor prospered well, by gracious suns and showers,
For mercies on the home, and for comforts on the hearth,
O happy heart of this broad land, praise the God of harvest!

All ye that have no tongue to praise, we will praise Him for you,
And offer on our kindling souls the tribute of your thanks;
Trees and shrubs and the multitude of herbs, gladdening the eyes
with verdure,
For all your leaves and flowers and fruits, we praise the God of
harvest!
Birds, and beetles in the dust, and insects flitting on the air,
And ye that swim the waters in your scaly coats of mail,
And steers, resting after labor, and timorous flocks afold,
And generous horses, yoked in teams to draw the creaking wains,
For all your lives, and every pleasure solacing that lot,
Your sleep, and food, and animal peace, we praise the God of
harvest!
And ye, O some who never prayed, and therefore cannot praise;
Poor darkling sons of care and toil and unillumined night,
Who rose betimes, but did not ask a blessing on your work,
Who lay down late, but rendered no thank-offering for that blessing
Which all unsought He sent, and all unknown ye gathered, —
Alas, for you, and in your stead, we praise the God of harvest!
O ye famine-stricken glens, whose children shrieked for bread,
And noisome alleys of the town where fever fed on hunger, —
O ye children of despair, bitterly bewailing Erin,
Come and join my cheerful praise, for God hath answered prayer.
Praise him for the better hopes, and signs of better times,
Unity, gratitude, contentment; industry, peace, and plenty;
Bless Him that his chastening rod is now the sceptre of forgiveness,
And in your joy remember well to praise the God of harvest!

Come, come along with me, and swell this grateful song,
Ye nobler hearts, old England's own, the children of the soil:
All ye that sowed the seed in faith, with those who reaped in joy,

And he that drove the plough afield, with all the scattered gleaners,
And maids who milk the lowing kine, and boys that tend the sheep,
And men that load the sluggish wain, or neatly thatch the rick,—
Shout and sing for happiness of heart, nor stint your thrilling cheers,
But make the merry farmer's hall resound with glad rejoicings,
And let him spread the hearty feast for joy at harvest-home,
And join this cheerful song of praise,—to bless the God of harvest!

M. T.

Forgotten?—not forgotten, kind, good man,
  Tho' seldom fully prized at thy great worth,—
I will embalm thy memory as I can,
  And send this blessing to the ends of earth!
For thou wert all things kindly unto all,
  Benevolent and liberal from birth,
Ever responsive to affection's call,
  And full of care for others,—full of care—
Weary with others' burdens, generous heart,
  And yet thine own too little strong to bear:
Father! I owe thee all, and cannot pay
  The happy debt, until I too depart;
Then, will I bless and love it all away
  In that bright world, my Father, where thou art!

TWO PSALMS.

I. THE 19TH.

Heav'n declares its Makers glory,
  And the firmament His might;
Day to day the wondrous story
  Echoes on, and night to night:

All is silence, yet Creation
  Knows and hears that voiceless speech
Which to every tribe and nation
  Doth their Maker's glory teach.

From his chamber bright in heaven
  Lo, the bridegroom of the earth
Gladness by his smile hath given,
  And awakes the morn to mirth:
Not less full of life and pleasure
  Is God's truth, nor less complete;
'Tis more precious than all treasure,
  Than the honeycomb more sweet.

It rejoices, heals, and teaches,
  Ever holy, just, and good;
To the inmost feeling reaches,
  And leads up the heart to God.
Warned by that, thy servant turneth
  To the path that tends to bliss;
Yet, who all his faults discerneth?
  Cleanse me, if I err in this.

Let not pride be ruler in me,
  But deliver, guide, forgive,
Thus, corruption quenched within me,
  I shall be upright and live.
Let my words and meditation,
  Ever pleasing in thy sight,
Meet with gracious acceptation,
  My Redeemer and my Might!

II. THE 20TH.

GOD in time of trouble hear thee,
  And the name of Jacob's Lord
From his sanctuary near thee,
  Out of Zion help afford;
Crown thy sacrifice with fire,

All thy gifts remembered still,
Grant thee all thy heart's desire,
And thy choicest wish fulfil!

We will joy in Thy salvation,
And will set our banners high
In our God! — Thy supplication
Be accomplished at thy cry.
Now I know the Lord from heaven
Saveth still his Christ from harm;
Now to Him will strength be given
By the might of his right arm.

Some in chariots, some on horses, —
We in God Jehovah trust:
And while He our sure Resource is,
They are fallen in the dust:
Save, Jehovah, save and hear us,
King of glory, King of might!
When we call be ever near us, —
Ever for thy servants fight!

CONFESSION.

Alas, how many vain and bitter things
My zeal, and pride, and natural haste have wrought;
Yea, thou my soul, by word and deed and thought,
The curse of selfishness hath scorch'd thy wings:
There is a fire within, I feel it now,
A smouldering mass of strong imaginings
That heat my heart, and burn upon my brow,
And vent their hissing lava on my tongue,
Scathing, unsparing: — yet, my will is just,
My wrath is ever quickened by a wrong,

I flame — to strike oppressors to the dust,
  To crush the cruel, and confound the base,
To welcome insolence with calm disgust,
  And brand the scoffer's forehead with disgrace.

A SONG.

Ah Memory! why reproach me so
  With shadows of the past,
The thrilling hopes of long ago
  That came and went so fast?
Ye tender tones of that dear voice,
  Ye looks of those loved eyes, —
Return, — and bid my heart rejoice,
  For true love never dies!

Rejoice? — O word of hope! I may
  When those indeed return:
For looks and tones so past away
  In solitude I yearn!
Let others fancy I forget
  The light of those dear eyes, —
  love, — O how I love thee yet!
  For true love never dies.

CHEER UP.

FOR MUSIC.

NEVER go gloomily, man with a mind!
  Hope is a better companion than fear,
Providence, ever benignant and kind,
  Gives with a smile what you take with a tear;
All will be right,
Look to the light,—
Morning is ever the daughter of night,
All that was black will be all that is bright,
Cheerily, cheerily then! cheer up!

Many a foe is a friend in disguise,
  Many a sorrow a blessing most true,
Helping the heart to be happy and wise,
  With lore ever precious and joys ever new.
Stand in the van!
Strive like a man!
This is the bravest and cleverest plan,
Trusting in God, while you do what you can,
Cheerily, cheerily then! cheer up!

"TOGETHER."

FOR MUSIC.

THE elm tree of old felt lonely and cold
  When wintry winds blew high,
And, looking below, he saw in the snow
  The ivy wandering nigh;
And he said, Come twine with those tendrils of thine

My scathed and frozen form,
For heart and hand together we'll stand,
And mock at the baffled storm,
Ha, ha! Together.

And so when grief is withering the leaf,
And checking hope's young flower,
And frosts do bite with their teeth so white
In disappointment's hour,
Tho' it might o'erwhelm either ivy or elm
If alone each stood in the strife,
If heart and hand together they stand,
They may laugh at the troubles of life,
Ha, ha! Together.

FRIENDS.

I CANNOT move a mile upon this earth,
I could not, did I walk from end to end,
But there I find a heart of wit and worth,
Some gracious spirit to be hailed a friend:
O there are frequent angels unawares,
And many have I met upon my way,
Kind Christian souls, to make me rich with prayers,
Whilst in like coin their mercies I repay;
And oft the sun of praise hath lit mine eyes,
Generous praise and just encouragement,
From some who say I help them to be wise,
And teach them to be happy in content:
Ah soul, rejoice! for thou hast thickly sown
The living world with friendships all thine own.

A GREETING.

It were not well to vex thee with my praises,
Yet I am quick to read thy gifts aright,
Loving, sincere, and wise, — in three best phases,
Young heart, I note thy characters of light;
Spirits are keen to make such instant guesses;
For time is nothing to the Soul that lives;
Therefore my spirit thy good spirit blesses,
Therefore my Mind its cordial greeting gives, —
Its greeting? — of a moment, sad to tell,
For all my greeting is a true Farewell!

HORACE'S PHILOSOPHY.

III. 29.

Wisely for us within night's sable veil
God hides the future; and, if men turn pale
For dread distrusting, laughs their fear to scorn.
For thee, the present calmly order well:
All else as on a river's tide is borne,
Now flowing peaceful to the Tuscan sea
Down the mid-channel on a gentle swell;
Now, as the hoarse, fierce mandate of the flood
Stirs up the quiet stream, time-eaten rocks
Go hurrying down, with houses, herds, and flocks,
And echoes from the mountain and the wood.
He stands alone, glad, self-possessed, and free,
Who grateful for to-day can say, I live;
To-morrow let my Father take or give:

II.

As He may will, not I — with dark or light
Let God ordain the morrow, noon, or night.
He, even He, can never render vain
The past behind me; nor bring back again
What any transient hour has once made fact.
Fortune, rejoicing in each cruel act,
And playing frowardly a saucy game,
Dispenses changeful and uncertain fame.
Now kind to me, and now to some beside.
I praise her here: but if it should betide
She spreads her wings for flight, I hold no more
  The good she gave, but in mine honest worth,
  Clad like a man, go honorably forth
To seek the undowried portion of the poor.

"THE LAST TIME."

Another year? another year!
  Who dare depend on other years?
The judgment of this world is near,
  And all its children faint for fears:
Famine, pestilence, and war,
  Mixt with praises, prayers, and tears
Civil strife and social jar,
  Spurr'd by pen, and stirr'd by sword,
Herald Him who comes from far,
In Elijah's fiery car,
  Our own returning Lord!

Look around — the nations quail!
  All the elements of ill
Crowd like locusts on the gale,
  And the dark horizon fill:

Woe to earth, and all her seed!
  Woe, they run to ruin still: —
He that runneth well may read
  Texts of truth the times afford,
How, in earth's extremest need
Cometh, cometh soon indeed
  Our own redeeming Lord!

Lo, the marvels passing strange
  Every teeming hour brings,
Daily turns with sudden change
  The kaleidoscope of things;
But the Ruler, just and wise,
  Orders all, as King of kings, —
Hark! His thunders shake the skies,
  Lo! His vials are outpour'd!
Earth in bitter travail lies,
And creation groans and cries
  For our expected Lord!

Stand in courage, stand in faith!
  Tremble not as others may;
He that conquers hell and death
  Is the friend of those who pray.
And in this world's destined woe
  He will save his own alway
From the trial's furnace glow, —
  Till the harvest all is stor'd,
Rescu'd from each earthly foe,
And the terrible ones below,
  By our avenging Lord!

Yea, come quickly! Savior, come
  Take us to thy glorious rest,
All thy children yearn for home,
  Home, the heaven of thy breast
Help, with instant gracious aid!
  That in just assurance blest,
We may watch — nor feel afraid,

Every warning in thy word,
Signs and tokens all array'd
In proof of that for which we pray'd,
The coming of the Lord!

THE POET'S WEALTH.

I NUMBER you by thousands, unseen friends,
And dearly precious is your love to me;
Yea, what a goodly company ye be!
Far as the noble brotherhood extends
Of Saxon hearts and tongues o'er land and sea:
How rich am I in love! — the sweet amends
For all whatever little else of pain
Some few unkindly cause; — most rich in love,
From mine own home to earth's remotest ends:
Let me then count my store, my glorious gain,
This wealth, that my poor merit far transcends,
Your loving kindness, echoing from above
The Highest Blessing on my works and ways,
Εὖ δοῦλε ἀγαθέ, my Father's praise:

Yea, let me thank you; let my heart outpour
Unbidden notes of honest gratitude
To all whose yearnings follow me with good,
Loving my mind and all its humble store:
O generous friends! — a cordial multitude
Hived in the West, upon that busy shore
Where fair Columbia, Britain's child, is throned
Imperial, yet with empire all unowned, —
O generous friends! — another cordial band,
From far Australia to the Arctic seas,
And crowds around me in my own dear land, —
How, how to thank for mercies rich as these?
Lo, let me stand and bless from East to West,

From North to South, — because I thus am blest!
Aye: blest indeed above the lot of men,
And rich in joys that reach the true sublime!
For that the magic-music of my pen
Hath won such wealth of love in every clime,
And still shall win such treasure for all time,
Therefore my soul is glad: judge me, my friends,
Is not the poet wealthier in his joys
Than Attalus with all his golden toys?
And, as his growing dynasty extends
To children's children, reigning in the mind,
Is he not great, a monarch of his kind?
Ah me! not so: this thought of pride destroys:
Give God the praise: His blessings send this store
Of unseen friends by thousands evermore!

ΘΕΩ ΔΟΞΑ.

GERALDINE,

AND

OTHER POEMS.

PREFACE.

INCLUDING A SKETCH OF CHRISTABEL.

The Christabel of Coleridge is a poem of which it is almost impossible to give shortly a fair and perfect abstract. Every word tells; every line is a picture: simple, beautiful, and imaginative, it retains its hold upon the mind by so many delicate feelers and touching points, that to outline harshly the main branches of the tree, would seem to be doing the injustice of neglect to the elegance of its foliage, and the microscopic perfection of every single leaf. Those who now read it for the first time, will scarcely be disposed to assent to so much praise; but the man to whom it is familiar, will remember how it has grown to his own liking, how much of melody, depth, nature, and invention, he has found from time to time hiding in some simple phrase, or unobtrusive epithet. Most gladly, therefore, do I refer my readers to the Christabel itself, however it may tell to the disadvantage of Geraldine: at the same time, inasmuch as there may be many to whom the sequel will be obscure, from having had no opportunity of perusing the prior poem, I trust I shall be pardoned, if, in consulting the interest of some of my readers, I mar the fair memory of Christabel by a sketch so imperfect, as only to serve the purpose of explaining myself.

The heroine of Coleridge is a "blue-eyed" girl, "O call her fair, not pale;" and is introduced as "praying in the midnight wood," "beneath the huge oak tree," "for the weal of her lover that's far away." While thus engaged, she is startled by "moanings," and on the "other side of the oak," finds "a damsel bright" "in sore distress" and "weariness;" in fact, the dark-eyed Geraldine, whose sudden appearance is by herself very suspiciously explained. Christabel, "comforting her," takes her home to Langdale-Hall, the castle of Sir Leoline, where the howl of "the mastiff-bitch" seems to bode evil, and some wild expressions addressed by Geraldine to Christabel's "guardian spirit," her dead mother (who had "said that she should hear the castle-bell strike twelve upon her [daughter's] wedding day"), gives the first clue to the wicked and supernatural character of Geraldine. The maidens now retiring to rest together, the beautiful stranger's "bosom and half her side," — "old" "and cold," suggest vague alarms, and "for an hour" Christabel in "her arms" is dreaming fearfully, — from which state of terror she is delivered by her guardian mother.

The second part opens with the introduction of Geraldine to Sir Leoline, who recognises in the "lofty lady," the daughter of his once "friend in youth," "Roland de Vaux, of Tryermaine," who had parted from Sir Leoline many years ago "in disdain and insult." At her tale, (which I am pleased to consider a fabrication, as also the likeness to Roland's daughter to be a piece of witchcraft,) the Baron is highly indignant, and vows to avenge "the child of his friend." Meanwhile, poor Christabel is under a mysterious spell, subjected to "perplexity of mind," "a vision of fear," and "snake-like looks" of the rival beauty; albeit "comforted" by a "vision blest." Sir Leoline, glad of the opportunity of a reconciliation to his long-lost friend, sends "Bracy the bard," with "harp" and "solemn vest," by "Irt-(hing) flood," &c., to Roland's border-castle, commissioning him to "greet Lord Roland," acquaint him that "his daughter is safe in Langdale-Hall," and bidding him "come" with "all his numerous array" to meet Sir Leoline "with his own numerous array," on "panting palfreys," and to be friends once more. "Bard Bracy" hesitates, on account of having dreamt that Christabel — "the dove" — had "a green snake" "coiled around its wings and neck," "underneath the old tree;" and having "vowed," "with music strong and saintly song," to exorcise the forest. The Baron interprets it as of "Lord Roland's beauteous dove," and when Christabel, who had ever and anon been tortured by "looks askance" of "dull and treacherous hate," entreats him by her "mother's soul to send away that woman," he, accounting "his child" jealous of the radiant stranger, and no doubt alienated by black arts from his daughter, as the lover is afterwards, seems full of wrath, and, "in tones abrupt, austere," sends the reluctant Bracy on his mission.

Thus far Christabel: for the "Conclusion to part the second," however beautiful in itself, is clearly out of place, unless it was intended as a mystification.

And now, on my own portion, I may be permitted to make a few remarks. My excuse for continuing the fragment at all, will be found in Coleridge's own words to the preface of the 1816 pamphlet edition, where he says, "I trust that I shall be able to embody in verse the three parts yet to come, in the course of the present year;" a half-promise, which, I need scarcely observe, has never been redeemed.

In the following attempt I may be censured for rashness, or commended for courage: of course, I am fully aware that to take up the pen where COLERIDGE has laid it down, — and that in the wildest and most original of his poems, — is a most difficult, nay, dangerous proceeding: but, upon these very characteristics of difficulty and danger I humbly rely; trusting that, in all proper consideration for the boldness of the experiment, if I be adjudged to fail, the fall of Icarus may be broken; if I be accounted to succeed, the flight of Dædalus may apologize for his presumption.

I deem it due to myself to add what I trust will not be turned against me, viz.: that, if not written literally *currente calamo*, GERALDINE has been the pleasant labor of but very few days: also, that until I had just completed it, I did not know of the existence of the proposed solution of Christabel in a recent life of Coleridge, and at that period saw no reason to make any change in mine: and finally, that I should wish to be judged by the whole volume, and not by GERALDINE alone.

M. F. T.

GERALDINE.

PART I.

(BEING THE THIRD OF CHRISTABEL.)

It is the wolf on stealthy prowl,
Hath startled the night with a dismal howl,
It is the raven, whose hoarse croak
Comes like a groan from the sear old oak,
It is the owl, whose curdling screech
Hath peopled with terrors the spectral beech;
For again the clock hath tolled out twelve,
And sent to their gambols the gnome and the elve,
And awoken the friar his beads to tell,
And taught the magician the time for his spell,
And to her cauldron hath hurried the witch,
And aroused the deep bay of the mastiff bitch.

The gibbous moon, all chilling and wan,
Like a sleepless eyeball looketh on,
Like an eyeball of sorrow behind a shroud
Forth looketh she from a torn grey cloud,
Pouring sad radiance on the black air, —
Sun of the night, — what sees she there?
O lonely one, O lovely one,
What dost thou here in the forest dun,
Fair truant, like an angel of light

Hiding from heaven in deep midnight?
Alas! there is guilt in thy glittering eye,
As fearfully dark it looks up to the sky;
Alas! a dull unearthly light
Like a dead star, bluely white;
A seal of sin, I note it now,
Flickers upon thy ghastly brow;
And about the huge old oak
Thickly curls a poisonous smoke,
And terrible shapes with evil names
Are leaping around a circle of flames,
And the tost air whirls, storm-driven,
And the rent earth quakes, charm-riven,--
And — art thou not afraid?

All dauntless stands the maid
In mystical robe array'd,
And still with flashing eyes
She dares the sorrowful skies,
And to the moon, like one possest,
Hath shown, — O dread! that face so fair
Should smile above so shrunk a breast,
Haggard and brown, as hangeth there, —
O evil sight, wrinkled and old,
The dug of a witch, and clammy cold, —
Where in warm beauty's rarest mould
Is fashioned all the rest;
O evil sight! for, by the light
From those large eyes streaming bright,
By thy beauty's wondrous sheen,
Lofty gait and graceful mien,
By that bosom half reveal'd,
Wither'd, and as in death congeal'd,
By the guilt upon thy brow,
Ah! Geraldine, 'tis thou

Muttering wildly through her set teeth,
She seeketh and stirreth the demons beneath,
And — hist! — the magical mandate is spoken,

The bonds of the spirit of evil are broken,
There is a rush of invisible wings
Amid shrieks and distant thunderings,
And now one nearer than others is heard
Flapping his way as a huge seabird,
Or liker the deep-dwelling ravenous shark
Cleaving through the waters dark.

It is the hour, the spell hath power!
Now haste thee, ere the tempest lower.

Her mouth grows wide, and her face falls in,
And her beautiful brow becomes flat and thin,
And sulphurous flashes blear and singe
That sweetest of eyes with its delicate fringe,
Till, all its loveliness blasted and dead,
The eye of a snake blinks deep in her head;
For raven locks flowing loose and long
Bristles a red mane, stiff and strong,
And sea-green scales are beginning to speck
Her shrunken breasts, and lengthening neck;
The white round arms are sunk in her sides,—
  As when in chrysalis canoe
A may-fly down the river glides,
  Struggling for life and liberty too,—
Her body convulsively twists and twirls,
This way and that it bows and curls,
And now her soft limbs melt into one
Strangely and horribly tapering down,
Till on the burnt grass dimly is seen
A serpent monster, scaly and green.
Horror!—can this be Geraldine?
Haste, O haste,—'tis almost past,
The sand is dripping thick and fast;
And distant roars the coming blast.

Swiftly the dragon-maid unroll'd
The burnished strength of each sinewy fold,
And round the old oak trunk with toil

Hath wound and trailed each tortuous coil,
Then with one crush hath splitten and broke
The hollow black heart of the sear old oak.

The hour is fled, the spell hath sped;
And heavily dropping down as dead,
All in her own beauty drest,
Brightest, softest, loveliest,
Fair faint Geraldine lies on the ground,
Moaning sadly;
And forth from the oak,
In a whirl of thick smoke,
Grinning gladly,
Leaps with a hideous howl at a bound
A squat black dwarf of visage grim,
With crutches beside each twisted limb
Half-hidden in many a flame-colored rag, —
It is Ryxa the Hag!

Ho, ho! what wouldst thou, daughter mine,
Wishes three, or curses nine?
Wishes three to work thy will,
Or curses nine thy hate to fulfil?

Ryxa, spite of thy last strong charm,
Some pure spirit saves from harm
Her, who before me was loved too well,
Our holy hated Christabel:
Her who stole my heart from *him*,
One of the guardian cherubim,
Hovers around, and cheers in dreams,
Thwarting from heaven my hell-bought schemes
Now, — for another five hundred years,
O mother mine, will I be thine,
To writhe in pains, and shriek in fears,
And toil in chains, and waste in tears,
So thy might will scorch and smite
The beautiful face of Christabel,
And will drain by jealous pain

Love from the heart of Christabel, —
And her own betrothed knight,
O glad sight! shall scorn and slight
The pale one he hath loved so well,
While in my arms, by stolen charms
And borrowed mien, for Geraldine
He shall forget his Christabel.

It is done, it is done, thy cause is won!
Quoth Ryxa the Hag to Geraldine;
Thus have I prest my seal on thy breast,
Twelve circling scales from a dragon's crest,
And still thy bosom and half thy side
Must shrivel and sink at eventide,
And still, as every Sabbath breaks,
Thy large dark eyes must blink as a snake's.
Now, for mine aid: — De Vaux doth come
To lead his seeming daughter home,
Therefore I fit thee a shape and a face
Differing, yet of twin-born grace,
That all who see thee may fall down
Heart-worshippers before thy throne,
Forgetting in that vision sweet
Thy former tale of dull deceit,
And tranc'd in deep oblivious joy,
Bask in bliss without alloy:
He too, thou lovest, in thine arms,
Shall grace the triumph of thy charms,
While thy thirsty rage thou satest
In the woes of her thou hatest.
Yet, daughter, hark! my warning mark!
Hallowed deed, or word, or thought,
Is with deadliest peril fraught;
And if, where true lovers meet,
Thou hearest hymning wild and sweet,
O stop thine ears, lest all be marr'd, —
Beware, beware of holy bard!
For that the power of hymn and harp
Thine innermost being shall wither and warp,

And the same hour they touch thine ears,
A serpent thou art for a thousand years.

Hush! how heavily droops the night
  In sultry silence, calm as death;
Gloomy and hot, and yet no light,
  Save where the glow-worm wandereth,
For the moon hath stolen by,
Mantled in the stormy sky,
And there is a stillness strange,
An awful stillness, boding change,
As if live nature holds her breath,
And all in agony listeneth
Some terror undefin'd to hear
Coming, coming, coming near!
Hush'd is the beetle's drowsy hum,
And the death-watch's roll on his warning drum,
Hush'd the raven, and screech owl,
And the famishing wolf on his midnight prowl, —
          Silent as death.
Hark, hark! he is here, he has come from afar,
The black-rob'd storm in his terrible car;
Vivid the forkéd lightning flashes,
Quick behind the thunder crashes,
Clattering hail, a shingly flood,
Rattles like grape-shot in the wood;
And the whole forest is bent one way,
Bowing as slaves to a tyrant's sway,
While the foot of the tempest hath trampled and broke
Many a stout old elm and oak.

And Geraldine? O who could tell
That thou who by sweet Christabel,
Softly liest in innocent sleep,
Like an infant's, calm and deep,
Smiling faintly, as it seems
From thy bright and rosy dreams,
Who could augur thou art she
That around the hollow tree,

With bad charm and hellish rite
Shook the heav'ns, and scar'd the night?

Alas! for gentle Christabel,
Alas! for wasting Christabel;
From evil eye, and powers of hell,
And the strong magic of the spell,
Holy Mary, shield her well!

CONCLUSION TO PART I.

THE murderer's knife is a fearful thing,
But what, were it edg'd with a scorpion's sting?
A dagger of glass hath death in its stroke,
But what, should venom gush out as it broke?
And hatred in man's deep heart
Festereth there like the barb of a dart,
Maddening the fibres at every beat,
And filling its caverns with fever-heat;
But jealous rage in a woman's soul
Simmers and steams as a poison-bowl:
A drop were death, but the rival maid
Must drain all dry, e'er the passion be staid:
It floodeth the bosom with bitterest gall,
It drowneth the young virtues all,
And the sweet milk of the heart's own fountain,
Chok'd and crush'd by a heavy mountain,
All curdled, and hardened, and blackened, doth shrink
Into the sepia's stone-bound ink;
The eye of suspicion deep sunk in the head
Shrinks and blinks with malice and dread,
And the cheek without and the heart within
Are blistered and blighted with searing sin,
Till charity's self no more can trace
Aught that is lovely in feature or face,

But the rose-bud is canker'd, and shall not bloom,
Corruption hath scented the rich perfume,
The angel of light is a demon of gloom,
And the bruise on his brow is the seal of his doom.
Ah! poor unconscious rival maid,
How drearily must thou sicken and fade
In the foul air of that Upas-shade!

Her heart must be tried, and trampled, and torn
With fear, and care, and slander, and scorn;
Her love must look upon love estranged,
Her eye must meet his eye, how changed!
Her hand must take his hand unpressing,
Her hope must die, without confessing;
And still she'll strive her love to smother,
While in the triumphs of another
The shadow of her joys departed
Shall scare and haunt her broken-hearted;
And he, who once lov'd her, his purest, his first,
Must hate her and hold her defil'd and accurst,
Till, wasted and desolate, calumny's breath
Must taint with all guilt her innocent death.

PART II.

(BEING THE FOURTH OF CHRISTABEL)

How fresh and fair is morn!
  The dew-beads dropping bright
Each humble flower adorn,
  With coronets bedight,
And jewel the rough thorn
  With tiny globes of light,—
How beautiful is morn!
  Her scatter'd gems how bright

There is a quiet gladness
  In the waking earth,
Like the face of sadness
  Lit with chasten'd mirth·
There is a mine of treasure
  In those hours of health,
Filling up the measure
  Of creation's wealth.

The eye of day hath opened grey,
  And the gallant sun
Hath trick'd his beams by Rydal's streams
  And waveless Coniston;
From Langdale Pikes his glory strikes,
  From heath and giant hill,
From many a tairn, and stone-built cairn,
  And many a mountain rill:

Helvellyn bares his forehead black,
And Eagle-crag, and Saddleback,

And Skiddaw hails the dawning day,
And rolls his robe of clouds away.

Ho, warder, ho! in chivalrous state,
A stranger-knight to the castle gate,
With trumpet, and banner, and mailed men,
Comes this way winding up the glen:
His vizor is down, and he will not proclaim
To the challenge within his lineage or name,
Yet by his heralds, and esquires eight,
And five-score spearmen, tall and straight,
And blazon rich with bearings rare,
And high-bred ease, and noble air,
And golden spurs, and sword, can he be
Nought but a knight of high degree.

Alas! they had lov'd too soon, too well,
Young Amador and Christabel;
Life's dawn beheld them, blithe and bland
Little playmates, hand in hand,
Over fell and field and heather
Wandering innocent together,
Alone in childhood's rosy hours
Straying far to find wild flowers;
Life's sun above the eastern hill
Saw them inseparable still
In the bow'r, or by the brook,
Or spelling out the monkish book,
Or as with songs they wont to wake
The echoes on the hill-bound lake,
Or as with tales to while away
The winter's night, or summer's day;
Life's noon was blazing bright and fair,
To smile upon the same fond pair,
The handsome youth, the beauteous maid,
Together still in sun or shade:
Warmer, good sooth, than wont with friends,
While he supports, and she depends,
As to some dangerous, craggy height

They climb with terror and delight,
Nor guess that the strange joy they feel,
The rapture making their hearts reel,
Springs from aught else than — sweet Grasmere,
Or hill and valley far and near,
Or Derwent's banks and glassy tide,
Lowdore, or hawthorn'd Ambleside:
Nor reck they what dear danger lies
In gazing on each other's eyes;
On her bright cheek, fresh and fair,
Blooming in the mountain air,
On his form, and agile limbs,
As from rock to rock he climbs,
Her unstudied, natural grace,
  Loosen'd vest and tresses flowing,
Or his fine and manly face
  With delighted ardor glowing.

Thus they grew up in each other,
  Till to ripen'd youth
They have grown up for each other;
  Yet, to say but sooth,
She had not lov'd him, as other
  Than a sister doth,
And he to her was but a brother,
  With a brother's troth:
But selfish craft that slept so long,
And, if wrong were, had done the wrong,
Now, just awake, with dull surprise
  Read the strange truth,
And from their own accusing eyes
  Condemned them both, —
That they, who only for each other
  Gladly drew their daily breath,
Now must curb, and check, and smother,
  Through all life, love strong as death;
While the dear hope they just have learnt to prize,
  And fondly cherish,
The hope that in their hearts deep-rooted lies,

Must pine and perish:
For the slow prudence of the worldly wise,
In cruel coldness still denies
The fondling youth to woo and win
The heiress daughter of Leoline.

And yet how little had he err'd,
That on his ear the bitter word
Of harsh reproach should fall, —
"Is it then thus, ungrateful boy,
Thou wouldst his dearest hope destroy
Who lent thee life and all?
Why did I save thee, years agone,
Beneath the tottering Bowther-stone,
An infant weak and wan?
Why did I warm thee on my hearth,
Nor crush the viper in its birth,
O thou presumptuous one?"

They met once more, in sweet, sad fear,
At the old oak tree in the forest drear,
And, as enamor'd of bitterness, they
Wept the sad hour of parting away,
The bursting tear, the stifled sob,
The tortur'd bosom's first-felt throb,
The fervent vow, the broken gold,
Their hapless hopes too truly told;
For, alas! till now they never had known
How deep and strong their loves had grown,
But just as they sip the full cup of the heart,
It is dashed from the lip, — and they must part:
Alas! they had lov'd, yet never before
The wealth of love had counted o'er,
And just as they find the treasure so great,
It is lost, it is sunk in the billows of fate.

Yea, it must be with a fearful shock
That the pine can be torn from its root-clasp'd rock,

Or the broad oak stump, as it stands on the farm,
Be rent asunder by strength of arm;
So, when the cords of love are twin'd
Among the fibres of the mind,
And kindred souls by secret ties
Mingle thoughts and sympathies,
O what a wrench to tear in twain
Those that are lov'd and love again,
To drag the magnet from its pole,
To chain the freedom of the soul,
To freeze in ice desires that boil,
To root the mandrake from the soil,
With groans, and blood, and tears, and toil!

He is gone to the land of the holy war,
The sad, the brave young Amador,
Not to return, — by Leoline's oath,
When all in wrath he bound them both,
Not to return, — by that last kiss,
Till name, and fame, and fortune are his.
Aye, he is gone; — and with him went,
As into chosen banishment,
The bloom of her cheek, and the light of her eye,
And the hope of her heart, so near to die:
He is gone o'er Paynim lands to roam,
But leaves his heart, his all, at home;
And years have glided, day by day,
To watch him warring far away,
Where, upon Gideon's hallowed banks,
His prowess hath scattered the Saracen ranks,
And the Lion-king with his own right hand
Hath dubb'd him knight of Holy Land:
The crescent wan'd where'er he came,
And Christendom rung with his glorious fame,
And Saladin trembled at the name
Of Amador de-Ramothaim.

He hath won him in battle a goodly shield
Three wild boars Or on an azure field,

While scallop-shells three on an argent fess
Proclaim him a pilgrim and knight no less;
Enchased in gold on his helmet of steel
A deer-hound stands on the high-plumed keel,
Hafiz, his hound, who hath rescued his life
From the wily Assassin's secret knife,
Hafiz, his friend, whom he loveth so well
As the last gift of Christabel:
And over his vizor, and round his arm,
And grav'd on his sword as a favorite charm,
And on his banner emblazoned at length,
Love's motto, "HOPE IS ALL MY STRENGTH."

Oh then with how much pride and joy
And hope which fear could scarce alloy,
With heart how leaping, eye how bright,
And fair cheek flushed with deep delight,
Heard Christabel the wafted story
Of her far-off lover's glory:
  For her inmost soul knew well
That he hoped and spake and thought
  Only of his Christabel,
That he liv'd and lov'd and fought
  Only for his Christabel;
So she felt his honor her's,
  His welfare her's, his being her's,
And did reward with rich largesse
The stray astonish'd messengers
  Who brought her so much happiness.

Behold! it is past,—that many a year!
The harvest of her hope is near;
Behold! it is come,—behold *him* here!
Yes, in pomp and power and pride,
And joy and love how true, how tried,
He comes to claim his long-lov'd bride;
Her own true knight, O bliss to tell!

Her Amador she loves so well
Returns for his sweet Christabel!

He leapt the moat, the portal past,
He flung him from his horse in haste,
    And in the hall
He met her: — but how pale and wan! —
He started back, as she upon
    His neck would fall:
He started back, — for by her side
(O blessed vision!) he espied
    A thing divine, —
Poor Christabel was lean and white,
But oh, how soft, and fair, and bright,
    Was Geraldine!
Fairer and brighter, as he gazes
All celestial beauty blazes
    From those glorious eyes,
And Amador no more can brook
The jealous air and peevish look
    That in the other lies!
Alas, for wasting Christabel,
Alas, for stricken Christabel,
How had she long'd to see this day,
And now her all is dash'd away!
How many slow sad years, poor maid,
Had she for this day wept and pray'd,
And now the bitterest tears destroy
That honied hope of cherish'd joy,
For he hath ceas'd, — O withering thought,
With burning anguish fully fraught,
    To love his Christabel!
Her full heart bursts, and she doth fall
Unheeded in her father's hall,
And, oh, the heaviest stroke of all!
    By him she loves so well.

) save her, Mary Mother, save!
.et not the damned sorceress have

Her evil will;
O save thine own sweet Christabel,
Thy saint, thine innocent Christabel,
And guard her still!

CONCLUSION TO PART II.

For it doth mark a godlike mind,
Prudence, and power, and truth combin'd,
A rare self-steering moral strength,
To over-love the dreary length
Of ten successive anxious years,
Unwarp'd by hopes, untir'd by fears;
Still, as every teeming hour,
Glides away in sun or shower,
Though the pilgrim foot may range,
The heart at home to feel no change,
But to live and linger on,
Fond and warm and true — to one!
O love like this, in life's young spring,
Is a rare and precious thing;
A pledge that man hath claims above,
A sister-twin to martyrs' love.
A shooting-star of blessed light,
Dropt upon the world's midnight,
A drop of sweet, where all beside
Is bitterest gall in life's dull tide,
One faithful found, where all was lost,
An Abdiel in Satan's host.

To love, unshrinking and unshaken,
Albeit by all but hope forsaken,
To love, through slander, craft, and fear,
And fairer faces smiling near,

Through absence, stirring scenes among,
And harrowing silence, suffering long,
Still to love on, — and pray and weep
For that dear one, while others sleep,
To dwell upon each precious word
Which the charm'd ear in whispers heard,
To treasure up a lock of hair,
To watch the heart with jealous care,
To live on a remember'd smile,
And still the wearisome day beguile
With rosy sweet imaginings,
And all the soft and sunny things
Look'd and spoken, ere they parted,
Full of hope, though broken-hearted, —
O there is very virtue here,
Retiring, holy, deep, sincere,
And self-pois'd virtue, working still
To compass good, and combat ill,
Which none but worldlings count earth-born
And they who know it not, can scorn.

Ah yes, let common sinners jeer,
And Mammon's slaves suspect and sneer,
While each idolator of pelf,
Judging from his gross-hearted self,
Counts Love no purer and no higher
Than the low plot of base desire; —
Let worldly craft nurse its false dreams
Of happiness, from selfish schemes
By heartless, hungry parents plann'd,
Of wedded fortune, rank and land, —
There is more wisdom, and more wealth
More rank in being, more soul's health,
In wedded love for one short hour,
Than endless wedded pelf and power:
Yes, there is virtue in these things:
A balm to heal the scorpion-stings
That others' sins and sorrows make
In hearts that still can weep and ache;

There is a heavenly influence,
A secret spiritual fence,
Circling the soul with present power
In temptation's darkest hour,
Walling it round from outward sin,
While all is soft and pure within.

PART III.

(BEING THE FIFTH AND LAST OF CHRISTABEL.)

HAST thou not seen, world-weary man,
Life's poor pilgrim white and wan, —
A gentle beauty for the cheek
  Which nothing gives but sorrow,
A sweet expression, soft and weak,
  Joy can never borrow?
Where lingering on the pale wet face
The rival tears run their slow race
  Each in its wonted furrow;
And patience, eloquently meek,
  From the threaten'd stroke unshrinking,
In mild boldness can but speak
  The burden of its sadden'd thinking, —
"Dreary as to-day has been,
And sad and cheerless yestereen,
  'Twill dawn as dark to-morrow!"

Desolate-hearted Christabel,
Hapless, hopeless Christabel, —
Nightly tears have dimm'd the lustre
  Of thy blue eyes, once so bright,
And, as when dank willows cluster
  Weeping over marble rocks,
O'er thy forehead white
  Droop thy flaxen locks:
Yet art thou beautiful, poor girl,
  As angels in distress,
Yea, comforting the soul, sweet girl,
  With thy loveliness;

For thy beauty's light subdued
  Hath a soothing charm,
In sympathy with all things good
  That weep for hate and harm;
And none can ever see unmov'd
  Thy poor wet face, with sorrow white,
O none have seen, who have not lov'd
  The sadly sweet religious light
That doth with pearly radiance shine
From those sainted eyes of thine!

A trampling of hoofs at the cullice-port,
A hundred horse in the castle-court!
From border-wastes, a weary way,
  Through Halegarth wood and Knorren moor,
A mingled numerous array,
On panting palfreys black and grey,
  With foam and mud bespatter'd o'er,
Hastily cross the flooded Irt,
And rich Waswater's beauty skirt,
And Sparkling-Tairn, and rough Scathwaite,
And now that day is dropping late,
Have passed the drawbridge and the gate.

By thy white flowing beard, and reverend mien,
And gilded harp, and chaplet of green,
And milk-white mare in the castle-yard,
Welcome, glad welcome to Bracy the bard!
And, — by thy struggle still to hide
This generous conquest of thy pride,
More than by yon princely train,
  And blazon'd banner standing near,
And snorting steed with slacken'd rein,
  Hail, O too long a stranger here,
Hail, to Langdale's friendly hall,
Thou noble spirit, most of all,
Roland de Vaux of Tryermaine!

Like aspens tall beside the brook
The stalwart warriors stood and shook,
And each advancing fear'd to look
Into the other's eye;
'Tis fifty years ago to-day
Since in disdain and passion they
Had flung each other's love away
With words of insult high:
How had they long'd and pray'd to meet!
But memories cling; and pride is sweet;
And — which could be the first to greet
The haply scornful other?
What if De Vaux were haughty still, —
Or Leoline's unbridled will
Consented not his rankling ill
In charity to smother?

Their knees give way, their faces are pale,
And loudly beneath the corslets of mail
Their aged hearts in generous heat
Almost to bursting boil and beat;
The white lips quiver, the pulses throb,
They stifle and swallow the rising sob, —
And there they stand, faint and unmann'd,
As each holds forth his bare right hand!
Yes, the mail-clad warriors tremble,
All unable to dissemble
Penitence and love confest,
As within each aching breast
The flood of affection grows deeper and stronger,
Till they can refrain no longer,
But with, — "Oh, my long-lost brother!" —
To their hearts they clasp each other,
Vowing in the face of heaven
All forgotten and forgiven!

Then the full luxury of grief
That brings the smothered soul relief,

Within them both so fiercely rushed
That from their vanquish'd eyes out-gush'd
A tide of tears, as pure and deep
As children, yea as cherubs weep!

Quoth Roland de Vaux to Sir Leoline:
"No lady lost can be daughter of mine,
For yestereen at this same hour
My Geraldine sat in her lattic'd bow'r,
And merrily marvell'd much to hear
She had been found in the forest drear:
Nathless, of thee, old friend, to crave
Once more the love I long to have
Ere yet I drop into the grave,
Behold me here!
I hail'd the rich offer, and hither I sped,
Glad to reclaim our friendship fled,
And see that face, — e'er yet it be dead, —
I feel so dear;
And my old heart danced with the joy of a child,
When out of school he leaps half wild,
To think he could be reconcil'd."

"Thy tale is strange," quoth Leoline,
"As thy return is sweet;
Yet might it please thee, brother mine,
In knightly sort to greet
This wondrous new-found Geraldine,
For sure she is a thing divine,
So bright in her doth beauty shine
From head to feet,
Yea, sure she is a thing divine,
For angels meet."

O glorious in thy loveliness!
Victorious in thy loveliness!
From what strong magnetic zone,
Circling some strange world unknown,
Hast thou stolen sweet influence

To lull in bliss each ravished sense?
That thine eyes rain light and love
Kindlier than the heavens above, —
That the sunshine of thy face
Shows richly ripe each winning grace, —
That thine innocent laughing dimple,
And thy tresses curling simple,
Thy soft cheek, and rounded arm,
And foot unsandalled, white and warm,
And every sweet luxurious charm,
Fair, and full, and flush'd, and bright,
Fascinate the dazzled sight,
As with a halo of delight?

Her beauty hath conquer'd: a sunny smile
Laughs into goodness her seeming guile.
Aye, was she not in mercy sent
To heal the friendships pride had rent?
Is she not here, a blessed saint,
To work all good by subtle feint?
Yea, art thou not, mysterious dame,
Our Lady of Furness? — the same, the same!
O holy one, we know thee now,
O gracious one, before thee bow;
Help us, Mary, hallowed one,
Bless us, for thy wondrous Son. —

The name was half spoken, the spell was half broken,
And suddenly, from his bent knee
  Upleapt each knight in fear,
All warily they look'd around,
Sure, they had heard a hissing sound,
And one quick moment on the ground
  Had seen a dragon here!
But now before their wildered eyes
Bright Geraldine, all sweet surprise,
With her fair hands in courteous guise,
Had touch'd them both, and bade them rise;

Alas, kind sirs, she calmly said,
I am but a poor hunted maid,
Hunted, ah me! and sore afraid,
That all too far from home have stray'd,
For love of one who flies and hates me,
For hate of one who loves and waits me.

Wonder stricken were they then,
And full of love, those ancient men,
Full-fired with guilty love, as when
In times of old
To young Susannah's fairness knelt
Those elders twain, and foully felt
The lava-streams of passion melt
Their bosoms cold:
They loved, — they started from the floor, —
But, hist! within the chamber-door
Softly stole Sir Amador: —
Nor look'd, nor wondered as they passed
(Speeding by in shame and haste,
Meekly thinking of each other
As a weak and guilty brother,)
For all to him in that dark room,
All the light to pierce its gloom,
All he thought of, car'd for, there,
Was that lov'd one, smiling fair,
Wondrous in her charms divine,
Glad and glorious Geraldine.

The eye of a hawk is fierce and bright
As a facet-cut diamond scattering light,
Soft and rayed with invincible love,
As a pure pearl is the eye of a dove·
And so in flashes quick and keen
Look'd Amador on Geraldine,
And so, in sweet subduing rays,
On Amador did fondly gaze,
In gentle pow'r of beauty's blaze,
Imperial Geraldine.

His head is cushion'd on her breast,
  Her dark eyes shed love on his,
And his changing cheek is prest
  By her hot and thrilling kiss,
While again from her moist lips
The honey-dew of joy he sips,
And views, with rising transport warm,
Her half-unveil'd, bewitching form. —

A step on the threshold! — the chamber is dim,
And gliding ghost-like up to him,
While entranced in conscious fear
He feels an injured angel near,
Sad Christabel with wringing hands
Beside her faithless lover stands,
Sad Christabel with streaming eyes
In silent anguish stands and sighs;
Ave, Maria! send her aid,
Bless, oh bless the wretched maid!

It is done, — he is won! — stung with remorse
He hath dropt at her feet as a clay-cold corse,
And Christabel with trembling dread
Hath rais'd on her knee his pale, dear head,
And bath'd his brow with many a tear,
And listen'd for his breath in fear,
And when she thought that none was near
But guardian saints, and God above,
Set on his lips the seal of her love.

But Geraldine had watch'd that kiss,
And with involuntary hiss,
And malice in her snake-like stare,
She gnash'd her teeth on the loving pair,
And shed on them both a deadly glare.

Softly through the sounding hall,
  In rich melodious notes,
With many a gentle swell and fall,
  Holy music floats,

Like gossamer in a sultry sky,
Dropping low, or sailing high:
Bard Bracy, bard Bracy, that touch was thine;
  On Cambria's harp with triple strings,
Wild and sweet is the hymn divine,
  Fanning the air like unseen wings:
Thy hand, good Bracy, thine alone
Can wake so sad, so sweet a tone;
Nought but the magic of thy touch
Can charm so well, and cheer so much,
And wondrously, with strong control,
Rouse or lull the passive soul.
What aileth thee, O Geraldine?
Why waileth Lady Geraldine?
The body convuls'd groweth lank and lean,
Thy smooth white neck is shrivell'd and green,
Thine eyes are blear'd and sunk and keen,
O dreadful! art *thou* Geraldine?—

The spell is dead, the charm is o'er,
Writhing and coiling on the floor
Awhile she curl'd in pain, and then was seen no more.

CONCLUSION TO PART III.

Sweet Christabel, my Christabel,
I have riven thy heart that loved so well:
Oh weak, O wicked, to rend in its home
The love that I cherish wherever I roam!

As when with his glory the morning sun
  Floods on a sudden the tropical sky,
And startled twilight, dim and dun,
  Flies from the fear of his conquering eye,

So flash'd across the lighten'd breast
  Of Christabel, no more to moan,
A dawn of love, the happiest
  Her maiden heart had ever known;
For sure it was only through powers of hell,
And evil eye, and potent spell,
That Amador to Christabel
            Could faithless prove, —
And when she saw him kneeling near,
Contrite, yet more in hope than fear,
Oh then she felt him doubly dear,
            Her rescued love!

Ave, Maria! unto thee
All the thanks and glory be,
For thy gracious arm and aid
Saved the youth, and blest the maid.
So falls it out, that vanquish'd ill
Breeds only good to good men still,
And while its poison seethes and works
It yields a healing antidote,
Which, whether mortals use or not,
Like a friend in ambush, lurks
Deepest in the deadliest plot.

Not swift, though soon, next day at noon,
  Just at the wedding hour,
As hand-in-hand betrothed they stand
  Beneath the chapel tower,
A holy light — a vision bright —
  'Twas twelve o'clock at noon,
A spirit good before them stood,
Her garments fair and flowing hair
Shone brighter than the moon.

And thus in musical voice most sweet, —
"Daughter, this hour to grace and greet,
To bless this day as is most meet,
          Thy mother stoops from Heaven!

And, ancient men, who all so late,
Have stopp'd at Death's half-opened gate,
In tears of love to drown your hate,
        Forgiving and forgiven,
Hear, noble spirits reconcil'd,
Hear, gracious souls, now meek and mild,
Albeit with guilt so long defil'd,
        Love's lingering boon receive;
Roland de Vaux, — thy long-lost child,
Whom border troopers, fierce and wild,
An infant from his home beguil'd,
        Thy soul to gall and grieve
In Amador — behold!"

The spirit said, and all in light
Melted away that vision bright:
  My tale is told.

MISCELLANEOUS POEMS.

MISCELLANEOUS POEMS.

IMAGINATION.

Thou fair enchantress of my willing heart,
Who charmest it to deep and dreary slumber,
Gilding mine evening clouds of reverie, —
Thou lovely Siren, who, with still small voice
Most softly musical, dost lure me on
O'er the wide sea of indistinct idea,
Or quaking sands of untried theory,
Or ridgy shoals of fixt experiment
That wind a dubious pathway through the deep, —
Imagination, I am thine own child!
Have I not often sat with thee retired,
Alone, yet not alone, though grave, most glad,
All silent outwardly, but loud within,
As from the distant hum of many waters,
Weaving the tissue of some delicate thought,
And hushing every breath that might have rent
Our web of gossamer, so finely spun?
Have I not often listed thy sweet song
(While in vague echoes and Æolian notes
The chambers of my heart have answered it),
With eye as bright in joy, and fluttering pulse,
As the coy village maiden's, when her lover
Whispers his hope to her delighted ear?
And, taught by thee, angelic visitant,

Have I not learned to love the tuneful lyre,
Draining from every chord its musical soul?
Have I not learnt to find in all that is,
Somewhat to touch the heart, or raise the mind,
Somewhat of grand and beautiful to praise
Alike in small and great things? and this power,
This clearing of the eye, this path made straight
Even to the heart's own heart, its innermost core,
This keenness to perceive, and seek and find,
And love and prize all-present harmony,
This, more than choosing words to clothe the thought,
Makes the true poet; this thy glorious gift,
Imagination, rescues me thy son,
(Thy son, albeit least worthy,) from the lust
Of mammon, and the cares of animal life,
And the dull thraldom of this work-day world.

Indulgent lover, I am all thine own;
What art thou not to me?—ah, little know
The worshippers of cold reality,
The grosser minds, who most sincerely think
That sense is the broad avenue to bliss.
Little know they the thrilling ecstasy,
The delicate refinement in delight,
That cheers the thoughtful spirit, as it soars
Far above all these petty things of life;
And strengthened by the flight and cordial joys,
Can then come down to earth and common men
Better in motive, stronger in resolve,
Apter to use all means that compass good,
And of more charitable mind to all.
Imagination, art thou not my friend
In crowds and solitude, my comrade dear,
Brother, and sister, mine own other self,
The Hector to my soul's Andromache?
Triumphant beauty, bright intelligence!
The chastened fire of ecstasy suppressed
Beams from thine eye; because thy secret heart,
Like that strange sight burning yet unconsumed,

Is all on flame, a censer filled with odors,
And to my mind, who feel thy fearful power,
Suggesting passive terrors and delights,
A slumbering volcano: thy dark cheek,
Warm and transparent, by its half-form'd dimple
Reveals an under-world of wondrous things
Ripe in their richness, — as among the bays
Of blest Bermuda, through the sapphire deep,
Ruddy and white fantastically branch
The coral groves; thy broad and sunny brow,
Made fertile by the genial smile of heaven,
Shoots up an hundred-fold the glorious crop
Of arabesque ideas; forth from thy curls,
Half hidden in their black luxuriance,
The twining sister-graces lightly spring,
The muses, and the passions, and young love,
Tritons and Naiads, Pegasus, and Sphinx,
Atlas, Briareus, Paæton, and Cyclops,
Centaurs, and shapes uncouth, and wild conceits:
And in the midst blazes the star of mind,
Illumining the classic portico
That leads to the high dome where Learning sits:
On either side of that broad sunny brow
Flame-color'd pinions, streak'd with gold and blue,
Burst from the teeming brain; while under them
The forked lightning, and the cloud-rob'd thunder,
And fearful shadows, and unhallow'd eyes,
And strange foreboding forms of terrible things,
Lurk in the midnight of thy raven locks.

And thou hast been the sunshine to my landscape,
Imagination; thou hast wreathed me smiles,
And hung them on a statue's marble lips;
Hast made earth's dullest pebbles bright like gems:
Hast lent me thine own silken clue, to rove
The ideal labyrinths of a thousand spheres;
Hast lengthen'd out my nights with life-long dreams,
And with glad seeming gilt my darkest day;
Helped me to scale in thought the walls of heaven,

While journeying wearily this busy world;
Sent me to pierce the palpable clouds with eagles,
And with leviathan the silent deep;
Hast taught my youthful spirit to expand
Beyond himself, and live in other scenes,
And other times, and among other men;
Hast bid me cherish, silent and alone,
First feelings, and young hopes, and better aims,
And sensibilities of delicate sort.
Like timorous mimosas, which the breath,
The cold and cautious breath of daily life,
Hath not as yet had power to blight and kill
From my heart's garden; for they stand retired,
Screen'd from the north by groves of rooted thought.

Without thine aid, how cheerless were all time,
But chief the short sweet hours of earliest love;
When the young mind, athirst for happiness,
And all-exulting in that new-found treasure,
The wealth of being loved, as well as loving,
Sees not, and hears not, knows not, thinks not, speaks not,
Except it be of her, his one desire;
And thy rose-color'd glass on every scene
With more than earthly promise cheats the eye,
While the charm'd ear drinks thy melodious words,
And the heart reels, drunk with ideal beauty.
So too the memory of departed joy,
Walking in black with sprinkled tears of pearl,
Passes before the mind with look less stern
And foot more lighten'd, when thine inward power,
Most gentle friend, upon that clouded face
Sheds the fair light of better joys to come,
And throws round Grief the azure scarf of Hope.

As the wild chamois bounds from rock to rock,
Oft on the granite steeples nicely poised,
Unconscious that the cliff from which he hangs
Was once a fiery sea of molten stone,
Shot up ten thousand feet and crystallized,

When earth was laboring with her kraken brood;
So have I sped with thee, my bright-eyed love,
Imagination, over pathless wilds,
Bounding from thought to thought, unmindful of
The fever of my soul that shot them up
And made a ready footing for my speed,
As like the whirlwind I have flown along,
Winged with ecstatic mind, and carried away,
Like Ganymede of old, o'er cloud-capt Ida,
Or Alps, or Andes, or the ice-bound shores
Of Arctic or Antarctic, — stolen from earth
Her sister-planets and the twinkling eyes
That watched her from afar, to the pure seat
Of rarest Matter's last created world,
And brilliant halls of self-existing Light.

THE SONG OF AN ALPINE ELF.

Ha, ha, ha! — My coy Jungfra
Is tall and robed in snow,
Yet at a leap to the cloudy steep
I bound from the glen below;
On her dizziest peak I sit and shriek
To the winds that around me blow,
And heard from afar is my ha, ha, ha!
The wild laugh echoes so.

In the forest dun round Lauterbrunn,
That line each dark ravine,
I hide me away from the garish day
Till the howling winter's e'en;
Then I jump on high through the coal-black sky,
And light on some cliff of snow
That nods to its fall like a tottering wall,
And I rock it to and fro!

My summer's home is the cataract's foam,
As it floats in a frothing heap;
My winter's rest is the weasel's nest,
Or deep with the mole I sleep:
I ride for a freak on the lightning-streak,
And mingle among the clouds,
My swarthy form with the thunder-storm,
Wrapped in its sable shrouds.

Often I launch the huge avalanche,
And make it my milk-white sledge,
When, unappall'd, to the Grindelwald
I slide from the Shrikehorn's edge:
Silent and soft to the ibex oft
I have stolen, and hurried him o'er
The precipice to the bristling ice
That smokes with his scarlet gore.

But my greatest joy is to lure and decoy
To the chasm's slippery brink
The hunter bold, when he's weary and old,
And there let him suddenly sink,—
A thousand feet—dead!—he dropp'd like lead,
Ha, he couldn't leap like me;
With broken back, as a felon on rack,
He hangs in a split pine-tree.

And there 'mid his bones, that echoed with groans,
I make me a nest of his hair;
The ribs dry and white rattle loud as in spite,
When I rock in my cradle there:
Hurrah, hurrah, and ha, ha, ha!
I'm in a merry mood,
For I'm all alone in my palace of bone,
That's tapestried fair with the old man's hair,
And dappled with clots of blood:
And when I look out all around and about,
The storm shouts high to the coal-black sky,

And the icicle sleet falls thick and fleet,
And all that I hear on the mountain drear,
And all I behold in the valleys cold,
 Is death and solitude.

DREAMS.

A DREAM — mysterious word, a dream!
 What joys and sorrows are enshrin'd
In those still hours we fondly deem
 A play-time for the truant mind:

It is a happy thing to dream,
 When rosy thoughts and visions bright
Pour on the soul a golden stream
 Of rich luxurious delight:

It is a weary thing to dream,
 When from the hot and aching brain,
As from a boiling cauldron, steam
 The myriad forms in fancy's train.

It is a curious thing to dream,
 When shapes grotesque of all quaint things,
Like laughing water-witches seem
 To sport in reason's turbid springs:

It is a glorious thing to dream,
 When full of wings and full of eyes,
Borne on the whirlwind or sunbeam,
 We race along the startled skies:

It is a wondrous thing to dream
 Of tumbling with a fearful shock
From some tall cliff where eagles scream,
 — To light upon a feather rock:

It is a terrible thing to dream
  Of strangled throats and heart-blood spilt,
And ghosts that in the darkness gleam,
  And horrid eyes of midnight guilt.

I love a dream, I dread a dream,
  Sometimes all bright and full of gladness,
But other times my brain will teem
  With sights that urge the mind to madness.

INFANT CHRIST, WITH A WREATH OF FLOWERS.

FROM A PICTURE BY CORREGGIO.

Yes,—I can fancy, in the spring
  Of childhood's sunny hours,
That nature's infant, priest, and king,
  Lov'd to gaze on flowers:

For lightly, 'mid the wreck of all,
  When torn from Eden's bowers,
Above the billows of the fall
  Floated gentle flowers.

Unfallen, sinless, undefil'd,
  Fresh bath'd in summer showers,
What wonder that the holy child
  Lov'd to play with flowers?

In these he saw his Father's face,
  All Godhead's varied powers,
And joy'd each attribute to trace
  In sweet unconscious flowers:

In these he found where Wisdom hides,
  And modest Beauty cowers,
And where Omnipotence resides,
  And Tenderness, — in flowers.

Innocent child, a little while,
  Ere yet the tempest lowers,
Bask thy young heart in Nature's smile
  Her lovely smile of flowers;

Thy young heart, — is it not array'd
  In feelings such as ours? —
Yes, being now of thorns afraid,
  I see thee crown'd with flowers.

PAST, PRESENT, AND FUTURE.

A SAD, sweet gladness, full of tears
  And thoughts, that never cloy,
Of careless childhood's happier years,
  Is memory's tranquil joy.

A rapturous and delusive dream
  Of pleasures, ne'er to be,
That o'er life's troubled waters gleam,
  Is Hope's sweet reverie.

Yet, before Memory can look back,
  When Hope is lost in sight,
Ah! where is Memory's fairy track,
  Ah! where is Hope's delight?

The present is a weary scene,
  And always wish'd away;
We live on "*to* be," and "*has* been"
  But never on "to-day."

ON A BULBOUS ROOT,

WHICH BLOSSOMED, AFTER HAVING LAIN FOR AGES IN THE HAND OF AN EGYPTIAN MUMMY.

What, wide awake, sweet stranger, wide awake?
And laughing coyly at an English sun,
And blessing him with smiles for having thawed
Thine icy chain, for having woke thee gently
From thy long slumber of three thousand years?
Methinks I see the eye of wonder peering
From thy tall pistil, looking strangely forth
As from a watch-tow'r at thy fellow-flowers,
Admiring much the rich variety
Of many a gem in nature's jewel-case
Unknown to thee, — the drooping hyacinth,
The prim ranunculus, and gay geranium,
And dahlias rare, and hearts-ease of all hues,
Mealy auriculas, and spotted lilies,
Gaudy carnations, and the modest face
Of the moss rose: methinks thy wondering leaves
And curious petals at the long-lost sun
Gaze with a lingering love, bedizen'd o'er
With a small firmament of eyes to catch
The luxury of his smile; as o'er the pool,
Hovering midway, the gorgeous dragon-fly
Watches his mates with thousand-facet vision;
Or as when underneath the waterfall,
Floating in sunny wreaths, the fretted foam
Mirrors blue heaven in its million orbs.
Methinks I see thy fair and foreign face
Blush with the glowing ardor of first love,
(Mindful of ancient Nile, and those warm skies,
And tender tales of insect coquetry,)
When some bright butterfly descends to sip
The exotic fragrance of thy nectarous dew;
Even so, Jabal's daughters in old time

Welcomed the sons of God, who sprang from heaven
To gaze with rapture on earth's fairest creatures,
And fan them with their rainbow-colored wings.

Didst ever dream of such a day as this,
A day of life and sunshine, when entranced
In the cold tomb of yonder shrivelled hand?
Didst ever try to shoot thy fibres forth
Through thy close prison-bars, those parchment fingers,
And strive to blossom in a charnel house?
Didst ever struggle to be free, — to leap
From that forced wedlock with a clammy corpse, —
To burst thy bonds asunder, and spring up,
A thing of light, to commerce with the skies?
Or didst thou rather, with endurance strong,
(That might have taught a Newton passive power,)
Baffle corruption, and live on unharmed
Amid the pestilent steams that wrapped thee round,
Like Mithradates, when he WOULD not die,
But conquered poison by his strong resolve?

O life, thy name is mystery, — that couldst
Thus energize inert, be, yet not be,
Concentrating thy powers in one small point;
Couldst mail a germ, in seeming weakness strong,
And arm it as thy champion against Death;
Couldst give a weed, dug from the common field,
What Egypt hath not, Immortality;
Couldst lull it off to sleep ere Carthage was,
And wake it up when Carthage is no more!
It may be, suns and stars that walked the heavens,
While thou wert in thy slumber, gentle flower,
Have sprung from chaos, blazed their age, and burst:
It may be, that thou seest the world worn out,
And look'st on meadows of a paler green,
Flowers of a duskier hue, and all creation,
Down to degenerate man, more and more dead,
Than in those golden hours, nearest to Eden,
When mother Earth and thou and all were young

And he that held thee, — this bituminous shape,
This fossil shell once tenanted by life,
This chrysalis husk of the poor insect man,
This leathern coat, this carcase of a soul, —
What was thy story, O mine elder brother?
I note thee now, swathed like a Milanese babe,
But thine are tinctur'd grave-clothes, fathoms long:
On thy shrunk breast the mystic beetle lies,
Commending thee to Earth, and to the Sun
Regenerating all; a curious scroll,
Full of strange written lore, rests at thy side;
While a quaint rosary of bestial gods,
Ammon, Bubastes, Thoth, Osiris, Apis,
And Horus with the curl, Typhon and Phthah,
Amulets ciphered with forgotten tongues,
And charmed religious beads, circle thy throat.
Greatly thy children honored thee in death,
And for the light vouchsafed them they did well, —
In that they hoped, and not unwisely hoped,
Again in his own flesh to see their sire;
And their affection spared not, so the form
They loved in life might rest adorned in death.

But this dry hand, — was it once terrible,
When among warrior bands thou wentest forth
With Ramses, or Sesostris, yet again
To crush the rebel Ethiop? — wast thou set
A taskmaster to toiling Israël,
When Cheops or Cephrenes raised to heaven
Their giant sepulchres? — or did this hand,
That lately held a flower, with murderous grasp
Tear from the Hebrew mother her poor babe,
To fling it to the crocodile? — or rather
Wert thou some garden-lover, and this bulb
Perchance most rare and fine, prized above gold,
(As in the mad world's dotage yesterday
A tulip root could fetch a prince's ransom,) —
Was to be buried with thee, as thy praise,
Thy Rosicrucian lamp, thine idol weed? —

Perchance, O kinder thought and better hope,
Some priest of Isis shrined this root with thee
As nature's hyeroglyphic, her half-guess
Of glimmering faith, that soul will never die.
What emblem liker, or more eloquent
Of immortality, whether the Sphinx,
Scarab, or circled snake, or wide-winged orb,
The azure-colored arch, the sleepless eye,
The pyramid four-square, or flowing river,
Or all whatever else were symbols apt
In Egypt's alphabet, — as thou, dry root,
So full of living promise? — yes, I see
Nature's "resurgam" sculptured there in words
That all of every clime may run and read:
I see the better hope of better times,
Hope against hope, wrapped in the dusky coats
Of a poor leek, — I note glad tidings there
Of happier things: this undecaying corpse
A little longer, yet a little longer
Must slumber on, but shall awake at last;
A little longer, yet a little longer, —
And at the trumpet's voice, shall this dry shape
Start up, instinct with life, the same though changed,
And put on incorruption's glorious garb:
Perchance for second death, — perchance to shine,
If aught of Israel's God he knew and lov'd,
Brighter than seraphs, and beyond the sun.

CRUELTY.

WILL none befriend that poor dumb brute,
  Will no man rescue him? —
With weaker effort, gasping, mute,
  He strains in every limb;

Spare him, O spare: — he feels, — he feels
  Big tears roll from his eyes;
Another crushing blow! — he reels,
  Staggers, — and falls, — and dies.

Poor jaded horse, the blood runs cold
  Thy guiltless wrongs to see;
To heav'n, O starv'd one, lame and old,
  Thy dim eye pleads for thee.

Thou too, O dog, whose faithful zeal
  Fawns on some ruffian grim,
He stripes thy skin with many a weal,
  And yet, — thou lovest him.

Shame! that of all the living chain
  That links creation's plan,
There is but one delights in pain, —
  The savage monarch, — man!

O cruelty, — who could rehearse
  Thy million dismal deeds,
Or track the workings of the curse
  By which all nature bleeds?

Thou meanest crime, — thou coward sin,
  Thou base, flint-hearted vice, —
Scorpion! — to sting thy heart within
  Thyself shalt all suffice;

The merciless is doubly curst,
  As mercy is "twice blest;"
Vengeance, though slow, shall come, — but first
  The vengeance of the breast.

Why add another woe to life,
  Man, — are there not enough?
Why lay *thy* weapon to the strife?
  Why make the road more rough?

Faint, hunger-sick, old, blind, and ill,
  The poor, or man or beast,
Can battle on with life uphill,
  And bear its griefs at least;

Truly, their cup of gall o'erflows!
  But, when the spite of men
Adds poison to the draught of woes,
  Who, who can drink it then?

Heard ye that shriek? — O wretch, forbear,
  Fling down thy bloody knife:
In fear, if not in pity, spare
  A woman, and a wife!

For thee she toils, unchiding, mild,
  And for thy children wan,
Beaten, and starv'd, — with famine wild,
  To feast thee, selfish man:

Husband and father, drunkard, fiend'
  Thy wife's, thy children's moan
Has won for innocence a friend,
  Has reach'd thy Judge's throne:

Their lives thou madest sad; but worse
  Thy deathless doom shall be;
"No mercy," is the withering curse
  Thy Judge has passed on thee:

Heap on, heap on, — fresh torments add, —
  New schemes of torture plan·
No mercy: Mercy's self is glad
  To damn the cruel man.

God! God! thy whole creation groans,
  Thy fair world writhes in pain;
Shall the dread incense of its moans
  Arise to Thee in vain?

The hollow eye of famine pleads,
  The face with weeping pale,
The heart that all in secret bleeds,
  The grief that tells no tale,

Oppression's victim, weak and mild,
  Scarce shrinking from the blow,
And the poor wearied factory child,
  Join in the dirge of woe.

O cruel world! O sickening fear
  Of goad, or knife, or thong;
O load of evils ill to bear!
  —How long, good God, how long?

CHILDREN.

Harmless, happy little treasures,
  Full of truth, and trust, and mirth,
Richest wealth, and purest pleasures,
  In this mean and guilty earth.

How I love you, pretty creatures,
  Lamb-like flock of little things,
Where the love that lights your features
  From the heart in beauty springs:

On these laughing rosy faces
  There are no deep lines of sin,
None of passion's dreary traces
  That betray the wounds within;

But yours is the sunny dimple
  Radiant with untutor'd smiles,
Yours the heart, sincere and simple,
  Innocent of selfish wiles;

Yours the natural curling tresses,
  Prattling tongues, and shyness coy,
Tottering steps, and kind caresses,
  Pure with health, and warm with joy.

The dull slaves of gain, or passion,
  Cannot love you as they should;
The poor worldly fools of fashion
  Would not love you if they could.

Write them childless, those cold-hearted,
  Who can scorn Thy generous boon,
And whose souls with fear have smarted,
  Lest — Thy blessings come too soon.

While he hath a child to love him,
  No man can be poor indeed;
While he trusts a Friend above him,
  None can sorrow, fear, or need.

But for thee, whose heart is lonely,
  And unwarm'd by children's mirth,
Spite of riches, thou art only
  Desolate and poor on earth.

All unkiss'd by innocent beauty,
  All unlov'd by guileless heart,
All uncheer'd by sweetest duty,
  Childless man, how poor thou art!

SONNET TO MY BOOK,

"PROVERBIAL PHILOSOPHY;" BEFORE PUBLICATION.

My soul's own son, dear image of my mind,
I would not without blessing send thee forth
Into the bleak wide world, whose voice unkind
Perchance will mock at thee as nothing worth;
For the cold critic's jealous eye may find
In all thy purposed good little but ill,
May taunt thy simple garb as qnaintly wrought,
And praise thee for no more than the small skill
Of masqueing as thine own another's thought:
What then? count envious sneers as less than nought:
Fair is thine aim, and having done thy best,
Lo, thus I bless thee; yea, thou shalt be blest!

TO THE SAME:

AFTER PUBLICATION.

That they have praised thee well, and cheered thee on
With kinder tones than critics deign to few,
Child of my thoughts, my fancy's favorite son,
Our courteous thanks, our heartfelt thanks are due.
Despise not thou thine equal's honest praise;
Yet feast not of such dainties; thou shalt rue
Their sweetness else; let rather generous pride
Those golden apples straightly spurn aside,
And gird thee all unshackled to the race:
On to the goal of honor, fair beginner,
A thousand ducats thou shalt yet be winner!

SONNET,

ON THE PUBLICATION OF THE SECOND EDITION OF MY "PROVERBIAL PHILOSOPHY."

Yet once again, not after many days
Since first I dared this voyage in the dark,
Borne on the prosperous gale of good men's praise,
To the wide waters I commit mine ark,
And bid God speed thy venture, gallant bark!
For I have launched thee on a thousand prayers,
Freighted thee well with all my mind and heart,
And if some contraband error unawares,
Like Achan's wedge, lie hid in any part,
Stand it condemned, as it most justly ought;
Yet be the thinker spared, if not his thought;
For he that with an honest purpose errs,
Merits more kind excuse than the shrewd world confers

MONSIEUR D'ALVERNON.

AN INCIDENT FOUNDED ON FACT.

Poor Monsieur D'Alvernon! I well remember
The day I visited his ruinous cot,
And heard the story of his fallen fortunes.
It was a fine May morning, and the flowers
Spread their fair faces to the laughing sun,
And look'd like small terrestrial stars, that gleam'd
With life and joy; the merry lark was high
Careering in the heavens, and now and then
A throstle from the neighboring thicket pour'd
His musical and hearty orisons.
The cot too truly told that poverty

Found it a home with misery and scorn
No clambering jessamine, no well-train'd roses
There linger'd, like sweet charity, to hide
The rents unseemly of the plaster'd wall:
No tight-trimm'd rows of box, or daisy prim,
Mark'd a clean pathway through the miry clay,
But all around was want and cold neglect.
With curious hand (and heart that beat with warm
Benevolence) I knock'd, lifted the latch,
And in the language of his mother-land
Besought a welcome; quick with courteous phrase,
And joy unfeign'd to hear his native tongue,
He bade me enter.—'Twas a ruined hovel;
Disease and penury had done their worst
To load a wretched exile with despair,
But still with spirit unbroken he lived on,
And, with a Frenchman's national levity,
Bounded elastic from his weight of woes.
I listed long his fond garrulity,
For sympathy and confidence are aye
Each other echoes, and I won his heart
By pitying his sorrows; long he told
Of friends, and wife, and darling little ones,
Fortunes, and titles, and long-cherish'd hopes
By frenzied Revolution marr'd and crush'd;
But oft my patience flicker'd, and my eye
Wander'd inquisitive round the murky room,
To see wherein I best might mitigate
The misery my bosom bled to view.
I sat upon his crazy couch, and there,
With many sordid rags, a roebuck's skin
Show'd sleek and mottled; swift the clear gray eye
Of the poor sufferer had mark'd my wonder,
And as in simple guise this touching tale
He told me, in the tongue my youth had lov'd,
Many a tear stole down his wrinkled cheek.

"Yon glossy skin is all that now remains
To tell me that the past is not a dream!

Oft up my Château's avenue of limes,
To be caress'd in mine ancestral hall,
Poor '*Louis*' bounded—(I had call'd him Louis
Because I lov'd my King);—my little ones
Have on his forked antlers often hung
Their garlands of spring flowers, and fed him with
Sweet heads of clover from their tiny hands.
But on a sorrowful day a random shot
Of some bold thief, or well-skill'd forester,
Struck him to death, and many a tear and sob
Were the unwritten epitaph upon him;
For children would not lose him utterly,
But prayed to have his mottled beautiful skin
A rug to their new pony-chaise, that they
Might oftener think of their lost favorite.
Aye, there it is!—that precious treasury
Of fond remembrances—that glossy skin!
O thou chief solace in the wintry nights,
That warms my poor old heart, and thaws my breast
With tears of,—Mais, Monsieur, asseyez vous!"—
But I had started up, and turn'd aside
To weep in solitude.—

WISDOM'S WISH.

Ah, might I but escape to some sweet spot,
  Oasis of my hopes, to fancy dear,
Where rural virtues are not yet forgot,
  And good old customs crown the circling year;
Where still contented peasants love their lot,
  And trade's vile din offends not nature's ear,
But hospitable hearths, and welcomes warm,
To country quiet add their social charm:

Some smiling bay of Cambria's happy shore,
  A wooded dingle on a mountain side,
Within the distant sound of ocean's roar,
  And looking down on valley fair and wide,
Nigh to the village church, to please me more
  Than vast cathedrals in their Gothic pride,
And blest with pious pastor, who has trod
Himself the way, and leads his flock to God;—

"There would I dwell, for I delight therein!"
  Far from the evil ways of evil men,
Untainted by the soil of others' sin,
  My own repented of, and clean again:
With health and plenty crown'd, and peace within,
  Choice books, and guiltless pleasures of the pen,
And mountain rambles with a welcome friend,
And dear domestic joys that never end.

There, from the flowery mead, or shingled shore,
  To cull the gems that bounteous nature gave,
From the rent mountain pick the brilliant ore,
  Or seek the curious crystal in its cave;
And learning nature's Master to adore,
  Know more of Him who came the lost to save;
Drink deep the pleasures contemplation gives,
And learn to love the meanest thing that lives.

No envious wish my fellows to excel,
  No sordid money-getting cares be mine;
No low ambition in high state to dwell,
  Nor meanly grand among the poor to shine:
But, sweet benevolence, regale me well
  With those cheap pleasures and light cares of thine,
And meek-eyed piety, be always near,
With calm content, and gratitude sincere.

Rescued from cities, and forensic strife,
  And walking well with God in nature's eye,
Blest with fair children, and a faithful wife,
  Love at my board, and friendship dwelling nigh,

Oh thus to wear away my useful life,
  And, when I'm call'd, in rapturous hope to die,
Thus to rob heaven of all the good I can,
And challenge earth to show a happier man!

THE MOTHER'S LAMENT.

My own little darling — dead!
The dove of my happiness fled!
    Just Heaven, forgive,
    But let me not live,
Now my poor babe is dead:

No more to my yearning breast
Shall that sweet mouth be prest,
    No more on my arm,
    Nestled up warm,
Shall my fair darling rest:

Alas, for that dear glaz'd eye,
Why did it dim or die?
    Those lips so soft,
    I have kissed so oft,
Why are they ice, oh why?

Alas, little frocks and toys,
Shadows of bygone joys;
    Have I not treasure
    Of bitterest pleasure
In these little frocks and toys?

O harrowing sight to behold
That marble-like face all cold,
    That small cherish'd form
    Flung to the worm,
Deep in the charnel-mould!

Where is each heart-winning way,
Thy prattle, and innocent play?
    Alas, they are gone,
    And left me alone
To weep for them night and day.

Yet why should I linger behind?
Kill me too, — death most kind:
    Where can I go
    To meet thy blow,
And my sweet babe to find?

I know it, I rave half-wild!
But who can be calm and mild,
    When the deep heart
    Is riven apart
Over a dear dead child?

I know it, I should not speak
So boldly, — I ought to be meek,
    But love it is strong,
    And my spirit is stung,
Lying all numb'd and weak.

TRUST.

"My times are in thy hand."

Yet will I trust! in all my fears,
Thy mercy, gracious Lord, appears,
To guide me through this vale of tears,
        And be my strength;
Thy mercy guides the ebb and flow
Of health and joy, or pain and woe,
To wean my heart from all below
        To Thee at length.

Yes, — welcome pain, — which Thou hast sent, —
Yes, — farewell blessings, — Thou hast lent,
With Thee alone I rest content,
For Thou art Heav'n, —
My trust reposes, safe and still,
On the wise goodness of Thy will,
Grateful for earthly good — or ill,
Which Thou hast giv'n.

O blessed friend! O blissful thought!
With happiest consolation fraught, —
Trust Thee I may, I will, I ought, —
To doubt were sin;
Then let whatever storms arise,
Their Ruler sits above the skies,
And lifting unto Him mine eyes,
'Tis calm within.

Danger may threaten, foes molest,
Poverty brood, disease infest,
Yea, torn affections wound the breast
For one sad hour.
But faith looks to her home on high,
Hope casts around a cheerful eye,
And love puts all the terrors by
With gladdening power.

FLOWERS.

Wilt thou gaze with me on flowers,
And let their sparkling eyes,
Glancing brightly up to ours,
Teach us to be wise?

The pale narcissus tells of youth
Nurtured in purity and truth;
Violets on the moss-bank green,
Of sweet benevolence unseen;
A rose is blooming charity;
A snow-drop, fair humility;
Yon golden crocus, smiling sweetly,
Smiles, alas, to perish fleetly;
That hyacinth, with cluster'd bells,
Of sympathy in sorrow tells;
This young mimosa, as it trembles,
Affection's thrilling heart resembles;
And the glazed myrtle's fragrant bloom
Hints at a life that mocks the tomb.

What is a flower? a beauteous gem
Set in nature's diadem,
A sunbeam o'er her tresses flung,
A word from her poetic tongue;
A silent burst of eloquence,
A plaything of Omnipotence;—
The poet's eye sees much in these
To learn, and love, and praise, and please.

WEDDING GIFTS.

Young bride,—a wreath for thee!
  Of sweet and gentle flowers;
For wedded love was pure and free
  In Eden's happy bowers.

Young bride,—a song for thee!
  A song of joyous measure,
For thy cup of hope shall be
  Fill'd with honied pleasure.

Young bride, — a tear for thee!
  A tear in all thy gladness;
For thy young heart shall not see
  Joy unmix'd with sadness.

Young bride, — a smile for thee!
  To shine away thy sorrow,
For heaven is kind to-day, and we
  Will hope as well to-morrow.

Young bride, — a prayer for thee!
  That all thy hopes possessing,
Thy soul may praise her God, and he
  May crown thee with his blessing.

MARRIAGE.

It is most genial to a soul refined,
  When love can smile unblushing, unconcealed,
When mutual thoughts, and words, and acts are kind,
  And inmost hopes and feelings are revealed;
When interest, duty, trust, together bind,
  And the heart's deep affections are unsealed,
When for each other live the kindred pair, —
Here is indeed a picture passing fair!

Hail, happy state! which few have heart to sing,
  Because they feel how faintly words express
So kind, and dear, and chaste, and sweet a thing
  As tried affection's lasting tenderness; —
Yet stop, my venturous muse! and fold thy wing
  Nor to a shrine so sacred rudely press;
For, marriage, — thine is still a silent boast,
"Like beauty unadorned, adorned the most."

A GLIMPSE OF PARADISE.

Not many rays of heaven's unfallen sun
  Reach the dull distance of this world of ours,
Nor oft dispel its shadows cold and dun,
  Nor oft with glory tint its faded flowers:
But, oh, if ever yet there wandered one,
  Like Peri from her amaranthine bowers,
Or ministering angel, sent to bless, —
'Twas to thy hearth, domestic happiness! —
Where, in the sunshine of a peaceful home,
Love's choicest roses bud, and burst, and bloom,
And bleeding hearts, lull'd in a holy calm,
Bathe their deep wounds in Gilead's healing balm.

A DEBT OF LOVE.

Thou, more than all endeared to this glad heart
  By gentle smiles, and patience under pain,
I bless my God and thee, for all thou art,
  My crowning joy, my richest earthly gain!
  To thee is due this tributary strain
For all the well-observed kind offices
  That spring spontaneous from a heart, imbued,
With the sweet wish of living but to please;
  Due for thy liberal hand, thy frugal mind,
  Thy pitying eye, thy voice for ever kind,
For tenderness, truth, confidence, — all these:
  My heaven-blest vine, that hast thy tendrils twin'd
Round one who loves thee, though his strain be rude,
Accept thy best reward, — thy husband's gratitude.

TO LITTLE ELLEN.

My precious babe, my guileless little girl,
  The soft sweet beauty of thy cherub face
Is smiling on me, radiant as a pearl
  With young intelligence, and infant grace;
  And must the wintry breath of life efface
Thy purity, fair snow-drop of the spring?
  Must evil taint thee, — must the world enthrall
Thine innocent mind, poor harmless little thing?
  Ah, yes! thou too must taste the cup of woe,
  Thy heart must learn to grieve, as others do,
Thy soul must feel life's many-pointed sting:
  But fear not, darling child, for well I know
Whatever cares may meet thee, ills befall,
Thy God, — thy father's God, — shall lead thee safe through all.

ON THE BIRTH OF LITTLE MARY.

Lo, Thou hast crowned me with another blessing,
  Into my lot has dropt one mercy more; —
All good, all kind, all wise in Thee possessing,
  My cup, O bounteous Giver, runneth o'er,
  And still thy princely hand doth without ceasing pour:
For the sweet fruit of undecaying love
  Clusters in beauty round my cottage door,
And this new little one, like Noah's dove,
  Comes to mine ark with peace, and plenty for my store.
O happy home, O bright and cheerful hearth!
  Look round with me, my lover, friend, and wife,
  On these fair faces we have lit with life,
And, in the perfect blessing of their birth,
Help me to live our thanks for so much heaven on earth.

DAYS GONE BY.

THOUGH we charge to-day with fleetness,
  Though we dread to-morrow's sky,
There's a melancholy sweetness
  In the name of days gone by:

Yes, though Time has laid his finger
  On them, still with streaming eye
There are spots where I can linger,
  Sacred to the days gone by.

Oft as memory's glance is ranging
  Over scenes that cannot die,
Then I feel that all is changing,
  Then I weep the days gone by.

Sorrowful should I be, and lonely,
  Were not all the same as I,
'Tis for all, not my lot only,
  To lament the days gone.

Cease, fond heart, — to thee are given
  Hopes of better things on high,
There is still a coming heaven
  Brighter than the days gone by:

Faith lifts off the sable curtain
  Hiding huge eternity,
Hope accounts her prize as certain,
  And forgets the days gone by.

Love in grateful adoration
  Bids distrust and sorrow fly,
And with glad anticipation
  Calms regret for days gone by.

THE CRISIS.

Hush — O heaven! a moment more,
A breath, a step, and all is o'er;
Hark — beneath the waters wild!
Save, O mercy, save my child.

Swiftly from her heaving breast
The mother tore the snowy vest, —
Her little truant saw and smil'd,
Turn'd, — and mercy sav'd the child.

Thus, the face of love can win
Where fear is weak to scare from sin,
Thus, when faith and conscience slept,
Jesus look'd, — and Peter wept.

CHARITY.

Fair Charity, — thou rarest, best, and brightest!
  Who would not gladly hide thee in his heart,
With all thine angel guests? — for thou delightest
  To bring such with thee, — guests that ne'er depart;
Cherub, with what enticement thou invitest,
  Perfect in winning beauty as thou art,
World-wearied man to plant thee in his bosom,
And graft upon his cares thy balmy blossom.

Fain would he be frank-hearted, generous, cheerful,
  Forgiving, aiding, loving, trusting ALL, —
But knowledge of his kind has made him fearful
  All are not friends, whom friends he longs to call;
For prudence makes men cold, and misery tearful,
  And interest bids them rise upon his fall,

And while they seek their selfish own to cherish,
They leave the wounded stag alone to perish.

Man may rejoice that thy sweet influence hallows
His intercourse with all he loves — in heaven;
But canst thou make him love his sordid fellows,
Nor mix with them untainted by their leaven?
How can he not grow cautious, cold, and callous,
When he forgives to seventy times seven,
And still-repeated wrongs, unwept for, harden
The heart that's never sued nor sought to pardon?

Reserve's cold breath has chilled each warmer feeling,
Ingratitude has frozen up his blood,
Unjust neglect has pierced him, past all healing,
And scarred a heart that panted to do good;
Slowly, but surely, has distrust been steeling
His mind, much wronged, and little understood;
Would Charity unseal affection's fountain?
Alas! 'tis crushed beneath a marble mountain!

Yet the belief that he was loved by other
Could root and hurl that mountain in the sea,
Oblivion's depth the height of ill would smother,
And all forgiven, all forgotten be;
Man then could love his once injurious brother
With such a love as none can give but he:
The sun of love, and that alone has power
To bring to bright perfection love's sweet flower.

Soft rain, and zephyrs, and warm noons can vanquish
The stubborn tyranny of winter's frost;
Once more the smiling valleys cease to languish,
Drest out in fresher beauties than they lost;
So springs with gladness from its bed of anguish
The heart that loved not, when reviled and crost,
For, though case-hardened by ill-usage, often
Love's sunny smile the rockiest heart will soften.

SONNET

TO THE UNDYING SPIRIT OF FREDERICK KLOPSTOCK.

(The allusions herein are to expressions contained in his letters.)

IMMORTAL mind, so bright with beautiful thought,
And robed so fair in loveliest sympathy,
"Thou Christian," by thy "guardian angel" taught
The master-touches of all melody,
Am not I "one of those" unworthy, sought
By thy rapt soul with "love's prospective eye?"
I feel I love thee, "brother," as I ought, —
Look down and love me too, where'er thou art:
I too am cherish'd by as kind a heart
As beat in "gentle Cidli's" breast divine,
I too can bless the hand which made her mine;
And within me, congenial feelings dart,
Whether to glow, or thrill, or hope, or melt,
My soul attuned to thine can feel as thou hast felt.

THE FORSAKEN.

I THOUGHT him still sincere,
I hoped he loved me yet;
My poor heart pants with harrowing fear, —
O canst thou thus forget?

I gazed into his face,
And scann'd his features o'er, —
And there was still each manly grace
That won my love before:

But coldly looked those eyes
  Which oft had thrilled my breast,
He was too great, too rich, too wise,
  To make me his confest.

Couldst *thou* know what I felt
  To see thee light and gay,
Thy frozen heart would warm and melt,
  And weep its ice away:

Yes, *I* can tell of tears
  These eyes for thee have shed,
In daily, hourly, nightly prayers
  For blessings on thy head.

I name thee not, through shame
  That truth should fade and flee:
Fear not, — thy love, thy vows, thy name,
  Are known to none but me.

Farewell! 'tis mine to prove
  Of blighted hopes the pain;
But, O believe, I ne'er can love,
  As I have lov'd, again:

Farewell; 'tis thine to change,
  Forget, be false, be free;
But know, wherever thou shalt range,
  That none can love like me.

THE STAMMERER'S COMPLAINT.

Ah! think it not a light calamity
To be denied free converse with my kind,
To be debarred from man's true attribute,
The proper glorious privilege of Speech.

Hast ever seen an eagle chain'd to earth?
A restless panther in his cage immur'd?
A swift trout by the wily fisher check'd?
A wild bird hopeless strain its broken wing?
Hast ever felt, at the dark dead of night,
Some undefined and horrid incubus
Press down the very soul,—and paralyze
The limbs in their imaginary flight
From shadowy terrors in unhallowed sleep?
Hast ever known the sudden icy chill
Of dreary disappointment as it dashes
The sweet cup of anticipated bliss
From the parched lips of long-enduring hope?

Then thou canst picture,—aye, in sober truth,
In real, unexaggerated truth,—
The constant, galling, festering chain that binds
Captive my mute interpreter of thought;
The seal of lead enstamp'd upon my lips,
The load of iron on my laboring chest,
The mocking demon that at every step
Haunts me,—and spurs me on—to burst with silence!
Oh! 'tis a sore affliction to restrain,
From mere necessity, the glowing thought;
To feel the fluent cataract of speech
Check'd by some wintry spell, and frozen up,
Just as it's leaping from the precipice!
To be the butt of wordy captious fools,
And see the sneering, self-complacent smile
Of victory on their lips, when I might prove
(But for some little word I dare not utter),
That innate truth is not a specious lie:
To hear foul slander blast an honored name,
Yet breathe no fact to drive the fiend away;
To mark neglected virtue in the dust,
Yet have no word to pity or console;
To feel just indignation swell my breast,
Yet know the fountain of my wrath is sealed;
To see my fellow-mortals hurrying on

Down the steep cliff of crime, down to perdition,
Yet have no voice to warn, — no voice to win!

'Tis to be mortified in every point,
Baffled at every turn of life, for want
Of that most common privilege of man,
The merest drug of gorged society,
Words, — windy words.

And is it not in truth,
A poisoned sting in every social joy,
A thorn that rankles in the writhing flesh,
A drop of gall in each domestic sweet,
An irritating petty misery,
That I can never look on one I love,
And speak the fulness of my burning thoughts?
That I can never with unmingled joy
Meet a long-loved and long-expected friend,
Because I feel, but cannot vent my feelings, —
Because I know I ought — but must not speak,
Because I mark his quick impatient eye
Striving in kindness to anticipate
The word of welcome, strangled in its birth!
Is it not sorrow, while I truly love
Sweet social converse, to be forced to shun
The happy circle, from a nervous sense,
An agonizing poignant consciousness
That I must stand aloof, nor mingle with
The wise and good, in rational argument,
The young in brilliant quickness of reply,
Friendship's ingenuous interchange of mind,
Affection's open hearted sympathies,
But feel myself an isolated being,
A very wilderness of widow'd thought!

Aye, 'tis a bitter thing, — and not less bitter
Because it is not reckoned in the ills,
"The thousand natural shocks that flesh is heir to;"
Yet the full ocean is but countless drops,

And misery is an aggregate of tears;
And life, replete with small annoyances,
Is but one long protracted scene of sorrow.

I scarce would wonder, if a godless man,
(I name not him whose hope is heavenward,)
A man, whom lying vanities hath scath'd
And harden'd from all fear, — if such an one,
By this tyrannical Argus goaded on,
Were to be wearied of his very life,
And daily, hourly foiled in social converse,
By the slow simmering of disappointment,
Become a sour'd and apathetic being,
Were to feel rapture at the approach of death,
And long for his dark hope, — annihilation.

BENEVOLENCE.

"It is more blessed to give, than to receive."

There is indeed one crowning joy,
A pleasure that can never cloy,
The bliss of doing good;
And to it a reward is given
Most precious in the sight of heaven,
The tear of gratitude.

To raise the fallen from the dust,
To right the poor by judgment just,
The broken heart to heal,
Pour on the soul a stream as bright
Of satisfying deep delight
As happy spirits feel!

Yes, high archangels wing their way
Far from the golden founts of day

To scenes of earthly sadness,
That they may comfort the distress'd —
And feel in blessing, deeply blest,
In gladd'ning, full of gladness.

The choicest happiness there is,
Godhead's essential perfect bliss,
Is born of doing good;
He looks around, and sees the eye
Of all creation spangled by
The tear of gratitude!

All hail, my country's noble sons,
Ye generous and unselfish ones,
Who foreign shores have trod
Smit with the love of doing good, —
O that my portion with you stood!
For ye are like your God.

And lives there one, who never felt
His heart with zeal or kindness melt,
Nor ever shed a tear
Of sympathy for other's woe?
If such a man exist below
A fiend in flesh is here.

Brethren, unsatisfied with earth,
Who heave a sigh 'mid all your mirth,
And feel it empty joy,
Ye may, — there only wants the will, —
Your dearest hope of bliss fulfil,
Of bliss without alloy:

Most glad a thing it is and sweet,
To sit and learn at Wisdom's feet,
And hear her dulcet voice;
First in her comforts to be glad,
And then to comfort other sad,
And teach them to rejoice:

How sweet it is to link again
Estranged affection's broken chain,
And soothe the tortured breast;
To be the favored one that may
Recall to love hearts torn away,
And thus by both be blest!

Rich men and proud, who fain would find
Some new indulgence for the mind,
Some scheme to gladden self,
If ye will feed the famish'd poor,
Happiness shall ye buy, far more
Than with a world of pelf:

Ye cannot see the tearful eye,
Ye cannot hear the grateful sigh,
Nor feel yourself belov'd
By the pale children of distress,
Whom ye have been the gods to bless, —
With hearts unthrill'd, unmoved.

And you, who love your fellow-men,
And feel a sacred transport when
Ye can that love fulfil, —
Go, rescue yonder tortured brute,
Its gratitude indeed is mute,
But, oh! it loves you still.

Children of science, who delight
To track out wisdom's beauty bright
In earth, or sea, or sky, —
While nature's lovely face you scan,
Go, seek and save some erring man,
And set his hope on high.

But still, reflect that all the good
Ye do, demands your gratitude,

For 'tis a heavenly boon,
That should for its own sake be sought,
Though to itself is kindly brought
A blessing sweet and soon:

It *is* reward to imitate,
In comforting the desolate,
That gracious One who stood
A ransom for a ruined world,
And still, himself to ruin hurl'd,
Found evil for his good.

And what an argument for pray'r
Hath yearning mercy written there,
For if indeed "to give
Is blessed rather than the gift"—
Go thou, to heaven the voice uplift,
And then thou must receive.

A CABINET OF FOSSILS.

Come, and behold with curious eye
These records of a world gone by,
These tell-tales of the youth of time,—
When changes, sudden, vast, sublime
(From chaos, and fair order's birth,
To the last flood that drowned the earth),
Shattered the crust of this young world,
Into the seas its mountain's hurl'd,
And upon boisterous surges strong
Bore the broad ruins far along
To pave old ocean's shingly bed,
While bursting upwards in their stead
The lowest granites towering rose
To pierce the clouds with crested snows.

Where future Apennine or Alp
Bared to high heaven its icy scalp.

Look on these coins of kingdoms old,
These medals of a broken mould;
These corals in the green hill-side,
These fruits and flowers beneath the tide,
These struggling flies, in amber found,
These huge pine forests underground,
These flint sea-eggs, with curious bosses,
These fibred ferns, and fruited mosses
Lying as in water spread,
And stone-struck by some Gorgon's head.
The chambers of this graceful shell,
So delicately formed, — so well
None can declare what years have past
Since life hath tenanted it last,
What countless centuries have flown
Since age hath made the shell a stone;
Gaze with me on those jointed stems,
A living plant of starry gems,
And on that sea-flower, light and fair,
Which shoots its leaves in agate there;
Behold these giant ribs in stone
Of mighty monsters, long unknown,
That in some antemundane flood
Wallow'd on continents of mud,
A lizard race, but well for man,
Dead long before his day began,
Monsters, through Providence extinct,
That crocodiles to fishes link'd;
And shreds of other forms beside
That sported in the yeasty tide,
Or flapping far with dragon-wing
On the slow tortoise wont to spring,
Or ambush'd in the rushes rank
Watch'd the dull mammoth on the bank,
Or lov'd the green and silent deep,
Or on the coral-bank to sleep,

Where many a rood, in passive strength,
The scaly reptiles lay at length.
For there are wonders, wondrous strange,
To those who will through nature range,
And use the mind, and clear the eye,
And let instruction not pass by:
There are deep thoughts of tranquil joy
For those who thus their hearts employ,
And trace the wise design that lurks
In holy nature's meanest works,
And by the torch of truth discern
The happy lessons good men learn;
O there are pleasures, sweet and new,
To those who thus creation view,
And as on this wide world they look,
Regard it as one mighty book,
Inscribed within, before, behind,
With workings of the Master-mind;
Ray'd with that wisdom, which excels
In framing worlds, — or fretting shells, —
Filled with that mercy, which delights
In blessing men, — or guiding mites, —
With silent deep benevolence,
With hidden mild Omnipotence,
With order's everlasting laws,
With seen effect, and secret cause,
Justice and truth in all things rife,
Filling the world with love and life,
And teaching from creation round
How good the God of all is found,
His handiwork how vast, how kind,
How preärrang'd by clearest mind,
How glorious in his own estate,
And in his smallest works, how GREAT!

THE MAST OF THE VICTORY.

A BALLAD; FOUNDED ON AN ANECDOTE HERE DETAILED.

PART I.

NINE years the good ship's gallant mast
  Encountered storm and battle,
Stood firm and fast against the blast,
  And grape-shot's iron rattle :

And still, though lightning, ball, and pike,
  Had stricken oft, and scor'd her,
The Victory could never strike, —
  For Nelson was aboard her!

High in the air waved proudly there
  Old England's flag of glory, —
While see! below the broad decks flow
  With streaming slaughter gory;

Each thundering gun is robed in dun, —
  That broadside was a beauty, —
Hip, hip, hurrah! the battle 's won,
Hip, hip, hurrah! each man has done
  This day a sailor's duty.

But, woesome lot! a coward shot
  Struck Nelson as he vanquish'd,
And Britain in her griefs forgot
Her glories, where her son was not, —
  Her lion-heart was anguish'd.

For, hit at last, against that mast
  The hero faintly lying,
Felt the cold breath of nearing death,
  nd knew that he was dying.

PART II.

And past is many a weary day,
  Since that dark glorious hour,
And half the mast was stow'd away
  In Windsor's royal tower;

But three feet good of that old wood
  So scarr'd in war, and rotten,
Was thrown aside, unknown its pride,
  Its honors all forgotten:

When, as in shade the block was laid,
  Two robins, perching on it,
Thought that place best to build a nest. —
  They plann'd it, and have done it:

The splintered spot which lodged a shot
  Is lined with moss and feather,
And chirping loud, a callow brood
  Are nestling up together:

How full of bliss, — how peaceful is
  That spot the soft nest caging,
Where war's alarms, and blood-stained arms
  Were once around it raging!

And so in sooth it is a truth
  That where the heart is stricken,
Sweeter at last, for perils past
  That used the soul to sicken,

Comes a soft calm, with healing balm,
  Where sorrow deeply smarted,
And peace with strength is sent at length
  To bless the broken-hearted.

AN INQUIRY CONCERNING THE SOULS OF BRUTES.

"INCERTUS ERRO PER LOCA DEVIA."—HOR.

Are these, then, made in vain? is man alone
Of all the marvels of creative love
Blest with a scintillation of His essence,
The heavenly spark of reasonable soul?
And hath not yon sagacious dog, that finds
A meaning in the shepherd's idiot face,
Or the huge elephant, that lends his strength
To drag the stranded galley to the shore,
And strives with emulative pride to excel
The mindless crowd of slaves that toil beside him,
Or the young generous war-horse, when he sniffs
The distant field of blood, and quick and shrill
Neighing for joy, instils a desperate courage
Into the veteran trooper's quailing heart —
Have they not all an evidence of soul
Of soul, the proper attribute of man),
The same in kind, though meaner in degree?
Why should not that which hath been, — be for ever?
And death, — O can it be annihilation?
No, — though the stolid atheist fondly clings
To that last hope, how kindred to despair!
No, — 'tis the struggling spirit's hour of joy,
The glad emancipation of the soul,
The moment when the cumbrous fetters drop,
And the bright spirit wings its way to heaven!

To say that God annihilated aught,
Were to declare that in an unwise hour
He plann'd, and made somewhat superfluous.
Why should not the mysterious life, that dwells
In reptiles as in man, and shows itself
In memory, gratitude, love, hate, and pride,

Still energize, and be, though death may crush
Yon frugal ant or thoughtless butterfly,
Or with the simoom's pestilential gale
Strike down the patient camel in the desert?

There is one chain of intellectual soul,
In many links and various grades, throughout
The scale of nature; from the climax bright,
The first great Cause of all, Spirit supreme,
Incomprehensible, and unconfin'd,
To high archangels blazing near the throne,
Seraphim, cherubim, virtues, aids, and powers,
All capable of perfection in their kind;—
To man, as holy from his Maker's hand
He stood, in possible excellence complete
(Man, who is destin'd now to brighter glories,
As nearer to the present God, in One
His Lord and substitute, — than angels reach);
Then man as fall'n, with every varied shade
Of character and capability,
From him who reads his title to the skies,
Or grasps with giant-mind all nature's wonders,
Down to the monster shap'd in human form,
Murderer, slavering fool, or blood-stained savage;
Then to the prudent elephant, the dog
Half-humanized, the docile Arab horse,
The social beaver, and contriving fox,
The parrot, quick in pertinent reply,
The kind-affectioned seal, and patriot bee,
The merchant-storing ant, and wintering swallow,
With all those other palpable emanations
And energies of one Eternal Mind
Pervading and instructing all that live,
Down to the sentient grass, and shrinking clay.
In truth, I see not why the breath of life,
Thus omnipresent, and upholding all,
Should not return to Him, and be immortal,
(I dare not say the same,) in some glad state
Originally destined for creation,

As well from brutish bodies, as from man.
The uncertain glimmer of analogy
Suggests the thought, and reason's shrewder guess;
Yet revelation whispers nought but this, —
"Our Father careth when a sparrow dies,"
And that — "the spirit of a brute descends,"
As to some secret and preserving Hades.

But for some better life, in what strange sort
Were justice, mixed with mercy, dealt to these?
Innocent slaves of sordid, guilty man,
Poor unthank'd drudges, toiling to his will,
Pampered in youth, and haply starved in age,
Obedient, faithful, gentle, though the spur
Wantonly cruel, or unsparing thong,
Weal your galled hides, or your strained sinews crack
Beneath the crushing load, — what recompense
Can He who gave you being render you,
If in the rank full harvest of your griefs
Ye sink annihilated, to the shame
Of government unequal? — In that day
When crime is sentenced, shall the cruel heart
Boast uncondemn'd, because no tortur'd brute
Stands there accusing? shall the embodied deeds
Of man not follow him, nor the rescued fly
Bear its kind witness to the saving hand?
Shall the mild Brahmin stand in equal sin
Regarding nature's menials, with the wretch
Who flays the moaning Abyssinian ox,
Or roasts the living bird, or flogs to death
The famishing pointer? — and must these again,
These poor, unguilty, uncomplaining victims,
Have no reward for life with its sharp pains? —
They have my suffrage: Nineveh was spared,
Though Jonah prophesied its doom, for sake
Of six-score thousand infants, and "much cattle;"
And space is wide enough, for every grain
Of the broad sands that curb our swelling seas,
Each separate in its sphere to stand apart

As far as sun from sun: there lacks not room,
Nor time, nor care, where all is infinite:
And still I doubt: it is a Gordian knot,
A dark deep riddle, rich with curious thoughts;
Yet hear me tell a trivial incident,
And draw thine own conclusion from my tale.

Paris kept holiday; a merrier sight
The crowded Champs Elysées never saw:
Loud pealing laughter, songs, and flageolets,
And giddy dances, 'neath the shadowing elms,
Green vistas throng'd with thoughtless multitudes,
Traitorous processions, frivolous pursuits,
And pleasures full of sin, — the loud "hurra!"
And fierce enthusiastic "Vive la nation!" —
Were these thy ways and works, O godlike man,
Monopolist of mind, great patentee
Of truth, and sense, and reasonable soul?
My heart was sick with gayety; nor less,
When (sad, sad contrast to the sensual scene,)
I marked a single hearse through the dense crowd
Move on its noiseless melancholy way:
The blazing sun half quench'd it with his beams,
And show'd it but more sorrowful: I gaz'd,
And gaz'd with wonder that no feeling heart,
No solitary man followed, to note
The spot where poor mortality must sleep:
Alas! it was a friendless child of sorrow,
That stole unheeded to the house of Death!
My heart beat strong with sympathy, and loath'd
The noisy follies that were buzzing round me,
And I resolved to watch him to his grave,
And give a man his fellow-sinner's tear:
I left the laughing crowd, and quickly gained
That dreary hearse, and found, — he was not friendless!
Yes, there was one, one only, faithful found
To that forgotten wanderer, — *his dog!*
And there, with measured step, and drooping head,
And tearful eye, paced on the stricken mourner.

Yes, I remember how my bosom ached,
To see its sensible face look up to mine,
As in confiding sympathy, — and howl!
Yes, I can never forget what grief unfeigned,
What true love, and unselfish gratitude,
That poor, bereaved, and *soulless* dog betrayed.

Ah, give me, give me such a friend, I cried;
Yon myriad fools and knaves in human guise,
Compared with thee, poor cur, are vain and worthless;
While man, who claims a soul exclusively,
Is sham'd by yonder "mere machine," — a dog!

——"EQUIDEM CREDO QUI SIT DIVINITUS ILLIS INGENIUM."
[*Virgil.*

THE CHAMOIS-HUNTER.

A LESSON OF LIFE.

THE scene was bathed in beauty rare,
For Alpine grandeur toppled there,
With emerald spots between;
A summer-evening's blush of rose
All faintly warmed the crested snows,
And tinged the valleys green;

Night gloom'd apace, and dark on high
The thousand banners of the sky
Their awful width unfurl'd,
Veiling Mount Blanc's majestic brow,
That seem'd among its cloud-wrapt snow,
The ghost of some dead world:

When Pierre, the hunter, cheerly went
To scale the Catton's battlement
Before the peep of day;
He took his rifle, pole, and rope,
His heart and eyes alight with hope,
He hasted on his way.

He crossed the vale, he hurried on,
He forded the cold Arveron,
The first rough terrace gain'd.
Threaded the fir wood's gloomy belt,
And trod the snows that never melt,
And to the summit strained.

Over the top, as he knew well,
Beyond the glacier in the dell
A herd of chamois slept;
So down the other dreary side,
With cautious tread or careless slide,
He bounded, or he crept.

And now he nears the chasmed ice;
He stoops to leap, — and in a trice,
His foot hath slipped, — O heaven!
He hath leapt in, and down he falls
Between those blue tremendous walls,
Standing asunder riven.

But quick his clutching nervous grasp
Contrives a jutting crag to clasp,
And thus he hangs in air; —
O moment of exulting bliss!
Yet hope so nearly hopeless is
Twin-brother to despair.

He look'd beneath, — a horrible doom!
Some thousand yards of deepening gloom,

Where he must drop to die!
He look'd above, and many a rood
Upright the frozen ramparts stood
Around a speck of sky.

Fifteen long dreadful hours he hung,
And often by strong breezes swung,
His fainting body twists;
Scarce can he cling one moment more,
His half-dead hands are ice, and sore
His burning, bursting wrists;

His head grows dizzy, — he must drop,
He half resolves, — but stop, O stop,
Hold on to the last spasm;
Never in life give up your hope, —
Behold, behold a friendly rope
Is dropping down the chasm!

They call thee, Pierre, — see, see them here,
Thy gather'd neighbors far and near,
Be cool, man, hold on fast:
And so from out that terrible place,
With death's pale paint upon his face,
They drew him up at last.

And he came home an alter'd man,
For many harrowing terrors ran
Through his poor heart that day;
He thought how all through life, though young,
Upon a thread, a hair, he hung
Over a gulf midway.

He thought what fear it were to fall
Into the pit that swallows all,
Unwing'd with hope and love;
And when the succor came at last,
O then he learnt how firm and fast
Was his best Friend above

NATURE.

I STRAYED at evening to a sylvan scene
  Dimpling with nature's smile the stern old mountain,
A shady dingle, quiet, cool and green,
  Where the mossed rock poured forth its natural fountain,
And hazels clustered there, with fern between,
  And feathery meadow-sweet shed perfume round,
  And the pink crocus pierced the jewelled ground;
    Then was I calm and happy: for the voice
  Of nightingales unseen, in tremulous lays,
    Taught me with innocent gladness to rejoice,
  And tuned my spirit to informal praise!
  So among silvered moths, and closing flowers,
    Gambolling hares, and rooks returning home,
    And strong-winged chafers setting out to roam,
  In careless peace I passed the soothing hours.

ART.

THE massy fane of architecture olden,
  Or fretted minarets of marble white,
Or Moorish arabesque, begemmed and golden,
  Or porcelain Pagoda, tipped with light,
  Or high-spanned arches, — were a noble sight:
Nor less yon gallant ship, that treads the waves
  In a triumphant silence of delight,
    Like some huge swan with its fair wings unfurled,
  Whose curvéd sides the laughing water laves,
    Bearing it buoyant o'er the liquid world:
  Nor less yon silken monster of the sky,
    Around whose wicker car the clouds are curled,
  Helping undaunted man to scale on high
  Nearer the sun than eagles dare to fly; —
  Thy trophies these, — still but a modest part
  Of thy grand conquests wonder-working Art.

CHEERFULNESS.

AN INVOCATION.

Come to my heart of hearts, thou radiant face!
So shall I gaze for ever on thy fairness;
Thine eyes are smiling stars, and holy grace
Blossoms thy cheek with its exotic rareness,
Trellising it with jasmin-woven lace:
Come, laughing maid, — yet in thy laughter calm,
Be this thy home,
Fair cherub, come!
Solace my days with thy luxurious balm,
And hover o'er my nightly couch, sweet dove,
So shall I live in joy, by living in thy love!

MALICE.

A DEPRECATION.

White Devil! turn from me thy lowering eye,
Let thy lean lips unlearn their bitter smile,
Down thine own throat I force its still-born lie,
And teach thee to digest it in thy bile, —
But I will merrily mock at thee the while:
Such venom cannot harm me; for I sit
On a fair hill of name, and power, and purse,
Too high for any shaft of thine to hit,
Beyond the petty reaching of thy curse,
Strong in good purpose, praise, and pregnant wit:
Husband thy hate for toads of thine own level,
I breathe an atmosphere too rare for thee:
Back to thy trencher at the witches' revel,
Too long they wait thy goodly company:
Yet know thou this, — I'll crush thee, sorry devil,
If ever again thou wag thy tongue at me.

THE HAPPY HOME.

O NAME for comfort, refuge, hope, and peace,
  O spot by gratitude and memory blest!
Where, as in brighter worlds, "the wicked cease
  From troubling, and the weary are at rest,"
  And unfledged loves and graces have their nest:
How brightly here the various virtues shine,
  And nothing said or done is seen amiss;
While sweet affections every heart entwine,
  And differing tastes and talents all unite,
  Like hues prismatic blending into white,
In charity to man, and love divine:
  Thou little kingdom of serene delight,
Heaven's nursery and foretaste! O what bliss
Where earth to wearied men can give a home like this.

THE WRETCHED HOME.

SCENE of disunion, bickering, and strife,
  What curse has made thy native blessings die?
Why do these broils embitter daily life,
  And cold self-interest form the strongest tie?
  Hate, ill concealed, is flashing from the eye,
And muttered vengeance curls the pallid lip;
  What should be harmony is all at jar;—
Doubt and reserve love's timid blossoms nip,
  And weaken nature's bonds to ropes of sand;
  While evil indifference takes the icy hand—
(O chilling touch!)—of constrained fellowship:
  What secret demon has such discord fanned?
What ill committed stirs this penal war,—
Or what omitted good?—Alas! that such things are.

THEORY.

How fair and facile seems that upland road,
  Surely the mountain air is fresh and sweet,
And briskly shall I bear this mortal load
  With well-braced sinews, and unweary feet;
  How dear my fellow-pilgrims oft to meet
O'ertaken, as to reach yon blest abode
  We strive together, in glad hope to greet,
With angel friends and our approving God,
  All that in life we once have loved so well,
So that we loved be worthy: her bright wings,
My willing spirit plumes, and upward springs
  Rejoicing, over crag, and fen, and fell,
And down, or up, the cliff's precipitous face,
To run or fly her buoyant happy race!

PRACTICE.

This body, — O the body of this death!
  Strive as thou wilt, do all that mortal can,
  This is the sum, a man is but a man,
And weak in error strangely wandereth
  Down flowery lanes, with pain and peril fraught,
  Conscious of what he doth, and what he ought.
Alas, — but wherefore? — scarce my plaintive breath
  Wafts its faint question to the listening sky,
When thus in answer some kind spirit saith;
  "Man, thou art mean, altho' thine aim be high;
All matter hath one law, concentring strong
  To some attractive point, — and thy world's core
Is the foul seat of hell, and pain, and wrong:
  Yet courage, man! the strife shall soon be o'er,
And that poor leprous husk, sore travailing long,
  Shall yet cast off its death in second birth,
  And flame anew a heavenly centred earth!"

RICHES.

HEAPS upon heaps, — hillocks of yellow gold,
Jewels, and hanging silks, and piled-up plate,
And marble groups in beauty's choicest mould,
And viands rare, and odors delicate,
And art and nature, in divinest works,
Swell the full pomp of my triumphant state
With all that makes a mortal glad and great;
— Ah no, not glad: within my secret heart
The dreadful knowledge, like a death-worm lurks,
That all this dream of life must soon depart;
And the hot curse of talents misapplied
Blisters my conscience with its burning smart,
So that I long to fling my wealth aside:
For my poor soul, when its rich mate hath died,
Must lie witn Dives, spoiled of all its pride.

POVERTY.

THE sun is bright and glad, but not for me,
My heart is dead to all but pain and sorrow,
Nor care nor hope have I in all I see,
Save from the fear that I may starve to-morrow;
And eagerly I seek uncertain toil,
Leaving my sinews in the thankless furrow,
To drain a scanty pittance from the soil,
While my life's lamp burns dim for lack of oil.
Alas, for you, poor famishing patient wife,
And pale-faced little ones! your feeble cries
Torture my soul; worse than a blank is life
Beggared of all that makes that life a prize:
Yet one thing cheers me, — is not life the door
To that rich world where no one can be poor?

LIGHT.

A GLORIOUS VISION; as I walked at noon,
  The children of the sun came thronging round me,
In shining robes and diamond-studded shoon;
And they did wing me up with them, and soon
  In a bright dome of wondrous width I found me,
Set all with beautiful eyes, whose wizard rays,
  Shed on my soul, in strong enchantment bound me;
And so I looked and looked with dazzled gaze,
  Until my spirit drank in so much light
That I grew like the sons of that glad place,
  Transparent, lovely, pure, serene, and bright:
Then did they call me brother; and there grew
  Swift from my sides broad pinions gold and white,
And with that happy flock a brilliant thing I flew!

DARKNESS.

A TERRIBLE dream: I lay at dead of night
  Tortured by some vague fear; it seemed at first
Like a small ink-spot on the ceiling white,
To a black bubble swelling in my sight,
  And then it grew to a balloon, and burst;
Then was I drowned, as with an ebon stream,
  And those dark waves quenched all mine inward light,
That in my saturated mind no gleam
  Remained of beauty, peace, or love, or right:
I was a spirit of darkness! — yet I knew
  I could not thus be left; it was but a dream;
Still felt I full of horror; for a crew
  Of shadowy ITS hemmed in my harried mind,
And all my dread was waking mad and blind.

POETRY.

To touch the heart, and make its pulses thrill,
  To raise and purify the grovelling soul,
To warm with generous heat the selfish will,
  To conquer passion with a mild control,
And the whole man with nobler thoughts to fill,
  These are thine aims, O pure unearthly power!
These are thine influences; and therefore those
Whose wings are clogged with evil, are thy foes;
And therefore these, who have thee for their dower,
The widowed spirits with no portion here,
  Eat angels' food, the manna thou dost shower:
For thine are pleasures, deep, and tried, and true,
  Whether to read, or write, or think, or hear,
By the gross million spurned, and fed on by the few.

PROSE.

THAT the fine edge of intellect is dulled,
  And mortal ken with cloudy films obscure,
And the numbed heart so deep in stupor lulled
  That virtue's self is weak its love to lure,
  But pride and lust keep all the gates secure,
This is thy fall, O man; and therefore those
Whose aims are earthly, like pedestrian prose,
  The selfish, useful, money-making plan,
Cold language of the desk, or quibbling bar,
  Where in hard matter sinks ideal man:
Still, worldly teacher, be it from me far
  Thy darkness to confound with yon bright band,
Poetic all, though not so named by men,
Who have swayed royally the mighty pen,
  And now as kings in prose on fame's clear summit stand.

FRIENDSHIP, CONSTRAINED.

GENTLE, but generous, modest, pure, and learned,
  Ready to hear the fool, or teach the wise,
With gracious heart that all within him burned
  To wipe the tears from virtue's blessed eyes,
  And help again the struggling right to rise;
Such an one, like a god, have I discerned
  Walking in goodness this polluted earth,
And cannot choose but love him: to my soul,
Swayed irresistibly with sweet control,
  So rare and noble seems thy precious worth,
That the young fibres of my happier heart,
  Like tendrils to the sun, are stretching forth
    To twine around thy fragrant excellence,
  O child of love; — so dear to me thou art,
    So coveted by me thy good influence!

ENMITY, COMPELLED.

COARSE, vain and vulgar, ignorant and mean,
  Sensual and sordid in each hope and aim,
Selfish in appetite, and basely keen
  In tracking out gross pleasure's guilty game
  With eager eye, and bad heart all on flame,
Such an one, like an Afreet, have I seen,
  Shedding o'er this fair world his baleful light,
And can I love him? — far be from my thought
To show not such the charities I ought, —
  But from his converse should I reap delight,
Nor bid the tender sproutings of my mind
  Shrink from his evil, as from bane and blight,
    Nor back upon themselves my feelings roll? —
O moral monster, loveless and unkind,
    Thou art as wormwood to my secret soul!

PHILANTHROPIC.

COME near me, friends and brothers; hem me round
With the dear faces of my fellow-men;
The music of your tongues with magic sound
Shall cheer my heart and make me happiest then,
My soul yearns over you; the setting hen
Cowers not more fondly o'er her callow brood
Than in most kind excuse of all your ill,
My heart is warm and patient for your good;
O that my power were measured by my will;
Then would I bless you as I love you still,
Forgiving, as I trust to be forgiven:
Here, vilest of my kind, take hand and heart,
I also am a man — 'tis all thou art,
An erring, needy pensioner of heaven.

MISANTHROPIC.

How long am I to smell this tainted air,
And in a pest house draw my daily breath, —
Where nothing but the sordid fear of death
Restrains from grander guilt than cowards dare?
O loathsome, despicable, petty race,
Low counterfeits of devils, villanous men,
Sooner than learn to love a human face,
I'll make my home in the hyæna's den,
Or live with newts and bull-frogs on the fen:
These at least are honest; — but for man,
The best will cheat and use you if he can;
The best is only varnished o'er with good;
Subtle for self, for damning mammon keen,
Cruel, luxurious, treacherous, proud, and mean, —
Great Justice, haste to crush the viper's brood:
And I too am — a man! — O wretched fate
To be the thing I scorn — more than I hate.

COUNTRY.

Most tranquil, innocent, and happy life,
Full of the holy joy chaste nature yields,
Redeemed from care, and sin, and the hot strife
That rings around the smoked unwholesome dome
Where mighty Mammon his black sceptre wields, —
Here let me rest in humble cottage home,
Here let me labor in the enamelled fields:
How pleasant in these ancient woods to roam,
With kind-eyed friend, or kindly-teaching book:
Or the fresh gallop on the dew-dropt heath,
Or at fair eventide, with feathered hook,
To strike the swift trout in the shallow brook,
Or in the bower to twine the jasmin wreath,
Or at the earliest blush of summer morn
To trim the bed, or turn the new-mown hay,
Or pick the perfumed hop, or reap the golden corn!
So should my peaceful life all smoothly glide away.

TOWN.

Enough of lanes, and trees, and valleys green,
Enough of briery wood, and hot chalk-down,
I hate the startling quiet of the scene,
And long to hear the gay glad hum of town:
My garden be the garden of the Graces,
Flowers full of smiles, with fashion for their queen,
My pleasant fields be crowds of joyous faces,
The brilliant rout, the concert, and the ball,
These be my joys in endless carnival!
For I do loathe that sickening solitude,
That childish hunting up of flies and weeds,
Or worse, the company of rustics rude,
Whose only hopes are bound in clods and seeds;
Out on it! let me live in town delight,
And for your tedious country-mornings bright,
Give me gay London with its noon and night.

WORLDLY AND WEALTHY.

IDOLATOR of gold, I love thee not,
The orbits of our hearts are sphered afar,
In lieu of tuneful sympathies, I wot;
My thoughts and thine are all at utter jar,
Because thou judgest by what men have got,
Heeding but lightly what they do, or are:
Alas, for thee! this lust of gold shall mar,
Like leprous stains, the tissue of thy lot,
And drain the natural moisture from thy heart;
Alas! thou reckest not how poor thou art,
Weighed in the balances of truth, how vain;
O wrecking mariner, fling out thy freight,
Or founder with the heavily sinking weight;
No longer dote upon thy treasured gain,
Or quick, and sure to come, the hour shall be,
When MENE TEKEL shall be sentenced thee.

WISE AND WORTHY.

RATHER be thou my counsellor and friend,
Good man, though poor, whose treasure with thy heart
Is stored and set upon that better part,
Choice of thy wisdom, without waste or end,
And full of profits that to pleasures tend:
How cheerful is thy face, how glad thou art!
Using the world with all its bounteous store
Of richest blessings, comforts, loves, and joys,
Which thine all-healthy hunger prizeth more
Than the gorged fool whom sinful surfeit cloys;
Still, not forgetful of thy nobler self,
The breath divine within thee, — but with care
Cherishing the faint spark that glimmereth there
Nor, by Brazilian slavery to pelf,
Plunging thy taper into poisoned air

LIBERALITY.

GIVE while thou canst, it is a godlike thing,
Give what thou canst, thou shalt not find it loss,
Yea, sell and give, much gain such barteries bring,
Yea, all thou hast, and get fine gold for dross:
Still, see thou scatter wisely; for to fling
Good seed on rocks, or sands, or thorny ground,
Were not to copy Him, whose generous cross
Hath this poor world with rich salvation crowned.
And when thou lookest on woes and want around,
Knowing that God hath lent thee all thy wealth,
That better it is to give than to receive,
That riches cannot buy thee joy nor health,—
Why hinder thine own welfare? thousands grieve,
Whom if thy pitying hand will but relieve,
It shall for thine own wear the robe of gladness weave.

MEANNESS.

WHERE vice is virtue, thou art still despised,
O petty loathsome love of hoarded pelf;
E'en in the pit where all things vile are prized,
Still is there found in Lucifer himself
Spirit enough to hate thee, sordid thing:
Thank Heaven! I own in thee nor lot nor part;
And though to many a sin and folly cling
The worse weak fibres of my weedy heart,
Yet to thy withered lips and snake-like eye
My warmest welcome is, Depart, depart,
For to my sense so foul and base thou art,
I would not stoop to thee to reach the sky:
Aroint thee, filching hand, and heart of stone!
Be this thy doom, with conscience left alone,
Learn how like death thou art, unsated selfish one.

ANCIENT.

My sympathies are all with times of old,
I cannot live with things of yesterday,
Upstart and flippant, foolish, weak, and gay,
But spirits cast in a severer mould,
Of solid worth, like elemental gold:
I love to wander o'er the shadowy past,
Dreaming of dynasties long swept away,
And seem to find myself almost the last
Of a time-honored race, decaying fast:
For I can dote upon the rare antique,
Conjuring up what story it might tell,
The bronze, or bead, or coin, or quaint relique;
And in a desert could delight to dwell
Among vast ruins, — Tadmor's stately halls,
Old Egypt's giant fanes, or Babel's mouldering walls.

MODERN.

Behold, I stand upon a speck of earth,
To work the works allotted me, — and die,
Glad among toils to snatch a little mirth,
And, when I must, unmurmuring down to lie
In the same soil that gave me food and birth:
For all that went before me, what care I?
The past, the future, — these are but a dream;
I want the tangible good of present worth,
And heed not wisps of light that dance and gleam
Over the marshes of the foolish past:
We are a race the best, because the last,
Improving all, and happier day by day,
To think our chosen lot hath not been cast
In those old puerile times, discreetly swept away.

SPIRIT.

Throw me from this tall cliff, — my wings are strong,
The hurricane is raging fierce and high,
My spirit pants, and all in heat I long
To struggle upward to a purer sky,
And tread the clouds above me rolling by: —
Lo, thus into the buoyant air I leap,
Confident, and exulting, at a bound,
Swifter than whirlwinds, happily to sweep
On fiery wing, the reeling world around:
Off with my fetters! — who shall hold me back?
My path lies there, — the lightning's sudden track,
O'er the blue concave of the fathomless deep, —
Thus can I spurn matter, and space, and time,
Soaring above the universe sublime.

MATTER.

In the deep clay of yonder sluggish flood
The huge behemoth makes his ancient lair,
And with slow caution heavily wallows there,
Moving above the stream, a mound of mud!
And near him, stretching to the river's edge,
In dense dark grandeur, stands the silent wood,
Whose unpierced jungles, choked with rotting sedge,
Prison the damp air from the freshening breeze:
Lo! the rhinoceros comes down this way,
Thundering furiously on, — and snorting sees
The harmless monster at his awkward play,
And rushes on him from the crashing trees, —
A dreadful shock as when the Titans hurled
Against high Jove the Himalayan world.

LIFE.

O Life, O glorious! sister-twin of light,
  Essence of Godhead, energizing love,
Hail, gentle conqueror of dead cold night,
  Hail, on the waters kindly-brooding dove.
I feel thee near me, in me: thy strange might
  Flies through my bones like fire, — my heart beats high
With thy glad presence: pain, and fear, and care
  Hide from the lightning laughter of mine eye;
No dark unseasonable terrors dare
  Disturb me, revelling in the luxury,
The new-found luxury of life and health,
  This blithesome elasticity of limb,
  This pleasure, in which all my senses swim,
This deep outpouring of a creature's wealth!

DEATH.

Ghastly and weak, O dreadful monarch, Death,
  With failing feet I near thy silent realm,
Upon my brain strikes chill thine icy breath,
  My fluttering heart thy terrors overwhelm.
Thou sullen pilot of life's crazy bark,
  How treacherously thou puttest down the helm
  Just where smooth eddies hide the sunken rock;
While close behind follows the hungry shark
  Snuffing his meal from far, swift with black fin
  The foam dividing, — ha! that sudden shock
Splits my frail skiff; upon the billows dark,
A drowning wretch, awhile struggling I float,
  Till, just as I had hoped the wreck to win,
I feel thy bony fingers clutch my throat.

ELLEN GRAY.

THE EXCUSE OF AN UNFORTUNATE.

A STARLESS night, and bitter cold;
The low dun clouds all wildly rolled,
Scudding before the blast;
And cheerlessly the frozen sleet
Adown the melancholy street
Swept onward thick and fast;

When, crouched at an unfriendly door,
Faint, sick, and miserably poor,
A silent woman sate;
She might be young, and had been fair,
But from her eye looked out despair,
All dim and desolate.

Was I to pass her coldly by,
Leaving her there to pine and die,
The live-long freezing night?
The secret answer of my heart
Told me I had not done my part
In flinging her a mite.

She looked her thanks, — then drooped her head;
"Have you no friend, no home?" I said:
"Get up, poor creature, come,
You seem unhappy, faint, and weak,
How can I serve or save you, — speak,
Or whither help you home?"

"Alas, kind sir, poor Ellen Gray
Has had no friend this many a day,
And, but that you seem kind, —
She has not found the face of late
That looked on her in aught but hate,
And still despairs to find

"And for a home, — would I had none!
The home I have, a wicked one,
    They will not let me in,
Till I can fee my jailer's hands
With the vile tribute she demands
    The wages of my sin:

"I see your goodness on me frown;
Yet hear the veriest wretch on town
    While yet in life she may
Tell the sad story of her grief, —
Though heaven alone can bring relief
    To guilty Ellen Gray.

"My mother died when I was born:
And I was flung, a babe forlorn,
    Upon the work-house floor;
My father, — would I knew him not!
A squalid thief, a reckless sot, —
    I dare not tell you more.

"And I was bound an infant slave,
With no one near to love, or save
    From cruel, sordid men;
A friendless, famished factory child, —
Morn, noon, and night, I toiled and toiled —
    Yet was I happy then;

"My heart was pure, my cheek was fair, —
Ah, would to God a cancer there
    Had eaten out its way!
For soon my tasker, dreaded man,
With treacherous wiles and art began
    To mark me for his prey.

"And month by month he vainly strove
To light the flame of lawless love

In my most loathing breast;
Oh, how I feared and hated him,
So basely kind, so smoothly grim,
My terror and my pest!

"Till one day at that prison-mill,--
* * * * * *
* * * * * *
* * * * * *
* * * * * *
* * * * * *

"Thenceforward drooped my stricken head;
I lived, — I died, a life of dread,
Lest they should guess my shame;
But weeks and months would pass away,
And all to soon the bitter day
Of wrath and ruin came;

"I could not hide my altered form;
Then on my head the fearful storm
Of jibe and insult burst:
Men only mocked me for my fate,
But woman's scorn and woman's hate
Me, their poor sister, curst.

"O woman, had thy kindless face
But gentler looked on my disgrace,
And healed the wounds it gave! —
I was a drowning, sinking wretch,
Whom no one loved enough to stretch
A finger out to save.

"They tore my baby from my heart,
And locked it in some hole apart,
Where I could hear it cry,
Such was the horrid poor-house law; —
Its little throes I never saw,
Although I heard it die!

"Still the stone hearts that ruled the place
Let me not kiss my darling's face,
My little darling dead;
O I was mad with rage and hate,
And yet all sullenly I sate,
And not a word I said.

"I would not stay, I could not bear
To breathe the same infected air
That killed my precious child;
I watched my time, and fled away—
The livelong night, the livelong day,
With fear and anguish wild:

"Till down upon a river's bank,
Twenty leagues off, fainting, I sank,
And only longed to die;
I had no hope, no home, no friend,
No God!—I sought but for an end
To life and misery.

"Ah, lightly heed the righteous few,
How little to themselves is due,
But all things given to them;
Yet the unwise, because untaught,
The wandering sheep, because unsought,
They heartlessly condemn

"And little can the untempted dream,
While gliding smoothly on life's stream
They keep the letter-laws;
What would they be, if, tost like me
Hopeless upon life's barren sea,
They know how hunger gnaws.

"I was half starved, I tried in vain
To get me work my bread to gain;

Before me flew my shame;
Cold Charity put up her purse,
And none looked on me but to curse
The child of evil fame.

"Alas, why need I count by links
The heavy lengthening chain that sinks
My heart, my soul, my all?
I still was fair, though hope was dead,
And so I sold myself for bread,
And lived upon my fall:

"Now was I reckless, bold, and bad,
My love was hate, — I grew half-mad
With thinking on my wrongs;
Disease, and pain, and giant-sin
Rent body and soul, and raged within!
Such need to guilt belongs.

"And what I was, — such still am I;
Afraid to live, unfit to die, —
And yet I hoped I might
Meet my best friend and lover — Death,
In the fierce frowns and frozen breath
Of this December night.

"My tale is told: my heart grows cold;
I cannot stir, — yet, — kind good sir,
I know that you will stay, —
And God is kinder e'en than you, —
Can He not look with pity too,
On wretched Ellen Gray?"

Her eye was fixed; she said no more,
But propped against the cold street-door
She leaned her fainting head;
One moment she looked up and smiled
Full of new hope, as Mercy's child,
— And the poor girl was dead.

THE AFRICAN DESERT.

SYNOPSIS.

By contemplating a guilty death-bed, the mind is brought to that state in which it can best picture the desolation of nature. — The Desert. — Allusion to the fable of the cranes and pigmies. — The contrast afforded by surrounding countries. — The omnipresent God. — Man regarded as an intruder on the wastes of nature. — Exemplified by the journey and fate of a caravan crossing the desert. — In detail. — An African sunrise. — Approach of the caravan. — Solitude. — The father and child. — Mirage.— The well in sight. — The Simoom. — The stillness that succeeds.

Go, child of pity; watch the sullen glare
That lights the haggard features of despair,
As upon dying guilt's distracted sight
Rise the black clouds of everlasting night;
Drink in the fevered eye-ball's dismal ray,
And gaze again, — and turn not yet away,
Drink in its anguish, till thy heart and eye
Reel with the draught of that sad lethargy;
Till gloom with chilling fears thy soul congeal,
And on thy bosom stamp her leaden seal;
Till Melancholy flaps her heavy wings
Above thy fancy's light imaginings,
And Sorrow wraps thee in her sable shroud,
And Terror in a gathering thunder-cloud!

Go, call up Darkness from his dread abode,
Bid Desolation fling her curse abroad,
— Then gaze around on nature! — Ah, how dear,
How widow-like she sits in sadness here:
Lost are the glowing tints, the softening shades,
Her sunny meadows, and her greenwood glades;
No grateful flower hath gemmed its mother-earth,
Rejoicing in the blessedness of birth;
No blithesome lark has waked the drowsy day,
No sorrowing dews have wept themselves away;
Faded, — the smiles that dimpled in her vales;
Scattered, the fragrance of the spicy gales

That dewed her locks with odors, as they swept
The waving groves, or in the rose-bud slept!

Is this the desert? this the blighted plain
Where Silence holds her melancholy reign,—
Where foot of daring mortal scarce hath trod,
But all around is solitude,—and God!
And where the sandy * billows overwhelm
All but young Fancy's visionary realm,
In which, beneath the red moon's sickly glance,
Fantastic forms prolong the midnight dance,
And pigmy warriors, † marshalled on the plains,
Shout high defiance to the invading cranes?
Regions of sorrow,—darkly have ye frowned
Amidst a sunny world of smiles around;
Luxurious Persia, bowered in rosy bloom,
Breathes the sweet air of Araby's perfume,
And where Italian suns in glory shine,
To the green olive clings the tendrilled vine:
In yon soft bosom of Iberia's vales,
The orange-blossom scents the lingering gales,
That waft its sweets to where Madeira's plain
With emerald beauty gems the western main:
The winds that o'er the rough Ægean sweep,
Tamed into zephyrs, on its islands sleep,
And where rich Delta drinks the swelling Nile,
Auspicious Ceres spreads her golden smile.
But on Sahara ‡ Death has set his throne,
And reigns in sullen majesty alone:
Unfurled on high above the desert-king,
The red § simoom spreads forth its fiery wing;
The spirits of the storm his bidding wait,
Gigantic shadows swell his awful state,

* "The sands roll onward in waves like those of a troubled sea." — Goldsmith's Animated Nature, vol i., p 13.

† Some account of the Pigmies may be found in Philostratus. — Icon. ii., c. 22.

‡ Sahara, or Zara, the Great Desert of Africa.

§ "That extreme redness in the air, a sure presage of the coming of the simoom." — Bruce, vol. iv., p. 558.

And circling furies hover round his head,
To crown with flames the tyrant of the dead!
The desert shrank beneath him, as he passed,
Borne on the burning pinions of the blast;
He breathed, — and Solitude sat pining there;
He spake, — and Silence hushed the listening air;
He frowned, — and blighted nature scarce could fly
The lightning glances of her monarch's eye;
But where he looked in withering fury down,
A dying desert knit its giant frown!

Desolate wilds, — creation's barren grave,
Where dull as Lethe rolls the desert-wave,
How sparingly with warm existence rife
Have ye rejoiced in love, or teemed with life.
Can it then be in solitudes so drear,
That utter nothing has its dwelling here? —
Hence, — thought of darkness! — o'er the sandy flood
Broods the great Spirit of a present God:
HE is, where other being may not be:
Space cannot bind Him, — nor infinity!
Deeper than thought has ever dared to stray,
Higher than fancy winged her wondering way,
Beyond the beaming of the furthest star,
Beyond the pilgrim-comet's distant car,
Beyond all worlds, and glorious suns unseen,
HE is, and will be, and has ever been!
Nor less, — where the huge iceberg lifts its head,
Dim as a dream, from ocean's polar bed;
Or where in softer climes creation glows,
And Paphos blushes from its banks of rose,
Or where fierce suns the panting desert sear, —
HE is, and was, and ever will be, HERE!

But would thy daring spirit, child of man,
The secret chambers of the desert scan,
Curtained with flames, and tenanted by death,
Fanned by the tempest of Sirocco's breath?

With crested Azräel * shall a mortal strive,
Or breathe the gales of pestilence, and live?
O then, let avarice his hand refrain,
Nor tempt the billows of that fiery main;
Let patience, toil, and courage, nobly dare
Far other deeds than fruitless labors there;
Let dauntless enterprise, with generous zeal,
Toil, not unlaurelled, for her fellows' weal,
But be the howling wilderness untrod,
And trackless still, Sahara's barren flood.
Lo, from the streaming east, a blaze of light
Has swept to distant shores astonished night;
Darkness has snatch'd his spangled robe away,
And in full glory shines the new-born day; †
Rejoice ye flowery vales, — ye verdant isles
With the glad sunbeams weave your rosy smiles,
The bridegroom of the earth looks down in love,
And blooms in freshened beauty from above;
Ye waiting dews, leap to that warm embrace,
With fragrant incense bathe his blushing face,
Thou earth be robed in joy! — But one sad plain
Exults not, smiles not, to the morn again:
Soon as the sun is all in glory drest
The conscious desert heaves ‡ its troubled breast
Like one, aroused to ceaseless misery,
That, ever dying, strives once more — to die.
And can Sahara weep? — with sudden blaze
Deep in her bosom pierce the cruel rays,
But never thence one tributary stream
Shall soar aloft to quench the maddening beam
Tearless in agony, fixt in grief, alone,
Pines the sad daughter of the torrid zone,
A rocky monument of anguish deep,
The Niobe of Nature cannot weep!

---

* Azräel, the angel of death.

† A morning near the equator has no twilight.

‡ "The solar beams causing the dust of the desert (as they emphatically call it) to rise and float through the air." — Pottinger's Travels to Beloochistan, p. 133.

Yet from her bosom steams the sandy cloud,
And heavily waves above — a lurid shroud,
Dense as the wing of sorrow, flapping o'er
The withered heart, that may not blossom more.

Faint o'er that burning desert, faint and slow,
Failing of limb, and pale with looks of woe,
Parched by the hot Siróc, and fiery ray,
The wearied kafflè * winds its toilsome way,
'Tis long, long since the panther bounded by,
And howled, and gazed upon them wistfully; †
Long since the monarch lion from his lair
Arose, and thundered to the stagnant air:
No wandering ostrich, with extended wing,
Flaps o'er the sands, to seek the distant spring;
Bounding from rock ‡ to rock, with curious scan
No wild gazelle surveys the stranger, man;
Nor does the famished tiger's lengthening roar
Speak to the winds and wake the echoes more.

But o'er these realms of sorrow, drear and vast,
In hollow dirges moans the desert blast,
Or breathing o'er the plain, in smothered wrath,
Howls to the skulls § that whiten on the path.
And as with heavy tramp they toil along,
Is heard no more the cheering Arab song;
No more the wild Bedouin's joyous shriek
With startling homage greets his wandering sheik;
Only the muttered curse, or whispered prayer,
Or deep death-rattle, wakes the sluggish air.

---

* The kafflè or caravan.

† These animals are mentioned as inhabiting the skirts of the desert, but not found in the interior, by Mungo Park, vol. i., p. 142.

‡ Buffon, Hist. Nat., vol. vii, p. 248. — "Une terre morte, &c., laquelle ne presente que des rochers debout ou renversés."

§ Skeletons in the desert, Denham and Clapperton, vol. i., pp. 130, 131; also Buffon, in the passage above quoted. — "Une terre morte, et pour ainsi dire ècorchée, par les vents, laquelle ne presente que, &c. — des ossements."

Behold one here, who till to-day has been
A father, and with bursting bosom seen
His last, his cherished one, whose waning eye
Smiled only resignation, droop and die!
Parched by the heat, those lips are curled and pale,
As rose-leaves withered in the northern gale;
Her eye no more its silent love shall speak,
No flush of life shall mantle on her cheek;
Yet with a frenzied fondness to his child
The father clung, and thought his darling smiled;
Ah, yes! 'tis death that o'er her beauty throws
That marble smile of deep and dread repose.

What thrilling shouts are these that rend the sky,
Whence is the joy that lights the sunken eye?
On, on, they speed, their burning thirst to slake
In the blue * waters of yon rippled lake,—
Or must they still those maddening pangs assuage
In the sand-billows of the false mirage?
Lo, the fair phantom melting to the wind,
Leaves but the sting of baffled bliss behind.

Hope smiles again, as with instinctive haste, †
The panting camels rush along the waste,
And snuff the grateful breeze, that sweeping by
Wafts its cool fragrance through the cloudless sky,
Swift as the steed that feels the slackened rein,
And flies impetuous o'er the sounding plain,
Eager, as bursting from an Alpine source,
The winter torrent in its headlong course,
Still hasting on, the wearied band behold
—The green oase, an emerald couched in gold!
And now the curving rivulet they descry,
That bow of hope upon a stormy sky, ‡

* For a description of the mirage, see Capt. Lyon's Travels, p. 347, and Burckhardt's Nubia, p. 193.—"Its color is of the purest azure."

† The rush of a caravan to a stream in the desert is well described in Buckingham's Mesopotamia, vol ii, p. 8

‡ Bruce's Travels, vol. iv., p. 559.—"The simoom—I saw from the S. E. a haze

Now ranging its luxuriant banks of green,
In silent rapture gaze upon the scene:
His graceful arms the palm was waving there,
Caught in the tall acacia's tangled hair,
While in festoons across his branches slung
The gay kossóm in scarlet tassels hung;
The flowering colocynth had studded round
Jewels of promise o'er the joyful ground,
And where the smile of day burst on the stream,
The trembling waters glittered in the beam.

It comes, the blast of death! that sudden glare
Tinges with purple hues the stagnant air:
Fearful in silence, o'er the heaving strand
Sweeps * the wild gale, and licks the curling sand,
While o'er the vast Sahara from afar
Rushes the tempest in his wingéd car:
Swift from their bed the flame-like billows rise,
Whirling and surging to the copper skies,
As when Briareus lifts his hundred arms,
Grasps at high heaven, and fills it with alarms;
In eddying chaos madly mixt on high
Gigantic pillars dance † along the sky,
Or stalk in awful slowness through the gloom,
Or track the coursers of the dread simoom,
Or clashing in mid air, to ruin hurled,
Fall as the fragments of a shattered world!

Hushed is the tempest, — desolate the plain,
Stilled are the billows of that troubled main;

---

come, in color like the purple part of a rainbow, &c., a kind of blush upon the air, a meteor, or purple haze."

* Στρόμβοι δὲ κόνιν εἱλίσσουσι. — Æsch. Prom. v. 1091.

† Bruce (as above). "We were here at once surprised and terrified by a sight surely one of the most magnificent in the world. In that vast expanse of desert, from W. to N. W. of us, we saw a number of prodigious pillars of sand, at times moving with great celerity, at others stalking on with a majestic slowness; at intervals we thought they were coming in a few minutes to overwhelm us, &c. Sometimes they were broken near the middle, as if struck with a huge cannon-shot." See also Goldsmith's An. Nat. vol. i., p. 363.

As if the voice of death had checked the storm,
Each sandy wave retains its sculptured form:
And all is silence, — save the distant blast
That howled, and mocked the desert as it passed;
And all is solitude, — for where are they,
That o'er Sahara wound their toilsome way?
Ask of the heavens above, that smile serene,
Ask that burnt spot, no more of lovely green,
Ask of the whirlwind in its purple cloud,
The desert is their grave, the sand their shroud.*

THE SUTTEES.

SYNOPSIS.

The natural beauty of Hindostan contrasted with its moral depravity. — Approach of a funeral procession. — Hymn of the Brahmins. — The widow. — Her early history. — The scene of the funeral pile. — Enthusiastic feelings of the victim. — The pile is fired. — Address to British benevolence in behalf of the benighted Hindoos.

O GOLDEN shores, primeval home of man,
How glorious is thy dwelling, Hindostan!
Thine are these smiling valleys, bright with bloom,
Wild woods, and sandal-groves, that breathe perfume,
Thine, these fair skies, — where morn's returning ray,
Has swept the starry robe of night away,†
And gilt each dome, and minaret, and tower,
Gemmed every stream and tinted every flower.
But dark the spirit within thee; — from old time
Still o'er thee rolls the wheeling flood of crime,

---

* Denham and Clapp., i. 16. "The overpowering effect of a sudden sand-wind, when near the close of the desert, often destroys a whole kafila (caravan) already weakened by fatigue, &c" — and p. 63 — "The winds scorch as they pass; and bring with them billows of sand, rolling along in masses frightfully suffocating, which sometimes swallow up whole caravans and armies."

† Æsch. Prom. v. 24. ποικιλείμων νύξ, and Orph. Argon. 1026, ἀστροχίτων νύξ.

Still o'er thee broods the curse of guiltless blood,
That shouts for vengeance from thy reeking sod;
Deep-flowing Ganges in his rushy bed
Moans a sad requiem for his children dead,
And, wafted frequent on the passing gale,
Rises the orphan's sigh, — the widow's wail.
Hark, tis the rolling of the funeral drum,
The white-robed Brahmins see, they come, they come,
Bringing, with frantic shouts, and torch, and trump,
And mingled signs of melancholy pomp,
That livid corpse, borne solemnly on high —
And yon faint trembling victim, doomed to die.

Still, as with measured step they move along,
With fiercer joy they weave the mystic song;
Eswara,* crowned with forests, thee they praise,
Birmah, to thee the full-toned chorus raise;
To ocean, — where the loose sail mariners furl,
And seek in coral caves the virgin pearl,
And to the source of Ganga's sacred streams,
Bright with the gold of Surya's morning beams,
Where on her lotus-throne Varuna sings,
And weeping Peris lave their azure wings:
They shout to Kali, of the red right hand,
Bid Aglys toss on high the kindled brand,
And far from Himalaya's frozen steep,
In whirlwind car, bid dark Pavâneh sweep;
They chant of one whom Azräel waits to guide
O'er the black gulf of death's unfathomed tide;
Of her, whose spotless life to Seeva given,
Bursts for her lord the golden gates of heaven,
Of her, — who thus in dreadful triumph led,
Dares the unhallowed bridal of the dead!

---

* Eswara, goddess of Nature. Surya, the sun. Varuna, a water-nymph. Peris, or spirits of a certain grade, are excluded from paradise, from a gate of which Ganges flows. Kali, goddess of murder. Aglys, god of fire. Pavaneh, of wind. See Maurice's Indian Antiquities.

And there in silent fear she stands alone,
The desolate, unpitied, widowed one:
Too deeply taught in life's sad tale of grief,
In the calm house of death she hopes relief;
For few the pleasures India's daughter knows,
A child of sorrow, nursed in want and woes.
Curst from the womb, how oft a mother's fear
In silence o'er thee dropt the bitter tear,
Lest a stern sire to Ganga's holy wave
Should madly consecrate the life he gave:
Cradled on superstition's sable wing
In joyless gloom passed childhood's early spring,
And still, as budded fair thy youthful mind,
None bade thee seek, none taught thee, truth to find;
Poor child! that never raised the suppliant prayer,
Nor looked to heaven and saw a Father there.
Untutored by religion's gentle sway
To love, believe, be happy, and obey,
Betrothed in artless infancy to one
Thy warm affections never beamed upon,
How should'st thou smile, when ripe in beauty's pride
The haughty Rajah claimed his destined bride?
A trembling slave, and not the loving wife,
Passed the short summer of thy hapless life; *
And now to deck that bier, that pile to crown; †
His fiery sepulchre becomes — thine own.

And must it be, that in a spot so fair
Shall rise the madden'd shriek of wild despair?
The lovely spot, where glows in every part
The smile of nature on the pomp of art;
The banian spreads its hospitable shade,
The bright bird warbles in the leafy glade,
The matted palm, and wild anana's bloom,
The light pagoda, the majestic dome,

---

* On the miserable state of woman in India, see Ward on Hindostan, Letter vi. In p. 96 he says, "between eight and nine hundred widows are burnt every year in the Presidency of Bengal alone! 1818."

† Capt. Marr's Picture of India, p. 235.

With emerald plains, and ocean's distant blue,
Cast their rich tints and shadows o'er the view.
But murder here must wash his bloody hand,
And superstition shake the flaming brand,
And terror cast around an eager eye
To look for one to save, — where none is nigh!
Far other incense than the breath of day
From that dark corpse must waft the soul away,
Far other moans than of the muffled drum
Herald the lingering spirit to its home:
Yes, — thou must perish; and that gentle frame
Must struggle frantic with the circling flame,
Constant in weal and woe, for death, for life,
The victim widow, as the victim wife.
Hoping, despairing, — friendless, and forlorn,
The death she may not fly, she strives to scorn:
Lists to the tale that bright-winged Peris wait
To waft her to Kalaisa's crystal gate, —*
Thinks how her car of fire shall speed along,
Hailed by high praises, and Kinnura's song, —
And upward gazing in a speechless trance,
Darts earnestly the keen ecstatic glance,
Till rapt imagination cleaves the sky,
And hope delusive points the way — to die.
Who hath not felt, — in some celestial hour,
When fear's dark thunder-clouds have ceased to lower,
When angels beckon on the fluttering soul
To realms of bliss beyond her mortal goal,
When heavenly glories bursting on the sight,
The raptured spirit bathes in seas of light,
And soars aloft upon the seraph's wing, —
How boldly she can brave death's tyrant sting?
Thus the poor girl's enthusiastic mind
Revels in hope of blessings undefined,
Roams o'er the flowers of earth, the joys of sense,
And frames her paradise of glory thence:

* Kalaisa, the Indian heaven. Kinnura, the heavenly singer.

For oft as memory's retrospective eye
Glanced at the blighted joys of days gone by,
How sadly sweet appeared those smiling hours,
When hope had strewed life's thorny path with flowers;
How dark, and shadowed o'er with fearful gloom,
The unimagined horrors of the tomb!
When she remembered all her joy and pain,
And in a moment lived her life again;
Each sorrow seemed to smile, that frowned before, —
Her cup of blessing *then* was running o'er, —
Days passed in grief, beamed now in hues of bliss,
Fancy gilt them, — but terror clouded this!
Yet swift her spirit, resolutely proud,
Scorned every hope, by mercy disallowed:
The priests have long invoked their idol god,
The murd'rous pile, his altar, thirsts for blood, —
A horrid silence summons to the grave,
All wait for her, — and none stands forth to save.
O shall she tremble now, nor die the same, —
Shall she not fearless rush into the flame?
From her dark eye she strikes the rising tear,
And firmly mounts the pile — a widow's bier.
Instant, with furious zeal and willing hands,
Attendant Brahmins ply the ready brands;
And as the flames are raging fierce and high,
And mount in rushing columns to the sky,
Lest those wild shrieks, or pity's soft appeal
Should rouse one hand to save, one heart to feel,*
Madly exulting in their victim's doom
They heap with fiendish haste her fiery tomb, —
Clash the loud cymbals, wake the trumpet's note,
Roll the deep drum, and raise the deafening shout,
Till in dread discord through the startled air
Rise the mixt yells of triumph and despair!

Britain, whose pitying hand is stretched to save
From despot's iron chain the writhing slave;

---

* For a description of a Suttee, see Capt. Marr, as above. p. 243.

Where freedom's sons, at wild oppression's shriek,
Feel the hot tear bedew the manly cheek, —
Where the kind sympathies of social life
Sweeten the cup to one no more a wife,
Where misery never prayed nor sighed in vain, —
Shall India's widowed daughters bleed again?
Let wreaths more glorious deck Britannia's head
Than theirs, who fiercely fought, or nobly bled, —
Wreaths such as happy spirits wear above,
Gemmed with the tears of gratitude and love,
Where palm and olive, twined with almond bloom,
Tell of triumphant peace and mercy's rich perfume
And ye, whose young and kindling hearts can feel
The prayer of pity fan the flame of zeal,
Trace the blest path illustrious Heber trod,
And lead the poor idolator to God!
Thus, in that happy land, where nature's voice
Sings at her toil, and bids the world rejoice,
No guiltless blood her paradise shall stain,
No demon rites her holy courts profane,
No howl of superstition rend the air,
No widow's cry, no orphan's tear, be there, —
India shall cast her idol gods away,
And bless the promise of undying day.

A CARMEN SÆCULARE FOR CHRISTIAN ENGLAND.

ON THE PATTERN AND IN THE METRE OF THAT FOR HEATHEN ROME, BY HORACE.

Holy Creator, ruler of the kingdoms,
Glory of earth and heaven, the Almighty,
Thou to be praised and worshipped never ceasing,
Hear us, Jehovah!

While as in days of innocence aforetime,
We, with the choral voice of supplication,
Cry to the one great Spirit who beholds us,
Save, we beseech Thee!

May the bright sun, thy day-bestowing servant,
And at whose setting blushes modest even,
Still as he beams successive o'er the nations,
Favor old England!

Kindly may nature, providence approving,
Bless our homes with increase, and the matrons
Gently relieving, give us noble sons and
Virtuous daughters.

Rivet the golden links of happy wedlock,
And be the social sympathies unbroken,
While on her lord the wedded wife depending,
Smiles for him only.

Still against sect and heresy protesting,
Nursing her babes with motherly affection,
Loving to all, and tender, may the Church be
Faithful and holy:

And if Omniscience, never to be altered
In its decrees, be destiny presiding,
May Britain, by that destiny protected,
Prosper in greatness.

Pour on us kindly seasons, that abundant
Be the rich fruits of mother earth, and healthy
Still be the gale that wafts us o'er the ocean,
Conquerors ever!

Hear us, Redeemer, hear us, ever-blessed!
Hear, Thou that dwellest infinite in splendor,
Hear Thou that always lovest to be gracious,
Rise and be with us!

If yet thou smilest favoring on England,
If yet the rose, the thistle, and the shamrock,
Form a sweet garland offered on thine altar,
Keep us united.

Let not the thief or murderer infest us,
Let not the base incendiary be near us,
Let not the foul adulterer pollute us, —
Spare us from evil:

Bring up the youth in modesty and virtue
Grant to old age tranquillity and wisdom,
Give the glad sons of Britain health and honor,
Greatness and plenty.

May British mercy more than British valor
Gain from the world its laurel and its olive,
Till over all her enemies triumphant
Glories Britannia!

Help her to rule her own rebellious children,
That the wide West may honor and uphold her;
Aid her to spread the banner of protection
Over her conquests!

Save from intestine murmurings and discord,
Criminal sloth, and infidel compliance;
Scatter the curse of national rejection
Brooding above us!

Let open faith, integrity and firmness,
Primitive truth, and piety, and prudence,
Loyal content, and patriotic virtue,
Quickly returning,

Crown us with blessings, though we be unworthy,
Fill us with mercies forfeited, and rescue
From bitter hate and scorn among the Gentiles
Protestant Zion.

Friend of the needy, pity and relieve them:
Prosper our arts, and sciences, and commerce:
All that can bless and beautify a nation,
Ever be Britain's!

Long as the world rejoices in thy favor,
Holding it up, Omnipotent, — let England,
Let Caledonia, with her sister Erin,
Queen of the nations,

Reign, and be strong, acknowledging thy mercy;
Hear us in choral voice of supplication,
Who now invoke thy succor and thy blessing,
Father Almighty!

Yes, we accept the promise of thine answer,
Yes, we depend on pity for protection,
And upon God our confidence reposes,
Through the Redeemer.

A PRAYER FOR THE LAND.

Almighty Father! hearken,
Forgive, and help, and bless,
Nor let thine anger darken
The night of our distress;
A sin, and shame, and weakness,
Are all we call our own;
We turn to thee in meekness,
And trust on thee alone.

O God, remember Zion —
And pardon all her sin!
Thy mercy we rely on,
To rein thy vengeance in,

Though dark polution staineth
  The Temple thou hast built,
Thy faithfulness remaineth, —
  And that shall cleanse the guilt!

To Thee, then, Friend All-seeing,
  Great source of grace and love,
In whom we have our being,
  In whom we live and move, —
Jerusalem obeying
  Thy tender word, "draw near,"
Would come securely, praying
  In penitence and fear.

Thou knowest, Lord, the peril
  Our ill deserts have wrought,
If earth for us is sterile,
  And all our labor naught!
Alas! our righteous wages
  Are famine, plague, and sword,
Unless thy wrath assuages
  In mercy, gracious Lord!

For lo! we know thy terrors
  Throughout the world are rife,
Seditions, phrensies, errors,
  Perplexities, and strife!
Thy woes are on the nations,
  And thou dost scatter them, —
Yet, heed the supplications
  Of thy Jerusalem!

Truth, Lord, we are unworthy,
  Unwise, untrue, unjust,
Our souls and minds are earthy,
  And cleaving to the dust;
But pour thy graces o'er us,
  And quicken us at heart;
Make straight thy way before us,
  And let us not depart!

Turn us that we may fear thee,
  And worship day by day, —
Draw us, that we draw near thee,
  To honor and obey;
Be with us in all trouble,
  And, as our Savior still,
Lord, recompense us double
  With good for all our ill!

Though we deserve not pity,
  Yet, Lord, all bounty yield,
All blessings in the city,
  And blessings in the field;
On folded flocks and cattle,
  On basket and on store,
In peace and in the battle,
  All blessings evermore!

All good for earth and heaven!
  For we are bold to plead,
As through thy Son forgiven,
  And in Him sons indeed!
Yes, Father! as possessing
  In thee our Father — God —
God give us every blessing,
  And take away thy rod!

LABOR.

A BALLAD FOR OUR MINES AND MANUFACTORIES.

FAIR work for fair wages! it's all that we ask,
  An Englishman loves what is fair, —
We'll never complain of the toil or the task,
  If Livelihood comes with the care;

Fair work for fair wages! we hope nothing else
  Of the mill, or the forge, or the soil,
For the rich man who buys, and the poor man who sells,
  Must pay and be paid for his toil!

Fair work for fair wages, — we know that the claim
  Is just between master and man:
If the tables were turned we would serve him the same,
  And promise we will when we can!
We give to him industry, muscles, and thews
  And heartily work for his wealth,
So he will as honestly yield us our dues,
  Good wages for labor in health!

Enough for the day, and a bit to put by
  Against illness, and slackness, and age;
For change and misfortune are ever too nigh
  Alike to the fool and the sage:
But the fool in his harvest will wanton and waste,
  Forgetting the winter once more,
While true British wisdom will timely make haste,
  And save for the "basket and store!"

Aye; wantonness freezes to want, be assured,
  And drinking makes nothing to eat,
And penury's wasting by waste is secured,
  And luxury starves in the street!
And many a father with little ones pale,
  So racked by his cares and his pains,
Might now be all right, if, when hearty and hale,
  He never had squandered his gains!

We know that prosperity's glittering sun
  Can shine but a little, and then
The harvest is over, the summer is done,
  Alike for the master and men:
If the factory ship with its Captain on board
  Must beat in adversity's waves,
One lot is for all! for the great cotton lord
  And the poorest of Commerce's slaves.

One lot! if extravagance reigned in the home,
  Then poverty's wormwood and gall;
If rational foresight of evils to come,
  A cheerful complacence in all:
For sweet is the morsel that diligence earned,
  And sweeter, that prudence put by;
And lessons of peace in affliction are learned,
  And wisdom that comes from on high!

For GOD in his providence ruling above,
  And piloting all things below,
Is ever unchangeable justice and love
  In ordering welfare or woe:
He blesses the prudent for heaven and earth,
  And gladdens the good at all times,—
But frowns on the sinner, and darkens his mirth,
  And lashes his follies and crimes!

Alas! for the babes, and the pallid wife
  Hurled down with the sot to despair,—
Yet,—GOD shall reward in a happier life
  Their punishment, patience, and prayer!
But woe to the catiff, who, starved by his drinks,
  Was starving his children as well,—
O Man! break away from the treacherous links
  Of a chain that will drag you to hell!

Come along, come along, man! it's never too late,
  Though drowning, we throw you a rope!
But quick and be quit of so fearful a fate,
  For while there is life there is hope!
So wisely come with us, and work like the rest,
  And save of your pay while you can;
And heaven will bless you for doing your best,
  And helping yourself like a man!

For Labor is riches, and Labor is health,
  And Labor is duty on earth,
And never was honor, or wisdom, or wealth,
  But Labor has been at its birth!

The rich, — in his father, his friend, or himself,
  By head or by hand must have toiled,
And the brow that is canopied over with pelf,
  By Labor's own sweat has been soiled!

"WHAT IS A POET?"

AN OFF-HAND ANSWER TO THE QUESTION.

No jingler of rhymes, and no mingler of phrases,
No tuner of times, and no pruner of daisies,
No lullaby lyrist with nothing to say,
No small sentimentalist fainting away,
No Ardert of albums, no trifling Tyrtæus,
No bilious misanthrope loathing to see us,
No gradus-and-prosody maker of verses,
No Hector of tragedy vaporing curses, —
In a word — not a bad one — no mere "poetaster,"
The monkey that follows some troubadour master,
And filching from Tennyson, Shelley, or Keats,
With cunning mosaic his coterie cheats
Into voting the poor petty-larceny fool,
A charming disciple of Wordsworth's sweet school!

Not a bit of it! — Pilferers, duncy and dreary;
Human society's utterly weary
Of gilt insincerities hopping in verse,
And stately hexameters plumed like a hearse,
And second-hand sentiment sugared with ice,
And a third course of passions, warmed up very nice,
And peaches of wax, and your sham wooden pine,
The fitting dessert of a feast so divine!

With musical lies, and mechanical stuff,
The verse-ridden world has been pestered enough;

And yet in its heart, if unsmothered by words,
It still can respond, from its innermost chords,
To generous, truthful, melodious Sense,
To beautiful language and feelings intense,
To human affection sincerely poured out,
To Eloquence, — tagged with a rhyme, or without,
To anything tasteful, and hearty, and true,
Delicate, graceful, and noble, and new.

Aye, — find me the man, — or the woman, — or child,
Though modest yet bold, and though spirited, mild,
With a mind that can think, and a heart that can feel,
And the tongue and the pen that are skilled to reveal,
And the eye that hath wept, and the hand that will aid,
And the brow that in peril was never afraid, —
With courage to dare, and with keenness to plan,
And tact to declare what is pleasant to Man,
While guiding, and teaching, and training his mind,
While spurring the lazy, and leading the blind,
With pureness in youth, and religion in age,
And cordial affections at every stage, —
The harp of this woman, this man, or this youth,
By genius well-strung, and made tuneful by truth,
Shall charm and shall ravish the world at its will,
And make its old heart yet tremble and thrill,
While all men shall own it, and feel it, and know it,
Gladly and gratefully, — Here is the Poet!

"YE THIRTY NOBLE NATIONS."

A NEW BALLAD TO COLUMBIA.

YE Thirty noble nations
  Confederate in One!
That keep your starry stations
  Around the Western Sun —

I have a glorious mission,
  And must obey the call —
A claim! and a petition!
  To set before you all.

Away with party blindness,
  Away with petty spite!
My Claim is one of Kindness,
  My Prayer is one of Right:
And while in grace ye listen —
  For tenderness, I know
Your eyes shall dim and glisten,
  Your hearts shall thrill and glow!

For, on those hearts is written
  The spirit of my song, —
I claim your love for Britain,
  In spite of every wrong!
I claim it for — your mother,
  Your sister, and your spouse,
Your father, friend, and brother,
  The "Hector of your vows!"

In spite of all the evils
  That statesmen ever brewed,
Or busy printer's devils,
  Or Celtic gratitude, —
In spite of politicians,
  And diplomatic fuss,
Your feelings and traditions
  Are cordially with us!

O yes! your recollections
  Look back, with streaming eye,
To pour those old affections
  On scenes and days gone by;
Your Eagle well remembers
  His dear old island-nest,
And sorrow stirs the embers
  Of love within his breast.

Ah! need I tell of places
  You dream and dwell on still?
Those old familiar faces
  Of English vale and hill, —
The sites you think of, sobbing,
  And seek as pilgrims seek,
With brows and bosoms throbbing,
  And tears upon your cheek.

Or should I touch on glories
  That date in ages gone,
Those dear historic stories,
  When England's name was won, —
The tales your children thronging
  So gladly hear you tell,
And note their father's longing,
  And love that longing well.

For language, follies, fashions,
  Religion, honor, shame,
And human loves, and passions,
  Oh! we are just the same;
You, you are England growing
  To Continental state,
And we Columbia, glowing
  With all that makes you great.

Yes, Anglo-Saxon brother,
  I see your heart is right, —
And we will warm each other,
  With all our loves alight;
In feeling and in reason
  My Claim is stowed away, —
And kissing is in season
  For ever and a day! —

And now in frank contrition,
  Oh brother mine, give heed, —
And hear the just Petition
  My feeble tongue would plead,

I plead across the waters,
  So deeply crimson-stained,
For Afric's sons and daughters
  Whom freemen hold enchained!

I taunt you not unkindly
  With ills you didn't make,
I would not wish you blindly
  In haste the bond to break;
But tenderly and truly
  To file away the chain,
And render justice duly
  To Man's Estate again!

O judge ye how degrading —
  A Christian bought and sold!
And human monsters trading
  In human flesh for gold!
When ruthlessly they plunder
  Poor Afric's homes defiled,
And all to sell — asunder!
  The mother, and her child.

O free and fearless nation,
  Wipe out this damning spot,
Earth's worst abomination,
  And nature's blackest blot
Begin and speed thee rather
  To help with hand and eye
The children of your Father
  Beneath his tropic sky.

He — He who formed and frees us,
  And makes us white within,
Who knows how Holy Jesus
  May love that tinted skin!
For none can tell how darkly
  The sun of Jewry shed
Its burning shadows starkly
  On Jesus' homeless head!

And lo! One great salvation
  Hath burst upon The World, —
And God's Illumination
  Like noonday shines unfurled;
Shall bonds or color pale it?
  Candace's Eunuch — say, —
The first, though black, to hail it,
  And love the Gospel Day!

Columbia, well I note it
  That half your sons are strong
Against this ill, and vote it
  A folly and a wrong;
Yet, lurks there not a loathing,
  Aye, with your best inclined,
Against that sable clothing
  Of Man's own heart and mind?

I charge you by your power,
  Your freedom, and your fame,
To speed the blessed hour
  That wipes away this Shame;
By all life's hopes and wishes,
  And fears beyond the grave,
Renounce these blood-bought riches,
  And frankly free the slave!

So let whatever threaten,
  While God is on our side,
Columbia and Britain
  The world shall well divide, —
Divide? — No! in one tether
  Of Anglo-Saxon might
We'll hold the world together
  In peace and love and right!

CONCLUSION.

Alas! poor Muse, thy songs are out of time,
  Thy lot hath fallen on an iron age,
  When unrelenting war the sordid wage
Against thee, — counting it no venial crime
  To fling down in thy cause the champion's gage,
And utterly scorning him, who dares to rhyme:
  O that thy thoughts had filled an earlier page,
And won the favoring ears of holier men!
Whose spirits might with thee have soared sublime,
Far above selfish Mammon's crowded den:
Thou hadst been more at home and happier then:
Yet be thou of good courage; there are still
Those "left seven thousand," whose affections will
Yearn on thy little good, and pardon thy much ill.

THE END.

www.ingramcontent.com/pod-product-compliance
Lightning Source LLC
LaVergne TN
LVHW020919110826
845150LV00004B/718

9781425555221